3ds max® 6 Animation

CG Filmmaking

FROM CONCEPT TO COMPLETION

Barrett fox

OSBORNE

New York Chicago San Francisco
Lisbon London Madrid Mexico City
Milan New Delhi San Juan
Seoul Singapore Sydney Toronto

The McGraw·Hill Companies

McGraw-Hill/Osborne
2100 Powell Street, 10th Floor
Emeryville, California 94608
U.S.A.

To arrange bulk purchase discounts for sales promotions, premiums, or fund-raisers, please contact **McGraw-Hill**/Osborne at the above address. For information on translations or book distributors outside the U.S.A., please see the International Contact Information on the opposite page.

3ds max® 6 Animation: CG Filmmaking from Concept to Completion

234567890 CUS CUS 01987654

Book p/n 0-07-222895-4 and CD p/n 0-07-222894-6
parts of
ISBN 0-07-222893-8

Publisher
Brandon A. Nordin

**Vice President
& Associate Publisher**
Scott Rogers

Acquisitions Editor
Marjorie McAneny

Project Editor
Patty Mon

Acquisitions Coordinator
Jessica Wilson

Technical Editor
Danny Riddell

Copy Editor
Bart Reed

Proofreader
Pam Vevea

Indexer
Valerie Perry

Composition
Tara A. Davis, Elizabeth Jang

Illustrators
Kathleen Edwards,
Melinda Lytle, Lyssa Wald

Series Designers
Lyssa Wald, Peter F. Hancik

Insert Designer
Wil Voss

Cover Designer
Theresa Havener

This book was composed with Corel VENTURA™ Publisher.

INTERNATIONAL CONTACT INFORMATION

AUSTRALIA
McGraw-Hill Book Company
Australia Pty. Ltd.
TEL +61-2-9900-1800
FAX +61-2-9878-8881
http://www.mcgraw-hill.com.au
books-it_sydney@mcgraw-hill.com

CANADA
McGraw-Hill Ryerson Ltd.
TEL +905-430-5000
FAX +905-430-5020
http://www.mcgraw-hill.ca

**GREECE, MIDDLE EAST, & AFRICA
(Excluding South Africa)**
McGraw-Hill Hellas
TEL +30-210-6560-990
TEL +30-210-6560-993
TEL +30-210-6560-994
FAX +30-210-6545-525

MEXICO (Also serving Latin America)
McGraw-Hill Interamericana Editores
S.A. de C.V.
TEL +525-1500-5108
FAX +525-117-1589
http://www.mcgraw-hill.com.mx
carlos_ruiz@mcgraw-hill.com

SINGAPORE (Serving Asia)
McGraw-Hill Book Company
TEL +65-6863-1580
FAX +65-6862-3354
http://www.mcgraw-hill.com.sg
mghasia@mcgraw-hill.com

SOUTH AFRICA
McGraw-Hill South Africa
TEL +27-11-622-7512
FAX +27-11-622-9045
robyn_swanepoel@mcgraw-hill.com

SPAIN
McGraw-Hill/
Interamericana de España, S.A.U.
TEL +34-91-180-3000
FAX +34-91-372-8513
http://www.mcgraw-hill.es
professional@mcgraw-hill.es

**UNITED KINGDOM, NORTHERN,
EASTERN, & CENTRAL EUROPE**
McGraw-Hill Education Europe
TEL +44-1-628-502500
FAX +44-1-628-770224
http://www.mcgraw-hill.co.uk
emea_queries@mcgraw-hill.com

ALL OTHER INQUIRIES Contact:
McGraw-Hill/Osborne
TEL +1-510-420-7700
FAX +1-510-420-7703
http://www.osborne.com
omg_international@mcgraw-hill.com

Dedication

There is a good reason why so many books are dedicated to the author's spouse. But there are more reasons than I can count for this book to be dedicated to my wife, Deanna.

About the Author

Barrett Fox has over nine years of experience with real-world animation productions and has been teaching and writing about 3-D graphics for nearly eight years. His work has been published in *3DGate, 3D Magazine, Cadence,* and other prominent publications. Fox's real-time and rendered animations have been shown at numerous conferences, animation festivals, and web venues including the Webby Awards Siggraph and the Game Developers' Conference. After starting his career as a videogame artist, Fox has written, produced, animated, and directed dozens of widely variegated 3-D animated projects—from the earliest examples of real-time 3-D characters on the Web, to animating characters with markerless, camera-based motion capture. Currently an instructor in San Francisco State University's Multimedia Studies Program, Fox lives in San Francisco with his wife, Deanna.

About the Technical Editor

Danny Riddell has been working with 3-D graphics and animation for over ten years and has taught Maya, Flash, and other design applications for several years, in both corporate and college environments. Riddell heads his own design firm, Riddell Design Group (www.riddelldesign.com), which specializes in high-end web and print design. He's also a best-selling author, and continues to train and write for various colleges, publishers, and magazines.

Contents

II   The First Production Phase: Building

14 Facial Animation: Keyframing Expressions 353

15 Secondary Animation and Effects: Bringing the Background to Life 381

Acknowledgments

Thank you, Margie McAneny, for this opportunity, your candor, and your steadfastness. Thank you, Patty Mon, for your patience, resourcefulness, and kindness. Thank you, Danny Riddell, for bringing your excellent knowledge and invaluable eye for detail to bear. Thank you Bart Reed, for patiently fielding homonyms and non-sequiturs.

Many thanks to the team who put this book together: Kathleen Edwards, Melinda Lytle, Tara Davis, Elizabeth Jang, and Wil Voss. I've been moved and blessed by your enthusiasm for this project.

I'm very grateful to my dear friend Matthew Carter for the long hours he devoted to creating the excellent music and sounds. Thanks to Tony Parisi and David Ewers for the enjoyable story and script collaborations. Thanks David, Heather Dunn, and Michael Siebielec for their voices and excellent acting. And, of course, thanks to Kristin Dunn, Michael Siebielec, and Alan Stewart for loaning me their skin. Also, thanks to Alan for his expert audio advice.

Thanks to Michael Comet, whose brilliant character Maxscript created the character rigs. A sincere thanks to Randall Ho, Jim Stewartson, and Rory Lutter for the invaluable, savage beat down they gave me. Thank you, sir, may I have another? Thanks to Cathy Flight for the endorsement. Thanks to Lance Alameda, Dave Campbell, and Kevin Clark at Discreet for their generous assistance. Thanks to Erich Werner and Kara Jonsson for their generosity, sacrifices, and companionship. Thank you Marc Heft for your tireless searching.

And thank you, to the Fox family—my parents, my brothers, my sisters-in-law, and my nephews and niece—for your prayers and for cheering me on.

Finally, thank you to anyone who gave me any encouragement during this project. Time and again this is what pulled me through.

Introduction

CG Cinematics with 3ds max 6: A Holistic Approach

For the last decade, a monumental engineering effort has been underway with an army of programmers on one side of a grand chasm and an army of artists on the other side, building brick by brick a bridge between pure fantasy thought and tangible, visible reality. Today, computer graphics artists are presented with the current results of this effort, what very nearly amounts to a magic box with the power to make our thoughts real. And even though this magic is currently conjured through hard work and technical skill, CG filmmakers are presented with an awe-inspiring and unprecedented artistic freedom to cross the divide between imagination and realization.

The current incarnation of the magic box that you are likely looking at is a fast PC running 3ds max 6. And what makes this CG toolset even more unprecedented is the way it is empowering small-team and solo productions. 3ds max is being used to create state-of-the-art CG imagery, even Oscar-nominated short films, showing that creative limitations are being systematically stripped away for the 3ds max artist.

This is a particularly good time for CG artists in that it is a time when we can focus more on artistry than on technology. 3ds max 6 is an evolutionary release as opposed to a dramatic paradigm shift in the tools. This means that we can draw upon and build on modeling, animation, and rendering techniques that have been tested in the crucible of demanding real-world productions instead of having to play catch-up with the latest innovations. Furthermore, this is a time of fairly close parity between the toolsets of the major 3-D animation packages (Maya, Lightwave, and Softimage) and 3ds max. This means that more techniques and practices can be shared between users of these different packages, making for a wider, richer knowledge base.

This atmosphere gives CG artists the opportunity to be less preoccupied with the latest toolset and get down to the business of creating rich, evocative worlds and cinematic, emotionally compelling animation. By looking at how some of the best CG animation is created, we can derive a reasonably standard methodology for creating CG cinematics. This can go a long way from the overwhelming chaos of tools, techniques, and methodologies toward a flexible, practical approach to creating your own animations.

Yet, today there is still a shortage of educational resources that tie together all the disparate knowledge needed to create quality CG animation. A gap exists between what is being taught and the real world of animation, because much information is provided without the context of how and where a technique can be used and whether you actually need to know it. This book will explore the deep art of creating CG cinematic sequences for short films, broadcasts, and videogames, with a total approach that balances knowledge of tools and techniques with the creative skills needed to drive them effectively.

Who Should Read This Book

This book is made for those who want to move beyond random tutorials and proceed directly to creating their own finished animations. It is geared toward the serious beginners wanting to prepare a fully realized portfolio for professional work or wanting to create quality work on their own.

The way in which this book covers the entirety of the animated filmmaking process makes it useful for more experienced users who want to coalesce disparate areas of knowledge to form a more complete and cohesive approach using industry-standard techniques.

The materials of this book are relevant to those wanting to create independent short films, videogame cinematics, and broadcast animation. The production methodologies are described with smaller productions in mind, but they are equally relevant to larger groups and longer formats.

This book will also be useful for those seeking specific jobs in areas such as modeling, texturing, and character animating, but who want to understand the entire process of CG animation with 3ds max.

For those completely new to 3ds max, I recommend going through the first few tutorials that come with the software. These are located under the heading "Getting Started with 3ds Max."

How This Book Is Organized

CG filmmaking is a pursuit composed of many disciplines—from scriptwriting, sound design, and art direction, to modeling, rigging, and animating, to name just a few. Many of the individual disciplines that go into a CG animation are deep enough to merit their own separate profession. This makes for a potentially overwhelming quantity of information needed for neophyte CG artists. So many books and tutorials are devoted to 3ds max alone that one could not possibly study them all. And more importantly, most of this information is presented without a context of where and when to apply it and whether it is relevant to your work.

This book is intended to provide a holistic approach toward CG animation by covering all aspects of a typical animation project, using 3ds max 6 as the main toolset. Think of this book as a unified theory of CG animating. This is an all-encompassing approach to learning 3ds max 6 from the perspective of actually creating a finished project with it. This means planning, writing, design, direction, and postproduction, in addition to the work that is done within 3ds max itself. By seeing the entire CG filmmaking gestalt, you'll be given a context in which to place further learning as you move forward.

Almost all the 17 chapters in this book represent entire disciplines that, in larger CG productions, have professionals dedicated solely to them. Therefore, the subject of each chapter has numerous books and tutorials specifically dedicated to it. Following the lessons in this book will give you a solid introduction to each subject, and in their entirety, these lessons provide you with a clear roadmap to further learning. And, just as importantly, the book will take you through all the steps necessary to create your own original animated short film.

Although you will be able to do most of the lessons in this book without the electronic user reference and tutorials that come with 3ds max, this book is not meant to replace them. Also, it is not meant to cover every feature of 3ds max simply because it is there. Instead, this book is meant to be a guide to making rich, cinematic, character-based CG animation, leveraging the power of the latest version of 3ds max.

Therefore, this book will not cover the specifics of using Mental Ray and Reactor but rather will focus on teaching you the core of 3ds max. Each of these features alone is deep enough for its own book, and thorough documentation is available elsewhere. Furthermore, these features, although powerful, are secondary to and fit within the essential skill set presented here. The 3ds max techniques and methodologies in this book do not negate the use of these features, so they can easily be added into the projects presented here.

Techniques for CG animating change constantly and rapidly in fits and starts as the technology and tools evolve. However, some sets of techniques do become common. This is a snapshot of how to do CG cinematics with 3ds max today. This means that by learning the real-world methodologies and techniques in this book, you will have common ground to collaborate with other artists and, if you produce quality work, to fit into the professional animation environment.

A Context for the Lessons: The Example Film

The lessons in this book are tied together by taking you through the entire process of creating a short animated film. The film, called *The Game to Save the World,* is set in a fictional multiplayer online videogame and is about the conversation between three main characters as they play this game. It is presented humbly regarding the artistry of the film but confidently regarding the vital techniques and methodologies that its production illustrates.

The example film was created with this book in mind and with expediency and pragmatism to strike a balance between creating rich, quality work and making practical choices so *your* project can be finished in a timely manner. In keeping with the subject matter of the film, the characters are not only appropriate for prerendered cinematics but for real-time videogame cut scenes as well. The film was also created with only one plug-in (for the characters' hair) so that you would not be bogged down by needing external plug-ins to complete the lessons. Also, the characters, environments, animations, and effects are kept general enough so that you can easily go on to create your own distinctive animations after completing the lessons in this book.

From Concept to Completion: The Lesson Organization

Here's how the chapters are broken down.

Part I: The Preproduction Phase

This part of the book covers the critical preparation work of choosing a story concept carefully, planning your production so it proceeds smoothly, and writing the script to make your story flow and your characters convincing. It also covers the vital, creative visual arts work of designing characters and environments as well as planning the cinematography of your film through storyboarding. 3ds max is a deeply complex blank slate that can be used in an infinite variety of ways. Therefore, the animations that come out of max are only as good as the preparation and artistry that are put into it. This section will help you avoid the pitfalls of blindly rushing into a complex project and hopefully inspire you to create stories that are distinctive to you.

Part II: The First Production Phase: Building

This part of the book covers the nuts-and-bolts work of building and rigging characters and constructing environments. You'll acquire bedrock modeling skills by creating detailed and efficient models for a character's head and body. You'll learn to create "skins" for your models by creating and applying texture maps, and you'll learn to construct virtual sets for your characters to act in using a wide variety of modeling tools. The modeling techniques in this section are used by many of today's top CG modelers, and they will empower you as a digital sculptor and architect using 3ds max's highly evolved set of modeling tools. Then there are the detailed instructions for preparing characters for animation. The chapter on rigging features an in-depth introduction to the technically challenging task of creating custom animation controls for your characters using max bones, inverse kinematics, custom attributes, and wire parameters. This chapter teaches you to harness the built-in power of 3ds max to create flexible rigs designed specifically for your characters, and it serves as a firm foundation for learning to create professional-quality character rigs.

Part III: The Second Production Phase: Animating

The second production phase covers the artistic choreography work of animating your film. This section teaches you how to instill movement, believability, and emotion into your characters through the use of skillful keyframing. The lessons in this part of the book move beyond rudimentary tutorials to introduce you to the real work of animating your characters walking, talking, acting, and emoting. You'll get hands-on experience animating characters rigged with sophisticated professional-quality controls in the context of creating actual scenes from a short film. The chapter on body animation shows you how to achieve believable locomotion and body language and how to enable your characters' movements to communicate your story. The chapter on facial animation shows you how to enable your characters to employ a wide range of facial motions using morph targets. You'll use them to animate the face with eloquent expressions and convincing lip-synch. The chapter on animated effects will take you through examples of specific problem solving and finding the right 3ds max tools and techniques to create a wide variety of effects.

Part IV: The Postproduction Phase

Finally, the postproduction phase covers the process of putting the finishing touches on your animated film. The chapter on lighting and rendering takes you through lighting your scenes with evocative, cinematic illumination, and rendering them with efficient and advanced techniques such as global illumination. Also, the chapter on compositing shows you how to use Discreet's video-compositing program, combustion 3, to add special effects to your rendered footage and how to use Adobe Premiere to edit your final shots together into a completed film.

The CD-ROM

The accompanying CD-ROM for this book contains a host of 3ds max files and supporting texture files that not only support the lessons but give you direct access to the models and animations used to create the example film. The three detailed character models are richly textured and fully rigged with sophisticated animation controls, and the scene files contain all the characters, environments, textures, animations, lighting, and rendering setups to reproduce many of the shots from the example film in their entirety. These files can be examined to learn more about their construction as well as used for practice to prepare for your own work.

You Can Use This Book in a Number of Ways

Because this book presents an integrated approach for the entire process of CG filmmaking, working through the entire book will provide you with a well-rounded skill set, allowing you to create entire projects on your own. Beginners should follow all the exercises to practice the skills and become familiar with the tools. More advanced users can use the lessons as templates for creating their own project.

If you want to shore up your skill set by studying specific areas, you can do lessons individually. The sample files from almost every stage of completion allow you to pick up at any point in the production. You can also use each chapter as a branching-off point for further practice and study to master a particular skill or you can complete that portion of your own project before moving on.

Part **I**

The
Preproduction
Phase

Chapter 1

Story Ideas: Finding a Concept Worth Animating

Congratulations, you've come to the exciting decision, "I'm going to make a 3-D film!" Whether you're using 3ds max or any other 3-D animation package, the first step of any 3-D animation project—coming up with a story concept—is exhilarating. What will the film be about? The sky is the limit, for now at least.

Coming up with a story idea for a film is the most nebulous, ethereal, and intangible step of the entire process, while simultaneously being the most critical to the film's success and even completion. This first step is a time of great creative freedom, when a filmmaker has the fewest boundaries.

And for those of us who make films with 3ds max, we have the added fortune of choosing story ideas at a time when many long-standing technical limitations to the types of stories we can create continue to slough away. Today, 3ds max is being used virtually everywhere animation is being created. This means max filmmakers can make anything from web-based 3-D animation to real-time cinematics for video games to short film animations and even full-length feature animations.

Specifically relevant to this book, many recent solo and small team short films give us uncompromising examples of rich animation done with 3ds max. Filmmakers Andre Bessy, Jerome Combe, and Stephane Hamache have created an evocative and even touching story of a little girl who has to enter an artificial world for a chance to experience nature. Their film, *Respire,* was created with a distinctive cartoon look and is the music video for the song *Respire* by French artist, Mickey 3D. Mike Brown has created richly colored and expressively animated fantasy animations of glowing-eyed forest creatures, the Nyxies.

In 2001, max-based filmmaker Ruairi Robinson proved that the primary limitations left to 3ds max filmmakers are the artist's own storytelling abilities when his film, *50 Percent Gray*, was nominated for an Academy Award for Best Animated Short Film. His story is a tragic-comic look at heaven, hell, purgatory, and suicide. And proving that this was not a fluke, Tomek Baginski's haunting story of medial thieves, *Cathedral*, again created in max, was nominated in the same Oscar category in 2002.

To be clear, this is not a marketing pitch for 3ds max. Despite all the advances in 3ds max and computer graphics (CG) filmmaking in general, 3-D animation is still animation and a highly labor-intensive endeavor no matter which animation software you use. It pays to the give the conception part of the process its full due, because your entire project's success or failure may rest upon what you do here. Hollywood constantly demonstrates, in spectacularly huge fashion, that no matter how much time and money you put into a film, it will most likely flop miserably if the story is not compelling. And countless more productions, large and small, fail quietly when a story chosen turns out to be impossible to finish.

But despite the critical role story plays in an animated film, it is not something you can simply produce from a vending machine. Inspiration and instinct are the prime progenitors of good stories and good films. The best approach is to take your best inspiration and put it through a rigorous filter. For example, if your first creative impulse is to make a story about weasels, ask yourself, "Do I know how to create and animate a convincing weasel?" and "Do I know what's interesting or funny about weasels?" Now is the time in the filmmaking process, the time when you have the least investment, to ask yourself the hardest questions. Think of this chapter as that filtering process as you begin to think of the kinds of stories you'd like to create. Now that we've established that there are few, if any, limitations specific to 3ds max, we'll look at choosing a story from the viewpoint of CG filmmakers in general.

Two Types of Story Concepts: Your Stories and Someone Else's Stories

This is an arbitrary division, but for the sake of getting our brains around the vast world of creative possibility, let's say there are two top-level categories that most 3-D animated films' story concepts can fit into: your stories (stories of your own invention) and someone else's stories (where you realize the vision of another).

Type 1: Your Stories

The first type of story—one that springs forth from your own internal big bang of creativity— can take an extravagant variety of forms. Your idle musings, a complex fiction, a joke, a visual poem, a cautionary tale, an account from your life, daydreams, night dreams, nightmares, a love letter, a diatribe, or a speculation are all fine leaping-off points.

If you're struggling to find a story of your own that you feel compelled to devote some blood, sweat, and tears to, some of the following exercises and brief studies may be helpful to free your inner impresario. And if you have already hit upon the tale you want to tell, it's definitely worthwhile to dissect your idea at this point.

Finding Ripe Subject Matter

If you want a story that does not trigger a viewer's channel changing, web page flipping, or latent narcolepsy, serve up some fresh new imagery, ideas, or both, that all those hungry eyes out there have not seen before. This can seem daunting given the spectacular volume of stimulation continually frying people's eyeballs. So, how do you ensure the freshness of your precious story idea? Here are a few exercises that might help.

Looking Inward: What's Interesting to You Specifically?   A nearly surefire technique for divining a story that is unique is to tap into what is unique about you. Just as surely as everybody on the planet has a unique DNA fingerprint, you've got some perspective, experience, interest, neurosis, or hallucination that enough people haven't seen before. Although your love of *Star Wars* may not provide you with the most original story fodder, there is more than likely a host of things unique to you. Make a list of the things that make you unique. Maybe it's your weird neighbor, or maybe you have a fixation with chewing gum. Maybe you're the only person you know who ever fantasized about who invented maracas. If the items you come up with at first are too familiar, keep looking. The deeper you go, the more "surefire" this technique becomes.

Fresh Inspiration Through Brainstorming   If you really are struggling to find a story subject, you don't have to get a sore neck waiting for a light bulb to appear. Certain techniques can aid you in this process. Inspiration can be incubated by surrounding yourself with the right stimuli and keeping yourself in the right frame of mind.

Brainstorming is an important skill for any artist—and for more than coming up with an initial story concept. Brainstorming can be helpful in areas throughout the filmmaking process, from creating rich characters to even solving technical issues. And it is a skill that can be cultivated through practice. Some common brainstorming methods included free associating through the use of flash cards with relevant words written on them, browsing through random scrapbook or magazine images, and even thinking out loud with creative friends.

Mindmapping is a powerful technique used by many creative types that involves making a visual diagram of your ideas (see Figure 1-1). By listing ideas visually, you can categorize them with

FIGURE 1-1   These notebook pages show some of the brainstorming I did for my story idea.

icons and draw connections between them. This is an excellent way to see the breadth of your ideas and to map their relationships.

Of course, drawing can be a powerful brainstorming tool (see Figure 1-2). Many famous cartoon characters have come from the most idle, random, freeform scribbles. When you are trying to generate the creative raw material for your stories, drawing with the loose-and-free approach of a brainstorming exercise can be extremely fruitful.

All these brainstorming methods share common elements of free association, following a train of thought, and exploring multiple connections between ideas. Also, they are all most effective when you have cultivated a creatively fertile state of mind. Many creative people say that inspiration comes to them when they are falling asleep or waking up. We're not sure why this is—perhaps because of the relaxed state your mind enters when you're going to sleep. At any rate, it's a good idea to keep a drawing pad or notebook by your bed. But more than that, it's worth studying this relaxed freeform state of mind and learning to put yourself there at will. This may mean putting yourself in a relaxed environment and removing any pressure to come up with the ultimate story on demand.

FIGURE 1-2   I began sketching my story idea right from the start.

BRAINSTORMING EXAMPLE

Here's just one of the many different ways to start brainstorming. Think of any memorable thing you might have done in the last couple of months that didn't involve someone else's fiction, such as TV shows, movies, videogames, and so on. Perhaps you went to…

▶ The science museum

▶ A dance club

▶ A flea market

▶ The circus

Any one of these has fodder for a thousand great animations. Go with your gut and choose the most interesting one. How about the circus? What struck your fancy?

▶ The trapeze artists

▶ The weird guy sitting next to you

▶ The size of the tents

▶ Someone spinning from their teeth

Okay, how about the tightrope walker? Let's get granular on that one:

▶ What if he had the wrong shoes? Maybe roller skates, platform shoes, or Shaquille O'Neal's shoes?

▶ What if he had the wrong instrument to balance with? Such as a set of barbells, a fishing rod, a lightning rod, or a radio antenna?

▶ What if the tightrope walker is distracted? By birds, bees, bats—or any of these, only giant?

▶ What is the tightrope walker daydreaming about? A really wide tightrope? Meeting a tightrope walker of the opposite sex?

▶ What if the tightrope is actually a power line, a snake, a giant's nose hair?

▶ What is the tightrope walker walking between? Buildings? Buildings on fire? Cops wanting to arrest him on one side and gangsters wanting to kill him on the other?

▶ What is below the tightrope walker? Lava, a trampoline, raspberry jelly?

Now try applying this process to a motorcycle daredevil, a bike messenger, an animal trainer, or a celebrity personal trainer. Brainstorming is an exercise of possibilities, so go back up to any level in your brainstorming process and branch off again from there.

Type 2: Someone Else's Stories

The second type of stories we can tell are other people's stories. Maybe it's a myth or a fable, a chronicle, or a history. Maybe it's a short story or a novelette, hearsay, or gossip. To some, it may not be as satisfying to tell someone else's tale as it is bringing something from their own imagination to life. But it can be just as rewarding, especially if told in one's own creative voice. In their film *Shrek*, PDI showed how you could take worn-out old fairy tales and put a new twist on them. And this can be the best way to learn how to be a storyteller and artist. Telling a friend's story can be a rich experience for everyone involved. Crafting a story that complements a song to make a music video is also fine animation material.

For small teams and solo animators it can be impractical to imagine an entire world or reality on the scale of *Star Trek*, *Alice in Wonderland*, or a Dickens novel; coming up with such a vast fictional environment can be daunting for a whole team of people, let alone a solo artist or small team. Therefore, some people find that working within the creative constraints of a preexisting fictional world can be a fun experience (not to mention a more feasible undertaking). The Animatrix project, a collection of short animations that flesh out more of the world of the *Matrix* movies, has attracted several of the best animated storytellers from around the world. They were inspired and excited to tell part of the Wachowski brothers' *Matrix* story.

Much of the best CG animation today is being created to tell stories in support of video games. Here, the filmmakers are telling the stories of the videogame creators. They are finding a rich symbiosis in making stories that help visualize and dramatize the fictional worlds in which the games are played. It's a fascinating challenge to find the dramatic hooks to keep players emotionally engaged in the interactive experience.

Whether you're going to animate your own story or someone else's story, this is the time to free your mind and allow it soak in new ideas. Be prepared to spend a long time—several months—doing this, and give yourself a little breathing room to see what inspirations come to you over time.

These next exercises apply to pretty much any kind of film you're going to make, whether it's your own story concept or an adaptation of someone else's.

Looking Outward: Timeliness

Another way to bring some hot-off-the-presses freshness to your stories is to let them be informed by current events. It's so tiresome to hear the worn-out old saying "Everything has been done" again and again. The planet is full of new happenings to stimulate fresh ideas. Sure we've heard science-fiction stories about what would happen if Earth's population went over 6 billion, if we started genetically engineering plants, animals, and humans, or if we discovered new planets. But now all those things are *happening* for real and ready to spawn a new raft of inspiration.

Many everyday experiences would seem surreal and preposterous to us if they weren't actually happening. Until recently we'd never had the world's most famous pop star be someone without a nose or movie stars injecting botulism into their eyebrows. And we'd also never seen a recovering cancer victim win the Tour de France multiple times. We've never seen half the species of animals on this planet or half of the ocean floor. Keeping this kind of wide-eyed interest is what master storytellers such as Michael Crichton and Steven Spielberg do so well.

In 2001, San Francisco animation studio DotComix teamed up with cartoonist Garry Trudeau to create short 3-D animations based on Duke, from Trudeau's *Doonesbury* comic strip. Presented as campaign speeches and appearances, the animations portrayed the obnoxious and anachronistic Duke running for president against Al Gore and George Bush. These animations' timely political satire and up-to-the-minute humor showed how today's current events can always infuse fresh new ideas into animation.

Humor and Emotion

Of course, the real clincher for your story is to have it create an emotional response in the viewer. Stories that trigger emotion have been the meat of animation since its early stages and, indeed, stories in general. Moviegoers were famously touched for life when Bambi's mother died because of the powerful emotions it evoked. Not only are emotions the context for us to explore the human condition through art, they are an excellent sugarcoating if you want to communicate a personal idea or opinion.

Filtering

So let's say you have an idea for a story. The heavens have opened up above you and your perfect story idea has floated down on the wings of a dove. After you have had your honeymoon with your new idea, just enjoying the fact that one of the biggest obstacles has been overcome, it's time to put your idea through an unsentimental screening process. Think of this part of the process as sitting your story down in front of a big, intimidating desk for a lengthy and uncomfortable interview. Because you're going to be spending so much time with this story idea, it pays to know everything about it before you commit. Submit your story idea to a critical analysis, considering the history, strengths, and weaknesses of the animated medium as well as what your intentions and capabilities are. As the first phase of your idea-filtering process, here are some in-depth areas to explore.

Is the Idea Ripe to Be Animated?

To create your 3-D film you will be using cutting-edge, rocket science technology to bring to life a virtual world. But to breathe life into that virtual world, you have to make it move. And to make it move, you have to animate it. What's more, you'll be using virtually the same artistic skills used to move animated characters since the turn of the last century. In traditional animation productions, a keyframing animator draws a character at each key pose of an animated sequence, every few frames so. Through the power of illustration, these master artists make sure that every pose expressively communicates at least some small part of the story. Then, so-called "inbetweener" artists flesh out the motion by drawing the animated frames that go between the keyframing animator's drawings.

Although 3ds max now fills the role of inbetweener, today's CG animators create expressive motion by posing, or *keyframing*, 3-D models much the same way a traditional animator would pose a character as they drew it. This expressiveness is still at the heart of today's animation. So there may be some stories—such as an *exact* portrayal of a boring court case—that are simply better left to straight, courtroom video because animation wouldn't add anything. But indeed, if the drama were exaggerated and the people caricatured, the story might become an engaging animation. And, of course, if the lawyers were weasels and the judge a bald eagle….

As you are evaluating the worthiness of the story you want to animate, it's valuable to consider a little of what has been animated before. By taking a look at animation's strengths and weaknesses as a medium, you'll find some criteria to weigh your story idea against, and possibly help yourself find a story idea in the first place. Here are a few questions to ask.

What Is Animation Good At?

Some types of stories truly lend themselves to being animated. Let's look at some of animation's historic strengths to get a better idea of which story ideas are good candidates to try out in an animated film. Given that Disney and Warner Bros. cartoons are practically synonymous with cartoon animation, their emotionally powerful stories make it clear that animation excels at expressive characters and exaggerated performances. In fact, animation quickly elevated exaggeration itself to a deeply subtle and communicative art form.

Emotion At Disney, cartoon masters such as Ollie Johnson and Frank Thomas, authors of *The Illusion of Life*, showed us a powerful and broad range of emotions thanks to their ability to draw a face as though it were a malleable object. Thomas, Johnson, and the other masters of two-dimensional animation used their spectacular pencil drafting prowess to draw a character consistently from one animation frame to the next. This gave characters a fluidity of motion that allowed them to convey emotions with great facility.

Humor Meanwhile, artists such as Tex Avery and Chuck Jones, at Warner Bros., turned pencil drawings into physical comedians using that same illusion of elasticity. They highlighted animation's unique ability to convey squashing, stretching, weight, anticipation, and follow through, and used them to communicate physicality. Obviously, animation often excels at being gut-wrenchingly funny.

Nature and Tranquility   Dispelling the myth that animation as a medium is mainly for children or funny gags, the work of Japanese masters Hayao Miyazaki and Osamu Tezuka shows us animation's power to be evocative and even meditative. Films such as Miyazaki's *Princess Mononoke* and Tezuka's *Metropolis* are rife with scenes of raindrops making rings on puddles, cherry blossoms falling, and cloud formations metamorphosing. They show that with just the right ultra-subtle movements, animation can speak volumes about stillness.

Alternate Realities   The animated medium also excels in its ability to show other realities. Not just in the science-fiction sense, but to show realities that no other medium can visualize so succinctly. Fantasies, dreams, parables, hallucinations can be given a life outside the imaginer's mind. But a raft of today's animators are spotlighting another facet of this strength with the sharply stylized and illustrative qualities of their work. Animations such as Genndy Tartovsky's *Dexter's Laboratory*, Craig McCracken's *Powerpuff Girls*, and John Kricfalusi's *Ren & Stimpy* accentuate the fact that animations are illustrations in motion.

What Is 3-D Good at Historically?

Throughout its relatively short history, 3-D animation has always been similar to 2-D animation in the way movement is created. It's capable of almost everything 2-D animation can do. However, 3-D computer animation does differ dramatically from traditional animation in its constant and rapid evolution of what it can depict, from its humble beginnings of chrome spheres and teapots to today's furry monsters and photorealistic stunt doubles. Given that, let's consider what 3-D has been historically good at visualizing.

Some of the earliest examples of dramatic, narrative-driven 3-D animation came from Pixar. Films such as *Luxo Jr.* and *Tin Toy* have stories that focus on hard, shiny plastic and metal objects— things the software was capable of adequately rendering. This demonstrated early on that Pixar had a strongly pragmatic approach to choosing story topics that were practical in a medium that was then arcane and technically challenging. And, importantly, although they highlighted the fact that 3-D animation at that stage couldn't really portray much beyond smooth, shiny geometric objects, these films demonstrated that a potent story could be told in spite of the medium's limitations.

As Pixar moved on to their first feature film, *Toy Story*, 3-D artists were already starting to create photorealistic images of fairly complex subject matter. But to create an entire movie, Pixar chose the subject of shiny plastic toys. Given the daunting task of producing an all-CG feature, this was what was practical at the time.

For their next feature, *A Bug's Life*, a story about an ant colony, Pixar moved on to something incrementally more complex than toys—hard and shiny (but more flexible than toys) bugs. And this time, PDI underscored the logic of Pixar's decisions on subject matter by releasing their own feature about an ant colony, *Antz*, almost simultaneously with Pixar's *A Bug's Life*. The occurrence of both of these state-of-the-art, pioneering animation studios independently choosing similar subject matter from a world of possibilities illuminates what 3-D was good at during that time—objects and characters that were still shiny and plastic looking, but were now more flexible and in greater quantity.

The similarities continue with Pixar and PDI releasing *Monsters Inc.* and *Shrek* in the same year, and then again with two fish stories, Pixar's *Finding Nemo* and PDI's *Shark Slayer*. This forward progression traces the evolution of CG's ability to enhance an animated story by marking the increase in visual complexity with each new generation of films.

This is not to say that 3-D animation is made only for creating bugs, monsters, and fish. Instead, this progression reveals to us that as CG's capacity to show complexity increases, artists are given more freedom in the subject matter they choose. Even though these two giant studios both have several hundred people working on their films, they can inform us about what is practical to animate in a rubber-hits-the-road production scenario. It's good to keep the sense of the progression of the 3-D medium's sweet spot when thinking about what to animate.

What Is the State of the CG Art?

3-D animation's progression obviously continues. The animated portions of the latest *Lord of the Rings*, *Star Wars*, and the *Matrix* movies now feature CG stunt doubles, main characters, and giant crowds of characters. Gollum, from *The Lord of the Rings: The Two Towers*, demonstrated that when animated carefully enough, a CG character can now play an effective emotional lead in a film. These films show that given a large enough army of artists and enough computers crunching away, we can create visual complexity that seems to rival our eyeballs' ability to funnel it all in.

But besides enabling the amazing achievements of these high-profile examples, today's 3-D animation technologies are getting better at other things as well.

Empowering Smaller Productions   Faster computers and cheaper, more powerful software are combining to allow artists working on their own to create stories compelling to a wide audience. As mentioned at the beginning of this chapter, Ruairi Robinson's 2001 solo short film *50 Percent Gray* was nominated for an Academy Award. Using 3ds max, empowered with new character-animation tools and state-of-the-art, global illumination rendering, Robinson was able to create a film whose character was engaging emotionally and whose visuals transcended computer animation's traditionally plastic look. Because more powerful, less expensive tools have continued to get in the hands of more artists, the efforts of much smaller groups and solo animators are becoming more compelling. This means CG is getting better and better at telling more personal stories.

And this may mean a dramatic democratization of the CG art form. Productions for blockbuster animated feature films have by definition demanded giant, blockbuster budgets. To release this kind of money, there has had to be a promise of giant economic returns, which has meant limiting the subject matter of big-budget films. Their stories must have "universal" themes and appeal to the widest possible audience to be financially viable. But nowadays, a small team or even a solo animator can create films that do not have these limitations. We no longer need to make animated films that appeal to both children and adults, or even all children or all adults.

So far, this is similar to what happened in the history of live-action movies. Putting moviemaking tools in the hands of more artists made for a much richer and diverse cultural stew than a few giant movie factories could ever produce on their own. But CG animation stands to spawn an even more diverse mix of artistic expression than live-action movies because filmmakers can create animations virtually on their own.

What Are You Good At?

Another filter to pour your idea through is to ask yourself what you are good at. You may have already asked yourself what your interests are, but also ask yourself critically what your best talents and skills are.

By looking at the chapter titles in this book, you can get a broad sense of the different skills you'll need to pull off a 3-D film. Which of these have you trained for so far? And which ones do you want to learn the most? These questions can help you determine key elements of your story. If you have never created or animated a character before, it would be unwise to embark on a ten-character ensemble piece. If you have never modeled organic forms, it would not be recommended to set your story in a forest of trees.

But also do some self-examination and see where your inherent talents may lie. If you've always been a ham or gotten the lead in the school play, consider a story that focuses on the acting of a character. You may excel at getting the character to act. If you are always making home movies with your video camera, you might want to craft an action sequence that shows off your film-editing skills.

Why Are You Making This Film?

This is the part of the interview process where you slam your fist down on the big, intimidating interview desk and yell, "What are you doing with your life?" You need to know about your expectations for your film. Two questions that some will surely say you should answer before even starting to think of story ideas are who your audience is and what your goals are. These questions are undoubtedly critical to choosing a story topic. However, I choose to consider them later in the process so that the raw creative stages can be as unfettered and fertile as possible.

What Are Your Goals?

At some point you must examine your goals and your potential audience for your film and see if your story idea can serve them. First, what are your goals? That is, why are you making the film? There are, of course, any number of different goals, and you'll likely have several, but here are some common ones.

Expressing Yourself   One of the most basic goals is to simply scratch the creative itch. Films made for this reason often wind up being the most personal pieces.

Learning   When you are creating a film to learn—whether you're in school or on your own—some of your creative decisions will be informed by what you need to study. This type of film takes more careful planning upfront to ensure the tasks you don't yet have the skills for can wait until you learn how to execute them. For example, you would want to provide extra time in your schedule to learn the process of texturing your models before you proceed with animating them. You may also want to find a mentor or a teacher to help guide you through the process.

Communicating an Idea   Animated filmmaking is a strong communication tool that is capable of piercing many cultural, linguistic, generational, and even political divides. Especially when leveraging its strengths in showing emotion and humor, animated filmmaking becomes an effective medium for personal expression, education, and political satire.

Making the Audience Laugh   This goal is similar to the goal of expressing yourself. But some people are possessed with an undeniable need to make people laugh. This goal often makes for some of the most simplistic films. (Not that there's anything wrong with that.) It's helpful to write your goals down to carefully delineate them (see Figure 1-3). As you move through the steps of producing your film, it is wise to refer back to your original goals.

Who Is Your Audience? Would Grandma Like Your Film?

If your story is well conceived and skillfully told, the issue of who your audience is becomes somewhat less critical. But discerning your demographic early on can enable you to communicate more effectively. Here are a few flavors of audience and how they might change your film.

Everyone   To make a film that appeals to "everyone," you'll definitely want to be aware of those "universal" themes, the almost generic ideas of "integrity ", "love", "courage", and so on. And to be sure, the biggest Hollywood studios, which pay a lot of people a lot of money to know what "everyone" likes, are infamous for putting their films through focus groups to try to find the answer. Knowing what "everyone" likes is really an instinct more than anything.

And, this brings up practical matters such as language and cultural barriers. This is partly why it's common in animations for characters to speak in gibberish.

FIGURE 1-3   Early in the conception process, I began writing down the goals of my film to define its central idea. The goal of my film was to explore the idea of what a game about socializing would be like, as well as serving as a portfolio piece.

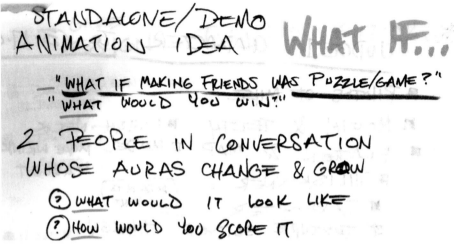

Kids   Many artists who are around children a lot take great pleasure in crafting stories just for them. This can be an enjoyable and therapeutic way to make sure that inner child is still in you somewhere. Of course, the other day I was renting some films and heard a mother ask her daughter which one she would like. She responded by yelling "Barney! Barney!" And I heard the mother shudder and sigh deeply. Fortunately for her and the rest of the world, animators like SpongeBob Squarepants creator Stephen Hillenburg are showing us that films made for kids do not have to be the kind that torture adults.

Young Men   Here is a demographic that is highly overserved. Because the vast predominance of 3-D animators, at least right now, is young men, the vast predominance of 3-D animated content is made largely for them.

More Specific Audiences   The more specific your audience becomes, the smaller it gets. But it also gets easier to understand how to speak to that audience. An effective scale to use may be to consider how much effort you'll be putting into an animation and weighing that against how large your potential audience is. For someone who would appreciate the effort, it could be an extraordinary experience to have an animation crafted just for them.

Once you have a sense of who your audience is, you can then imagine seeing your story through their eyes and visualize how they may react to it. Also, talk to people in your potential audience early on. Does the soundbyte of your story make your friends laugh, or does it inspire blank stares? If it's the latter, you may want to reconsider your story.

Avoiding Pitfalls and Perils

So you are starting to think you want to marry this story and live happily ever after? At this juncture, it's time to ask if it has any scandalous baggage that will doom its success. Here are a few hazards that often cause creative casualties in CG.

Clichés

Certain subject matter is so overwhelmingly prevalent that it definitely warrants marking as a minefield. Once again, largely because 3-D animators are usually young men, subject matter that appeals to them tends to take the guise of a dead horse that gets beaten so often somebody needs to report the cruelty. Allow me to share a list of story subjects many would like to put a bullet through:

- ▶ Dragons
- ▶ Dungeons
- ▶ Robots
- ▶ Dinosaurs
- ▶ Spaceships
- ▶ Unrealistically endowed women (this, unfortunately, might not be totally true for games)
- ▶ *Matrix*-style "bullet time"
- ▶ *Star Wars* re-creations

Now, before you call me a prude, I'm not saying this to impose my personal taste. However, I have heard these categories flagged not only by art directors but by many objective observers outside our industry. So my advice is not to ever touch these subjects but rather to think twice before embracing them. Remember, no matter how cool you think that dinosaur you've made is, the dinosaurs in any of the three *Jurassic Park* movies are probably way better.

Obviously if you're trying to get an animation job at Blizzard, the makers of *Warcraft III*, or ID, the makers of *Quake* and *Doom*, you had better be able to create awesome dungeons and/or dragons. But even in this case, you have a rich opportunity for creativity. Instead of exactly duplicating a potential employer's existing character, you can create a new character that fits in their creative universe. This allows you to go beyond simply showing your technical skills to showing that you can be creative within external parameters.

Not Having a Story

All too often, animators pass up opportunities to tell a fun or even rewarding story. With alarming frequency filmmakers will go through an enormous amount of work to create a piece of CG without any story all. The only thing worse than another story about a large-breasted woman riding a dragon is another story featuring a large-breasted woman and a dragon that doesn't go anywhere.

Another manifestation of this type of pitfall is when animators create technology-driven stories. Each time a revolutionary new CG tool becomes available, a rash of animations that abuse that tool magically appear. When the first global illumination renderers became available, animators reveled in the fact that they could finally make computer animations that didn't look like shiny plastic. But an alarmingly large number of films began to surface that featured little else but an uninteresting object that was globally illuminated.

The way to avoid this pitfall is to make sure there is a story-driven reason to use a particular tool. If you're going to use crowd-control software to create a flock of birds, make a character to go with it with a head made of birdseed. That is to say, make the technologies you use serve your story, instead of vice versa.

Gratuitous Photorealism

Photorealism is certainly one of the areas where CG shines with a perfectly convincing glint. But stylistically and aesthetically there are a couple of issues with photorealism worth considering. One, our medium is an animated medium. This means that by definition we are imparting the illusion of life to something fictitious. CG animators will undoubtedly create an indistinguishable virtual human. But when that finally happens, many will be asking the question, "Why?" By the time we can completely reproduce reality, why not just videotape it?

The animated film *Final Fantasy: The Spirits Within* illustrates quite eloquently the issues involved here. Most will agree that this was the most photorealistic animation to date when the film came out, but it highlighted for many a strange quality: The closer you get to realistic human characters, the more apparent the animation's shortcomings become. At the same time, the Gollum character in the *Lord of the Rings* movies shows that using photorealism to bring the fictional to life can be deeply effective.

Biting Off More Than You Can Chew

As a teacher and as an animator myself, attempts to create overly ambitious projects are something I've witnessed many times. This is by far the most frequent and most damaging pitfall for new animators. A surefire way to ensure your film will not be finished is to start one you *can't* finish. It is also an understandably common thing to do because it is difficult to know your full capabilities when just starting out. This is by far the most common and most damaging of pitfalls for CG animators and leads us to the next phase of our story-filtering process—"Feasibility."

Feasibility

By now, you're probably growing quite fond of your story idea and starting to get the feeling that it simply must see the light of day. You're still in the glow of creative inspiration and chomping at the bit to commence your Frankenstein dreams. But this is the part of the process where you hear the record needle scratch painfully, stopping the music abruptly. The last thing you have to do before starting your film is the toughest: It's time to take your precious, inspired idea through the security gate and give it a humiliating full-body cavity search. It is precisely here, before you do any actual work, that you have to turn mercilessly critical of your story. By taking this step, you can save yourself a lot of suffering down the road.

Take a sober and objective view as you consider the feasibility of each aspect of your story. What's at stake is nothing but the life or death of your project. Choosing a story is a simple proposition compared to choosing a story about which you can complete a well-crafted animation. A key point to remember is that you can make *anything*, but you can't make *everything*. CG's magical capabilities can be a seductive drug, especially to those starting out, causing you to attempt projects much larger and more complex than you can finish.

And to be clear, many find this challenge an enjoyable puzzle—to take a complex story and figure out which tools and techniques will make it digestible and feasible. As you look around the world of completed CG animation, one of the things you see is artists who have learned to finesse their limitations. Animations, whether the traditional 2-D or today's 3-D, are often simple stories for a reason. Many films consist of visual elements as simple as a single, modestly textured character performing in a minimalist environment. Victor Navone's short film *Alien Song* features exactly this. In this famous short, a very simple, cartoonish alien sings the beginning of the song "I Will Survive" and is promptly squashed by a disco ball. Navone focused on the one-eyed alien character's diva-style singing movements, leaving the rest of the film understated. This simplicity not only allowed him to finish the film, but it allowed his simple, funny little story to shine. *Alien Song* became a viral Internet phenomenon on a par with the dancing baby from *Ally McBeal* and also landed Navone a character-animation job at Pixar.

So here are a few elements to examine to aid you in discovering whether your story is practical to animate.

Your Experience Level

The amount of training and experience you have should be a prime indicator of how large or complex your story can be. Obviously, if you haven't made any films before, only entertain the simplest story ideas. Something along the lines of a single, unadorned character in an abstract or impressionistic environment. Many traditional animators would often create their first films by doing a "sack of flour" animation, where they would study the art of character animation with the exercise of putting a sack of flour through its emotional paces. Creating a simple pantomime of the most minimal of characters is an excellent way to do some relatively quick practicing.

For those of you who have some experience in CG, it is advisable to consider how many unfamiliar tasks or skills your story will require of you. I recommend a story that does not demand that you learn more than a few major areas. For example, if you have never modeled extensive environments before, do not attempt a film with a chase scene that goes through multiple settings. If you have never animated characters before, do not attempt to create a crowd scene.

Time

Next, consider the window of time you have to make this film. Does it have to be done during a semester of school? Before your money runs out and you have to get a job? Before the jokes and references in your story get old?

Because the complexity of films spans a giant spectrum, it is fairly common for filmmakers to make a one-to-three-minute-long film, featuring one or two characters in a simple setting, in a few months. This can be a simple barometer to measure your project's complexity.

Resources

Although we'll consider the tools and resources at your disposal briefly in the next chapter, it's important to at least do a sanity check immediately. Do you have the tools necessary to create your story? Have you seen a story of the scope and magnitude you are considering, created with software and hardware similar to what you will be using? If your equipment is slow and outdated, simply tell an even less complicated story. CG filmmakers have been creating effective stories for many years now, which means that computers a couple years old can still be used to tell good stories.

Scope

Next, do some high-level dissection of the story to ascertain the breadth of work ahead of you. Here are some of the types of questions you should ask.

How Long Is the Story?
Even though you don't have a script yet, visualize your characters going through your story in as much detail as you can. Act out the motions physically and time yourself with a stopwatch. Although it is too early in the process to be at all accurate, this can at least get you in the ballpark of how many minutes your film will be.

How Many Characters?

This is a simple question. Each character in your story adds its own set of tasks (Figure 1-4). But you need to consider that complexity more than doubles when you add a second character. Not only will you have two characters moving around, but they might be talking to each other, or physically interacting with each other. Adding a third more than triples the complexity.

How Complex Are They?

Many different features determine the complexity of your characters. How realistic and how detailed are they? How many limbs and digits do they have? How close to the camera will they get? Do they talk? What is the range of physical movement they must perform?

How Many Environments?

How many different scenes will you need to model? How realistic and detailed do they need to be? How much background animation is necessary?

How Many Special Effects?

Does your story call for water, pixie dust, laser beams, clouds, or any other special effects? Do you plan to use tools that simulate physics, cloth, hair? These types of features can quickly balloon the complexity and length of your production.

FIGURE 1-4   Each character you add brings a host of tasks to your production.

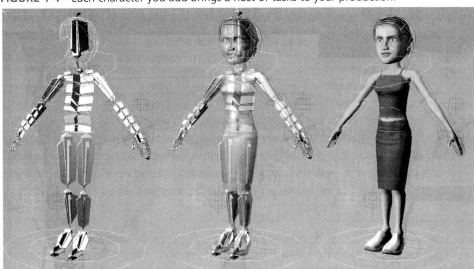

What Is the Stylization?

How will your artistic style simplify or complicate your production? If you want to be hyper-detailed, plan for more complexity and maybe a shorter story. If your characters are stylized like simple *Pokemon* monsters, you may be able to have more story.

How Much Dialogue?

How much will your characters be talking? Lip-synching can be a laborious, time-consuming element in a production.

What Is the Nature and Quantity of Action?

An animation of characters having a conversation is quite a bit simpler than an animation of characters in a violent fight. How much physical action will your characters have, and how much interaction will they have with each other? Does your story call for actions that you understand how to animate?

You can also accompany each of these questions with "Have I done that before?" and continue adding and answering as many of these types of questions as you can. Walk through your story again to help yourself find more questions to ask.

Two Final Filters

You may not have the answers to all these questions at this juncture. But for each of these types of questions you do not have answers for, and for each task you have never done before, you must make a mental red flag. And if doing this type of analysis brings up too many of these red flags, you must consider a simpler story to tell. But two key directives will help you navigate the tricky terrain of choosing a story.

Keep It Short

Especially for your first few films, it will be difficult to have an accurate sense of how long it will take you to complete them. Therefore, it is highly recommended that your first attempts err on the side of brevity. Even completing an animation of less than one minute can provide an enormous amount of information that you can apply to future projects. Typically two to three minutes of quality animation is an ambitious undertaking and room enough to tell a compelling story. Making a piece that is any longer only thins out your ability to make it good. Most viewers would rather see one minute of quality animation than ten minutes of mediocre work.

Keep It Focused

Make sure your film highlights what you are best at, what you are most interested in and most importantly, your story. Make sure that nothing obfuscates that focus. Resist the urge to add in gratuitous special effects simply because you've been experimenting with them, or putting in irrelevant 3-D objects simply because you've had them built. This will not only make your story more effective, but paring it down to its essentials will make it easier to produce.

I Now Pronounce You "Artist and Story"

It is a rigorous process to come up with a story that merits being brought to life through CG animation. But being thorough in your examination can provide you with added confidence as you move to the next step in the filmmaking odyssey, preproduction. Keep in mind that the process of settling on a final story can and should continue through the tasks of the next several chapters. This examination can be ongoing, but remember to keep it tough and show no mercy.

The Example Film's Story

I had several goals in mind when I set about finding a story for my film. I wanted to have a strong portfolio piece for getting my next job. I wanted to improve upon my character-animation and character-acting skills because I want to continue to focus on character work in the future. Specifically, I wanted to have a conversation between three characters because this seemed like a reasonable challenge given my previous work.

The Example Film's Subject Matter

I decided to collaborate on my story idea with a friend, Tony Parisi. Tony and I had worked together in the past, and he is one of the pioneers in the field of Internet virtual reality. His knowledge made collaborating on a story an enjoyable experience. Over the course of several brainstorming conversations we began to hit upon a topic I could make a film about.

We wanted to make a story about a next-generation socialization videogame. Through our experience with shared virtual reality and watching the phenomenon of massive online games, we became interested in the behaviors these games bring out in people.

I've had a love/hate relationship with videogames for many years. I do enjoy playing them, but I have always been irritated by the juvenile nature of their subject matter. I've always felt that playing is an important part of a healthy person's life, but I've also been sickly fascinated with people's behavior when playing goes out of balance and becomes escapism.

Tony and I enjoyed our mental exercise of pretending to be game designers and fleshing out what this fictional videogame would be like. It was fascinating to think about having to a turn a conversation or the act of making friends into a videogame.

I allowed myself to mull these things over for awhile. Then the actual story idea came to me when my wife and I were on the freeway and another driver cut us off. When my wife beeped the horn at him, he slammed on his brakes just to be a jerk and then sped away. That led me to thinking about jerks....

The story idea involves two fun-loving people playing a socializing game who are then accosted by a jerk. By adding this little conflict to the setting of the videogame environment, I started to have all the elements I was hoping to create.

Initial Feasibility

The story went through the entire gauntlet laid out in this chapter, and then some. Although its scope is definitely on the large side, it also has the special requirement of needing enough features to be used as an example for all the chapters in this book. Here are some of the many issues I had to consider for my story idea:

▶ I would use relatively low-polygon characters, something like what a next-generation videogame would feature. This not only fits stylistically but allows me to keep rendering times reasonable.

▶ The story would be largely conversational and gestural. Because I have spent the last two years focusing on facial and gestural animation, conversational animation plays to my strengths.

▶ Lastly, because I'm always ambitious, creating a fictitious videogame environment with interface elements and special effects would give me all the challenges I could handle.

Chapter 2

Production: 3ds max and the Animation Pipeline

Planning and scheduling comprises a chunk of work CG filmmakers must do that at first may not feel like CG filmmaking at all. But it could mean the difference between deftly finishing your film with a grand sense of accomplishment and finding yourself six months down the road with a virtual room full of virtual junk. Not only will thorough planning of your film project provide you with a crucial roadmap to navigate the complexities of your project, but it will also give you work habits that make you more valuable to a team.

Due to the long list of disciplines required to create a CG film, even short projects can quickly take on the complexity of a moon rocket. To handle this aspect of production, one must have a strong sense of all the individual tasks involved, how they interact with each other, and how long they take to complete.

Wearing the Producer's 50-Pound Hat

Most of the tasks in this chapter fall under a producer's job description. So it's worth briefly examining what a producer does because those tasks will need to be done for your film as well. To be sure, exactly what a producer does can vary greatly from studio to studio—from essentially administrative assistance all the way up to assistant directing. But there are plenty of commonalities that most producers share.

The producer is not unlike a shepherd, who must account for all the various tasks in a production and oversee the completion of each and every one. To do this, they must have enough knowledge about a given task to know whether it is being done correctly and efficiently. Furthermore, they must understand the interdependencies between each task and how they impact on the project as a whole. On even modest-size projects, this requires producers to be able to efficiently track an often staggering quantity of details, many of critical consequence.

But prior to the actual execution of a project, and of equal importance, producers will architect a strategy for a production, often referred to as a *production pipeline*. This involves identifying the different steps in the production process, choosing the tools and techniques to execute each step, and creating connections between all those steps. You can think of it as creating a factory assembly line. A simple example might be as follows: The art department creates concept art of characters and their environment. This art is passed on to the modeling department, which builds the 3-D models of the characters and environment. These 3-D models are passed on to the texturing department to apply digitally painted surfaces. The characters are then given to the rigging department, where skeletons and animation controls are placed in them. The finished character assets are then animated inside their environments by the animation department. Then finished lighting is placed in the scenes by the lighting department. And, finally, the finished scenes are rendered in the rendering department. The producer defines these steps and their connections. For example, the producer must make sure the rigging department can use the models that the modeling department creates.

This production pipeline strategy is then used as a template to flesh out a production plan. This plan defines all the nitty-gritty details of every task and the order in which they are executed.

The thoroughness of a production plan relates directly to how many unseen, production-delaying, all-nighter-necessitating, magically appearing tasks happen later in the project.

Preparing to Prepare

Now let's return to your story with the eye of a producer. In the last chapter we went through a fairly rigorous process to investigate your story. But that mainly amounts to a sanity check to weed out the "bad apple" ideas. Now it is time to define the myriad of particulars for your CG animation project. By first analyzing your story in as fine-grained detail as possible, you can begin to strategize your project's pipeline.

Scope of Work

Here is one of the many spots in this book where the tasks in a chapter will overlap. Hopefully, as you are moving forward, your story is coalescing into focus and therefore finer details are discernible to you. At this point, revisit the questions you used from the last chapter to determine your scope of work. Additionally you may want to start on the next chapter's task: scriptwriting. This only needs to be a rough approximation of the dialogue, with terse notes to indicate action. But the practical, scope-related questions combined with a more fleshed-out story can begin to reveal production tasks in more detail.

Another powerful tool for this stage is to draw thumbnail storyboards representing each scene of your story (see Figure 2-1). Because you'll be drawing extensive storyboards of each camera shot in Chapter 5, these thumbnails need only give you a sense of what will be in your film. Even if you draw stick figures at this point, these can reveal many important production points.

FIGURE 2-1   With these thumbnail sketches, I began answering many specific production questions for my film.

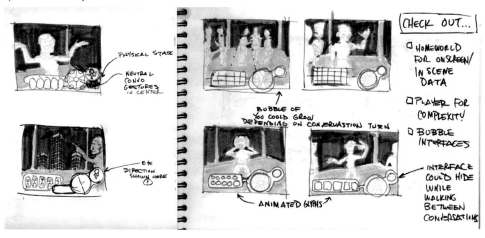

You don't need to be defining the appearance of your film at this point, so even a diagram can provide you with many answers. Maybe the thumbnails point out a prop or a set piece you hadn't thought about modeling yet. Maybe they show that you'll need to spend extra time planning camera moves. Think of these thumbnails as a diagnostic tool.

Attempt to catalog and identify every major element of your story at this point: characters, props, environments, special effects, rough number of camera shots, types and length of character animation, amount of background animation, and so on.

You also want a sense of how much music, dialogue, and sound effects will be required, as well as how much text and motion graphics you'll need for titling. You'll now want to have a broad but accurate assessment of the work entailed in your entire film project. This scope of work will be the foundation for you to draft a detailed production plan.

R&D and Learning

No matter what your skill level, it's likely by now you've identified several areas where you will need some learning to be able to accomplish the required task. Maybe you have never textured a character before and your story calls for a freckle-faced little boy. Maybe you have never created a lava flow and your story calls for a volcano. These types of gaps can create significant delays in a production. But with the right approach, you can avoid floundering and repeating work through too much trial and error.

First, by assessing the gaps in your skill set that pertain to the project at hand, you can narrow the focus of your learning. This will make you learn both faster and more effectively. For example, if your story calls for a lumberjack and you need to learn character rigging, you can focus on rigging a biped and ignore quadrupeds and winged characters.

You can treat this process as though you are being your own research and development (R&D) department. Most top production houses have a small crew specifically dedicated to inventing technologies and techniques to create innovative imagery. This is a prime indicator of R&D's importance in a production strategy. At PDI, this meant that films such as *Antz* and *Shrek* benefited from the fluid dynamics research of Nick Foster and Scott Peterson. Both films featured stunning and innovative fluid animations made possible by their work.

On a smaller scale, this may mean simply spending some time creating a better skin material or affecting moonlight through a window. Even if it doesn't necessarily mean innovation in the world of computer graphics at large, this type of study on your own or in a small production can greatly improve the quality of the imagery you produce. Also, focused time spent learning and innovating during preproduction can help you avoid significant delays during production as well as help you definitively answer questions of feasibility.

Feasibility Revisited

During the course of this chapter, much more of the true face of your story will be revealed to you. As more details become available to you, you must repeatedly weigh them against all the feasibility issues outlined in the previous chapter and additional pragmatic criteria as you move forward.

Within many of you, a pitched battle is being waged. On one hand, as you move forward you become more and more emotionally invested in the story you have chosen. On the other hand, as your feasibility picture becomes more accurate, realities of practicality become more apparent. It is imperative that you manage to keep a surgical objectivity about what you can and can't do. This may more than likely lead you to excising elements of your production unsentimentally. You might be saying, "It would be so awesome if my character was animated with the full set of muscles to make its movement totally accurate." But once you factor in the amount of time and effort it would take to create a fully functioning set of muscles, it will likely become clear that you will just never finish your project.

The key to keeping this from being a painful process is to at all times have a sense of your project as a whole. By weighing each individual feature against the entire film, you can begin to develop a sense of balance. First ask if a given feature is important to telling your story. And ask if focusing extra time on that feature will take away from other important elements. This balance may be one of the most valuable skills to develop as a CG filmmaker, because balance, combined of course with artistic skill, is at the very center of creating a quality project.

The areas of learning and research from the previous section play a significant role in determining feasibility during the planning stage. In a perfect world, even as a professional, you want to learn something new on every project. But the practical time requirements of learning new things can't be ignored. So naturally, if your planning unearths too many areas you need to learn about, you should consider paring down your story.

And even if you already know everything you need to reproduce *Final Fantasy: The Spirits Within* by yourself, you still have to consider the practicalities of your hardware. It is important to assess early on during preproduction whether your computer(s) can drive enough of your animation in real time for you to be able to animate effectively. And you need to investigate how long individual frame render times will be on your machine and extrapolate how much time it will take to render a scene. Then factor in that you might be rendering a scene several times before it is final.

You can't be expected to know, at this stage, everything you need to know to accurately calculate whether your story goals are achievable. Rough schematic sketches of your story idea may be helpful at this point (see Figure 2-2), but you should plan on investigating feasibility frequently throughout the preproduction of your film as details become clearer.

FIGURE 2-2   This is a page from my notebook that illustrates some of my planning with both notes and sketches.

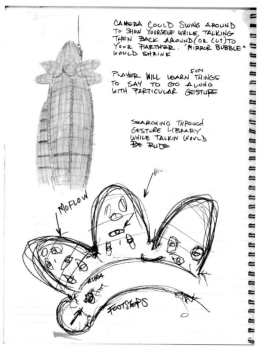

Planning

Once you have defined a scope of work you feel comfortable with, you can begin to form a production plan. In a small or solo production, this can consist of a pipeline description, a task list, and a schedule. Admittedly, for the very simplest of films, these items can be minimal, and it might be possible to complete your film without them. But it is worth remembering that the better you simulate a production environment, the more you can thrive in a real one. Without a doubt, if your project is anything beyond the very simplest, you will benefit greatly from a well-thought-out plan.

Defining the Max Animation Pipeline

3ds max is capable of a mind-numbing variety of tasks, and due to this program's flexibility, it is possible to do them in almost any order and practically all at once. But max does not have a built-in pipeline that defines how you should create your film. To create something as complex as an animated 3-D film, each artist must have a process of their own.

Architecting your project's pipeline can be a complex undertaking. In fact, expert producers with years of top-level experience often go through several iterations when settling on a pipeline strategy for an animation project. Therefore, it can help get you started to separate pipeline building into four steps:

▶ Defining your production steps

▶ Choosing the appropriate tools

▶ Choosing the appropriate methodologies to use those tools

▶ Identifying dependencies and recursiveness between the steps

The Steps of a Typical Production

You saw in the last chapter that the subject matter of stories 3ds max is capable of telling can be infinitely varied. Therefore, it is not possible to outline a series of production steps that apply to every story. However, because the vast predominance of stories involves characters of some kind, we can at least look at a series of steps that can be adapted to most productions. Fortunately, because Discreet equips 3ds max with industry-standard features and tools, this series of steps is similar no matter what professional 3-D animation software you are using.

A simple skeleton of steps to follow when creating your pipeline might look something like this:

PREPRODUCTION	PRODUCTION	POSTPRODUCTION
Story idea	Character modeling	Compositing
Scriptwriting	Character texturing	Motion graphics
Concept art	Character shader creation	Editing
Storyboarding	Body rigging	
Animatics	Head rigging	
Casting and recording	Environment modeling	
Sound effects and music	Environment texturing	
	Props modeling and texturing	
	Effects modeling	
	Scene layouts	
	Facial animation	
	Body animation	
	Background and effects animation	
	Rendering	

Assembling a Max-Centered Toolset

The stated goal of this book is to provide a description of a production that is as typical as possible. And indeed, this was my intent all along when planning the pipeline of my film. To this end, we will indeed use max as the foundation for our toolset and keep that toolset as compact and simplified as possible.

Max Plug-ins   There is a vast, kaleidoscopic multitude of third party plug-ins to augment 3ds max with, created to meet specific needs. For purposes of simplicity in your production and keeping your learning curve from getting too steep, I recommend limiting the number of plug-ins you attempt learning to use for your film. The best rule of thumb in sifting through the large array of plug-ins is to purchase and use only those which are specifically needed to tell the story you are currently working on.

MAXScripts   Additionally, 3ds max has the MAXScript scripting language, which allows people to solve specific workflow issues simply. Communities are online to support max with large libraries of free, downloadable scripts and plug-ins. These free, downloadable scripts are an invaluable resource for independent animators. They can be easily installed by copying them to the appropriate folder. MAXScripts have been created to augment almost all areas of 3ds max. They can take the form of anything from scripts that allow a simple, repetitive task to be done with a keyboard shortcut, all the way up to full-blown plug-ins. Again, even though any 3ds max filmmaker should be familiar with using MAXScripts, the same rule of thumb of using only those needed for your specific work should apply.

Image Creation and Editing   Here, the industry standards are clear, so the choice is easy. Adobe Photoshop and Corel Painter are the main options. One or both of these programs will be used throughout your production for everything from concept art (if you choose to create it digitally), to texture maps for 3-D objects, to background images.

Combustion for Compositing and Motion Graphics   A couple recent trends in CG have led to a tighter integration of video compositing tools into CG pipelines. One trend is to move away from having to create 100 percent of an animation in 3-D. Pragmatic artists are finding that it can often be faster to create certain effects in a 2-D compositing package. Additionally, animators are discovering that by rendering a scene in multiple component layers, they can have more control over the look of their renderings after the fact. Programs such as Discreet's combustion can manipulate these video layers much like Photoshop manipulates still images.

Video Editing   To splice together finished footage, create text graphics for titles and credits, and output a finished piece of video, you can use video-editing programs such as Adobe Premiere and Final Cut Pro.

Choosing Methodologies

Once you have your toolset equipped, you can grab a hardhat and some steel-toed shoes and get down to the job site. Now you can set about actually defining your pipeline. For almost every production step you have, there are multiple techniques and methodologies to choose from to accomplish that particular goal. Choosing which techniques to use can be influenced by personal preference and training. And it is important to know your chosen tool thoroughly.

However, you can also learn which are the most standard and preferred methods by looking to online forums, mentors, and partners for guidance.

> ✎ NOTE   *Each of the chapters of this book outline specific methodology choices for the various production of tasks. I've attempted to make my technique and methodology decisions based on simplicity and what are common practices. This is, by no means, to infer that this book describes the only way to make a film with 3ds max.*

Defining a Pipeline

The next step of your planning stage is to define a pipeline for your project. Taking the set of tools you have chosen and the set of methodologies for using those tools, you can start to define a pipeline that guides you through the steps of production. This pipeline can then change from an abstract set of steps into a living and breathing production process. You can do this by visualizing a particular asset as it passes through the phases of production, and you can ferret out dependencies in this manner. For example, it may become evident that you can't know exactly how much of your environment will need to be detailed until you have placed and animated cameras in your scene. Or you may discover that you cannot animate some specific actions in your animation until sound effects have been placed in your soundtrack.

Besides these practical matters, you may find technology dependencies. For example, it may become apparent that the rendering solution you have chosen requires a different type of texturing. There is no way you will reveal all the potential problems and dependencies in your process. But by neutralizing potential obstacles during preproduction (Figure 2-3), it is much less likely those problems will result in you repeating work during the actual production.

Identifying Granular Tasks

At this stage, you can compare your pipeline to your story as it has evolved to this point. By breaking up your story into its component assets, you can then imagine sending these individual items through your pipeline and begin to see the individual tasks each asset will require. You can see that a character will need sketches, design drawings, modeling, texturing, and so on, as it moves through the pipeline. And by drilling down into each step of this pipeline with a given asset, you can start to generate a thorough task list for your production.

The details of each of the steps can vary greatly, depending on the tools and methodologies you are using. So think of the following list as a top-level starting point for you to drill down into. The more details of your production that you reveal at this point, the more accurate a picture of the effort required you will paint for yourself.

FIGURE 2-3   This flowchart illustrates the production pipeline of my film.

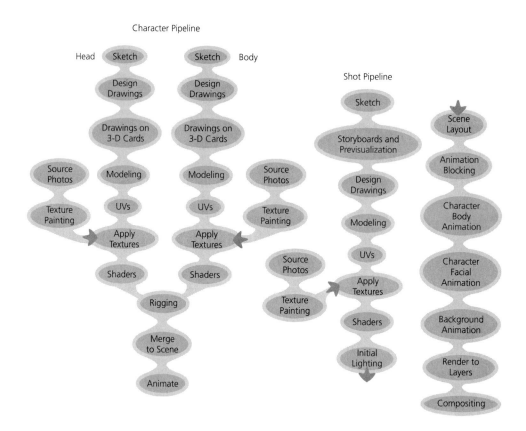

Organizational Methods

Here is where you'll really earn your producer stripes. Starting at this point before you have created any significant assets, you'll want to set up at least the shell of an organizational structure for your project. To many, this seems unnecessary on a small production. But there are many ways that bad organizational habits can frustrate your efforts. A single 3-D character can wind up with many dozens of individual components, from all the digits in just one hand, to multiple texture image files, to multiple animation handles. If all these objects are not named, grouped, stored, and backed up properly, they can become lost or difficult to handle. Avoiding these types of difficulties is absolutely critical to a smooth production.

A good way to approach organization is to pretend you are going to be working in a large group, even if you are working solo or with just a couple partners. This is doubly important because you will want to work with a team at some point and because you may take breaks in your production process and might need to return to your work after you have long since forgotten many of the details. Therefore, your organizational structure needs to function in a way that you or someone else can pick up the work you were doing and continue without having to play archeologist.

Good Practices

Your organizational structure should grow and adapt as you move through the phases of production, but there are a few practices to instill in yourself from the outset and carry with you throughout the process.

Name Everything and Name It Logically   This is a vitally important habit to develop. Naming conventions are a nuts-and-bolts mechanism in any type of collaboration. By default, max wants to name things sphere01 or line05. Once you have had the experience of being handed a 3-D character to animate on a deadline and found everything inside it named object01, object02, and so on, you'll never forget this practice.

Resist the urge to give objects funny names because you may not remember the joke three months later. Using a logical naming system will not only help you navigate and manage your scenes and assets more easily, it will assist you when referring to those objects from within scripts and in other technical situations as well.

This practice should apply to absolutely everything—every element in any 3-D scene and every file of any type. In a production of any significant size, you may actually want to create a crib sheet for yourself to catalog the various naming systems.

Create Logical Folder Structures   You will undoubtedly be creating a large number and variety of files for your project. Lost files can halt production dead in its tracks, and having to hunt for them at all is an avoidable slowdown. By creating a well-organized, logical tree structure, you not only make files easy to find but easier to move as well. 3-D files that reference many external texture image files is just one example of where the use of file paths is a critical issue. Trying to move a 3-D model file when its texture maps are all over the hard drive can turn a two-second job into one that can make you reach for the Prozac.

Iterate Your Files Frequently   I also recommend periodically saving the file you are working on as a new and separate file. This, in a sense, provides you with an archive of your work at its various stages. 3ds max, with a host of third-party plug-ins added, running a large and complex 3-D scene can most definitely crash. Occasionally, it will crash in such a lovely way that the file you are working on becomes corrupted and unusable. Creating iterations of your work can partially alleviate that perennial problem as well as give you, in effect, a more powerful "undo" system.

Use Layers   Layers are an organizational feature that shows up in many tools, particularly Photoshop, max, and combustion. They provide a powerful way to organize your work and speed your workflow. Having logically grouped layers within your max scenes can allow you to turn off everything but what you are focused on—be it the lights, characters, backgrounds, or whatever. This can increase your ability to understand what's going on in a complex 3-D scene as well as speed up your real-time interactivity. By putting characters in separate layers, you can quickly move from one to another when animating and keep yourself from accidentally grabbing the wrong objects.

Back Up Your Files   This one is a no-brainer, I hope. But more than just backing up your files, think about your backup strategy at the outset of production. You can quickly create more material than will fit on one burnable CD. But once again, through careful organization of your file structures you can create folders that contain all the latest versions of your files in one place for quick and easy backup. If you are creating a large and long project, I recommend hiring an armored car service, creating copies of your work, and sending them to a hard target bunker (or a buddy's house) for safekeeping.

Use Collaboration Tools   When working in a small team, from remote locations or not, rich and rapid team communication plays a paramount role in a project's success. Besides the now-obvious e-mail and instant messaging, other simple web-based collaboration tools, such as message boards and picture galleries can aid a production by aiding collaboration and critique. These are valuable tools even for the solo animator because there are often a couple tasks you'll look to others for help on. Having a "work in progress" web page is an excellent resource for showing others your work and, if planned carefully, can turn into a website to support, promote, and distribute your film once you release it. A web-based message board is a simple and powerful way to invite critiques of your work in progress as well as communicate day-to-day with collaborators. It's good to have a high-bandwidth website with lots of file space so that you can store and display production clips of your final film.

Scheduling: Putting a Gun to the Head of Invention

Once you have a task list that has been informed by your story and production pipeline, you can set about arranging those tasks in time. This can be a difficult chore at first, but it takes on greater and greater importance as your productions climb the evolutionary tree, from a mere hobby to professional-grade work. If you are seeking a job, being able to prove that you can schedule your work is a big plus. And if you are trying to get your project funded by outside sources, showing your client or investor that your project will be done before their money runs out will be much more than a big plus.

Certainly for the solo and small group endeavors this book is geared toward, scheduling will not carry the $50 million weight that a feature film carries. Because you are either new to CG filmmaking or attempting to create a film that's more ambitious than anything you've created before, the many unknown factors will make realistic scheduling difficult. Indeed, this is one of the reasons R&D is separated from production. This makes more of the tasks of production "known entities" and therefore you know how long they will take.

Still, comparing the work ahead of you against the time you have available is important. This comparison is the final word in feasibility and the key to making you an efficient filmmaker.

Production Documents

As you complete your project plan, it is wise to create a couple production documents for yourself and especially your partners, if you have them. Create a task list and a schedule. For large projects, there are tools specifically for this purpose, such as Microsoft Project and NXN's alienbrain. But frankly, these are only necessary if your crew is more than a few people and your project is more than a few minutes long. For small independent projects, I recommend a simple spreadsheet for your task list and a program such as Microsoft Outlook for scheduling.

Factors That Affect Scheduling

Given that it is likely CG filmmaking is new to you, accurately planning your film will be difficult. But this makes it even more important that you at least attempt to assess the scope of your work. This is also an absolutely vital practice to have if you plan to move into the professional world. Here are a few areas to examine to assist in your understanding of scheduling.

Task List Detail
Your scheduling is only as accurate as the detail of your task list (Figure 2-4). A task such as texture-mapping a face is a multistep process that can take several days for an expert. But the more tasks such as this are broken down into subtasks, the better chance you have of calculating how much time they will take.

How Much Is New to You?
As noted earlier, you should assess how many of the production tasks are new to you. It's difficult to determine exactly how long it will take somebody to learn a task before being able to accomplish it in a production situation. So unless you've done a particular task under the demands of a production environment, you'll not only need to factor in time to learn it, but you should double or triple the time it normally takes a professional to perform that task.

FIGURE 2-4   These pages from my notebooks show some of the many task lists I created for myself during my production.

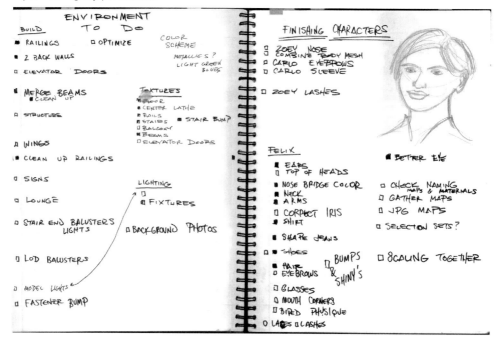

Quality and Detail

The quality and detail level you intend for your work will also factor greatly into any scheduling you do. Take, for example, a couple of the bulkiest tasks. If you want to do feature film–quality character animation, you can count on taking a full day just to do a few seconds of animation—for complex scenes it may take a week. And that's if you're a professional-level animator. If you choose to do something more like television-quality character animation, you can figure that professional animators often accomplish as much as 30 seconds to even a full minute of animation per week.

The same type of assessment applies toward another of the larger tasks: modeling. A character such as Dr. Aki Ross from *Final Fantasy: The Spirits Within* or Gollum from *The Lord of the Rings: The Two Towers* takes a small crew of artists several months to create. On the other hand, simple cartoonish 3-D characters can be modeled in an afternoon. It's common, though, for accomplished modelers to take two or three weeks to model and texture a quality character.

Priorities

Another point in the preproduction process is to ask yourself, "What is the bare-bones set of features my story needs?" The answers to this question, combined with the dictates of your pipeline, may give you some guidance in scheduling your tasks. For example, if you've modeled and animated a great flock of bats, but your vampire isn't scary, it's a sure sign your priorities are out of whack. Also, anything that falls under the "That Would Be Cool" category should definitely be moved to the end of your production schedule.

Go Get 'em, Tiger!

Armed with a solid plan, you can move ahead into the preproduction of your film with more confidence. And you can make sure your planning efforts are not wasted by updating your plan often throughout the course of production. Stay in the habit of knowing not only what it will take to execute the entire film but also what it will take to finish from any given point. Be prepared to ax unnecessary parts mercilessly while allowing for flexibility and adaptation to keep your overall plan a living entity.

Planning the Example Film

As I set about planning my film, my story was starting to settle down, but it was still slightly evolving. It was also getting more ambitious than any film I had made so far. I needed a plan thorough enough to help me manage the complexity of my project but also flexible enough to evolve as my story did and, indeed, as changes occurred in my life.

Top-level Considerations

One of the main issues I had to be realistic about from the outset was the large amount of new things I would have to learn to tell this story. But because this was my own project, I could set my own deadlines and give myself the time I needed.

Another key consideration was the length of time it would take to render a frame of animation. As I examined each element of my project, I thought about how detailed my models could be and how "high resolution" my textures could be from the perspective of how long they would take to render. It was no accident that my story was about a real-time 3-D videogame. This way, even though my film would be prerendered, it made stylistic sense to have the characters and environment be relatively "low resolution."

Scope of Work

By this time I knew many more details of my story, and I had an accurate vision of the scope of work I was biting off. I also knew there would be three characters, they would have colorful, animated auras around their heads, and there would be background animation representing the fake videogame interface. Here are the considerations I had compiled at this point in the process:

▶ **Scriptwriting**   My story is fairly subtle and therefore more difficult to write well, so the scriptwriting will take some extra time.

▶ **Lots of conceptual work**   This includes sketches and construction drawings of characters, sketches of the environment and the videogame elements, as well as design work for the graphic identity of the project.

▶ **Storyboarding and cinematic planning**   This involves drawing storyboards to help define camera shots and block out action. Although this is pretty straightforward, I did not know at the time how many storyboards I would be drawing.

▶ **Recording dialogue**   There needs to be dialogue with acting good enough to tell my tricky story.

▶ **Composing music and creating sound effects**   Soundtrack music and sound effects will play key roles in setting the mood and communicating many of the videogame-oriented story points.

▶ **Modeling and texturing three main characters**   I now know I have three main characters—two men and a woman. They should look as realistic as possible but with larger heads and hands.

▶ **Hair**   Because many 3-D graphics card manufacturers have been showing real-time hair in their demos, I thought the characters in my "videogame" should also have hair. Because I have used a hair plug-in before, I know it's a significant factor in both the amount of work and its impact on render time.

▶ **Character rigging**   Because all my previous character animation has been done with Character Studio, I want to use a more "industry-standard" bone-based rigging approach. I also want to do this to show a more industry-standard type of character rigging, similar to the type of rigs seen in *Maya*. This will be a significant challenge technically and because of time demands. I also know that the controls I will be able to give the character skeletons will affect the way I am able to animate the characters.

▶ **Modeling and texturing the architectural environment and interior**   I need to have an architectural environment that helps make my fictitious videogame look interesting to play.

▶ **Architectural exterior**   I want to have an establishing shot of the building where my story's conversation takes place.

▶ **Character auras**   The characters need to have a sculptural animated special effect around their heads—this is an important plot point. I have to work out some special-effects animation to go with my concept ideas.

▶ **Background characters**   There needs to be some background characters to establish that other players are playing this videogame. But these have to be created with some dirty tricks and finesse to minimize my workload. Luckily, they're mainly in the background.

▶ **Four to five minutes of conversational and gestural animation**   This will be a large chunk of work, but it can be minimized through careful camera cuts and framing. This is my favorite part of the process and the skill I am most interested in improving. I have animated one minute of two characters talking in one week for a past project, so this gives me a rough idea of a significant batch of time.

▶ **Lighting**   I want a colorful palette for this film, and I know I can achieve a lot of that through the lighting.

▶ **Rendering**   I want to do advanced rendering and depth of field, if possible. But setup issues and render times might play a factor. This isn't necessarily important to my story, so I'll leave it as a question to figure out later in production.

▶ **Fake videogame interface**   There needs to be an onscreen videogame interface that takes some graphic design work. It also requires some animating and compositing within a compositing package as well.

▶ **Videogame elements**   There needs to be game items and in-scene, 3-D game information that's animated after the characters.

▶ **Motion graphics**   I want my film to have some animated motion graphics to introduce the title and credits as well as establish a visual identity for the project.

▶ **Compositing**   I know I have compositing work to do for the interface, but there's also the possibility I will be compositing render layers, depending on the rendering solution.

The Example Film's Toolset

For the most part, I knew what my toolset consisted of for my production, but I did reserve making a final decision on a couple options until I was further along. Here are the tools I decided to use:

▶ **3ds max 5**

▶ **Photoshop and Painter**   For texture maps creation and many other tasks.

▶ **Shag hair**   Plug-in for max.

▶ **Automated lip-synch**   Possibly Ventriloquist, possibly Eyematic's FaceStation for facial motion capture.

▶ **Numerous free MAXScripts**   Notably for building character rigs automatically.

▶ **Plug-in renderer**   Use of a plug-in renderer depends on time constraints.

▶ **Adobe Illustrator**   For videogame interface design.

> ▶ **Discreet's combustion**   For compositing and possibly some color correction.
> ▶ **Adobe Premiere**   For final videoediting.

Feasibility

The key feasibility issues for me to consider were the general size and complexity of my production. I knew that it would take a very long and sustained effort, but it would also take working as smartly as I possibly could. Organization and planning would be critical.

Also, I knew learning character rigging would take some time. And frankly, as I started my film I did not know how big a challenge that would be. But it was definitely something I was interested in and really enjoyed. So the difficulty of the challenge was acceptable to me.

I simply was not sure about the feasibility of doing some advanced rendering such as global illumination. All my experiments at this point had produced render times much longer than with standard rendering. But I knew that this production would be long and that rendering came close to the end. So I knew that I had a good chance of picking up some knowledge before it became time to render my project. Because it fell under the "That Would Be Cool" category, I risked leaving this as an open issue.

I knew there would be a lot of facial animation, which is a labor-intensive task. But my job for the past two years had focused on facial animation, so I was confident enough to attempt this.

A lot of character animation would be needed, and I wanted it to be better than anything I had done before. But because this was supposed to be in a videogame where the players were supposedly making user-triggered gestures, the animation could have a little repetition, which could save a lot of work for me. Some of it was even supposed to look bad, which isn't hard to do at all.

Recording the dialogue would be a significant job, but I had directed dozens of dialogue-recording sessions in the past. Furthermore, I had several friends—David Ewers, Heather Dunn, and Michael Siebielec—who I knew would be comfortable acting and were willing to do this for me as a favor. And my good friend Matt Carter had agreed to do sound engineering as well as music and sound effects composition for this project. These were significant tasks that were beyond my skill set and I did not have time for.

What Got Cut

As my production got underway, I started to get a more accurate picture of my scope of work, and indeed it got pretty big. It became utterly critical that I follow my own teaching. I decided I had to cut the exterior scenes from my film. This was painful, because at that point I had already started designing building exteriors (see Figure 2-5). But looking back, it was definitely the right decision. This would have been a significant chunk of work.

FIGURE 2-5   Here are a few of the many drawings I had already done for exterior shots for my film. I cut the exterior shots when the scope of work for my film started to become clearer.

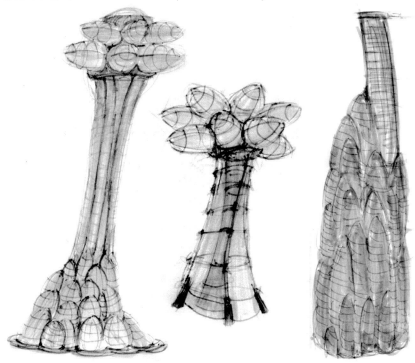

But an even more significant and difficult decision had to be made later on after the dialogue was recorded (see Chapter 6 for details). Although I was very clear from the outset that my film would be ambitious in length, I was planning for under six minutes. But once the dialogue was recorded, it came out to a whopping eight minutes, which was simply more animation than I would be able to finish. At that juncture, I chose to split my script into a two-part story to make my production feasible. This had a great impact on many aspects of my planning, but it highlights perfectly the unsentimental decision-making needed to finish a film project.

Key Methodology Decisions

Here's a rundown of some of the key features in my production. These are the methodology choices that stuck out to me during the planning phase of my project:

▶ **Traditional concept work**   Since I work on the computer so much, I welcome any excuse to spend time away from it. Doing traditional drawing is pure joy. I will occasionally draw on the computer.

▶ **Subdivision surface modeling for characters**   For many years my CG work has been mostly "real time," so I have done a lot of polygon modeling. Because subdivision surface modeling uses the same toolset, this will allow me to easily use this more powerful technology.

▶ **Lots of procedural modeling for the environment**   I plan on using lots of modeling tricks to make creating the environment faster and more editable. This means a lot of lofting, beveling, instancing, and referencing.

▶ **Separate heads**   To make rigging my characters simpler, I've decided to make the heads separate objects from the body. Aesthetically this is a compromise with an eye toward making the characters easier to manage.

▶ **Character textures starting from photographs**   This is a technique I have some training and practice in. But it also fits stylistically with my videogame theme. This way, it looks as if the people playing the game have put pictures of themselves on their characters.

▶ **Standard bone rigging with scripted controls**   Besides being more of an animation industry standard, this approach allows me to make character rigs customized to the way I want animated and specifically what I need to animate.

▶ **Facial morph targets**   This is probably the most common way to animate faces and the way I have been doing them for years.

▶ **Pose-to-pose animation**   This is also a very standard approach to animation, and it's also a fairly expedient technique.

▶ **Mouse and joystick motion capture**   I used this technique a lot at my last job. It's a fun and new way to animate and can save me a lot of time. I can sneak this technique in wherever possible for incidental animation and wherever it is appropriate.

▶ **Lighting for environment**   For the environment I'll focus on setting the mood for my animation through the color scheme.

▶ **Separate lighting for characters**   Digital characters are much like movie stars in that some lighting makes them look good, and other lighting is, well... unflattering. Therefore, I want the characters to have a separate set of lights to give myself more control.

Chapter 3

Scriptwriting: Story and Character Through Dialogue

Once again, it's time to reach into your CG filmmaker's closet stuffed to the gills with all the different hats you wear. After living in 3-D animation land, switching gears to scriptwriting mode may seem like the equivalent of taking off a space helmet and putting on a feathered headdress. But as part of our holistic approach to filmmaking, scriptwriting can transcend simply defining what your characters will say and become an additional method of inventing and crafting your story. So get out your trusty notebook or your not-so-trusty word processor and enjoy being a writer for a few hours.

Studying a Little Eugene O'Neill

Approaches to animation scriptwriting can take as many forms as the stories they describe—from a half awake, inspirational scribbling to a thoroughly researched, classically formal short story. But there are a number of time-tested and often-used exercises scriptwriters of all kinds can perform to help them pen something that makes sense and engages the viewer. By examining the work and process of screenwriters such as Quentin Tarantino and Woody Allen, and indeed playwrights such as Eugene O'Neill and Arthur Miller, we can start to see similar methods used by many successful writers.

Preparation

A key point to note about scriptwriting is that very few scripts and even fewer *good* scripts are started by simply typing out dialogue. It's best to think of dialogue as the last step in the scriptwriting process. By taking a bit of time to flesh out the surrounding details of your story, you can make your actual story and characters much richer, more compelling, and easier to write.

Background Reference

First, do a little bit of good old-fashioned research on the subject matter of your story. The more that the world and characters you create makes sense internally, the more viewers will be drawn into that world. Realistic elements give your stories credibility and make it easier for people to swallow the fictions you conjure. If your project is about samurai, study them as a scholar would. This will allow your story to move beyond garden-variety samurai stories and possibly create something fresh in that genre. And not just for serious subject matter either. If your film is about cartoon weasels, then, for the love of all that is decent, do a little bit of weasel research! Maybe you'll discover that they have really stinky scent glands, almost like skunks. Maybe this will give your weasel character a little special something the other cartoon weasels don't have.

Outlining the Plot

Hopefully, after going through the first chapter, you've already begun to create the mental picture of your story. But now it's a good idea to give your story a formal skeleton. Ask a couple of analytical questions to help you. What are the major advances in your story? How does your story flow? Most stories have an arc that starts with introducing a character, presents a conflict, and then shows a resolution. Of course, this dramatic rule can be broken, but it is wise to understand the mechanics of a typical story.

Creating a Back Story

A vital technique for giving your story a sense of the believability and immersion is to give your setting a history and context. To do this it might be valuable to put yourself in the mind of a 5-year-old, one that is at that exhaustively questioning stage. For example, if your story is set on top of a mountain, ask questions such as, How tall is the mountain? What type of animals live there? What is in the valley below the mountain? What is the weather like? What can you see from the mountain? Are there avalanches, rockslides, or volcanic eruptions? Is there a swami at the top?

Even if something is not directly a part of your story, it can have an impact. To use a typical example, many science fiction stories are set in a post-apocalyptic world. In these stories, people often wear primitive costumes and gas masks. These types of details are a direct result of the catastrophic events that happened before the actual story begins.

Knowing What Your Character Would Do

Creating biographies is a necessary step in creating engaging and believable characters. It is also a step that can make you feel as though your script is magically writing itself. By finding out what a character's personality and motivation is, you can provide yourself a very strong sense of what your character's reaction would be to a particular stimulus. In the book *The Art of Dramatic Writing* (Simon and Schuster, 1960), Lajos Egri posits that sufficiently developed characters can "plot their own play." Egri goes on to say, "Regardless of the medium in which you are working, you must know your characters thoroughly. And you must know them not only as they are today, but as they will be tomorrow or years from now."

Although it may seem that the lofty world of playwriting is far removed from animation, if you're trying to craft a funny cartoon, a richly rounded character can do wonders to inform the action. In the Warner Brothers cartoon "The Daffy Doc" (Clampett, 1938), Daffy and Porky find themselves in an operating room. Porky usually plays the straight man, and one can almost predict that when Daffy sees the table full of mallets and bone saws, much brandishing, chasing, clobbering, and general hilarity is imminent. Furthermore, when Daffy sees the iron lung machine in the corner, you know he's not going to simply ignore it. For the writers, it was a foregone conclusion that Porky would be stuffed in the iron lung, having his head and limbs inflated and deflated repeatedly before you could lisp "sufferin' succotash!"

A typical method of creating a character biography is to make a questionnaire and fill it out for each of your characters. You can do this before, during, or even after creating concept art of your character. This description can inform the visual aspects of your character, and vice versa. Think of these questions as more than just an aimless exercise and consider how each could manifest itself as an element in your story. I do not recommend a specific list of questions. Instead, you need to learn which questions will provide answers you need to further flesh out your story. However, here are some examples:

- ▶ **Physical and external** Age, sex, appearance, eating habits, sleeping habits, occupation, abilities and talents, quirks and where they came from, accents or language

- ▶ **Personality** Goals and aspirations, demeanor, prejudices, religion, politics, fears and phobias

- ▶ **History** Birthplace, education, ethnicity, lineage, past triumphs and tragedies

Sample Biography

For my character Carlo—the young, overconfident, abrasive villain of my film—I wanted somebody who was overly hip, a victim of fashion. And he needed to be somebody who was intelligent but whose arrogance was a main weakness. By answering questions similar to those in the preceding exercise, I came up with the following biography.

▶ **Name** Carlo

▶ **Age** 23

▶ **Love life** Player

▶ **Lives in** Williamsburg, in Brooklyn, NYC (trés trendy)

▶ **Occupation** Dropped out of college psychology studies to pursue modeling

▶ **Motivations** Similar to playing with ants with a magnifying glass

▶ **Enjoys** Searching for parties with celebrities

▶ **Idiosyncrasies** On a quest to get his picture in *Paper and Interview* magazine's monthly New York nightlife photo spreads.

▶ **Listens to** Andrew W. K. (his song, "It's Time to Party" was featured in one of those obnoxious beer commercials), Moby, Lenny Kravitz

Scriptwriting

Once you have enough research, back story and biography fodder fermenting in your head, you will probably reach creative critical mass, feeling a noticeable urge to get writing. As you begin writing your script, bear in mind the purpose it will serve in your production. Job number one for your script is simply to have in writing the words your characters will say. You can decide beyond that for your own purposes which descriptions and events are worth writing down. The script does not need to visualize your story or define its appearance, nor does it need to define physical behaviors. Most of this planning will be done visually in the conceptual design and storyboarding stages.

During your writing, you'll want to consider the following issues.

What Does a Given Phrase Make You Animate?

With each new piece of dialogue or event you add to your script, you'll want to visualize exactly what animation will be required. Artistically, what interesting facial expression or gesture will accompany a particular phrase? What physical act will your character perform given this specific situation? You may want to sketch expressions and gestures to allow yourself to think visually about these questions (Figure 3-1).

And here, feasibility, this time at its most granular, should enter your process once again. Consider each piece of dialogue and each minute event to see if you can execute all the production tasks it reveals and requires. These questions should inform and enrich every piece of dialogue you write.

FIGURE 3-1   Carlo's personality was fleshed out through a combination of sketching and scriptwriting.

Character Acting Starts with the Script

This is one of the first of several spots in your animation where you'll begin to transform your character into an actor. Acting and animation are tightly intertwined. And instilling believability into a fictional animated character is a deeply similar process to that of an actor informing their actions and line deliveries based on their character studies. In this case, the dialogue you write is informed by the biography and motivations of your character, with an eye toward how your voice actor and animation will combine to deliver a line through the character you model. The meat of this process will take place during the body and facial animation stages, as well as some during storyboarding. But the voice acting, character biography and even animation tests will all cross-pollinate with the script, one informing the other.

Writing Dialogue

So far, most of the topics discussed in this chapter are geared toward the content of your script and story. But as you are writing the character dialogue itself, you need to consider a few factors that will aid you in writing quality dialogue.

Internal Dialogue

For scenes where a character does not talk, it can be highly valuable to write out internal dialogue. This can richly dictate facial expressions and body language for a deeply communicative pantomime. Writing this inner voice can also be done during the animation phase as well because it can be changed even after audio dialogue has been recorded.

Here's a simplistic example: Say you need to animate a character stealing a cookie from a cookie jar. You could simply animate the character walking to the cookie jar, opening the lid, taking the cookie, and exiting the scene. Or by following the character's train of thought, you'll be given many rich cues to bring drama to the action:

1 As the character enters the room, he thinks, "Is everybody gone? Am I alone?" This might mean furtive glances, or even pulling the blinds and locking the door.

2 The character thinks, "Mmm...cookies. I love you!" This might manifest itself as licking of the lips or wringing of the hands.

3 The character has a sudden spasm of guilt thinking, "No! I mustn't. It would be evil!" This might result in the character halting abruptly in the middle of grabbing the cookie with an expression of agony.

4 The agonized expression gives way to one of fiendish glee as the character thinks, "I am the King of Cookies! They're mine! All mine!"

5 Cookie devouring ensues....

Communicate Through Narrative, Not Exposition

This may be rule number one for narrative writers and certainly one that beginning writers often fail to recognize. Avoiding expository dialogue essentially means not having a character verbally explain things that can be shown through a story point. For example, when a cartoon mouse stabs a cartoon cat in the rear end with a big pin, the cat does not say, "I have just been stabbed and am in great pain." Instead, he launches 30 or 40 feet in the air, clutching his backside and screaming like a fire engine. Avoiding expository dialogue is part of maintaining the fourth wall—that is, the imaginary wall between the characters and the viewers. When characters cross this wall by explaining too much to the audience, a viewer is reminded of their reality, sitting in a seat watching animation, and are taken out of the narrative illusion you are attempting to create.

Rhythm

This may not apply perfectly to every story, but a technique that I have found very useful is to be conscious of the rhythm of a given piece of dialogue. This is by no means saying that everything should rhyme. But all spoken language has a cadence and rhythm, whether regular or not. Particularly for animation, this is another way to make character dialogue interesting, catchy, and entertaining.

Concision

Choosing words accurately and economically is important—once again, both artistically and feasibly. Communicating your story to other people, one of the main roles of your script, takes crafting phrases and sentences clearly and concisely. Colorful and flowery speech is fine if it serves a vital role in your story, such as illuminating your character's personality or serving a particular plot point. But again, dialogue is extravagant. Make every phrase count, and pick every word carefully.

Wittiness and Humor

Because wit and humor are the epitome of subjectiveness, I won't presume to explain how to write funny or even smart dialogue. But regardless of whether you have penned something funny or clever, it is certainly worth some forethought and creative strategy when deciding how your character will turn a phrase. Regardless of voice characterizations or accents, many memorable characters—from Popeye to Ren & Stimpy to Yoda—choose their words in distinct and catchy ways. Funny characters often have funny speech patterns.

Who Will Deliver These Lines?

Consider the actor you will be casting to play the role of the character you are writing dialogue for. Can this person deliver the performance your writing requires? And how will those words sound delivered by that person's voice? Taking these factors into account will go a long way toward helping your characters come across more natural and believable.

Writing Action

Writing the action parts of your script should be a quick process because it is not the script's role to illustrate events and movements. Describe just enough action to outline your story, not to provide details. Simply refer to any props or set changes, particularly those that serve plot points to advance the story. Even Hollywood movie scripts (many of which you can buy in book form) provide only terse descriptions of settings and props and actions. During the concept art and storyboarding phases of your production, you will figure out most things visually.

Revisions

As with any writing process, your script will likely go through a number of drafts. Depending on the amount of dialogue in your film, it is good to revisit your script after some time away from it for a fresh take at refining and enhancing. I would go so far as to recommend arbitrarily giving yourself several days away from your script to allow yourself to return to it with a fresh perspective. Also, it is always good to try out your script by reading it aloud to others. Don't shy away from acting out the parts physically and speaking in a voice that sounds like your character.

During the process of creating concept art and storyboards, you can continue to refine the dialogue or make minor changes to the pacing and plot. But bear in mind that an inherent dependency exists in your production in that you can only revise your script up until you record the dialogue.

Finally, even though scriptwriting can seem a little strange when compared to all the other, visually oriented tasks of a CG animator, it can be such a rewarding pursuit that many choose to do it full time. By giving scriptwriting its proper attention during your production, you will greatly enhance the story you tell.

Writing the Example Film's Script

Of the many varied undertakings for my film, scriptwriting was one I felt fairly comfortable with. I have written 30 or 40 scripts for short animations during the past six or seven years, ranging from very straight corporate animations to smart-mouthed political satire. Despite this, due to the complex and ambitious nature of my story, writing this particular script turned out to be a real challenge. Nevertheless, I wanted from the start to write some convincing conversational dialogue, which this script demanded (Figure 3-2).

One of the challenges was that my story is about real people sitting at their computers playing a videogame and chatting through microphones with each other. So although the animation would be of their videogame characters, the conversation needed to seem as though the voices of convincing and believable people were speaking through these game characters. This meant working out character biographies before I started writing, and also thinking about why these people were playing this videogame. I had also cast three actors to play the parts of my three characters by this time and had been thinking about their voices and what would sound natural for them to say.

FIGURE 3-2   One of the main desires I had when starting this film was to simply animate a conversation with all of its nuanced facial expressions and gestures.

Another challenge was communicating what this videogame was like without bogging down my narrative. These people are supposed to be playing a massively multiplayer online role-playing game (known to videogamers as MMORPG) with an added twist. This meant that a lot of details about this fictional videogame would have to be communicated through the dialogue without being too expository. I wanted to keep the dialogue limited to what people might actually say to each other if they were playing this game and not have them explaining the game play.

My script went through at least eight drafts and revisions, with some minor last-second changes done at the time of recording. The original plan for my film was only to show a snippet of this fictional videogame that my collaborator Tony and I had been concocting. But then it began to occur to me that I was embarking on a very large production and that it would be silly to create all that animation without at least some drama to make it interesting. This is also what led me to introduce Carlo, the jerk, to stir things up for the other two characters.

Fine-tuning the Dialogue

Here's a small example of how we fine-tuned the dialogue. This is an excerpt of my script, after several revisions where Carlo interrupts the two other characters:

Felix: Yes girl, smart people play smart. You know some kids would play football or cops and robbers all day while others read books and draw pictures. Come on, wolves and dolphins and otters all play, people can, too.

Zoey: Okay, okay! I'm playing! *<Gestures accordingly>* So you're going to tell me that there are bio-ethicists running around in this game?

Felix: *<Felix hits the whisper button.>* Hey, I told you the drama would come to us. Here comes Gandhi!

Carlo: Hello, small people. I couldn't help but overhear you two spell-checkers attempting to discuss human cloning.

Zoey: How have you got such a big green aura if you're so rude?

Carlo: Oh, please! Don't get all touchy-feely with me. I've been enlightening people on all the daily topics for ten days running.

And here is the same excerpt, after Dave gave the dialogue another pass:

Felix: Listen, some people might content themselves as big barbarians in a D&D game but remember, play smart, live smart. I mean, dolphins, otters, and polar bears all play. Wolves, crows....

Zoey: Okay, okay! I'm playing! *<Gestures accordingly. The interface sounds, indicating an achievement of a goal>* Hey! Know what? I just accidentally engaged you in a conversation about a social issue without getting chatblocked! I guess that was a goal!

Felix: *<Felix hits the whisper button.>* Hey, I told you the drama would come to us. Here comes Gandhi boy....

Carlo: Hello, small people. Meet Carlo. Pleased to make *my* acquaintance, I'm sure.

Felix: Hello, I'm Felix, and this is Zoey.

Carlo: Acknowledged. I'm feeling you two spell-checkers are going to need some *assistance-du-Moi* if you're going to have any chance at getting over up in here.

Zoey: How have you got such a big green aura if you're so rude?

Carlo: Oh, no! You looking for a group hug, too? See sweetheart, I've been *enlightening* people on all the daily topics for three nights running.

Finally, after I had written several drafts with full dialogue and had refined most of the details I planned to animate, I still was not happy with my characters' dialogue. Although I had done a fair amount of homework to flesh out their personalities, their dialogue didn't feel natural enough. So I turned to my friend David Ewers, who has written many short stories with rich characters, to make the dialogue feel more natural. Conveniently, he had also been cast to play the part of the witty and irritating Carlo. This made for the added bonus that Dave would be more comfortable delivering Carlo's lines because he had had a hand in writing them.

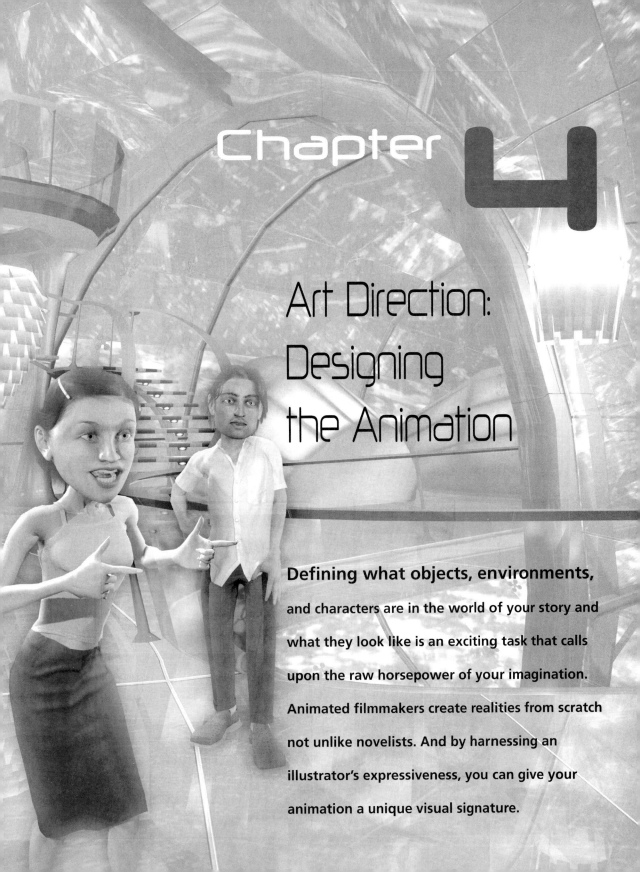

Chapter 4

Art Direction: Designing the Animation

Defining what objects, environments, and characters are in the world of your story and what they look like is an exciting task that calls upon the raw horsepower of your imagination. Animated filmmakers create realities from scratch not unlike novelists. And by harnessing an illustrator's expressiveness, you can give your animation a unique visual signature.

Art Direction

On any larger CG animation or videogame production you'll find many different creative artists designing and modeling characters, sets, animated special effects, textures and all the other creative elements that comprise a project's visuals. It is up to a project's art director to ensure that all the art assets created by the team hang together visually, thus creating a consistent world. As an extreme example, if you're working on a somber, moody, post-apocalyptic film and one of your fellow artists creates a background character with big cartoon eyes and day-glow colors, the art director must step in to correct the oversight. The art director is the one who defines the overall visual aesthetic for a project, so it falls to them to see that all the assets created form a consistent whole instead of a disparate patchwork.

In a smaller project, particularly your own, this task will belong to you. Thinking of yourself as an art director can put you in the right mindset to guide your inspirations, funneling your raw creative impulses into a cohesive, visionary animation. Character set and prop designs, color palettes, lighting, and all other visual elements combine to tell your story. By considering the way each element fits in an overall creative strategy, you can ensure that they work in concert.

Establishing an Aesthetic

Consider a few films that feature outstanding art direction, such as Terry Gilliam's *Brazil*, Jeunet and Caro's *City of Lost Children,* and the Coen brothers' *Hudsucker Proxy* and *Barton Fink*. Videogames such as *Oddworld's Munch's Odyssey* and *Jetset Radio Future* show distinctly illustrative worlds where you can almost see the artist's hands at work. Luc Besson's film *The Fifth Element* is a particularly good example. It not only features the freaky and exuberant costume designs of Jean-Paul Gauthier, but also visual designs by the comic book artist Jean Giraud (a.k.a. Moebius). Here you can see deep art direction at work by looking at the comics of Moebius and then seeing his visual signature all over *The Fifth Element*. All these projects epitomize the strong aesthetic made possible by skillful art direction.

Defining your project's visual identity can be a very rewarding process, giving you the opportunity to research and explore areas of interest to you and infuse them into your work. This can take the form of researching historic periods or cultures or aspects of nature or science. It can also take the form of defining your own voice as an illustrator, giving yourself a visual style with which to craft your own imaginary world and its characters (see Figure 4-1). Whatever your approach, actively define as many of the visual elements as possible to create a consistent world. This will create a uniformity that is a large part of what draws viewers in and allows them to suspend their disbelief.

Reference

Artists and reference go hand in hand. It is rare to find a professional concept artist whose workspace is not full of coffee table books, magazines, action figures, and all manner of visual

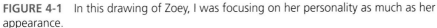

FIGURE 4-1   In this drawing of Zoey, I was focusing on her personality as much as her
appearance.

stimulation. This is not by accident, because saturating yourself with visual information is often
the professional artist's "secret" source of inspiration. Being creative about where you search
for reference can be a pivotal launching point in crafting a fresh and original vision. For the
LucasArts game *Grim Fandango*, director Tim Schafer chose to mix stylish, skeletal Mexican Day
of the Dead–inspired characters with architecture that combined Aztec and Mayan influences
with Art Deco. For the sentinel robots in *The Matrix,* concept artist Geoff Darrow studied squid
for inspiration. And the *Star Wars* art department is famous for creating alien creatures by
combining features from real-world animals. Artist Terry Whitlatch studied animal anatomy
extensively before being called upon to invent alien creatures.

Sources for artistic reference and inspiration can take countless forms. The common places
to start looking are relevant books, magazines, websites, and television documentaries to
name an obvious few. And it is wise to develop the habit of keeping on the lookout for sources
of reference at all times to build your own reference library. But the best source of reference by
far is direct observation. Being able to sketch or photograph the raw material that inspires your
story directly allows you to see it for yourself and make your own unfiltered observations.

》TIP   *Bookstore bargain bins are great for picking up cheap reference
materials; you can find a lot of the "complete visual references" on subjects such
as guns, planes, and so on.*

Creating Concept Art

For many who are new to the high-tech, nearly magical world of 3-D animation, it may seem strange that the ancient art of drawing is such an integral part of the process. But this is true for many reasons. And by noting these reasons, you can discern what two-dimensional illustration's strengths are and how to best leverage them for your work.

To begin, drawing is still a simpler, more portable, and in most cases much faster practice than 3-D modeling. This means that an artist is freer to experiment and iterate with far less time and effort invested, and therefore less consequence. Artists can quickly scribble iterations of visual ideas, allowing for thorough exploration of design variations. Also, being able to draw in remote locations is great for observing a subject directly. Even if you are adept at drawing on the computer with a pen tablet, bringing a sketchbook to a cafe, park, or zoo is not only pleasurable but can be more stimulating as well.

Artistically, because drawing is done with a pencil in the hand, it brings with it an inherent gestural expressiveness that is often lacking in computer animation. Because the hand is a series of bones and rotating joints, drawing naturally tends toward creating expressive, arcing lines. Animations such as Blue Sky's *Ice Age* have evocative character designs whose three-dimensional shapes obviously originated on an artist's sketchpad.

Next, drawing is another powerful way of seeing. To be able to accurately and artistically draw something requires keen observation and strong dimensional perception. This perception of form and detail that drawing cultivates translates in a palpably direct way to do computer modeling and animation. Classical sculptors usually draw before sculpting, and 3-D modeling is closely analogous to sculpture. So it's almost assured that the better you draw, the better you'll model.

Although some 3-D modelers out there essentially design "on the fly" while they model, this is actually a rare skill. It is good practice to draw all the major visual elements of your film, including characters, sets, and any props significant to the story, before you move on to modeling.

Approach: Communicating an Idea

When creating conceptual art for your project, a good basis to work from is the idea that these drawings and illustrations are being created to serve a purpose and not meant to be hung on your wall. The conceptual art is first meant to be a tool for exploring your design ideas and then it's a guide for the actual creation of your characters and sets in three dimensions. Next, accurate drawings of characters, props, and sets will greatly reduce guesswork during the modeling process, making it much faster and efficient. Quick and rough illustrations can be great tools for working out color palettes, lighting, staging, and many other cinematic aspects. Not only will this work save you time, but it will allow the cinematic aspects to have more cohesion and artistry than if you try to figure them out amid all the technical challenges of the 3-D software environment. These key tenants can help you efficiently focus your conceptual drawing efforts.

Character Design

As noted in the Chapter 3, a good place to start in designing characters is with the biography. This is a time-tested way to begin creating the appearance of your character with a solid, logical grounding. Even if you have had a visual inspiration and have begun visualizing your character already, going through the biographical exercise of the last chapter can help you refine your raw vision.

Character Reference

The next step is to gather reference that is relevant to your character's biography. At the most basic level, this should take the form of appropriate anatomy reference, whether your character is human, animal, or fantasy. A strong knowledge of anatomy is critical not only to creating a character that looks convincing but especially to making characters that *move* believably. The underlying bone and muscular structure should define much about the character's facial expressions, locomotion, and gestures. Then you can move on to more specific reference related to your character's culture, age, or other aspects of their biography.

Sketching

Loose, freeform sketching is an excellent way to rapidly explore many different variations of your character's appearance. My former art director, and excellent 3-D character artist, Randall Ho told me, "It's way more helpful to do 20 different one-minute sketches than it is to do one or two hour-long drawings." And by following his advice, I saw my drawing improve markedly. He was pointing out that it is a waste of time to shade and render (in the traditional sense of the word) a drawing that is not good in the first place. And indeed, realistic shading and rendering are what the computer excels at. So unless you are specifically designing a form or texture that you plan to later re-create, it's best to keep your sketches simple.

It is important to move beyond simply defining a character's appearance when sketching. The pose of a character is vital in making a sketch appear lifelike and expressive. Sketches that show the character with arms and legs straight to the sides and neutral expressions will almost always look lifeless and unnatural. But giving the character an expressive pose in a sketch not only gives it the breath of life, it also gives you a powerful way to begin defining the character's all-important personality.

NOTE *The ability to draw humans believably is a core skill needed to create engaging characters, even stylized and cartoony characters. This is why life drawing, that is drawing people live and in person, is bedrock training for any character artist. Taking classes in life drawing is invaluable for hands-on study in the human form, anatomy and believable posing. If you can't get to classes at a college or university, you can draw family members, friends, or even yourself to get the practice you need.*

Zoey's Facial Design

Having fleshed out the background details of my main character, Zoey, I would be using her biography as reference when creating her visual design. These types of fictional details would help me make decisions about what she would look like.

- ▶ **Age** 26
- ▶ **Love life** Single and dating
- ▶ **Lives in** Artsy neighborhood in downtown Seattle
- ▶ **Occupation** Writes for the Seattle Weekly, the local arts and entertainment paper
- ▶ **Motivations** Curiosity about the videogame, writing fodder
- ▶ **Enjoys** Going to music shows, art openings
- ▶ **Idiosyncrasies** Collects lunchboxes

Additionally, I would actually be building what was, according to my film's story, supposed to be the 3-D game avatar of this "real" person, Zoey. The idea is that players of this fictitious videogame might take pictures of their heads to use as "skins" for their game characters. This goes hand in hand with the fact that I knew I would be using photographic textures of real people when I built these characters.

In this game, I decided that people would make characters that looked more or less like themselves—that is, more or less like real people as opposed to movie or TV stars. My intention was to make Zoey cute and attractive, but not to have that be the central goal. Because I've seen enough fantasy sex symbol women designed by adolescent men, I wanted to make a female character who was not unlike women I knew. I started by finding and sketching as many pictures from books and magazines and even clothing catalogs as I could. Then, I continued drawing without reference so I could actively design her facial features as opposed to duplicating a real person's. Figure 4-2 shows a few of the many ideas I explored this way before hitting on something I liked. Next, I started looking at women's hairstyle websites for ideas on how she would wear her hair. This was extremely helpful in giving my character an air of believability.

Male Facial Design

I followed a process similar to the one I used for creating Zoey for my male characters as well. For Zoey's friend Felix, I knew I wanted a 40-something balding-yet-attractive type of man (more like an Ed Harris type as opposed to a Patrick Stewart type). It's easy to find lots of reference of handsome men. The images below show sketches simply testing out a facial idea with a male pattern baldness hairdo, for which I adhered only loosely to my reference.

The villain of my film, Carlo, was more challenging. I wanted him to look like a very specific archetype of male model. Pictures of male models with those exaggerated, pouty lips always make me laugh really hard, so I thought I would attempt to capture something like that. For

FIGURE 4-2 Exploratory sketches of Zoey

Carlo I looked at a lot of male fashion reference, which is easy to find in abundance. Again, I created many sketches in kind of an evolutionary process to come up with a face I liked.

These sketches of Carlo were done very quickly, with no more than five minutes spent on each, to allow me to quickly explore different ideas.

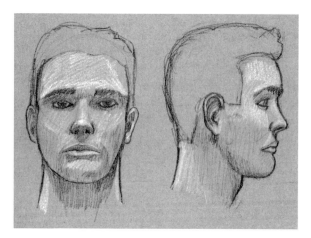

Further along in the character-design process for Carlo, I began to make more detailed drawings to help define his facial features more clearly.

Female Body/Costume Design

For Zoey's body, I looked to very basic reference from my various anatomy books. I wanted her body to look more like a normal woman's body, and anatomy books usually show women who are as average as possible. The image shown on the next page is an early sketch of Zoey that came before I decided to give the characters larger heads, hands, and feet to accentuate their expressions and gesturing.

For her clothes, I looked through many fashion magazines before I found *Delia's* clothing catalog. This was a great reference for the type of fashions a young woman such as Zoey would wear. I wanted to keep her clothes very simple and understated, with muted colors, because I knew my film would be visually busy. I did not want any of the characters' outfits competing with their colorful animated auras or with the videogame interface.

For her shoes and for the male characters' shoes, I looked through many online shoe websites. I devoted some time to this because I figured that for these types of real-world characters, the types of shoes they wear will say a lot about them. Also, because these characters have such simple costumes, the shoes are one of the main visual features.

Male Body/Costume Design

I wanted the Felix character to be very physically fit with well-defined musculature. Once again, this type of reference was readily available from anatomy books because they usually feature men with well-defined physiques. I also knew that Felix would be wearing a tight-fitting T-shirt and basic jeans. So I drew a basic male physique because I wouldn't need to model any complex clothing. As I sketched him, I was already thinking of the types of poses he would be in during a typical scene.

For Carlo, I wanted to have that fashionably unkempt look of many of today's male models. What I found after looking at a lot of male fashion reference was that just about anything goes these days. But I did see a lot of fashion pictures of men wearing retro 60s clothing. And although I myself am far from fashionable, my wardrobe conveniently consists of a lot of 60s thrift shop clothing. So I picked out a pair of pants and a shirt that fit the bill. Then I was able to be my own clothing model for sketches of Carlo. And for Carlo's shoes, I did a few sketches to design them myself. Carlo has a very standoffish and superior attitude, and sketches of him allowed me to learn what that meant visually. I pictured him as one of those guys who would wear shoes with the overly square toe.

Design Drawings: Showing the Shape of What You Are Going to Model

Once you come to a final character design, the next step is to create character model sheets. These usually take the form of front and side orthographic or nonperspective views of both the character head and body. Drawing horizontal construction lines between the major landmarks of the character can ensure that the front and side drawings are of the same dimension. These drawings can either be used for reference to keep with you as you model or, as is commonly done, they can be placed on 3-D planes in your 3-D environment to use directly as a modeling template.

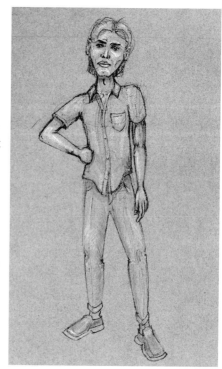

At this stage, your drawings should serve to define physical features as clearly as possible. The more accurate these drawings are, the easier your modeling process will be. Typically they do not need to be overly detailed but rather should simply describe the character's physical form. That being said, artists who are creating drawings for other modelers to build may need to put in more detail to lessen ambiguity.

Zoey's Design Drawings

For Zoey's head construction drawing, I drew in Procreate's Painter. This allowed me to quickly edit the drawings. This was helpful because I would be doing many subtle changes, and erasing that many times might have destroyed my drawings. I made a separate layer for blue construction lines and drew them at the top of the head, center of the eyes, tip of the nose, and the center of the mouth and chin.

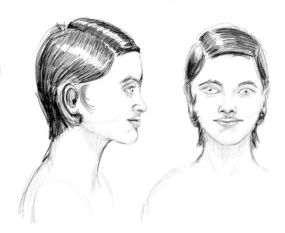

For Zoey's body, I drew in blue pencil on paper with several anatomy books open on my drawing table. For this construction drawing, I drew her in the neutral pose that she would be modeled in. I scanned this blue line drawing and used it as a base layer, this time in a Photoshop file. Then I created new layers to draw dark contour lines on top of my original blue line drawing. This allowed me to quickly create the contour lines without the tedious process of physically inking my drawing. I also cut and pasted Zoey's head from my other construction drawing, though this was just for context because I would model her head separately from the previous drawing.

While modeling characters in the computer based on two-dimensional construction drawings is the most common approach for character creation, there are other methods. It is possible to create characters by moving directly to a 3-D software package and modeling from scratch. But this is rare among professional 3-D character modelers. And it is even more rare to find successful 3-D modelers who do not have a strong grasp of traditional drawing. Another approach common in high-end studios, such as Pixar, is to create physical sculptures, called maquettes, of characters first. These maquettes are then either used as visual reference for modeling or they're scanned with 3-D object scanners. But this approach is rare for small independent filmmakers since it is typically labor-intensive to create the sculptures and expensive to obtain equipment to scan them.

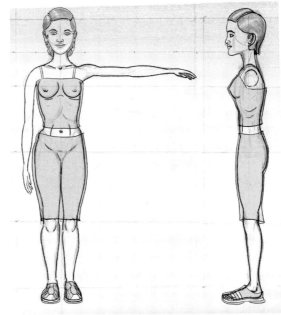

Felix and Carlo's Design Drawings

For Felix and Carlo's construction drawings, I repeated the process of creating blue line drawings and scanning them. I decided to cut corners in building the two male characters. Because Felix had an archetypical male physique with tight clothing, I made one drawing for his body. Once I had modeled Felix's body, I would use that as a template to build Carlo's more loose-fitting clothing around using my sketches of his clothes for reference. This meant that I could draw and model one body and use it for both characters.

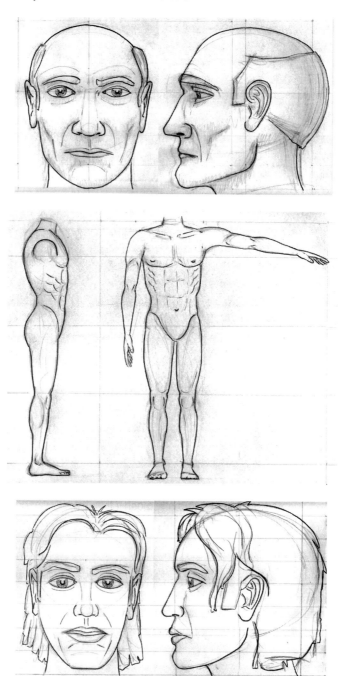

Set Design

The mechanics of set design is not unlike creating characters in that it involves gathering reference and creating sketches and then design drawings. But creatively, the set should first and foremost serve your story. If your story is about a wooden man trapped in a furniture factory, the set is obviously integral to the plot and can actually become a faceless character. If your story is a simpler conversation or pantomime, the set may need to be merely evocative of the story's mood. Either way, it is best to envision, as you design, the various "stages" your set will make possible. Specific staging and composition can be worked out in the storyboarding process described in the next chapter. Build your sets in a way that will frame and augment the key events in your story.

Cloud10 Set Design

For the design of my environment, I thought about the videogame idea within my story. This setting was to be at night in a club-style chat room on top of a futuristic, sculptural skyscraper. Though I wanted the environment to be architecturally believable, I did not care whether it was overly realistic because my film is set within a videogame. I looked through a large variety of reference on both real and virtual architecture, including many magazines, websites, and books from my own reference library. After extensive research, I began to pare down my focus to some of my old and new favorites. I've always liked the deconstructivist architecture of Zaha Hadid, Coop Himmelblau, and Lebbeus Woods as well as the spectacularly explosive virtual architecture of Marcos Novak. All this work features very complex forms created by combinations of many geometric shapes.

Sketching   The inspiration for my own space took the form of a glass bubble flower. The different stages of my story would take place in the different glass bubbles as my character Zoey passed through them. I started by sketching with colored markers many variations of my building's exterior. Once I had come to a design that I liked, I began to work out the interior forms. My story called for the main character, Zoey, to enter from an elevator and to look at the overall space from a balcony, seeing the activity going on in the videogame environment. She would then traverse through the entire space on her way to meet her friend, Felix. These story points dictated that there would be an elevator on the balcony and a staircase at the opposite end of the space from where Felix sits.

Because of the complexity of the interior space, composed of intersecting football shapes, I created a quick 3-D sketch in my 3-D package to help me visualize the interior volume (shown on the next page). It only took a few minutes to create the basic elliptical shapes, a simple floor, and a cylindrical wall. This allowed me to view the space from different perspectives quickly. I then created a few pencil sketches of the interior to help me solidify in my mind the shape and form of the space, shown here:

Then I began creating a large number of quick pencil sketches to explore and refine ideas for the various details of the space. Each aspect of the interior—elevator doors, lighting fixtures, stairs, hand railings, and furniture—went through several iterations in the design process. I wanted sculptural lamps with distinctive forms for the interior to provide visual interest. Furniture designs were intended to expand on the look and feel created by the interior. Because all these details were meant to be simple, I let these quick sketches suffice when it came to modeling.

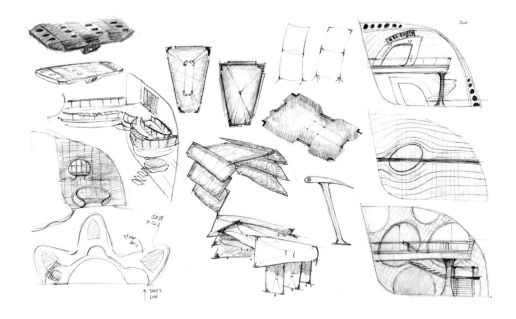

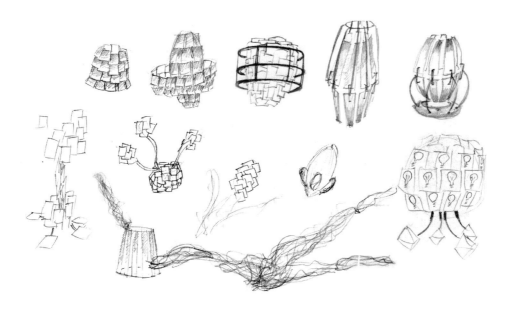

Design Drawings   Because of the geometrical complexity of my interior's intersecting ellipsoid forms and the fact that they are composed of many layers of glass, I knew I would be relying on the mathematical precision of my 3-D modeling tools to sculpt and visualize them. I also had a strong sense of the modeling procedures I would be using to create these forms. Therefore, I did not draw my interior in great detail for my design drawings. To be sure, if I were a professional concept artist working in a full-blown production, I would have drafted more elaborate illustrations. I did create a rough floor plan to use in conjunction with my numerous sketches.

The interior concept drawings did not need to be elaborate because I had a strong sense of how the space would be shaped and how it would be modeled.

Tying Your Aesthetic Elements Together

As you are designing the various visual elements that appear film, it is important to be conscious of the color palettes, lighting, and even the graphics of your credits and titles, and how they all work together. This is part of creating a fully realized aesthetic for your film.

Color Palettes

Taking conscious control of the color palette of your film can greatly enhance the power of your story. Even a rudimentary knowledge of major elements of color theory can be helpful. As you choose the colors for your characters, take into account the colors of the sets they will be in. Do the colors of your characters and other elements that are supposed to capture the viewer's attention stand out in relation to the background?

The Visual Identity for "The Game to Save the World"

The overall look and feel for my film would be largely defined by it's glassy and curved set with a backdrop of a nighttime city. For the color palette, I had seen several photos in my reference that showed lighting schemes I liked, consisting of saturated blues, greens, and oranges, creating pools of light in an overall dark environment. Because my story basically features a simple conversation, I wanted the set to provide a hypermodern, science fiction context and mood. I augmented this by choosing ultramodern and futuristic fonts that would seem at home in a science fiction context. And for the various graphical elements of my faux videogame interface and onscreen graphics, I chose elliptical blob-like forms that are evocative of the sophisticated interactions going on in the story. I'll get into more about designing these elements in Chapter 17.

In general, the saturation and brightness of a color scheme has a strong effect on the perceived mood of a scene. With a simple film, it's likely you'll be able to define the look of most of the scenes with one or two different palettes. For longer animations with multiple sets, color scripts, as mentioned in Chapter 5, are often created along with the storyboards to define color palettes for each individual scene.

Lighting

As anyone who has watched an Alfred Hitchcock movie or a gritty, black-and-white film noir knows, lighting is a powerful story-enhancing tool. It's also a powerful way to control the color palette of your film. And although we will get into lighting in Chapters 9 and 16, when we model and render the environment, you will want to consider the overall lighting strategy of your scenes early on.

Graphic Identity

Whatever the delivery medium your film is intended for, whether it's the Web, film festivals, your portfolio, or all of the above, presentation is important. Devoting some attention to the graphical identity of your film will greatly enhance your film's first impression. To be sure, it's possible to go overboard on this and end up creating a significant amount of extra work. Bear in mind that most of today's blockbuster films hire studios for the sole task of creating their elaborate opening title sequences.

But for short animations, simply choosing fonts and colors and movement styles for opening and closing graphics can do a lot to set the mood. Consider the theme of your story and its tone as you choose fonts. For example, if your film is a scary monster story, you can find many free, horror-themed fonts available on the Net.

When it comes to concept art, what matters most in the end is the final product. Painting illustration masterpieces may not mean you will model and animate one, and drawing stick figures does not necessarily mean you can't create expressive characters. But undoubtedly, creating good concept art will enrich your filmmaking process and make your film stronger.

Chapter 5

Storyboarding: Cinematic Planning

When you are ready to begin defining the cinematic framework of your film, it is a good time to remind yourself of an obvious point—that an animated film is, well… a film. And in traditional filmmaking there is usually a cinematographer or director of photography who helps the director translate the written script into the visual language of film. This involves tasks such as creating a list of shots, lighting and coloring a scene, choosing camera angles and movement—tasks that relate to the mechanics of the story. These tasks can be quite engrossing even when making animated films. Indeed, these pursuits are significant enough that large animated productions have people devoted full-time to cinematography.

The Cinematographer's Job

Fortunately for those who have to handle many or all of the filmmaking disciplines, cinematography has a long history and plenty of readily available and highly visible reference. There is a very rich and mature language of filmmaking that is almost as pervasive in our culture as written and spoken language. For example, almost anyone immediately understands that a shot of someone's wide-open eyes during an embrace is a clear indication that this person is holding something back from the person they are embracing. We know that if a film cuts from a speeding car to a truck full of glass crossing the street, a collision is impending. Most of us are fluent in a visual vocabulary that uses editing, camera angles and movements, lighting, and other devices to invoke emotional responses. And it is this vocabulary that we as CG filmmakers can leverage with storyboards for our storytelling plan.

Storyboarding

The tried-and-true way to make the cinematic choices dictate the way your story is told is through storyboarding. Storyboards are quickly drawn rough sketches of each camera shot and are a powerful visual tool for problem solving and removing guesswork when laying out your animated scenes. When done thoroughly, a series of storyboards can read much like a comic book. When combined with the script, they should be able to tell your story quite handily. In fact, animator Bill Plympton published the storyboards from his film, *Mutant Aliens,* as a thoroughly entertaining comic book (*Mutant Aliens,* NBN, 2000).

But to be clear, storyboards do not need to be seen by anyone but you and your partners. These drawings are meant to be a planning device, not works of art. They serve so many purposes that they are an invaluable part of almost any preproduction. The following sections detail some of the things for which storyboards are helpful, as well as some points you should keep in mind as you create them.

Blocking and Story Progression

First, in the broadest sense, the storyboards should reveal the story progression by defining each camera shot with a drawing. Where is the camera and what does it see in the first shot, in the next, and so on? In traditional filmmaking, this part of the process is also known as *camera blocking* and involves deciding how many cameras there will be and where they will be placed. As a CG animator, you can approach this in the same way, thinking of yourself as the director, deciding what needs to be in each scene to communicate each point in your story.

Character Choreography and Placement

The storyboards provide a lot of vital information about your characters. They define which characters are in a scene, where they stand, in what direction they are looking, and what they are doing. This is not only important for arranging your story so it will be understandable to the audience, it's critical for telling you where to place your character models when you set up a scene.

Action

Storyboards can tell a lot about what *happens* in each shot. Expressive drawings can show a lot about motion and action—and even though they are static, they can be *sequential*. You can create multiple storyboards for a single camera cut to show the major points of action. Additionally, you can annotate drawings with arrows or other symbols to indicate movements.

This element of storyboarding can provide thorough and accurate information about how much and what type of animation a particular shot will require.

Drama and Expressions

The poses and expressions of your characters are undoubtedly two of the most important aspects of communicating your story, and the storyboards (along with the conceptual art) can be a key tool to begin exploring the drama and emotion of your story and characters. Where possible, draw the characters in each storyboard exhibiting the key emotions or expressions of the shot. This will make your storyboards read much more effectively. It will also give you a head start when creating the character animation by giving you key poses and emotions for each shot.

Camera Composition and Camera Moves

Storyboards can define the framing of each camera shot. Composition in filmmaking is as important as it is in painting or illustration. Creating visual balance or purposeful imbalance and directing the focus of attention can all be accomplished through careful composition. How close your camera is to your subject, its angle, its focal length, and other details affect the composition of your shot and can be defined through your drawings.

A shorthand is used to describe several of the most common types of camera shots and provide examples of their use. You can think of these shots as building blocks from which to construct your story:

- **Extreme long shot**   Sometimes referred to as an *establishing shot*. These shots will often be the first in a sequence to show viewers where the action is taking place. Many movies start with helicopter shots for this reason.
- **Long shot**   These shots are often used to simulate the character's point of view as they see someone approach from the distance. These shots give a different feeling of drama to the actions of characters far away.
- **Medium shot**   These shots typically feature characters from the waist up for garden-variety conversation shots.
- **Close-up**   These shots are typically used to focus on one person at a time during a conversation.
- **Extreme close-up**   For heightened drama, the camera zooms in until only a character's face is visible to enhance the power of emotional expressions.

Camera Angle

The camera's angle in relationship to your scene also plays an important role in composition by giving you another way to decide what is in the shot and how it is framed. But more than that, camera angles are an effective tool for defining the mood and tone of a shot. A camera angle looking down on a subject can give the viewer a powerful, godlike feeling or the dispassionate feeling of a surveillance camera. Conversely, camera shots looking up at a character can make that character scene more impressive and powerful by accentuating its size.

Scene Elements

Most scenes are composed of a combination of foreground, middle ground, and background elements. Understanding the relationships, for example, between talking characters in the foreground, a window in the middle ground, and an onrushing tank in the background can allow you to frame your shot not just for the dramatic content but for the visual composition as well.

Camera Movement

You can also plan your camera's movements. Through the use of arrows or sequential drawings, you can choreograph the camera to pan, tilt, zoom, focus, or whatever else you want your camera to do. Most of the top CG animation directors adhere to the theory that

viewers will digest a story better if it is told with familiar, real-world camera moves. Although it is possible to animate a virtual camera through complex movements, impossible to duplicate physically, these moves can be disorienting. Therefore, unless you have a strong story-driven reason for a wildly animated camera shot, it is wise to stick with simple, traditional camera movements.

Animators Edit at the Beginning

When a live-action director blocks out a film, they will place several cameras in a given scene for what is known as *coverage*. Adequate camera coverage allows the director to have several film recordings of the scene shot from different angles. This way, not only can the director pick and choose from the different footage, but they can be mixed together, or *intercut,* for greater visual interest—and in some cases to provide more information than one camera could.

In traditional animation, creating extra coverage is an impossibility. Therefore, animation directors essentially do the bulk of the film's editing during the storyboarding process. Usually, each storyboard drawing represents a camera cut. This means that an animation storyboard artist not only defines the progression of the story but also its pace, rhythm, and punctuation.

Finally, in CG animation, we have the luxury of placing multiple cameras in a scene. But because animation does not feature live action's spontaneity or unpredictability, it is still wise to be able to know from your storyboards exactly what each camera cut will entail. This process of "editing upfront," if you will, gives you the power to present your story as a rapid-fire action piece with machine-gun-fast camera cuts, as a documentary with long stable shots, or anything in between. Because animation is a lot of hard work, the key is to make every shot count and do its part to tell your story, which leads us one final time back to the feasibility issue.

Storyboards Are the Ultimate Planning Tool

Storyboarding is the last step in your preproduction before major changes in your story begin to have major consequences in your work. But fortunately, the storyboards are the most informative indicator of practicality and feasibility.

What Is in a Scene

It can be very surprising, both serendipitously and terrifyingly, what storyboards can reveal about a given shot. When fulfilling their purpose properly, storyboards define many logistical aspects of your film. They show definitively how many characters, sets, props, and actions are in a given camera shot.

Maybe they reveal that the camera will have to see way off into the distance behind your subject. This might mean that at the very least you have to create a background image or maybe even that you have to model a huge set you hadn't planned on. They can tell you how close the camera will be to a character and therefore how high the resolution the texture maps need to be.

Animation Economy

Storyboards can also help you *make* your story feasible by letting you explore how to tell it efficiently.

One of the reasons Japanese anime features so many pensive, meditative, and evocative scenes undoubtedly stems not just from dramatic intent but from animation practicalities. Animating scenes with small movements and cycling movements is relatively easy compared to other types of action.

Framing shots creatively to show a significant detail can evoke the image of much larger subjects. A close-up of blood dripping from a hand, instead of a full shot of a character, can dramatically show that a character has been wounded. Showing a character's terrified reaction to a monster can be much more powerful than attempting to explicitly show the monster.

One thing I learned from my last art director, Randall Ho, is that efficient animators do not create *anything* that will not actually be seen. In CG animation, you can take cues from traditional Hollywood filmmaking. For example, if you have a scene at street level, you will not need to model the backs of any of the buildings. If your character wears a helmet, you probably won't need to create any hair. This type of streamlining has many ramifications—from file sizes to animation complexity to render times.

Drawing the Storyboards

Actual storyboard drawings can legitimately and effectively take many forms. Many say simple stick figure drawings will suffice, while professional storyboard artists can rapidly create rich, expressive and even beautiful works of art. For the sake of expedience without sacrificing their effectiveness, I recommend somewhere in between. Overly detailed storyboards can be overkill and a waste of time. This is especially true because you're likely to refine your choice of camera shots, requiring the adding and subtracting of storyboards before you settle on a final sequence.

Level of Detail

It is best to find a level of detail for your storyboards that is appropriate considering, as just noted, what they are supposed to communicate. And indeed, the more you can show in your drawings, the less guesswork you have during actual production. A loose rule of thumb is to not spend more than a couple of minutes on each drawing. Although this depends largely on the amount of complexity in your film, the point is to move through the storyboarding process quickly to get an overall plan for your film.

Materials and Technique

A wide variety of artistic mediums work well for storyboarding. First and foremost you should choose the medium you are the most comfortable with and the one that allows you to create your storyboards rapidly. Here are a few common techniques:

- ▶ **Pencil**   Straight pencil on paper is probably the most common because it is the simplest and most expedient.

- ▶ **Blue line**   Another common method is to use light blue-colored pencil and lay in dark pencil or ink lines on top.

- ▶ **Art markers**   Many professional illustrators favor scribbling with various values of gray art markers before laying in black lines on top.

- ▶ **Digital**   For some, digital drawing with a tablet in Painter or Photoshop is the fastest and most versatile method, allowing the artist to quickly change line weights or fill in the areas with different tonal values to indicate shadow and light.

Storyboard Presentation

Although there are common storyboard layouts in the animation industry, there is no standard. The storyboard sheets take many forms. They aid you in keeping your storyboards uniform and consistent and give you convenient space in which to annotate. But these are not necessary. Here are a few simple guidelines.

- ▶ **Aspect ratio**   Make sure your drawings are the aspect ratio intended for your finished film. For example, if you're planning your film to be sized for video (720 by 486 pixel resolution), make your drawings 4 by 3 inches or 8 by 6 inches.

- ▶ **Annotations**   Leave room for copious notes. Because storyboards are one of your prime planning tools, you'll need to place all manner of notes next to them. In particular, an annotation may take the form of the 3-D filename for that shot, the camera name, or other important details.

- ▶ **Script dialogue**   Write the appropriate dialogue from your script to accompany each drawing.

After you have completed your storyboards, plan on scanning your drawings in if needed. Many animators will then pin them up around their workstation to have as constant reference.

Once the Storyboards Are Complete

At this point, it is important to look through the entire group of storyboards in sequence. Try to assess objectively and critically—perhaps with the help of others—whether or not your story can be understood. One of the key reasons to keep the drawing of storyboards simple is that you'll often find ways to streamline or enhance your storytelling. Therefore, you should be prepared to storyboard a sequence again for better clarity. Once you have finished storyboarding, you should have a very clear and concise vision of every camera shot in your story and whether those shots add up to eloquently tell that story.

Previsualization: Beyond Storyboards

There are several other optional steps to the "previz" process. Depending on the complexity of your film, these may or may not be necessary. Either way, they are good exercises to give your filmmaking process a solid grounding.

Animatic

A very common practice in animated productions is to bring scanned storyboard drawings along with the soundtrack into a video-editing package such as Adobe Premiere or Final Cut Pro. The drawings can then be synchronized with the audio, providing what is called an animatic or "board blast." Backgrounds or cut-out elements can be easily animated to simulate panning and zooming and other simple movement. Animatics can powerfully illustrate the timing and pacing of your film and provide a strong sense of how your story flows.

Color Script

Another increasingly common method of previsualization is to create a second series of drawings or paintings expressly for the purpose of defining the colors of a particular shot. This is a way of creating a color palette for each shot in a film and is typically part of the art direction. These images are usually created very rapidly, with very broad strokes, and often look like Impressionist paintings. The power of color to create and manipulate moods and emotions is often underestimated and this method gives you conscious control of that power.

Previsualization Animations

As contemporary 3-D animation and special effects continue to grow more complex and involved, elaborate previsualization animatics are becoming more common. For the latest trilogy of *Star Wars* films, there exists almost an entire version of the film created for previsualization. In contrast to these giant productions with crews of several hundred using state-of-the-art tools, these previz versions of the films were created by a tiny crew of people working with inexpensive desktop computers and relatively inexpensive software such as Lightwave.

Often a complex piece of animation and camera work can require a large amount of rendering time before one can see enough for a critical analysis of the cinematography aspects. But by creating quick-and-dirty low-resolution models, often from just geometric primitives, one can quickly see whether a given camera move or animation path is working.

Balancing Good Planning Without Sacrificing Serendipity

I think the best approach to storyboarding and previsualization in general is to answer as many questions for yourself as you can regarding your ensuing production. Define your film as tightly as possible at this phase to give yourself a thorough production guide. This will keep you from getting lost in the myriad details of your film. But also give yourself a small bit of wiggle room for coming up with new ideas during your production.

It is important to remember that this is where a lot of the actual craft of *directing* your film occurs. By taking the time to storyboard thoroughly, you take advantage of an excellent opportunity to craft your story with finesse and impact.

Storyboards for "The Game to Save the World"

One of the main thrusts of my storyboarding focused on my scope of work. I drew all 60 of my storyboards in just a few hours. And indeed, I was flabbergasted when I realized that it would take *60* shots—a huge amount—to tell my story. But this spurred me on to examine each shot to see how I could simplify it.

Managing Complexity

I was daunted by the fact that in many shots, I would need multiple background characters. Creating and managing many characters was a task I did not have a simple solution for, yet. And animating these characters, even if I was able to reuse animations from one character to another, would certainly be tough. But on closer examination and some redrawing for tighter composition, I realized that just a shot here and there actually necessitated showing large chunks of my scene with many characters. Most of the shots focused on the main characters, and often one at a time. This was critical in that it meant I wouldn't need all those character models and all the animation throughout. It meant that I could trim down my 3-D scene files to contain only the character who was in that series of shots. This meant a dramatic reduction of complexity and in the amount of work.

Storytelling

Because my script is complex, I tried to be very obvious and as simple as possible in my storytelling approach. I wanted to make sure each step in my film was clearly delineated. In the back of my mind, I was thinking about the films of Alfred Hitchcock, where he would successfully tell a complex story by taking a very utilitarian and simple approach to his camera work and editing. Even though I really wanted my film to feel hypermodern, I felt that hyperfast camera cuts might distract and confuse.

Conversation Blocking

Because my story is largely a conversation between two and then three people, I studied and adhered to the traditional practices of blocking a conversation. Mainly this involved acknowledging what is called the *fourth wall*—that is, the wall that you, the viewer, look through. I tried to keep the cameras on one side of the conversation so that as I changed cameras to shift focus from one character to the other, the camera cuts would be less disorienting. Also, as in a typical conversation on a television show, I turned the characters slightly toward the camera.

Compositions

As for my compositions, I allowed myself a little leeway in this area. By framing my scenes so simply, I was able to crank out the storyboard drawings faster because I didn't give a lot of thought to the compositions. From past experience, I knew that I would be able to make slight adjustments to camera positions once the scene was animated. This would allow me to compose my scenes adequately for my purposes.

Drawing

I drew my storyboards with pencil in my sketchbook. I didn't spend any time with a ruler trying to measure things. Because I knew I would be tweaking camera angles in 3-D, I also wasn't exact about drawing my frames. Then, I scanned the drawings and gave them very quick washes of color value in Photoshop.

Example Storyboards

The following storyboards are from the sequence of the example film where Zoey, talking on her headset phone, walks past Carlo as he talks to two other game players.

This shot pans from left to right to show Zoey's point of view as she walks past Carlo.

Felix: Okay, brief eye contact and a casual wave.
Nothing fancy, so he doesn't think you're overeager.

This shot frames most of Zoey to show her full body gesture.

<Zoey picks the wrong wave from her game interface.>

This shot returns to the panning camera.

<Carlo responds coyly.>

This is a medium close-up shot to highlight Zoey's frustration.

Zoey: Oh Cripes! That was the wrong wave! And he's looking all nonchalant and everything! This guy's sooo smooooth. Oh yeah, he totally looks like somebody we need to know.
Felix: Yeah, but he *totally* blew off those two people he was talking with. Umm...rrruuude?!

The shot on the next page backs out from the previous shot to frame Carlo in the background as Zoey glances furtively over her shoulder.

Zoey: Hmmm! From the looks of him, aurawise, he's like the most enlightened, top citizen, oral historian, and brain surgeon all rolled into one! He couldn't have nailed all those goals by irritating people, could he?

Here, Zoey uses the same gesture that she used to wave to Carlo, so I have used the same storyboard. Now Zoey's videogame character actually approaches Felix's videogame character. She now hangs up her headset phone and greets Felix "in person".

<Zoey sees Felix sitting suavely in a lounge chair as she enters the skybox.>
Zoey: Oh, there you are!
<Strikes a movie star walk, gesture, and expression.>
Zoey: Heeeeeyyy!

This is a Zoey point of view shot to show Felix approaching to greet her.

**Felix: Well hello, daahhling! Look at you, girl!
You're looking like Miss Natural herself!**

The rest of the shots are blocked as a straightforward conversation. When this scene is blocked and animated, over-the-shoulder cameras and cameras at other angles can be added for further coverage. But these shots delineate the bulk of the story.

Zoey: Thanks! I have been messing with my menus a bit. Check this gesture out. I made it myself. It's my "you are *so* interesting" combo.
<Her body leans slightly forward with head tilted a bit to the side and an expression of concern.>

Felix: Ooh, that one's handy! Check out my new joke punch line delivery moves: "…so I said, I'll have what *she's* having!"
<Felix bends at the waist, grabbing his stomach with one hand and throwing the other in the air. He slaps his leg and laughs hysterically.>

Zoey: *<Laughing>* Impressive! You're a conversation sensation! These will be great the next time we tag-team a soiree! Oh! Oh! Here's my new gossip reaction: "… no *way!* You're not serious!"
<Zoey does "incredulous" take.>

Felix: Magnificent! You are going to be such an influence peddler! Everybody wants to talk to the expressive players because they're so much more fun.

Zoey: But hey, I hear they've totally hacked this place and it's full of freaky a-life animals and genetic sculptures. God! It sounds so... <wistful> but, I think you actually have to know stuff if you want to play up here. Snappy patter by itself just isn't going to cut it with this crowd, is it?

Felix: It's all right girl. By the time we're done with Cloud10, we'll have auras like Mardi Gras dancers! They're gonna love love *love* us!

<Zoey's body and face freeze with her mouth open and the TV news blares out. The camera zooms in slowly.>
Felix: Zoey. Zoey. Helloooo! Do you have your TV on?

Part II

The First Production Phase: Building

Chapter 6

Sound: Your Film's Sonic Identity

For almost any successful animated film, praise can be heard regarding the visual elements and motion. But take a closer look at almost any animated film that gets attention and acclaim, and you'll likely hear excellent voice work, sound effects, music, or all three. It's almost as if sound is the silent partner in any good film.

Despite the fact that *Ren & Stimpy* cartoons feature thoroughly distinctive and memorable character designs, fans of the cartoon are more likely to shout "You eeediot!" in the voice of Ren Hoek than they are to say "That Ren was so funny looking!" And it would be difficult to argue that fans of *South Park* are loyal because the animation is great. Its smart-mouth humor is mostly in the sound.

Whether it's the orchestral scores of Danny Elfman for *Batman* or John Williams for *Star Wars* setting the tone for adventure, or the often-atonal soundtrack of *The Matrix*, music alone has a massive impact on the viewer. And artfully matched sound effects such as those found in *Ren & Stimpy* can take a simple gag and turn it into a sidesplitting, tear-inducing experience. Sound and music can be informative, evocative, funny, and cinematic.

For independent animators, given the quantity and variety of skills that must be mastered, audio can be a daunting prospect. To be sure, it is preferable to have sound created in a professional recording studio by professional sound engineers, musicians, composers, and sound effects creators, known as *Foley artists*. This is also one of the best areas to seek collaborators for the solo filmmaker. But, if you give sound adequate attention and craft, it is possible to give your project a strong sonic identity, given even modest equipment and skill.

General Notes on Sound

In this chapter, we will approach the vast world of sound from the perspective of a small or solo film production, where audio may not be the main focus of the creators. We will discuss simple and inexpensive solutions for authoring audio of reasonable quality and a few top-level issues on the cinematic nature of sound.

Sound as a Storytelling Tool

An excellent guiding approach to sound for your film is to view it as a storytelling device. This can aid you in making decisions when presented with the endless possibilities of sound for your film. If you are creating a lighthearted story about a squirrel frolicking in a meadow, ominous and threatening music with sound effects of the grass crunching under his feet would likely make people think the poor squirrel is doomed.

Several aspects of sound make it a powerful storytelling tool, as detailed in the following subsections.

Evoking a Mood
Sound literally sets the tone for a film and is one of the most powerful tools the director has for putting viewers in a mood that is receptive to the action that the story is about to deliver. And it is good to bear in mind that moods and the sounds that invoke them can be more than simply the primary emotional colors of "happy," "sad," "frightened," and so on. Subtle variations of moods can be achieved through subtle sound and music choices.

These moods can be created not only with music but through the use of ambient sounds as well. Echoing street traffic, wind through leaves, distant battle noises, and spooky jungle sounds are all familiar to us, but they just hint at the possibilities.

Cinematic Pacing

Stories themselves have rhythm, tempo, and pace. In the most hyperkinetic, frenzied sequences of *The Matrix*, speed metal and bombastic techno music helped put the story's already frenetic pace into overdrive. And in many of the classic Warner Bros. cartoons, the music of Carl Stahling would change tempo on a dime to help all the many flavored gags of a given cartoon flow together. Skilled feature film directors understand that varying the pace of the story is critical to keeping viewers' attention. A film with too much over-the-top action can overwhelm viewers, whereas too slow of a pace can put them to sleep. The literally and dramatically quiet parts in James Cameron's *Terminator 2* gave him time to reveal more of the characters' personalities while giving viewers a breather before another explosive action and audio barrage.

Communicating and Accentuating Story Points

Artfully created sounds can greatly enhance and embellish specific story points. Crickets and owls underscore that night has fallen. Sudden silence in the wind can herald the onset of a hurricane, and the sound of an ice cream truck can warn you that that evil clown is coming back.

Sound can also be mission critical when it is the sole communicator of a story point. The whine of an artillery shell, muffled thumping behind a door, and the ticking of a bomb are all examples of sound playing a critical role in story advancement. And this is doubly important for filmmakers who need to tell a story as efficiently as possible. A sound can effectively communicate a dramatic element and alleviate the need to model and animate that element.

General Equipment and Process

It is likely that a solo or small project filmmaker will only be beginning to acquire audio equipment and skills. So here are some of the most basic audio issues relating to dialogue, sound effects, and music. By understanding at least the basic elements of sound, you can stay focused on the artistry aspects without getting bogged down by too many technical issues.

Signal Quality

Keeping out unwanted noise and ensuring good clarity in your audio is integral to its quality. The best way to ensure this is to consider the source—that is, make sure your original audio signal is of acceptable quality. Your microphones, sound card, and recording environment all combine to create the quality of your initial signal. A relatively small money investment in a quality, general-purpose microphone and microphone preamp, as shown in Figure 6-1, can spare you a lot of futile time spent trying to clean up poor quality audio.

FIGURE 6-1   This standalone preamp and microphone setup is a good starting point for simple audio production.

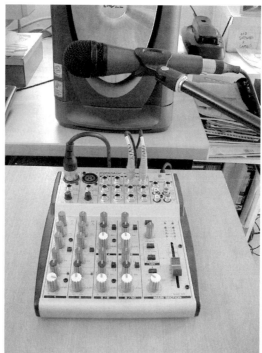

Sound Sampling and Resolution

Sound has a resolution not unlike bitmap images do. Sound resolution, coupled with the sample rate, affects not only the audio quality, but also the resulting file size. This in turn has an effect on how cumbersome the files are to load and manipulate and whether they will fit in your delivery medium. You will need to choose the proper sound sample rates and resolution when you record and when you finish your audio files. Here is a very simplified guide:

▶ **44.1 KHz sampling, 16-bit resolution, stereo**   On the high end of the quality spectrum is CD quality audio, and it should be used for your initial sound recordings wherever possible. Your sounds should also retain this level of detail if you intend on playing your film in a theater.

▶ **11 KHz sampling, 8-bit resolution, stereo**   Low-quality sound files are usually not acceptable for final delivery unless you're streaming your film over low-bandwidth web connections. But it can be useful to use lower-resolution sound files within your 3-D package when animating to save memory.

Although there are flavors of sampling rates and resolution in between, the basic rule of thumb is to always record initial audio at the highest quality possible. Then, preserve the high sampling and resolution of your audio throughout your editing process and create lower-quality copies if you need to deploy over a low-bandwidth medium such as the Web or to use as scratch audio during animating. Your audio file will be downsampled and compressed when you create your final video, as described in Chapter 15.

Recording and Editing

The centerpiece of your audio work will be a sound-editing software package. For nuts-and-bolts sound work, digital audio professionals typically use software such as Cakewalk's Sonar (see Figure 6-2) or ProTools. But even the freely downloadable Cool Edit can be sufficient for simpler sound-editing tasks. You will need to become comfortable with the basics of audio recording and editing, such as cropping and combining, simple noise reduction, and applying effects.

FIGURE 6-2   Cakewalk's Sonar is a popular audio recording and editing package.

Basic Recording Procedure   The details of digital recording will vary depending on your equipment and software. But whether you're creating dialogue, sound effects, or music, the actual recording requires a simple but important procedure:

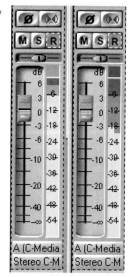

1 Create an empty file of the sample rate and resolution you desire—usually 44 KHz, 16-bit stereo.

2 Set the recording levels. This critical step is done by watching your editing software's recording input meter while actors talk or a sound effect is produced. By adjusting your microphone's volume level, you can make sure the meter is not going into the red zone, like the meter on the left. This will cause unwanted distortion in the recorded sound. Keep input levels high for a good signal but in the green, like the meter on the right.

3 Record, save, and then edit.

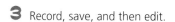

Audio Advice
from Industry Expert Alan Stuart

For some hard-core information on a few key audio issues, I turned to Alan Stuart, an accomplished musician, composer, and audio engineer. Alan has skillfully created music and sound effects and has performed audio engineering for a wide variety of technically challenging real-time and rendered 3-D animations. He is co-founder of Robotspeak, a provider of electronic music and audio equipment in San Francisco.

What would be the baseline audio hardware and software for a solo filmmaker or a small group?

A filmmaker can get surprisingly professional audio recordings using a decent condenser mic pair in tandem with a digital video camera or a minidisk recorder. For making field recordings and even recording dialogue, a number of small diaphragm condensers come configured in a stereo pair and are actually placed within the ears (much like a pair of walkman headphones). These in-ear mics are particularly well suited for a few reasons: In addition to sounding great, the mics pick up sound waves at exactly the same point they reach the ears, producing a realistic stereo image that remains in phase. The mics, which are designed for minidisk recorders, can often be plugged straight into a video camera's mic inputs. Because the camera operator is more often than not facing the action, pertinent dialogue is recorded cleanly in the center of the stereo field. The mics are also super-stealthy, giving you access to audio you may not otherwise be able to record with a pair of handheld mics and a shoulder-worn DAT machine.

For getting the audio into your computer, it's preferable to use a dedicated audio interface. A number of USB devices are on the market, from companies such as M-Audio and Creative Labs, that sport multiple audio I/O connectors and sometimes even studio-grade mic preamps.

A multitrack audio-recording software package such as Cool Edit or Pro Tools Free will let you record in sound effects, field recordings, and dialogue. Once all your audio material is recorded and edited in time, track volume can be automated to achieve the perfect mix.

Character Dialogue

The utterances of animated characters can be as memorable as the characters themselves, as evidenced by Homer Simpson's "Mmmm... doughnuts" or the mumbling and muttering of Popeye. The excellent, contrasting voice characterizations of all the characters on *King of the Hill* make its dialogue at least as important as its animation. Achieving quality dialogue involves casting the right voices, enabling good acting, and getting a good recording. And it is the foundation on which you can build engaging character animation (see Figure 6-3).

Voice Casting

Casting voice talent is an art in itself. It not only plays a pivotal role in the success of a given character, but it can also do a lot to *define* a character. Casting Woody Allen as the voice of "Z" provided PDI's *Antz* with a distinctive personality that perfectly fit the underdog, outcast theme of the character. And actor Kelsey Grammer's pompous and effete voice characterization gave the *Simpsons'* Sideshow Bob the perfect comedic counterbalance to his clown-like appearance.

Does the Voice Fit the Character?
When looking for the right voice for your character, I recommend closing your eyes and listening only to the person's voice you are considering. This is the best way to keep from being distracted by the way the real person looks and to focus on how that person's voice will sound coming out of your character. If your tall and skinny friend happens to have a booming base voice, he may be the perfect cast for your fat villain character.

Can That Person Act?
A truly skilled actor can bring a lot of serendipity to your character. The best actors may even be able to delve deeper into what the characters are like than you can. This can give you an even more authentic performance than if they were to follow your script precisely.

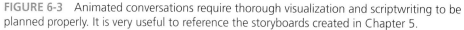

FIGURE 6-3 Animated conversations require thorough visualization and scriptwriting to be planned properly. It is very useful to reference the storyboards created in Chapter 5.

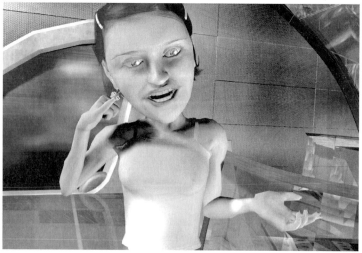

Because it's likely that you'll be casting amateur actors, one of the main things to consider—even more important than their acting skills—is how uninhibited your actors are. Even if your potential actor has the perfect voice and can act well in a casual setting, it may be difficult to get a good performance if they are overly shy or self-conscious when placed behind a microphone.

Then it is important to know whether or not this person can take direction. Amateur actors may not understand the process of storytelling and the importance of being receptive to the input of the storyteller. One of the best ways to discern this is to simply ask, "Will you be comfortable taking direction from me?"

Directing a Dialogue–Recording Session

The dialogue-recording session is a significant milestone in your preproduction. Unlike most of the other work in animated filmmaking, which can be iterated ad nauseam until completed, dialogue recording is essentially a performance-based process. Therefore, the successful session not only takes thorough preparation and process to get a good dialogue recording, it also takes a different mindset. Dialogue recording requires that you be able to effectively communicate your ideas while allowing the creativity of your collaborators to infuse and inform your work.

Directing Actors

The process of directing your actors starts as soon as you have cast them. It takes time for almost any voice actor to work out an effective voice characterization. And this usually requires discussing all the issues of the character biography with the actor. This not only makes for an accurate voice characterization but, importantly, gets the actor creatively engaged in the process.

Rehearsal

Then, for all but the smallest speaking roles, it is recommended that you have a rehearsal one or two days prior to the actual recording. This allows the actors to receive initial direction from you while still having time to practice and assimilate that direction. Rehearsal is a good opportunity for improvisation and creativity without pressure. And it may allow you to have time to revise your script based on input from your actors.

Creating a Productive Atmosphere

Despite the pervasive caricature of a director angrily barking orders at performers and being a temperamental artiste, this is the exact opposite behavior required to direct effectively. Recording sessions can be stressful for many reasons, including nervous actors, limited time, technical difficulties, interruptions, and a host of other complications. If left unchecked, the stress factors can wreak havoc on the recording process by distracting your actors. Critical to overcoming these obstacles is, of course, careful preparation but also the ability to create a calm and relaxed atmosphere for the session. Because everyone involved in the session will be looking to you for direction, it is likely that they will take cues from your demeanor as well. Achieving this type of relaxed atmosphere can greatly enhance the productivity of your session and leave you with a full head of hair. Here are some key factors to help you direct effectively.

Patience   Patience in both yourself and everyone involved will be important. It is wise to prepare both yourself and your actors for multiple takes, even if they are not ultimately necessary. It is highly unusual for the best performance in any situation to occur on the first take. Both you and actors will likely see specific spots in a performance that can be improved upon through fine-tuning.

Knowing What You're Looking For   Prior to the recording sessions, it is wise to go over your script and storyboards with a fine-tooth comb, with an eye toward what key vocalizations you will need to animate. You may find out that to voice a key fighting sequence may require timing some "Oof!" sounds or yelling to the action outlined in your storyboards. Or you may find that you need a character to laugh long enough for the camera to zoom in on them. You may even have in mind a particular gesture or expression you want your animated character to use that needs a specific voicing. This knowledge will allow you to be more informed and confident in your direction, and this confidence will reduce uncertainty and indecision in your actors.

Improvisation versus Precision   Lastly, based on your own directing experience and the experience level of your actors, you can allow for serendipity and improvisation in your session. This should be balanced with ensuring that a workable result is achieved. Improvisation can take the simple form of picking a particular line and delivering it with differing inflections, or it can become a full-blown improvisation with skilled actors responding spontaneously to one another.

In the end, the most important thing is to get a result that you can animate to, and this will likely require following your script closely and a thorough attention to detail during the recording process.

Recording Session Logistics

There are many mundane, practical issues when recording any significant dialogue that can greatly affect the final outcome:

▶ **Scheduling** Try to schedule your session early enough in the day so that people are fresh. Fatigue can disrupt the session through poor performances and added irritation.

▶ **Environment** If you're not recording in a professional studio, with a soundproof recording booth, attempt to at least record in a quiet environment, free from distraction and onlookers. Brief, incidental noises can often be dealt with simply by doing another take of a given passage. Particularly, watch out for the noise of your computer's cooling fans. You may want to get extension cords for your microphones to be able to get away from the noise of your computer.

▶ **Defining logical sections** If the dialogue for your script is more than 30 seconds long, it is advisable that you find logical breaks in your story that can be recorded in discrete sections. This will keep the actors from having to be perfect for uncomfortably long durations and make multiple takes much less tedious and stressful.

Zoey, Felix, and Carlo's Recording Session

Very fortunately for my project, and me, I was able to team up with a longtime friend, musician and songwriter Matt Carter, who agreed to do audio engineering, sound effects, and music for my animation. This was a pivotal partnership for my project, and I would not have even attempted this type of film without his help.

For the actors, I depended heavily on the good graces of family and friends. I had been thinking of specific people to voice my characters from the very outset of my character-design process. For the role of Zoey, I asked my sister-in-law, Heather Dunn, because she had the right voice, was comfortable and uninhibited, and had recently taken an acting class. For Felix, I called upon Michael Siebielec, an experienced stage actor who had skillfully voiced a wide variety of characters in my previous animation projects. And for the villain, Carlo, I cast my brother-in-law, David Ewers, because I knew he had the cheek and wit to play this irritating character, and he had actually helped me write Carlo's dialogue.

We recorded the dialogue at Matt's home studio on a quiet Sunday afternoon. I had held discussions with each of the actors about their characters, and everyone had been given a chance to read the

Alan Stuart on Dialogue Recording

What are the three or four major technical concerns when recording dialogue?

When recording dialogue, it's important to place the mic close enough (to the actor) that room reflections and environmental noise are kept to a minimum, but at such an angle to avoid unwanted sibilance (over accentuated *ess* and *th* sounds) and pops caused from a sudden rush of air from *p*-type consonants. A directional mic (or a mic with a cardiod or shotgun pickup pattern) held at or above the actor's forehead will help to keep room reflections at a minimum and nasty consonants at bay.

>> TIP   *A wire coat hanger bent into a circle with panty hose stretched over it can serve as a pop filter in a pinch. Seriously!*

script for couple of weeks. To get us into the flow of performing, the actors rehearsed the first passages into the microphones while Matt checked sound levels.

Performing and recording the dialogue then went extraordinarily smooth. I had broken up the script into five sections, and we recorded four or five takes of each section. I would read along in my script while the actors performed and mark particular phrases or even words where I was hoping to hear a different emphasis or inflection. I would then point out these spots between takes. The session lasted about three hours.

Sound Effects

The skillful use of sound effects can be a powerful tool for the visual storyteller. They can help to explain and sell a visual moment that might otherwise be difficult to understand. Adding the sound of screeching brakes is much more effective than simply seeing the wheels of a train stop turning. Sound effects help the viewers suspend their disbelief. The rumbling sounds of smashing concrete and glass give great credence to the fantastic image of a superhero blasting through a wall. When done creatively, they can help to create a convincing fiction, such as when the sound of an alien spaceship's engines has just the right otherworldly quality. You can choose to precisely match appropriate sound effects to each point in your story to give it an air of plausibility and realism—or you can juxtapose contrasting sounds for added emphasis or humor. A character's yelp can sound like a train whistle, or a group of people getting knocked down can sound like bowling pins.

Basic Sound Effect Techniques

There are numerous methods for creating and acquiring sound effects. Choosing them can be dictated by the type of sound required, your equipment resources, and by the method you are most comfortable with. A few of the major methods are included in the following list.

▶ **Recording in the field**   One of the best ways to ensure that your sounds are both appropriate and fresh is to record them at their source. An affordable MiniDisc recorder with a decent microphone, or even the microphone on a digital video camera, as explained earlier, can make this a simpler and more economical process than in the past.

▶ **Creating from scratch—the Foley artist**   Many convincing sound effects can be created through the creative use of just about any imaginable item that makes noise. Foley artists frequently record the smashing of watermelons for grizzly gore scenes or punch bags of flour to simulate the sounds of a fistfight. Most of these types of sounds can be created right by your computer for easy recording.

▶ **Using sound effect and sample libraries**   Professional sound designers regularly rely on CD- and Internet-based sound archives for a multitude of ready-made sounds. These can be highly valuable when properly cataloged and easily searchable.

Editing and Enhancing

Once the initial source for your sound effect has been acquired or created, you have many possibilities for enhancement, depending on what sound-editing software you use. These enhancements can take the form of effects such as reverb to match acoustics. It can also be helpful to combine different effects for more complex sounds.

Sound Effects for "The Game to Save the World"

Matt Carter used several techniques to create the many sound effects for my film. I wanted a distinctive shuffling sound for Zoey's flip-flop-style shoes. To do this, Matt recorded the sound of an actual shoe shuffling on the floor. For videogame interface and gadget sounds, he began by triggering samples from a library with his keyboard and then manipulated those sounds through editing and effects. For the ambient crowd noise, Matt cleverly used the actual recordings from the dialogue session, layering and manipulating them to create the background murmuring.

Music

Acquiring the right music to enhance your work is a challenging task. Ideally, it's usually preferable to have custom music scored specifically to your animation. This way, the music can cater perfectly to the cinematic demands of your story. But this depends on the resources of a composer, musicians, their equipment, and time.

Alan Stuart on Sound Effects

When you are not using a real-world recording as the base for a sound effect, what kinds of things do you start with?

Cabbage, pots and pans, and an electric razor. When you produce audio to match an image, you shouldn't feel obligated to exactly reproduce a real-world event. The psycho-acoustic effect of "non-real" audio events in synch with images can create a profoundly convincing result. Go for found objects that, when struck, brushed, squashed, or otherwise manipulated, produce sounds that in some way hint at the actual event. Record as many variations as possible and try layering, pitch shifting, reversing, and splicing your recordings within a multitrack audio software app to produce new sonic blends.

Fortunately, quality music creation is becoming more and more economical thanks to powerful computers and music-creation software, which enable more independent music creators to have a wide palette of instrumentation choices and a more fluid music-creation process. This means it may be easier to find musical collaborators than in the past.

Working with a Composer or Songwriter

If you have the opportunity to work with someone to create music for your film, it will be important to them to be able to communicate in a way that is meaningful to their creative process. If they are scoring music to your film, allowing them to work directly with the finished animation is probably best. But it is good to work with them prior to this so that they can begin working on musical ideas and themes.

It helps to be able to talk to songwriters in musical terms about the instrumentation, tempos, and musical styles you envision. Then it is good to describe the cinematic points you hope to accentuate and the feelings and moods you are trying to invoke in the viewer.

Setting the Tone for Cloud10

For my collaboration with Matt on my film's musical score, I tried to give broad ideas to allow him as much creative freedom as possible. In years past, Matt and I had composed dozens of songs together, so I was comfortable with what he would create once he had a sense of the story. One of our main considerations was that we did not want the music to compete with the dialogue that went through most of the film. We wanted something that would work with the flavor of the science-fiction atmosphere I was creating. So I asked Matt to attempt to create some technology-infused music that sounded as fresh as possible but would remain subtle and understated. This was a very tall order, but I was thrilled with the results of Matt's long hours and hard work.

Using Existing Music

If you are not able to create music specifically for your film, it is still possible, through inspired choices and creative editing, to use existing music to great effect for an animation soundtrack. When done with finesse, choosing music passages that fit with your scene and carefully adjusting volume to balance with the dialogue and sound effects can work almost as well as custom scoring.

In some cases, it is even preferable to animate to music, creating movements that match the rhythm and tempo of the soundtrack. To take this further, you can create a music video, making the music central to the animation.

>>TIP *Unless your film is simply for portfolio purposes, you'll need to get permission from the authors or publishers of the music to use it in your film. If you are attempting to use a song from a giant star such as Eminem, it may be difficult to get permission from the giant BMG Publishing. But getting permission from a local band that you like can be a much simpler and rewarding process.*

Audio Workflow for Your Animation

Because of logistical dependencies in the production process, it is helpful to create the soundtrack in phases to accommodate workflow needs at a few stages. Although these requirements can vary greatly from production to production, here is the rough audio workflow for an animated film:

1 *Record the dialogue*. Dialogue should be recorded first because you'll need to animate to it.

2 *Add sound effects*. You can use your sound-editing program to add the sound effects that, like the dialogue, will need animations to match them.

3 *Import sounds to your 3-D package*. Break your master soundtrack file into separate files that correspond to the length of each shot or group of shots in your scene files that you'll be setting up in Chapter 10. These sound files can be loaded as WAV audio files (I recommend scratch quality) into your 3-D package.

4 *Animate to the dialogue*. You can view your waveform for aligning facial and body animation keyframes (see Figure 6-4), as explained in Chapters 11 and 12.

5 *Add animation-dependent sound effects*. Use your sound-editing program to add sound effects (to your original, high-resolution soundtrack) that need to be timed to your animation, such as footsteps and punches. It may be simpler to perform this synchronization with rendered video in your video-editing package instead of in your 3-D package.

FIGURE 6-4   Viewing the waveforms in your 3-D package allows you to align keyframes for lip-synching directly to the corresponding syllables in your audio file.

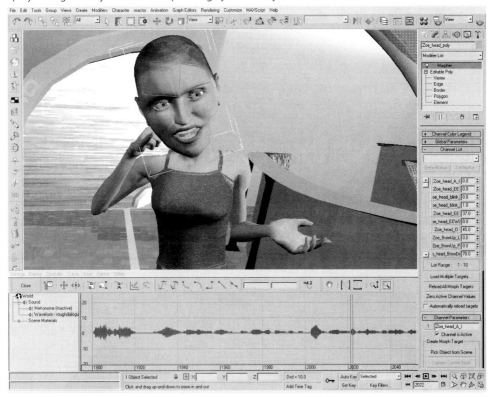

6 *Add music.* Now you can either compose your musical score or add the existing music you have chosen. Once again, it is best to use rendered video as reference in a video-editing package.

7 *Create the final mix.* To complete the soundtrack for your film, you'll want to mix the relative volume levels of the dialogue, sound effects, and music tracks in your sound-editing software and export a single high-resolution WAV audio file.

From here, you'll be importing your finished soundtrack file into a video-editing package such as Adobe Premiere (more on this in Chapter 17), where you will combine it with your final rendered frames (covered in Chapter 16).

Chapter 7

Modeling Character Heads: The Digital Sculptor I

Now it's time to create the face of a

CG film: the actors. Creating 3-D characters is

a task that requires proficiency in 3ds max's

modeling tools to realize your character designs

from Chapter 4. This process can be a rewarding

one because learning a small set of tools

combined with some artistic ability can allow

FIGURE 7-1   These are front and side views of the head mesh for Carlo, modeled with subdivision surfaces.

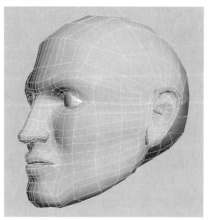 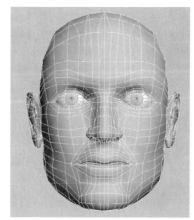

even beginning modelers to create rich and expressive forms. In this chapter, we'll go through the process of modeling the head mesh for the villain of the film, Carlo (see Figure 7-1), as an example of how to make your own.

Character Mesh Modeling

Today's 3-D modeler has a selection of several methods to choose from when it comes to modeling a character (see Figure 7-2). There are many ways to skin a cat—or any other 3-D character. Each of the major methods has its own strengths and weaknesses, and this leads to particular modeling methods being used more often in certain applications—some for film,

FIGURE 7-2   This image illustrates four of the dominant methods for creating a surface. Working with raw polygons using the Editable Mesh object requires directly manipulating every point, edge, or plane, while the other methods offer the ability to manipulate a surrounding area of polygons using control points or handles.

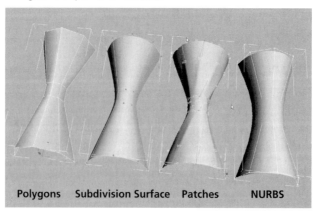

Polygons   Subdivision Surface   Patches   NURBS

some for games, and so on. These methods have evolved over the course of quite a few years now, with one gaining in favor over the other as its toolset evolves.

Editable Mesh Objects: Raw Triangles

One of the most basic choices has been raw triangular meshes found in 3ds max's Editable Mesh objects and objects with the Edit Mesh modifier applied. These meshes are most commonly found in video games because the object format is the simplest. An Editable Mesh object is composed of essentially three components: points in 3-D space (called *vertices*), the connections between these points (called *edges*), and then the planes that these points and edges form (called *polygons*). Because all the edges are straight lines, complex surfaces require more polygonal resolution to give the illusion of curvature. This simplicity makes models built as Editable Mesh objects easier to translate to real-time video game engines. However, the toolset specifically for Editable Mesh objects is no longer as powerful as those for other methods.

NURBS: Mathematically Precise Curved Surfaces

The acronym NURBS stands for *nonuniform rational B-splines,* which means that NURBS models are comprised of actual three-dimensional mathematical curves and therefore fewer vertices are required to create complex surfaces. Also, the curvature of the surfaces is resolution independent. This means that for applications such as movies, where highly detailed images are required, NURBS models can be viewed close up without revealing the telltale faceting of mesh models. NURBS models often have a fairly steep learning curve and a complex modeling process to be able to use them effectively.

Patches: User-friendly Curved Surfaces

Spline patches are a simpler, more user-friendly implementation of curved surfaces for modeling. Like NURBS, patches allow you to construct models from resolution-independent curves. However, their simpler mathematical underpinnings allow for more straightforward construction of complex shapes. Today, 3D rendering engines are moving beyond supporting simple mesh geometry, and some are even starting to support patch-based models.

Subdivision Surfaces

In this chapter, we'll explore another approach to modeling—subdivision surfaces—in some depth. A subdivision surface model, which in 3ds max is known as an Editable Poly object, can be built with a very mature and simple-yet-robust toolset that allows for fast and intuitive 3-D sculpting. This means that you can focus on learning a finite set of tools and techniques for creating and manipulating polygons, edges, and vertices. Also, like the toolset of a traditional sculptor, who might use a handful of different chisels to create anything from a human to a gargoyle, this simple set of polygonal tools allows you to create almost any three-dimensional form. Particularly for those learning modeling, this is an excellent way to weed through all of the bells and whistles—such as lofting, Booleans, and metaballs—and zero in on what is most important.

Subdivision Surface Tools and Techniques

For subdivision surface modeling, you'll need to become familiar with the Sub Object tools in the Editable Poly object, particularly those within the Vertex, Edge, and Polygon Sub Object modes. All these tools are located in the Modify panel when an Editable Poly object is selected. Near the top of the panel are buttons for each of the different sub object selection modes, as shown on the right. In each mode, you'll be presented with a different set of tools, although all the modes share many of the same tools and have other similarities.

Here are some of the more common operations you'll perform in the course of subdivision surface modeling. We'll get into these and a few other operations in the course of the tutorials in this chapter:

▶ **Connect vertices**   A very common and intuitive way to create an edge is to change to Vertex Sub Object mode, select two or more vertices, and use the Vertex Connect button located in the Edit Vertices rollout of the Modify panel. Figure 7-3a and Figure 7-3b show an example of this type of operation.

FIGURE 7-3   New edges are created between a selection of vertices (a) using the Vertex Connect tool (b).

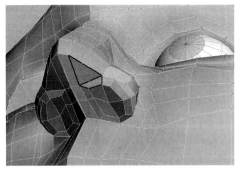

(a)

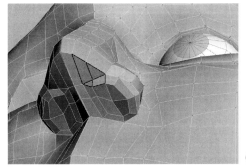

(b)

FIGURE 7-4   Edge loops can be created by selecting a ring of edges (a) and using the Connect Edge tool (b).

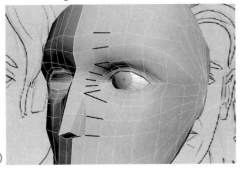

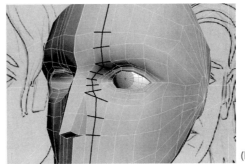

(a)   (b)

▶ **Connect edges**   Edges themselves can also be connected with the Edge Connect button located in the Edit Edges rollout of the Modify panel when in Edge Sub Object mode (see Figure 7-4a and Figure 7-4b). This is an efficient way to create edge loops—edges that form a continuous line.

NOTE   *Sub object selection sets of vertices, edges, or polygons appear in red in the 3ds max viewports. For clarity, sub object selections have been outlined in black for the images in this book.*

▶ **Insert vertices**   The Insert Vertex button is available in both Edge and Polygon Sub Object mode. Figure 7-5a and Figure 7-5b show inserting a vertex that can later be connected with the Vertex Connect tool.

FIGURE 7-5   Here, an edge is selected (a) and a vertex is inserted with the Insert Vertex tool (b).

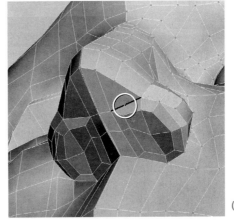

(a)   (b)

FIGURE 7-6   An edge is selected (a) and erased with the Remove Edge tool (b).

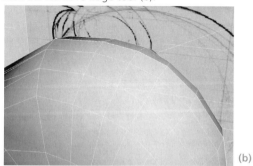

(a)   (b)

▶ **Remove edges and vertices**   Unnecessary edges, like the one shown in Figure 7-6a, can be erased with the Edge Remove tool, located in the Edit Edges rollout of the Modify panel in Edge Sub Object mode (see Figure 7-6b). This takes away an edge without deleting the underlying polygon, which would leave a hole in the mesh.

▶ **Collapse edges**   Areas of the mesh can be simplified in numerous ways. Figure 7-7a and Figure 7-7b show another example of reducing detail, this time with the Collapse Edge tool. It is found in the Edit Geometry rollout of the Modify panel in Edge Sub Object mode.

▶ **Collapse polygons**   Entire polygons can also be collapsed in a similar way with the Polygon Collapse tool, found in the Edit Geometry rollout of the Modify panel in Polygon Sub Object mode, as shown in Figure 7-8a and Figure 7-8b.

FIGURE 7-7   Areas can be simplified in several ways. Here, edges are selected (a) and collapsed using the Collapse Edges tool (b).

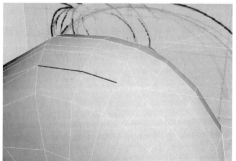

(a)   (b)

FIGURE 7-8   Selecting a polygon (a) and collapsing it with the Collapse Polygon tool (b) causes all the vertices that make up that polygon to be combined.

(a)

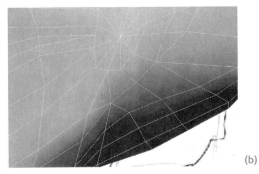

(b)

▶ **Extrude polygons**   Figure 7-9a and Figure 7-9b show how to make polygons "grow" out of a surface using the Polygon Extrude tool. This tool automatically creates polygons around the sides of the selected polygons. It is found in the Edit Polygons rollout of the Modify panel in Polygons Sub Object mode.

▶ **Bevel**   Next to the Extrude Polygon tool is the Bevel Polygon tool. The Bevel Polygon tool is very similar to the Extrude Polygon tool, except that it allows the outline of the selected polygons to be simultaneously scaled so that they can be "grown" out in tapering peaks, as shown in Figure 7-9c.

FIGURE 7-9   A polygon is selected (a) and extruded using the Extrude Polygon tool (b). Then the same polygon is beveled using the Bevel Polygon tool (c).

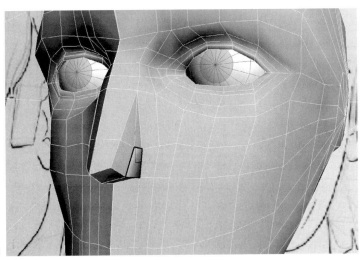

(a)

(b)

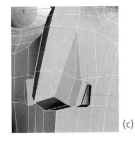

(c)

FIGURE 7-10 Within a selection of polygons (a), an edge loop that follows the outline of the selection is easily created (b).

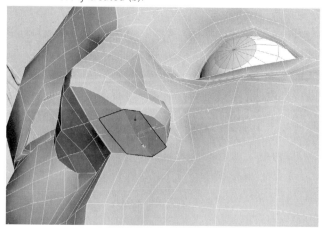

(a)

(b)

▶ **Inset** Next to the Bevel Polygon tool is the Inset Polygon tool. This tool works similarly to the Bevel Polygon tool, except that the selection is not extruded, as shown in Figure 7-10a and Figure 7-10b.

Modeling Methodology: Topology, Followed by Artistry

A simple, guiding methodology can help focus your modeling efforts and keep you from getting lost. Creating a complex 3-D object such as a character head or a body requires first creating the topology or grid work of your mesh and then molding that topology into the shape you desire artistically. These aspects certainly overlap, and a skilled modeler will factor both simultaneously as they model. However, conceptualizing these aspects separately will allow you to simplify the initially challenging task of modeling a complex surface.

Topology You have several overall considerations in creating the topology of your model. First, and most obvious, is making sure that the distribution of detail on the mesh allows for the contours that the form requires. This means that you'll need more polygons around the areas that have tighter curvature, such as nostrils, ears, and lips, than you will on flatter areas, such as the back of the head. But more than that, the topology of a mesh needs to *flow* along your surface's contours. For example, if you want your character to have a pronounced nasolabial fold (the wrinkle that runs from the nostril to the corner of the mouth), it is helpful to have a line of edges running along the fold, allowing the mesh to bend around that contour, as shown in Figure 7-11a. Also, your topology needs to be dictated by the movement the surface will need to perform. The mouth may need more polygons than are required to model it simply in a closed position. This is because when the mouth and other parts of the face are animated, they stretch out, and that stretching needs to be distributed over a number of polygons, as shown in Figure 7-11b.

FIGURE 7-11   When distinct contours are required in a surface, it is helpful to define them with edges that follow that contour (a). It is also helpful to have more polygons around areas that stretch when animated (b).

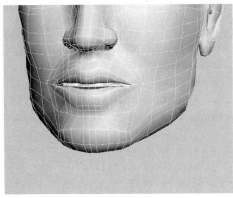
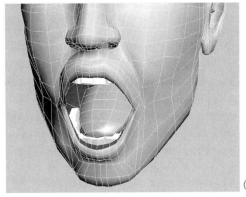

(a)

(b)

Another aspect of the topology to pay attention to as you model is to ensure that the mesh is composed of four-sided polygons, or *quads*, wherever possible. For a number of reasons, you should avoid any long and skinny polygons and allow for three-sided polygons only where necessary. First, this will keep your meshes organized to help you avoid getting lost in a confusing jumble of polygons. But more importantly, long skinny polygons and polygons with five sides or more can often cause splintery rendering artifacts in your model. The best way to ensure an organized topology is to pay attention to it after each addition or deletion of vertices, edges, or polygons. Figure 7-12a shows an area of problematic topology, and Figure 7-12b shows how adding edges can correct the problem.

FIGURE 7-12   This is a comparison between an area with a messy topology (a) and the same area once it has been cleaned up through the addition of edges (b).

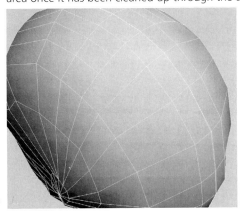
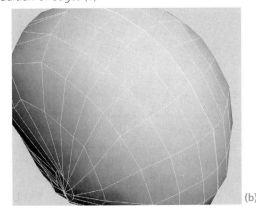

(a)

(b)

> **»TIP** *Creating a mesh with the right topology is a puzzle, but you can learn a lot from the way others have solved the problem. Many artists post images of the wireframes of their models when they show their work on web forums or in their web portfolios. These can be an excellent source of reference, and they're abundantly available because it is just as helpful to see a subdivision surface mesh created in other packages, such as Maya, Lightwave, or Softimage, as it is in 3ds max.*

Artistry   Once the topology of your mesh has been created, you can focus on sculpting—pushing, pulling, scaling and rotating polygons, edges, and vertices—with less focus on the technical aspects and more on realizing your artistic vision. This can be difficult when you're faced with the abstractness and unfamiliarity of a 3-D environment. However, thorough character designs and ample reference can alleviate creative guesswork at this stage and allow you to model decisively.

Modeling a Character Head

This tutorial will take you through the steps of creating the head of the character Carlo. To keep the characters as simple as possible, they have heads that are separate from the rest of their bodies. Also, the heads on my characters will be oversized, making their neck joints less obvious. I made this compromise to simplify the process of rigging them (see Chapter 10).

To do the tutorial in this chapter, you'll need to be comfortable with 3ds max's most rudimentary functions. Navigating the viewports through zooming, panning, rotating, and controlling the viewport display options will be necessary as well as moving, rotating, and scaling objects. These basic operations are covered thoroughly in the "Getting Started" tutorial that comes with 3ds max.

> **❤NOTE** *You can use this tutorial in several ways. You can follow closely and duplicate Carlo, or you can follow these same steps to create a character of your own. To aid you, the CD-ROM includes several .max files—named Carlo_Head01.max through Carlo_Head07.max—that I'll refer to if you want to follow along. These are located in \3dsmax6_CD\Carlo\Car_Head\.*

Setting Up a New Workspace

Many modelers bring their construction drawings directly into 3ds max by texture mapping them onto flat plane objects. This way the construction drawings can be used as referenced directly in the viewports. Here are the steps to do this and to set up your workspace for modeling:

1 In a new file, set your units to centimeters. From the Customize menu, select Units Setup and choose Metric Centimeters as the Display Unit Scale in the dialog box. Then click OK to close the dialog box.

2 While in a front viewport, click the Create panel on the right side of the 3ds max interface and then click the Plane button. Drag in the viewport to create a Plane primitive about 40 cm square and name it Portrait Plane. You can watch the dimensions of the Plane object change in the field of the Modify panel as you drag in the viewport.

3 Near the top of the Modify panel, click the drop-down modifier list and select a UVW Map modifier.

4 Open the Material Editor and in the first open slot, click the small blank button next to the Diffuse slot. In the Material/Map Browser dialog box that appears, make sure the New radio button is selected and then double-click Bitmap. Then choose the bitmap of your character's front and profile construction (\3dsmax6_CD\Carlo\Car_Head\car_drawing.jpg) drawings or photos. I chose to have the front and profile drawings together in the same bitmap so they are automatically aligned.

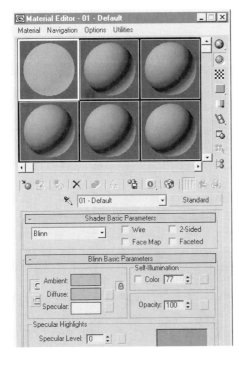

5 With your Plane objects selected, use the Assign Material to Selection button to place the material on it. Then use the Show Map in Viewport button to see the image on your Plane object.

6 In the Material Editor, navigate back up to the top level using the Go To Parent button shown here. Turn up the Self Illumination parameter in the Blinn Basic Parameters rollout and name your material Construction Portrait.

7 With the Portrait Plane selected, go to the Modify panel and click the Bitmap Fit button and choose the bitmap that you used in your material. This constrains the UVW map gizmo to the proportions of your bitmap.

8 To create the Profile Plane, hold down the SHIFT key and rotate the Portrait Plane 90 degrees in the view or world Z-axis and position it as shown in Figure 7-13. Name this object Profile Plane.

9 Now you can align the correct image on each of the Plane objects by simply sliding the UVW Map gizmo left or right. This is done by choosing Gizmo in the modifier stack and then using the normal Move tool in the viewport.

Starting with a Sphere

Depending on the shape of your character's head, you can start modeling with just about any basic primitive, or even one built from scratch. I like to start with a sphere laid on its side so that the "poles" will eventually become the ears of the character. This also provides a nice even quad grid for the cranium of the character. Now that the workspace is set up, follow these steps to begin modeling the head:

1 Create a sphere with a diameter of 10 to 15 cm and 20 segments. Name it Car_Head (you can replace "Car" with your character's name).

2 Rotate the sphere 90 degrees in the Y-axis. In the right viewport, move this sphere so the poles align with what will be the ears of your character. If you need to scale the sphere, do so by adjusting the Radius parameter in a Modify panel instead of using the Scale tool. It is best to avoid placing scale transforms on objects whenever possible, since it can complicate rigging as we'll see in Chapter 10.

FIGURE 7-13   This scene shows the Profile Plane and the Portrait Plane construction objects.

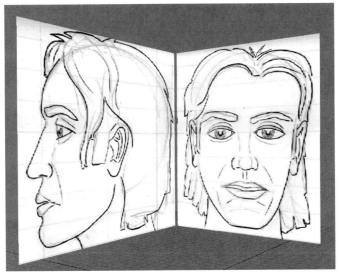

3   Right-click the sphere and, from the right-click menu, choose Convert to Editable Poly. Then in Polygon Sub Object mode, select and delete the left half of the sphere (what will be the character's right side).

4   Click the Polygon Sub Object Mode button again to get back in Object mode. Use the Mirror tool from the top toolbar with the Instance radio button clicked to create a flipped version of the sphere. You can allow 3ds max to automatically name this Car_Head01 because you'll delete it later. Now if you edit the original head object, your changes will be reflected in this new object because it is an instance. This essentially cuts your modeling time in half (see Figure 7-14).

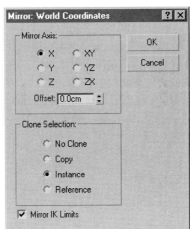

NOTE   *On the CD-ROM, the file \3dsmax6_CD\Carlo\Car_Head\\
Carlo_Head_01.max contains the completed tutorial to this point.*

FIGURE 7-14   This is the sphere, named Car_Head, once it has been cut in half and mirrored as an instance. Car_Head01 is on the left.

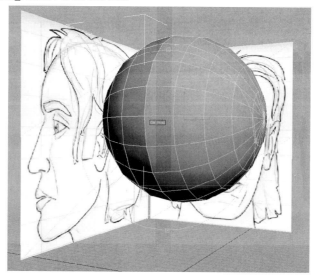

Extruding, Sculpting, and Refining

These next steps will outline a common procedure of extruding polygons and then sculpting this newly created geometry by moving vertices, edges, or polygons. We'll use this methodology often throughout the modeling process.

1 Select Car_Head. In Polygon Sub Object mode, select the bottom front polygons (see Figure 7-15a) and extrude them (see Figure 7-15b).

2 This operation creates a row of polygons that face the inside of the head. Select these and delete them.

3 Select the same set of polygons that you extruded. Move them toward the centerline where the mirrored halves of the head meet (see Figure 7-16a) and rotate them in the local Z-axis (see Figure 7-16b). These will become the face.

4 Fix any overlapping vertices around the ear area by moving them individually with the Move tool (see Figure 7-17).

FIGURE 7-15   The selection to be extruded (a), and the selection after extrusion (b). Note the polygons facing the center of the head that will need to be deleted.

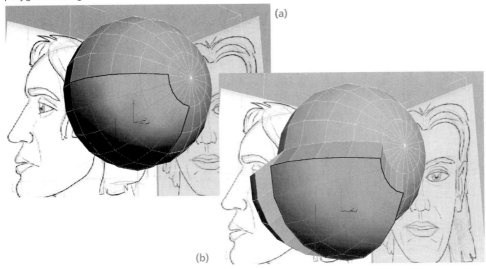

(a)

(b)

5   Right-click the head object and select Properties from the context menu. Click the See Through check box. This will allow you to see your construction drawings through the mesh. Then, click the word "Perspective" in the upper-left corner of the viewport and check Edged Faces from the pop-up menu.

FIGURE 7-16   Here, the extruded polygons have been moved inward toward the centerline (a). Then, the new vertices have been spread out with the move tool to arrange the topology (b).

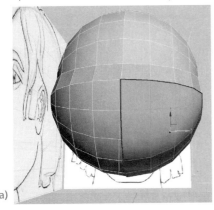
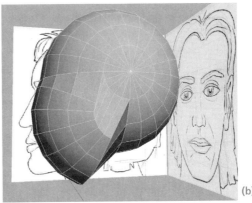

(a)

(b)

FIGURE 7-17 The vertices to the front and below the ear area have been spread out with the Move tool in Vertex Sub Object mode.

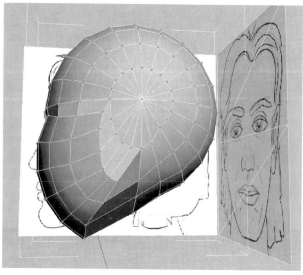

6 Now you can begin to sculpt the geometry you've created. In the right viewport, enter Vertex Sub Object mode and select the vertex that was the pole of your sphere. In the Soft Selection rollout of the Modify panel, turn on Soft Selection and adjust the falloff so that its influence extends about halfway past the ring of ear vertices to the next ring. Then, move this point so that it is centered on the ear of your profile construction drawing.

7 Repeat this same procedure for the chin and brow areas, each time adjusting your soft selection falloff so that the vertices remain evenly disbursed (see Figure 7-18).

8 Sculpt the mesh in a similar manner in the front viewport to match what you have created so far to the portrait construction drawing.

9 Now simplify the mesh around the ears by selecting edges, as shown in Figure 7-19a. Then click the Collapse button. The result is shown in Figure 7-19b.

10 Use the Arc Rotate button, located in the viewport controls in the bottom-right corner of the 3ds max interface, to look at the underside of the head. Then create a more even, grid-like topology underneath the head to compensate for the initial extrusion operation. Do this by selecting the large edges on the underside of the jaw (see Figure 7-20a). Then, in the Edit Edges rollout of the Modify panel, click the rectangle

FIGURE 7-18   Here is the mesh sculpted to match the profile drawings. This also shows the falloff of the soft selection with only the vertex at the center of the ear selected.

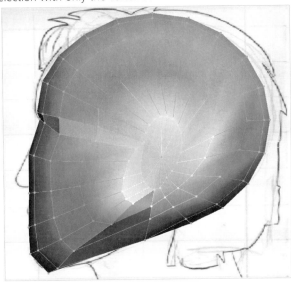

button next to the Connect button and connect the selected edges with a setting of 2 in the Connect Edges dialog box. The result is shown in Figure 7-20b.

FIGURE 7-19   This is the ear area with edges selected (a) and collapsed (b)

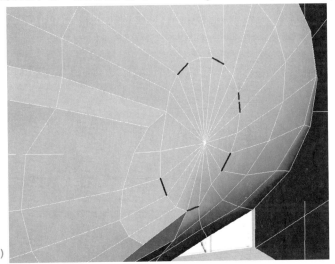

(a)

(b)

FIGURE 7-20 This is underneath the jaw with the long edges selected (a) and then connected using the Edge Connect tool (b).

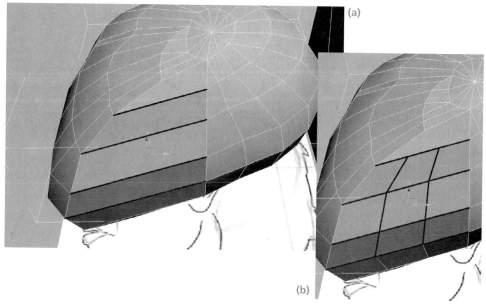

11 Select the polygons between the new edges that you created (see Figure 7-21a). Move these down in the view or world Z-axis and forward in the view or world Y-axis (see Figure 7-21b).

FIGURE 7-21 Here the selected polygons (a) have been moved down in the Z-axis and forward in the Y-axis (b).

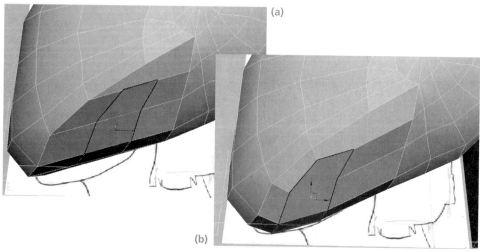

FIGURE 7-22   The selected edges (a) and the edges after they have been connected (b).

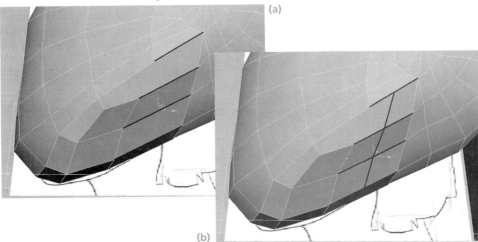

12   Select the same edges again, plus the one above them, as shown in Figure 7-22a.
Then use the Connect tool to connect these edges, as shown in Figure 7-22b.

13   Select the two pairs of vertices circled in Figure 7-23a and click the Connect tool.
The result is shown in Figure 7-23b. This is to keep the regular grid pattern of the
mesh wherever possible.

FIGURE 7-23   The selected vertices (a) and the vertices after being connected (b).

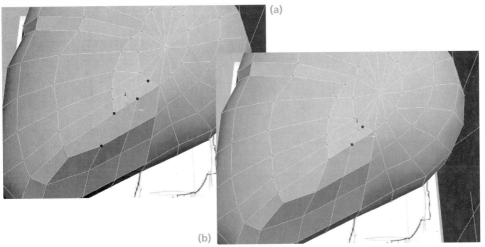

FIGURE 7-24 The right view (a) and the front view (b) after vertices have been sculpted to match the construction drawings.

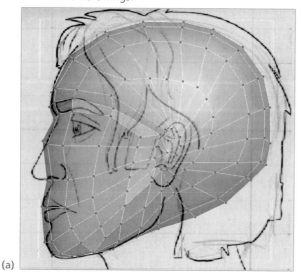
(a)

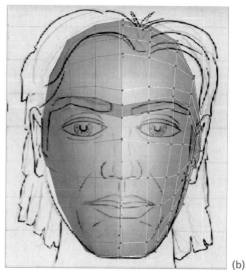
(b)

14 Arrange the vertices in the right view (see Figure 7-24a) and then in the front view (see Figure 7-24b) so that the mesh aligns with the construction drawings.

⌣NOTE **On the CD-ROM, the file \3dsmax6_CD\Carlo\Car_Head\ Carlo_Head_02.max contains the completed tutorial to this point.**

Modeling Around the Eye

To create the character's eyelids, we'll use another nuts-and-bolts modeling procedure. First, we'll create new edges to form contours that loop around the eye. Then we'll move the resulting vertices to sculpt the eye socket around a sphere that will become the eye itself. Here are the steps to follow:

1 Select the four edges under the brow (see Figure 7-25a) and connect them with the Edge Connect tool, this time with the setting of 1. The result is shown in Figure 7-25b. Then connect the two vertices on the right to create an unbroken loop of edges (see Figure 7-25c).

2 Select six edges, as shown in Figure 7-26a, and use the Edge Connect tool with a setting of 2 to create two loops around the eye (see Figure 7-26b).

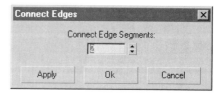

FIGURE 7-25 Here, edges have been selected (a) and then connected (b). The vertices at the end of this row of edges have been connected (c).

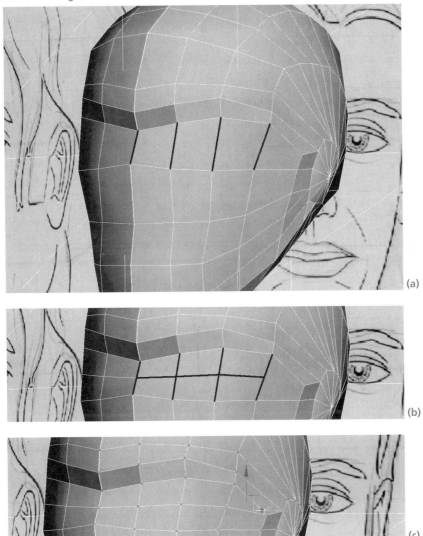

(a)

(b)

(c)

3 Select the edges inside the innermost loop (see Figure 7-27a) and use the Edge Remove button and to erase them. This will create a solid polygon that will become the back of the eye socket. Then, in the front view, arrange the vertices of the outer ring around the eye in the construction drawing (see Figure 7-27b).

FIGURE 7-26   Here, edges have been selected (a) and connected with a setting of 2 (b).

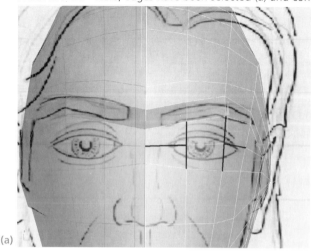
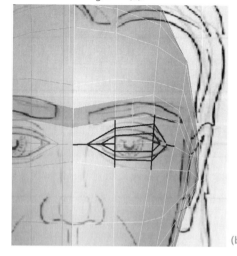

(a)   (b)

4   Select a single edge on the loop of edges closest to the centerline of the mesh. Then click the Loop button in the Selection rollout of the Modify panel. Use the ALT key to deselect the four edges on the eye (see Figure 7-28a) and then move the selection to the left in the Y-axis (see Figure 7-28b).

5   Now select one of the newly widened horizontal edges and select the Ring button in the Selection rollout of the Modify panel. This selects the ring of edges all the way around the head. Arc-rotate the head to the side and deselect the edges on the back half of the head (see Figure 7-29).

FIGURE 7-27   The edges at the center (a) of the eye have been removed and then vertices have been positioned according to the construction drawing (b).

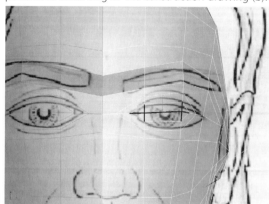
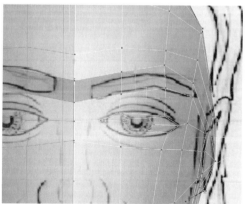

(a)   (b)

FIGURE 7-28   The selection set (a) is moved to the left in the Y-axis (b).

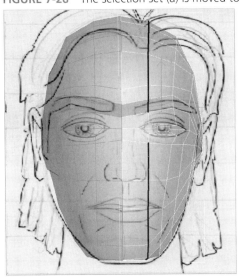
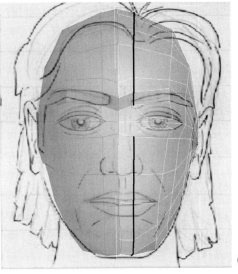

(a)

(b)

6   Use the Edge Connect tool with a setting of 2 to create two new loops of edges
    (see Figure 7-30). This will create messy topology at the top and bottom of the head.
    However, these are not critical areas because they will be covered by hair and the
    neck. To be thorough, you should clean up these areas later by collapsing vertices.

FIGURE 7-29   This selection of edges consists of about half of an edge ring that goes all the
way around the head.

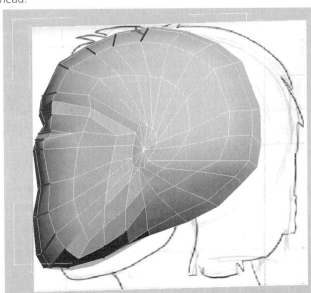

FIGURE 7-30   Connecting these edges gives you more detail to work with around the eye.

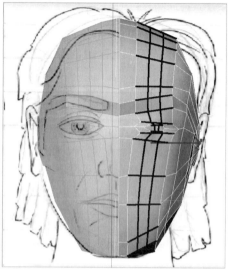

7 Once again, remove the innermost edges to preserve the single polygon in the center of the eye and arrange the new vertices in the front view (see Figure 7-31a) and then in the right view (see Figure 7-31b) according to the construction drawings.

8 In Edge Sub Object mode, click the Insert Vertex button and then click the midpoint of the edge that connects the bridge of the nose to the corner of the eye. Then in Vertices mode, connect this new vertex with the vertices above and below it (see Figure 7-32).

9 In Polygon Sub Object mode, select the polygon center of the eye that you removed the edges from. Move this polygon back into the head along the Y-axis, scale it up uniformly about 400 to 500 percent, and then nonuniformly scale it down along the X-axis about 50 percent so that it doesn't poke out of the side of the head (see Figure 7-33).

10 For a stand-in eye, exit Sub Object mode by clicking the button for Polygon Sub Object mode (or whatever Sub Object mode you are in). In the front view, create a sphere of 20 segments (see Figure 7-34a). My sphere has a radius of about 3.7 cm and is somewhat larger than is anatomically correct. However, you can size and position yours according to your construction drawings (consult an anatomy reference to see the size of a typical eyeball). Then, on the head, arrange the vertices of the eyelid around the sphere so that they do not intersect (see Figure 7-34b).

FIGURE 7-31   This shows the vertices of the eye arranged in the front view (a) and the right view (b) according to the construction drawings.

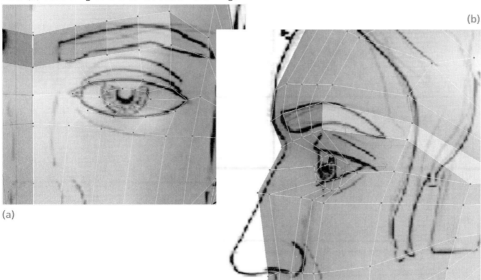

(b)

(a)

FIGURE 7-32   This shows the inserted vertex after it has been connected to the vertices above and below it.

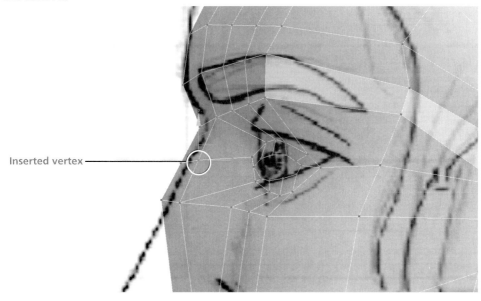

Inserted vertex

FIGURE 7-33   The selected polygon shown here was the center of the eye. It has been moved back and scaled.

FIGURE 7-34   Here, a sphere has been created and placed (a). Then the vertices have been positioned around a sphere (b).

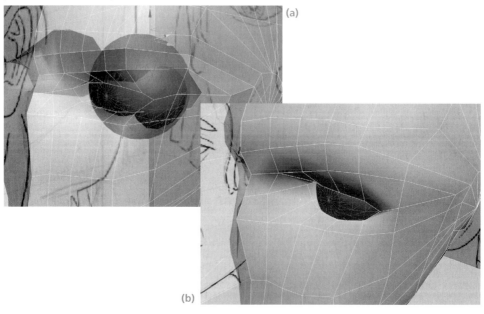

(a)

(b)

11 Select the ring of edges radiating out from the eye (see Figure 7-35a) and connect them to form a new loop. Move this new loop back toward the eye and arrange the vertices (see Figure 7-35b).

12 Reselect this new loop of edges and use the Edge Chamfer tool to duplicate the loop. Make sure that when you do this, the newly created loops do not overlap any of the surrounding vertices. Then select what is now the outermost loop around the eyes and chamfer it once more.

13 Now you can arrange the vertices to sculpt them into the form of the eyelid (see Figure 7-36). The vertices closest to the eye are close together because they will be stretching apart when the eyelid is animated closing.

At this point, there is still a long way to go on the head (see Figure 7-37). However, you have been introduced to and have used most of the tools and techniques needed to finish it.

NOTE   *On the CD-ROM, the file \3dsmax6_CD\Carlo\Car_Head \ Carlo_Head_03.max contains the completed tutorial to this point.*

FIGURE 7-35   The rings of edges around the eye (a) are connected, and the resulting vertices are moved to begin to form the eyelid (b).

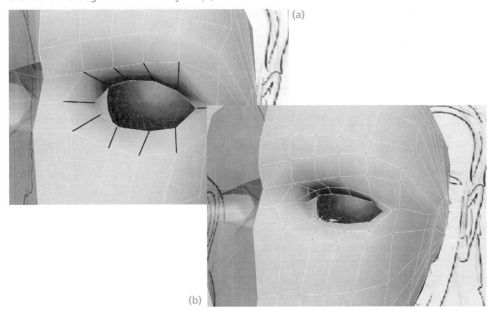

(a)

(b)

FIGURE 7-36 Chamfering the loops of edges around the eye gives you enough detail so that the new vertices created can be sculpted to form the finished eyelid.

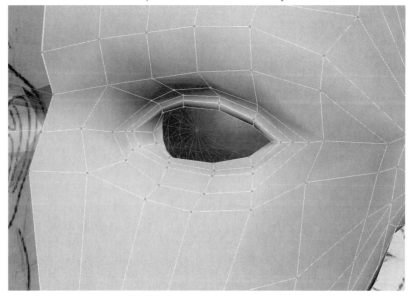

FIGURE 7-37 The head is now a solid framework on which to build the rest of the features.

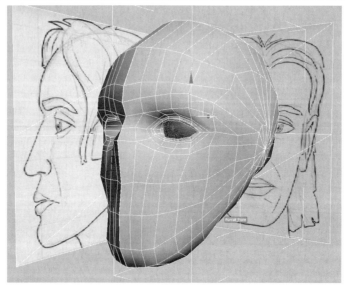

Modeling the Nose

Now we'll move on to building the rest of the features of the face using the same tools and techniques. In the following sections, I'll only be outlining the major steps. After each major operation that adds or changes topology, observe those areas around the operation and then clean up any messy topology as necessary. If you need to, you can see the process in great detail through the screen shots and the sequential models on the CD-ROM. Here are the broad steps to follow to model the nose:

1 Extrude the polygon in the nose area two times and collapse the vertices at the top (see Figure 7-38). Make sure you delete the polygons that face inside the head. Then move the new edges at the bottom front of the nose toward the center of the head to close the gap.

2 Using the Edge Connect tool, create edge loops that run horizontally across the nose (see Figure 7-39a) and vertically next to the nose (see Figure 7-39b). The horizontal line can continue all the way back to the ear, whereas the vertical line only needs to go to the top and bottom of the head.

3 You can bevel the polygon on the side of the nose twice to create the nostril (see Figure 7-40).

FIGURE 7-38   The nose polygon has been extruded twice, and the vertices at the top have been collapsed.

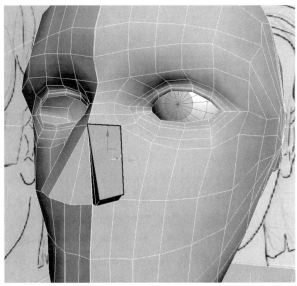

FIGURE 7-39 By connecting the edges to form horizontal (a) and vertical (b) edge loops, you begin to provide detail from which to sculpt the nose. The loops continue around the head to keep the topology organized.

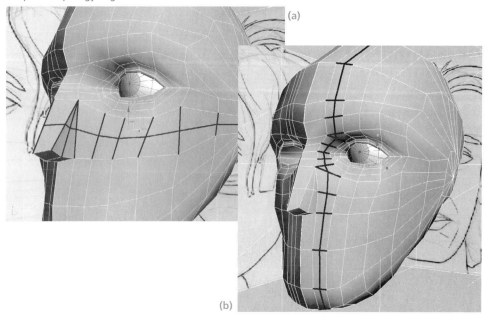

(a)

(b)

FIGURE 7-40 The polygon on the side of the nose has been beveled twice to form the nostril.

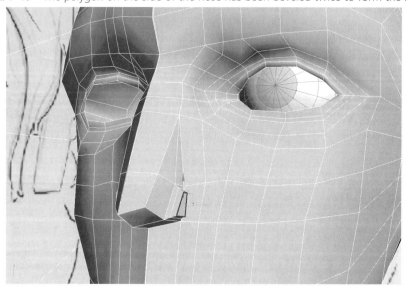

4 Repeat step 2 to add a vertical line along the nose, close to the center of the head, and a horizontal line across the nostril. Then, with the model's property set to See Through, you can switch to front and right views to sculpt the new vertices into place. Continue adding loops for detail and sculpting until you have enough curvature to form the nose.

5 On the underside of the nose, you can use the Inset Polygon tool to create a nostril outline, as shown in Figure 7-41a and Figure 7-41b. Then you can extrude these new polygons up into the nose.

6 Finally, you'll want to add finishing details by connecting some edges and vertices to round out the nose, as shown in Figure 7-42.

Correcting Rendering Artifacts

Some areas of the mesh may exhibit splintery rendering artifacts, which can occur when the angles between polygons become too great. You can correct these artifacts by controlling the smoothing groups and by editing the triangulation of polygons.

FIGURE 7-41 Here, polygons have been selected and inset (a). The new polygons at the center of the inset can now be extruded or beveled up into the nose to form the nostril opening (b).

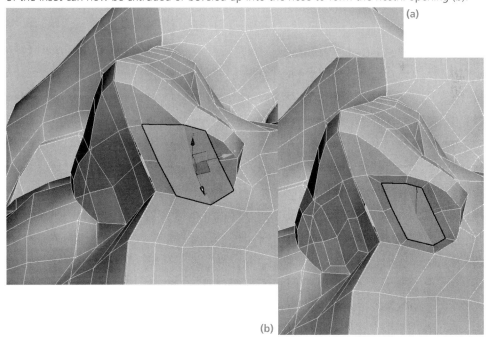

(a)

(b)

FIGURE 7-42   The finished nose has just enough detail to define the sharp contours of
the nostrils.

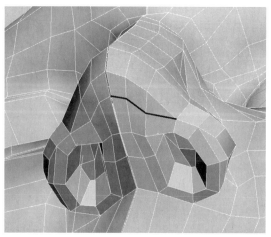

For multiple polygons to be rendered as one continuous surface, they
need to be in the same smoothing group. Smoothing groups are
controlled in the Polygon Properties rollout, shown here in the
Modify panel in Polygon Sub Object mode. Many times, as polygons
are created, they are not assigned to the same smoothing group as
the surrounding area. For example, to correct this in the nose area
(see Figure 7-43a), select the polygons of the nose (see Figure 7-43b)
and click the button for the first smoothing group twice. When the
button is depressed, all the selected polygons share that smoothing
group, and the mesh will appear smooth (see Figure 7-43c).

No matter how many sides a polygon has, it will be composed of
hidden triangles. When these triangles run perpendicular to the
way a surface is curving, or if they become too long and splintery,
rendering artifacts can occur (see Figure 7-44a). These artifacts can be corrected, as shown in
Figure 7-44b, using the Edit Triangulation tool in the Edit Polygons rollout of the Modify cap
panel in Polygon Sub Object mode. When this tool is turned on, dotted lines will show all
hidden triangles (see Figure 7-44c and Figure 7-44d). In this mode, you can simply click and
drag from one vertex to another to change the triangulation.

~~NOTE~~   *On the CD-ROM, the file \3dsmax6_CD\Carlo\Car_Head*
Carlo_Head_04.max contains the completed tutorial to this point.

FIGURE 7-43   Polygons that do not share the same smoothing group will not render smoothly (a). Selecting them (b) and placing them in the same smoothing group as the surrounding area can fix the problem (c).

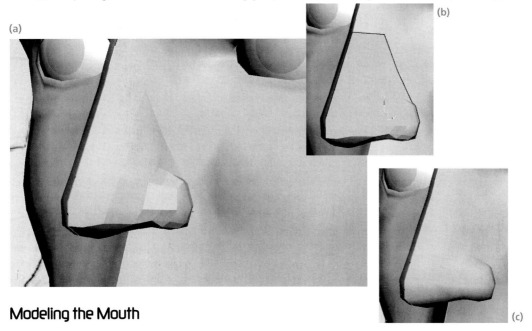

(a)

(b)

(c)

Modeling the Mouth

For the character to be able to open its mouth and speak, the interior of the mouth needs to be modeled. The polygons between the lips are extruded backwards into the head and expanded to form a cavity so that objects for the teeth and tongue can be added later. Here are the general steps to follow to build the mouth:

1 The process of creating the mouth starts with connecting edges to add loops of detail, like you did for the nose (see Figure 7-45a and Figure 7-45b).

2 Connect the edges to form concentric edge loops (see Figure 7-46a). Sculpt these new vertices into the shape of the lips (see Figure 7-46b) and then extrude the center inward like you did for the eyes (see Figure 7-46c).

3 More detail can be added by creating edge loops around the middle of the lips (see Figure 7-47a) and around the extruded inside of the mouth (see Figure 7-47b).

4 Sculpt the mouth vertices to fully form the lips (see Figure 7-48).

⤸ NOTE   *On the CD-ROM, the file \3dsmax6_CD\Carlo\Car_Head\ Carlo_Head_05.max contains the completed tutorial to this point.*

FIGURE 7-44 The top images show a rendering artifact before (a) and after (b) the triangulation is edit. The corresponding triangulation changes are illustrated in the bottom images (c and d).

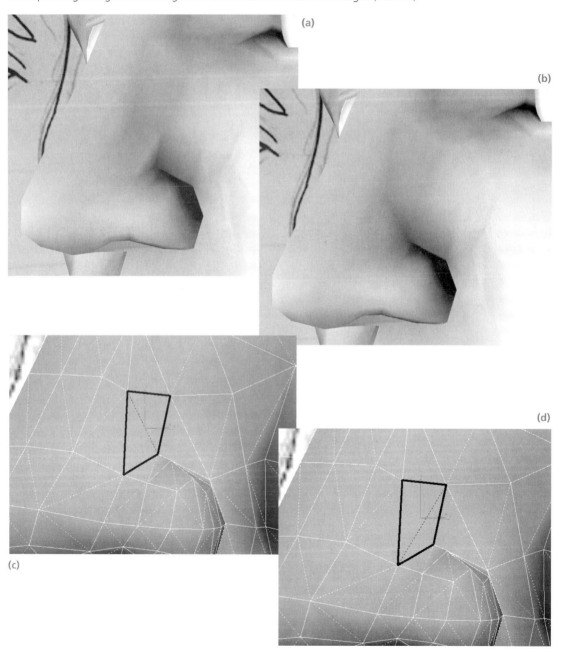

FIGURE 7-45   New edge loops are created by connecting edge rings that start under the nose (a) and continue back to the ear (b).

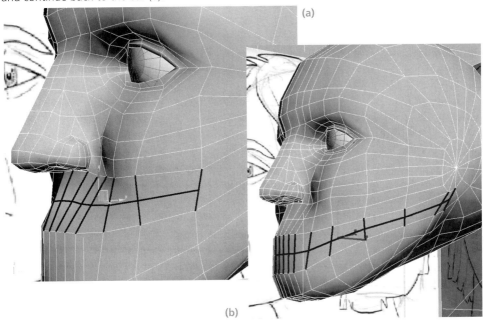

FIGURE 7-46   The process for creating the mouth is virtually the same as creating the eyes. Edges are selected and connected to form loops (a). The new vertices are sculpted and the process repeated (b). Then the center polygons are extruded back into the head and scaled.

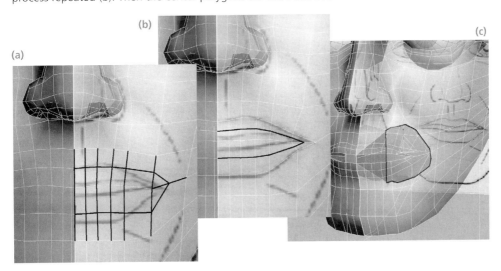

FIGURE 7-45   Here, the edges on the lips have been connected to create more detail (a). Then, the edges inside the mouth are connected so that the lips can form flaps that stretch over the teeth (b).

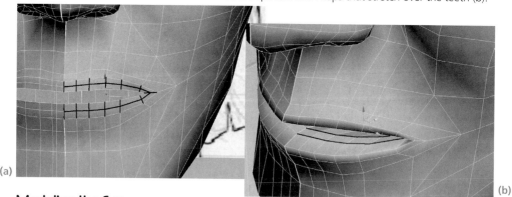

(a)

(b)

Modeling the Ear

The ear is undoubtedly the most difficult feature of the head to model. But with a simple, straightforward approach and some good anatomy reference, it becomes a manageable task. Here are the steps to follow:

1   The bulk of the ear is created with an uninterrupted series of bevels on the polygons at the base of the ear. First, bevel out the polygons, expanding them into a basic cone shape. Bevel them twice again to form a rounded edge, and then bevel them back in to form a funnel. Bevel them back out to form a new cone within the funnel. Finally, bevel the top of this new cone back inside the ear so that a ridge is formed inside the original outer funnel of the ear. This sequence is shown in Figure 7-49a through Figure 7-49i.

FIGURE 7-46   Here is the finished mouth. Note that vertices have been connected to create a loop of edges that forms the nasolabial fold.

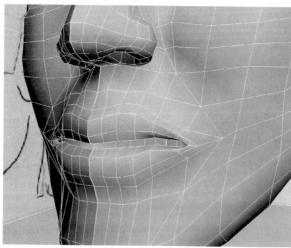

FIGURE 7-47 This sequence shows the operation of beveling the polygons at the base of the ear (a). This uninterrupted beveling starts by going outward, with the outline getting larger (b and c). The next steps go out a tiny bit with a smaller outline (d), then inward with smaller outlines (e and f), then outward with smaller outlines (g and h), and finally inward one last time with a smaller outline (i).

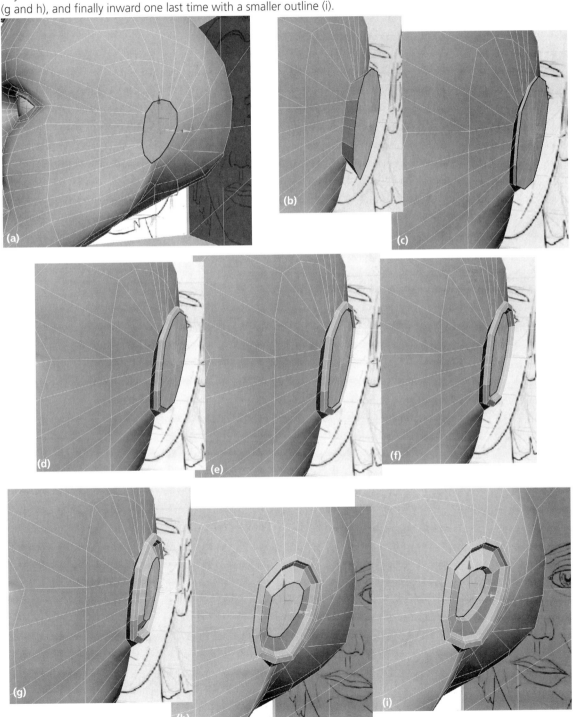

2 Extrude the bottom four polygons (see Figure 7-50a) downward two times, and then sculpt the new vertices to form the earlobe (see Figure 7-50b).

3 Collapse the edges at the front of the ear so that it becomes flush with the cheek (see Figure 7-51).

4 Now you can bevel out the polygons shown in Figure 7-52a to form the inner part of the spiral shaped helix (see Figure 7-52b).

5 The ear topology is basically complete and can now be sculpted further. The entire ear can then be selected and rotated in the view Z-axis so that it faces somewhat forward (see Figure 7-53).

♥NOTE *On the CD-ROM, the file \3dsmax6_CD\Carlo\Car_Head\ Carlo_Head_06.max contains the completed tutorial to this point.*

Finishing the Head Mesh

To complete the head mesh, we need to add some minor detail, clean up the topology, and finally weld the two halves together.

First, we'll add detail with extra edge loops.

1 The eyebrow ridge, the chin, and the area in front of the ears all need more detail to give a more rounded curvature to the surface. To add the detail while maintaining a clean,

FIGURE 7-48 The polygons at the bottom of the ear (a) are extruded down and sculpted to form the earlobe (b).

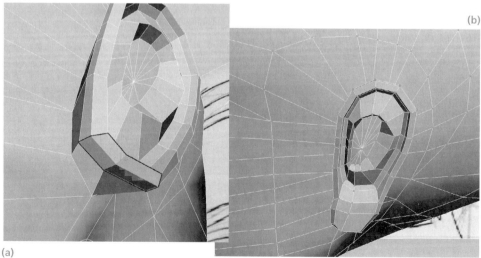

(b)

(a)

FIGURE 7-49   Several edges at the front of the ear have been collapsed.

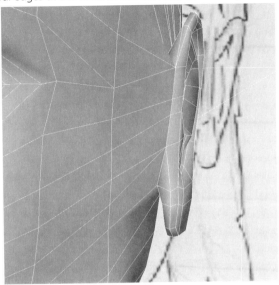

quad-strip topology, strategically select the edges in the edge rings throughout these areas (see Figure 7-54a) and connect them into one continuous loop (see Figure 7-54b).

FIGURE 7-50   Here, polygons have been selected (a) and beveled (b) to form the inner helical shape of the ear.

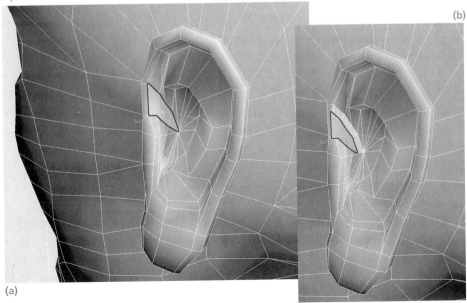

(b)

(a)

FIGURE 7-51 The finished ear. Note that the edges in the deepest center of the ear have been removed for simplicity. Because this multisided polygon will be inside the ear, rendering artifacts will not be apparent.

FIGURE 7-52 By selecting edges strategically (a), a continuous edge loop can be created to add more curvature to the chin, brow, and cheekbone areas simultaneously (b).

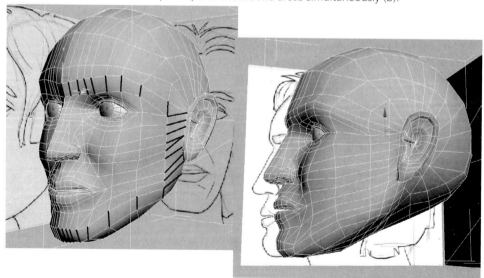

(a)

(b)

2 Several places on the mesh will need some cleanup of the topology. Problems such as polygons with five or more sides as well as areas where several three-sided polygons can be combined into cleaner four-sided polygons are created by various additions of detail.

For example, two instances of five-sided polygons appear above and below the outside corner of the eye (see Figure 7-55a). You can make these into quads simply by collapsing the edge that they both share (see Figure 7-55b). Then, by removing edges and reconnecting vertices, you can optimize the topology so that the quad strips continue back from the eye to the ear.

Now the two halves can be welded together.

3 Now select the other half of the head, right-click the Editable Poly entry in the Modifier Stack, and choose Make Unique from the pop-up menu (Figure 7-56). This breaks the instance connection between the two halves. Now select the original half of the head again, click the Attach button in the Edit Geometry rollout of the Modify Panel, and in the viewport click the other half of the head.

4 Now in the front, orthographic view, select the double row of vertices down the center of the head. In the Selection rollout of the Modify panel is a counter that tells you how many vertices you have selected. Click the button with the rectangular icon next to the Weld button in the Edit Vertices rollout of the Modify panel and then adjust the spinner until you see the vertices join. After clicking OK, you can look again at the vertex counter to confirm that you have exactly half as many vertices.

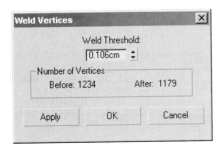

FIGURE 7-53　This is an example of cleaning up the topology. Collapsing the selected edge (a) turns two unwanted five-sided polygons into two four-sided polygons (b).

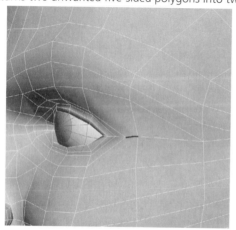
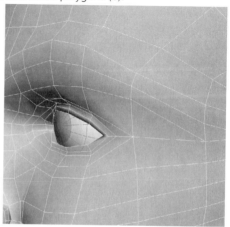

(a)

(b)

FIGURE 7-54　The mirrored and instanced right half of the head can be attached to the original left side of the head after you right-click on the Modifier Stack and choose Make Unique from the pop-up menu.

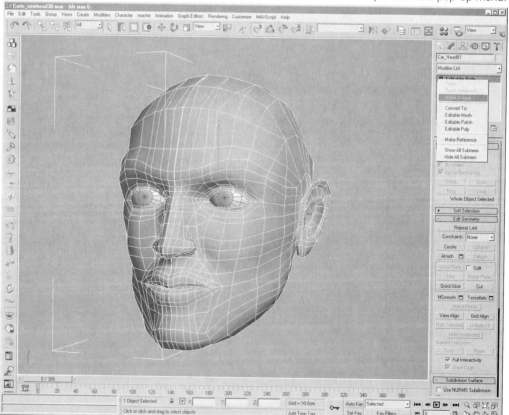

 **On the CD-ROM, the file \3dsmax6_CD\Carlo\Car_Head\ Carlo_Head_07.max contains the completed tutorial to this point.**

Subdivision Surfaces

Finally, our Editable Poly object has built-in subdivision surface properties located in the Subdivision Surface rollout of the Modify panel in any mode. This means that our relatively low polygon model (Car_Head is around 2,400 actual polygons) can now be automatically subdivided. This can create a smooth model for rendering close-ups, or the polygons of this higher-resolution version of the model can then be sculpted further for more detail. Creating the model with an even, organized topology means that the higher-resolution, subdivided model maintains an organized, animatable distribution of detail (see Figure 7-57a and 7-57b).

FIGURE 7-55   This is the finished Car_Head subdivided.

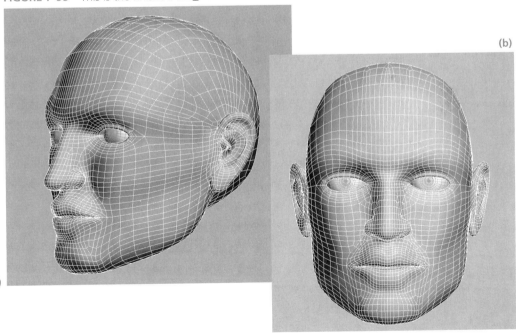

⌣ NOTE
3ds max 6 has a new feature that helps make Editable Poly objects easier to visualize. The new Isoline Display check box in the Subdivision Surface rollout allows you to show only the edges that are part of the base mesh. This enables you to see a smoothed, high-polygon model while still being able to see the underlying simpler topology.

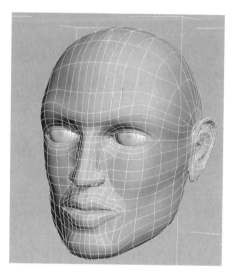
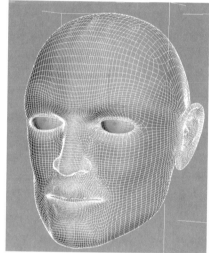

Artistically, modeling is much like drawing and takes practice and repetition for one to master the creative expression. Technically, there are many correct ways to solve the puzzle of a head's topology, and you might find a new solution each time you model. Becoming thoroughly familiar with the tools and techniques shown in this chapter will go long way toward making you a capable digital sculptor.

Chapter 8

Modeling Character Bodies: The Digital Sculptor II

The tools and process used for creating character bodies are very similar to those for creating character heads. Character bodies are typically simpler to model and therefore often take a shorter time to create. For this chapter, we'll use 3ds max's Editable Poly tools again—this time to create a body for Carlo (see Figure 8-1).

FIGURE 8-1   The body model of Carlo with the head model

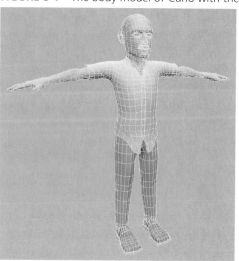 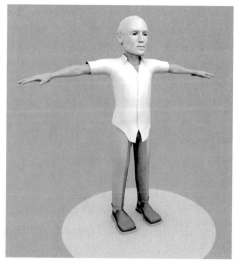

The keys to creating a good character body model are the same as creating the head: topology, animatability, and artistry. For the artistry aspect, surface anatomy knowledge (or ample reference) will again be important, maybe even more so for the body than for the head. Even if you're not modeling a human character, having an understanding of the body's underlying structure will provide added visual clarity as well as help the character *move* convincingly when you animate it.

Sculpting the Body

To create the body for this exercise, we'll sculpt a nude male body and then build clothes around it. To save time, we'll actually create the body of the character Felix because his tighter-fitting T-shirt will demand more definition in the torso. Once we create Carlo's looser fitting shirt and pants around this model, scale it to Carlo's height, and texture-map the hands, arms, and neck with different skin textures (see Chapter 9), the similarities will be less apparent.

The body is created by converting a geometry primitive to an Editable Poly object, just as it was done for Carlo's head. The body is created using the same sub object tools and methodologies as for the head. Because these techniques were covered in detail in the previous chapter, the steps in this chapter's tutorial will be broader. It's not important that you duplicate this model, vertex by vertex, but that you practice these nuts and bolts modeling techniques as you build and sculpt the body.

Setting Up a New Workspace and Starting with a Cylinder

We'll start modeling the body in the same manner that we started modeling the head in the last chapter. The construction drawings for Felix are placed on reference planes to set up the workspace. Here are the steps to follow:

1   Create two construction planes as before, and texture-map them with the body construction drawings (...\3dsmax6_CD\Carlo\Car_Body\felcar_body_cnst.jpg).

2   Make sure the drawings are proportionate to a 165 cm man. Also, remember to account for the head. (I size my drawings by creating a box that is 165 cm tall next to the construction planes and then scaling the UVW gizmos to match.)

3   Instead of using a sphere, start modeling the body with a 24-sided, five-segment-high cylinder roughly the size of the chest (see Figure 8-2) with 2-cap segments.

4   Name the cylinder Car_body.

⌣NOTE   *On the CD-ROM, the file ...\3dsmax6_CD\Carlo\Car_Body\ Carlo_body_00.max contains the completed tutorial to this point.*

Sculpting the Torso

The cylinder primitive is cut in half and mirrored as an instance so that only one half of the body needs to be modeled. The first part of the process is sculpting the vertices that are already there in the original cylinder to begin to form the shape of the torso. Again, I'm using the term "sculpt" to refer to pushing and pulling vertices as opposed to creating new topology

FIGURE 8-2   The workspace for the body is set up in the same way as the workspace for the head. This time, modeling starts from a cylinder.

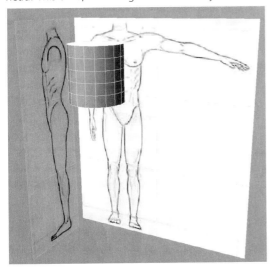
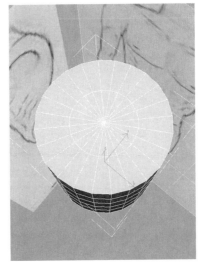

by adding any vertices, edges, or polygons. The vertices can be moved, rotated, and scaled individually or in groups with or without soft selection.

1 Convert the cylinder to an Editable Poly object and cut it in half. Do this by selecting half the polygons of the cylinder in a front view and deleting them. Then use the Mirror Selected Objects tool (icon) to mirror the half cylinder object as a new instance object.

2 You can begin sculpting the vertices of the original cylinder half to form the chest using the construction drawings as reference (see Figure 8-3a). First, scale the cylinder in Sub Object mode in a top viewport to narrow the torso. Angle the vertices on the top of the mesh to form a line that will become the clavicle, and angle the bottom to form the hip (see Figure 8-3b). This can be done in a front view using Soft Selection.

3 Extrude the bottom polygons to form the pelvic area, and sculpt the new polygons to form the buttocks and groin. By moving vertices (see Figure 8-4a and Figure 8-4b) and creating edges where needed with the Edge or Vertex Connect tool, you can create contour lines to define the bottom of the pectoral muscles, the bottom of the rib cage, and the hips (see Figure 8-4c and Figure 8-4d).

4 Create concentric edge loops at the top of the mesh to start sculpting a ridge for the clavicle and the start of the neck.

5 On the side of the shoulder, you can use the Edge Connect tool to create the outline for the base of the arm. When the faces within this outline are extruded, the number of the edges making up the outline determines the number of sides the cross-section of the arm will have. Of course, you can change the number of polygons at any stage along the arm, but making this beginning outline as close as possible to the rest of the arm's

FIGURE 8-3   Once the cylinder has been cut in half and mirrored, sculpting the torso is started by scaling all the polygons inward in a top viewport (a). Then you move the vertices of the cylinder, often with Soft Selection, to match the construction drawings (b).

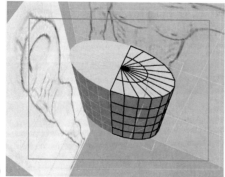
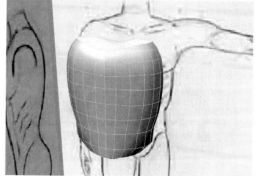

(a)

(b)

FIGURE 8-4   Contour lines under the pectoral muscles (a and b) and other areas (c and d) are created by moving vertices and creating new edges, where needed, to create continuous loops.

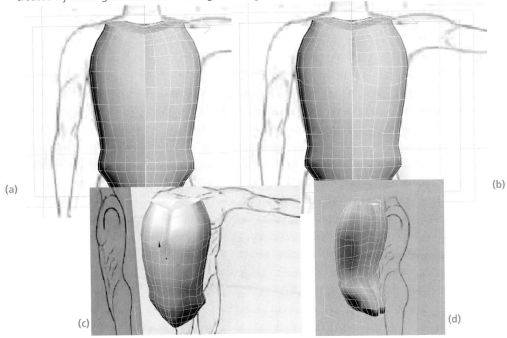

(a)

(b)

(c)

(d)

cross-section will give you the cleanest topology when the arm is extruded. Figure 8-5a through Figure 8-5c show this outline at the base of the arm for this model.

NOTE   *On the CD-ROM, the file ...\3dsmax6_CD\Carlo\ Car_Body\Carlo_body_01.max contains the completed tutorial to this point.*

FIGURE 8-5   Here, four edges on the top and bottom and six edges along the side have been selected to form the outline of the arm cross-section (a). The polygons within this outline (b) are extruded to form the beginning of the arm (c).

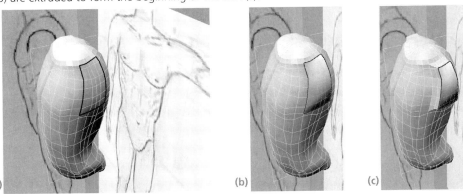

(a)

(b)

(c)

Creating the Shoulder and Arm

Unlike an elbow or knee, the shoulder rotates on several axes, making it one of the more difficult joints of the body to animate. This makes it important to have an adequate number of subdivisions so that the shoulder joint can deform smoothly during animation. However, it's also important to balance the amount of detail, because having too many vertices in that area can make the shoulder joint overly complex and therefore difficult to rig properly.

The shoulder and then the arm are created by arranging a base outline by moving vertices and connecting vertices to form new edges. Then, the polygons within that outline are extruded or beveled. As you begin to extrude the shoulder and base of the arm, you can then sculpt the new geometry as you go. Add contour lines where needed. To create a shoulder and arm:

1 Extrude the polygons within the outline that was created and then move the vertices into the shape of your cross-section. (I recommend extruding one ring of polygons at a time, sculpting at each step.) You can, of course, continue to sculpt the arm after it is completely created, but I find that part of the process moves faster if the arm is given at least a general form as I go. Following the surface of the shoulder as it flows out of the chest, the armpit curves up into the arm while the top of the deltoid muscle bulges out. Then as you continue extruding down the length of the arm, the concave armpit gives way to the triceps muscle to the rear and the bicep bulging forward (see Figure 8-6).

FIGURE 8-6 Sculpting the shoulder as you extrude each new section can be less confusing than having to move all the vertices once the arm has been created. The only operations that have been done to this newly extruded geometry are to move the vertices and to sculpt them. All the topology is a direct result of the outline used for the base of the arm. This figure shows the shoulder from the top (a), bottom (b), and back (c) at the same stage in the modeling process.

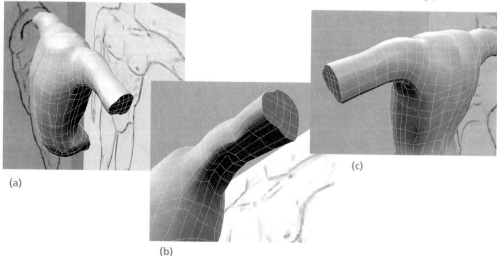

FIGURE 8-7   The arm is a simple extrusion of the original base outline. Contour lines can be created to better define the deltoids, biceps, and other muscles (a and b). The extrusion then continues down to the wrist. Note that more edge loops are created around the elbow because it will be bending when animated (c).

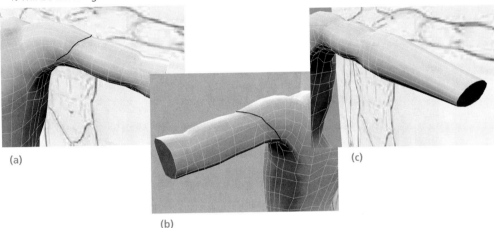

(a)

(c)

(b)

2   Cut contour lines to help define the deltoid and bicep muscles further (see Figure 8-7a and Figure 8-7b).

3   You can continue all the way down the arm in this manner, allowing the shape of each cross-section to change by following the bulges of the various muscles (see Figure 8-7c).

4   Scale the vertices at the end of the arm smaller in the local X-axis to form the start of the wrist.

Building the Hand

The wrist and palm of the hand are modeled in a similar way, by extruding and sculpting. Once the palm of the hand has been created, outlines of edges are cut into the end of the palm to form the base of the fingers. Each finger and the thumb is then extruded and sculpted individually.

1   Create the wrist and home by extruding the polygons above the arm. Then extrude to create enough edge loops in the wrist (two or three) so that it can bend without collapsing when animated (see Figure 8-8a).

2   To create the fingers, cut outlines for their bases in the end of the palm. For this model, cut eight-sided outlines for each finger (see Figure 8-8b) and extrude each one separately in the same manner as the arm (see Figure 8-8c).

FIGURE 8-8   A palm is extruded similarly to the arm, and new edges are cut in the end to form the base of the fingers (a). Each finger is extruded, once for the base knuckle, twice for the second knuckle, twice for the third, and two more times for the tip (b). Then the vertices of the fingers are sculpted and the edges between the fingers are chamfered to the create gaps between the fingers (c). The thumb is extruded from the polygons on the side of the hand (d and e).

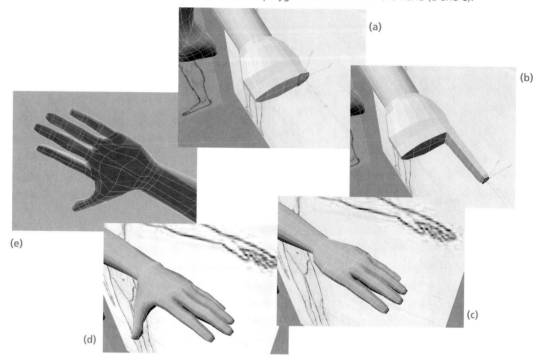

(a)

(b)

(e)

(d)

(c)

3 Create the thumb by extruding polygons out the side of the hand. Make sure all joints that need to bend have at least two or three edge loop subdivisions (see Chapter 10 for the reasons behind this). The edges between each finger can be chamfered to create polygons, allowing the base of the fingers to move more independently (see Figure 8-8d and Figure 8-8e).

⤳NOTE   *On the CD-ROM, the file ...\3dsmax6_CD\Carlo\Car_Body* *Carlo_body_02.max contains the completed tutorial to this point.*

Building the Leg

Again, you build the legs by extruding similarly to the arms. Polygons at the hips become the base of the leg. From the front, the edge loops of the hips should fan out, gradually rotating downward until the base of the thigh is horizontal to the ground plane. The vertices of the knee edge loops can be sculpted to form contour lines. The knee joint should have several edge loops to accommodate bending in the knee and providing sufficient geometry to sculpt the contours of the patella and the beginning of the calf muscles.

1 Extrude down and to the right for a few cross-sections. More detail is required around the hips since these joints rotate in multiple directions.

2 Rotate each of these cross-sections slightly more than the previous one until the last of them is horizontal to the ground.

3 Extrude and sculpt the leg (see Figure 8-9a and Figure 8-9b). Fewer edge loops are needed in the thighs while several loops are needed at the knee.

FIGURE 8-9   The legs are extruded and sculpted in the same manner as the arms. There are more polygons grouped around the pelvis and knees to accommodate for the bending during animation. Notice the contour lines at the top of the hips and the bottom of the calf muscles in both the back (a) and front (b) views.

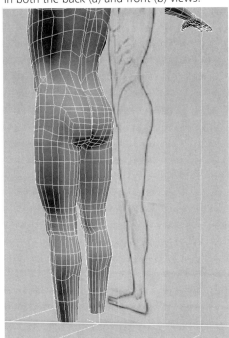
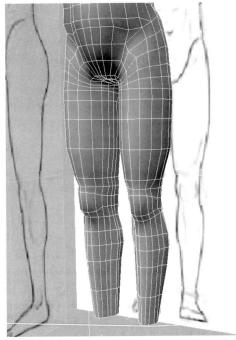

(a)

(b)

Building the Foot

Here are the steps to follow to create the feet:

1   Bevel the base of the leg and straight down about five times to create the ankle and heel (see Figure 8-10a and Figure 8-10b). Using the Bevel tool instead of the Extrude tool simply allows you to get a rough head start on sculpting as you go.

2   Extrude the front polygons outward to form the arch and toes (see Figure 8-10c and Figure 8-10d).

3   Sculpt vertices to form the protrusions of the ankle bones on either side.

4   Because the foot gets shorter and flatter as it moves forward, you'll want to collapse the edge rings along the sides. Also, because the feet will be inside shoes, it is not necessary to model the toes (see Figure 8-10e).

FIGURE 8-10   The feet are created by extruding polygons down several times to create the ankles and heels (a and b). Then the front polygons are selected, extruded forward, and finally sculpted to create the rest of the feet (c, d, and e).

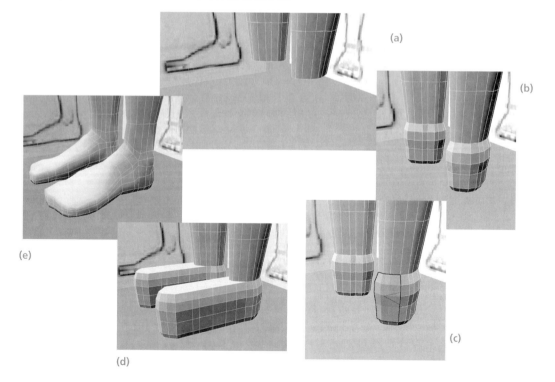

Building the Neck

Building the neck is slightly different from building the limbs in that the neck is divided in half by the mirrored centerline. If the polygons of the base of the neck were extruded, then the polygons would be created on the inside of the mesh at the centerline. Instead, the half loop of edges forming the base of the neck can be extruded. Follow these steps to create the neck:

1 Delete the polygons in the top center of the torso. This can be done easily by deleting the vertices that were originally the center of the top circle and the cylinder.

2 Select the resulting edge loop and move it up while holding down the SHIFT key. This, in effect, performs an extrusion, creating new polygons (see Figure 8-11a and Figure 8-11b). Give the neck two or three edge loops of detail so that it can bend during animation.

3 Sculpt the new geometry to form the larynx and the sternocleidomastoid muscle that curves from the base of the ear to the base of the clavicle in the front bottom of the neck (see Figure 8-11c).

The Finished Nude Body

You can finish the body by sculpting further (see Figure 8-12). If you wish to create a more detailed character, you can continue to add more subdivisions and more contour lines to define other muscles and anatomical features. For the purposes of our largely clothed, low-polygon character, this amount of detail is sufficient.

NOTE *On the CD-ROM, the file ...\3dsmax6_CD\Carlo\Car_Body\ Carlo_body_03.max contains the completed tutorial to this point.*

FIGURE 8-11   The neck is created by selecting the outline at the base of the neck (a) and moving it up while holding down the SHIFT key (b). Then the vertices can be sculpted to form the trachea and sternocleidomastoid muscle (c).

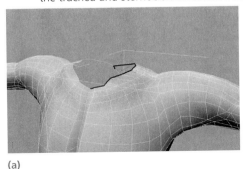

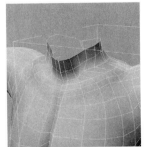

(a)   (b)   (c)

FIGURE 8-12   The finished nude body can be used as a starting point for other male characters around which to build clothing.

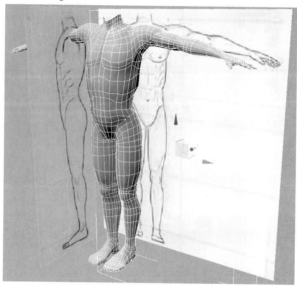

Creating Clothes

So far, we have essentially created the upper body of our other character, Felix. Although it may seem like redundant work to model polygons that will be hidden by clothing and removed anyway, as we continue, you'll see that the model we have created acts as an excellent template for making sure clothes are built as though there is a convincing body inside them. Also, you can quickly create clothes from the polygons of the body itself, making this an efficient modeling process. In creating the clothes we will make the character model specific to the Carlo character.

Tailoring a Shirt

A shirt for Carlo can be created relatively quickly and easily by using the existing polygons of the torso as a starting point. The polygons are first cloned, keeping the original torso intact for reference. These new polygons are expanded, smoothed, and simplified to become a shirt. The topology of the shirt model basically follows the seams in the fabric of the real shirt. The steps are as follows:

1   Select the polygons of the torso, upper arm (down to where the sleeve would extend to), and hips (to form the tail of the untucked shirt).

2   Detach these polygons as a clone to create a new object. Give this object a temporary name of Shirt.

FIGURE 8-13   The shirt is created by cloning the faces to create a new object, applying the Push modifier (a), applying the Relax modifier (b), and then sculpting vertices.

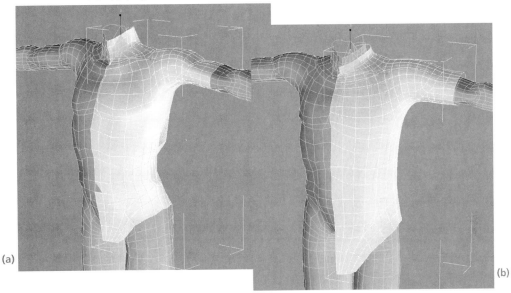

(a)

(b)

3 Add a Push modifier to the Shirt object to move the polygons of the shirt out off the surface of the skin (see Figure 8-13a).

4 Add a Relax modifier to smooth out the shirt and slightly redistribute its topology (see Figure 8-13b).

🔽 NOTE   *On the CD-ROM, the file ...\3dsmax6_CD\Carlo\Car_Body\ Carlo_body_04.max contains the completed tutorial to this point.*

5 From here, you can collapse the Shirt object back into an Editable Poly object.

6 Using the right-click menu, mirror this object.

7 Create a collar by selecting the top vertices of what was the neck, and then scale them out and move them down. The collar polygons will be invisible after that because they will be facing inward.

8 Each polygon faces one direction or the other based on what is called the *normal*. You can reverse the normals for these polygons by selecting them and clicking the Flip button in the Edit Polygons rollout (see Figure 8-14).

FIGURE 8-14 The shirt is created by scaling what was the neck outline out and moving it down, and then the normals of the collar polygons are flipped so that they face outward.

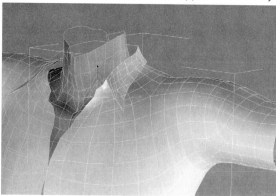

Stitching Some Pants

Carlo's straight-leg '60s style pants are simple to create: Essentially, a cylinder is tapered to the general shape of the leg. Most of their detail will come from the texture maps, so there needs to be just enough topology around the hips and knees to bend during animation.

1 Create a cylinder. The cylinder's pivot point is at its base. Move the cylinder so that its pivot point is at the base of the ankle of the character body. Then use the cylinder primitive's radius and height parameters to roughly size it around the leg.

2 To taper the pant leg quickly, temporarily add a Taper modifier to the pants model (see Figure 8-15a).

3 Mirror the cylinder as an instance and convert it into an Editable Poly object (see Figure 8-15b). Select and delete the polygons facing inwards toward the centerline, inside what would be the groin area.

4 Sculpt the vertices for the crotch of the pants by pulling the vertices in the middle top of the pant leg outward to form the front and back of the pants (see Figure 8-15c).

5 For Carlo, the long untucked shirttails will cover up the waist, so not much detail is needed for the top of the pants. Select the bottom ring of polygons and use the Detach button in the Edit Geometry rollout to detach it as an element and scale it out slightly from its center.

6 Scale this ring of polygons in the Z-axis to form the cuff of the pants (see Figure 8-15d).

FIGURE 8-15   The pants are created by starting with a cylinder and adding a Taper modifier (a). After the pant leg has been mirrored, the innermost polygons are removed (b), and the vertices in the middle of the body are pulled out toward the front and back to form the crotch of the pants (c). A cuff is formed by cloning polygons to create a new element and moving them into place (d).

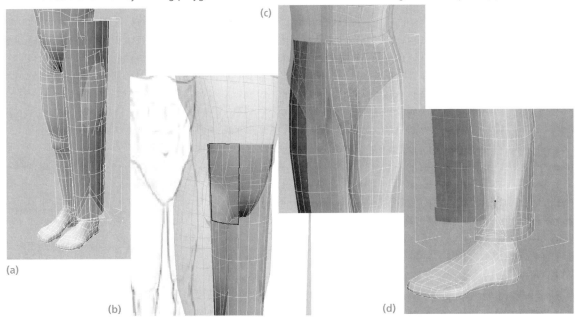

NOTE   *On the CD-ROM, the file …\3dsmax6_CD\Carlo\Car_Body\ Carlo_body_05.max contains the completed tutorial to this point.*

Polygonal Loafers

Shoes for Carlo can be created in the same way as the shirt. The polygons of the feet are cloned and expanded. These are then sculpted to follow the shoe designs in the concept art:

1 Clone the foot polygons as a new object and temporarily use the Push modifier to expand these new polygons outward so that they're just larger than the original foot polygons (see Figure 8-16a).

2 Create a sole for the shoes by beveling the bottom polygons (see Figure 8-16b).

FIGURE 8-16   Shoes are modeled using the same method as the shirt—by cloning the polygons of the foot to a new object and applying a Push modifier (a). The sole is formed by beveling the bottom polygons down and out (b).

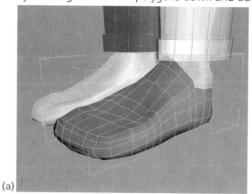

(a)

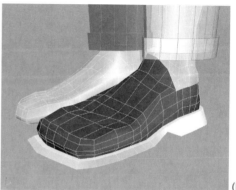

(b)

finishing the Body

Once the clothing is finished, you can delete all unnecessary polygons of the legs, torso, and feet from the Car_body object, leaving the ankles, neck, forearms, and hands. Also, mirror the shoe on the X-axis and move it into position on the right ankle.

So that they can be attached, make all the mirrored and instanced objects on the right side of the body unique. Do this by selecting each object, right-clicking its modifier stack, and choosing Make Unique from the pop-up menu. Then, with the Car_body object selected, click the Attach button and click all the right-side objects as well as both halves of the shirt and pants and both shoes. This creates a single object for the entire body, which will make the rigging process simpler.

Once all the objects are attached, weld all the vertices down the centerline of the body, except for those on the front of the shirt. Move the vertices of the right front of the shirt under those on the left. This way, the shirt will look as though it is buttoned together.

Carlo's body model comes in at about 6,000 polygons (when converted to the triangles of an Editable Mesh object), which makes the entire Carlo character come in around 10,000 polygons. This means the model is efficient enough for many real-time applications, such as videogames, and will render quickly. Furthermore, like the head, the body can be subdivided with the Editable Poly's built-in subdivision surface feature or with a Meshsmooth modifier.

 NOTE   *On the CD-ROM, the file …\3dsmax6_CD\Carlo\Car_Body\ Carlo_body_06.max contains the completed tutorial.*

The Specifics of Carlo and the Example Film

With Carlo's body, I made the creative decision to enlarge the character's hands, feet, and neck. I did this by selecting the polygons of each hand or foot individually, dialing Soft Selection to blend across the wrist or ankle, and scaling up those polygons.

For my film's pipeline, I left the heads of my characters as separate objects. Typically it is preferable, particularly for aesthetic reasons, to have the neck, head, and body a single contiguous mesh. However, because my characters' heads are oversized, I chose this path for the sake of a simpler rigging process.

Finally, the arms are angled downward to help the rigging process. It can be easier to model the arms by extruding straight outward along the X-axis. But when using the Skin modifier to attach the mesh to the character rig (see Chapter 10), it can be easier for the shoulder to deform properly if the arm is angled downward. The polygons in the arms and hands are selected with a Soft Selection radiating across the shoulder. Each arm is then rotated in the front view around a vertex in the center of the shoulder.

Modeling Other Characters

There are certainly many other valid approaches to modeling human characters, and I recommend experimenting with other variations of topology with the Editable Poly object. These modeling techniques are very similar to traditional drawing, and you will get better with practice. The general process of building topology, sculpting the form, and enhancing the topology with contour lines can be used to create virtually any character from the infinite variety of people, animals, and beyond.

Chapter 9

Texture Mapping and finishing Characters: Costumes and Makeup

Texture mapping a character can be a challenging and time-consuming endeavor. The technical aspects demand a methodical approach and good organization, whereas the artistic aspects require keen observation and illustration skills. We'll go through the entire process of texture mapping by finishing the Carlo model.

This chapter shows just one of an infinite variety of valid approaches to texturing. We'll cover creating textures and materials for the head and body as well as creating and texturing the eyeballs, teeth, and tongue for Carlo. For Carlo, shown in Figure 9-1a and Figure 9-1b, I've taken the approach of starting from photographs to create the textures. This is a good starting point for texturing, but it can be augmented or even replaced by painting textures by hand.

Texture Mapping the Head

Creating and applying a facial texture map is a process that involves many steps. The broad outline is to first apply UVW mapping coordinates that allow the facial texture map to be stretched and projected on the complex contours of the face. Then you create a facial texture map that corresponds with these UVW mapping coordinates.

Assigning Material IDs

Although the head is a single mesh object, it will need to have several materials assigned to it. This is accomplished by using 3ds max's Multi/Sub Object material. This way, a parent material can contain sub materials for the face and inside of the mouth, the eye sockets, and eventually the teeth and tongue. To accommodate this, we'll prepare the head mesh by assigning all

FIGURE 9-1   Here is the finished, textured model of Carlo. Many separate photographs were used as starting points for the various texture maps.

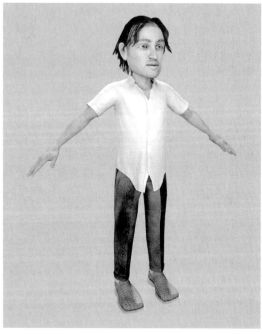

polygons material IDs that the Multi/Sub Object material can reference. This way, each object can have a single material for easier organization, but different parts of an object can have their own sub materials. Here are the steps for assigning material IDs to Carlo's head and creating a Multi/Sub Object material that references them.

1 Open the …\3dsmax6_CD\Carlo\Car_Texture_00.max.

2 With the Car_Head object selected, enter Polygon Sub Object mode and select all the polygons for the entire head. Assign these a material ID of 1 by entering **1** in the Set ID spinner box in the Polygon Properties rollout of the Modify panel.

3 Select the polygons for the inside of the eye sockets and the inside of the mouth. Although this may seem tricky, you can do it easily in a side viewport. Using the Select tool, window select around the flat polygons at the rear of the eye sockets and use the Grow button in the Selection rollout of the Modify panel. Assign these polygons a material ID of 2. Repeat this process for the mouth polygons, this time clicking the Grow button twice. Then assign those polygons a material ID of 2 as well.

4 In the Material Editor, click the button labeled Standard and choose Multi/Sub Object from the list. Click the Set Number button and set the number of materials to 2. In the field above the Multi/Sub Object Basic Parameters rollout, name this material car_head, and then click the first sub material entry to access it. Name this sub material car_face. Use the Go to Parent button to navigate back to the top level of the Multi/Sub Object material and then choose and name this second entry car_Mouth & eyes. Also, enter the shorter names, Face and Mouth Eyes in the Name column to the left of the Sub Material column. This leaves your Material Editor looking like Figure 9-2.

5 Click the Diffuse Color swatch to make the diffuse color of the car_Mouth and eyes sub material a dark red color.

6 With the head object selected, use the Assign Material to Selection button to give it this material. Because the second Sub Material slot has a dark red diffuse color, you should see the mouth and eye sockets of your mesh turn red because they have both been assigned material ID 2.

Unwrapping the Head

Applying a texture to a face without stretching is a difficult task thanks to the complex curvature of the facial features. UVW or mapping coordinates must be applied to the mesh in order to project a bitmap onto its surface. The standard cylindrical and spherical projection methods will

FIGURE 9-2 Here, the Material Editor shows the Multi/Sub Object for Carlo's head. The material sample sphere changes to a checkerboard, indicating that this sample represents multiple sub materials. Below is the sub material list. The ID number of each sub material shows that any polygons in the mesh having that material ID will be assigned that sub material. The names in the first name field are relevant only for organizing this Sub Object material, whereas the names in the Sub Material list are the names of the actual sub materials.

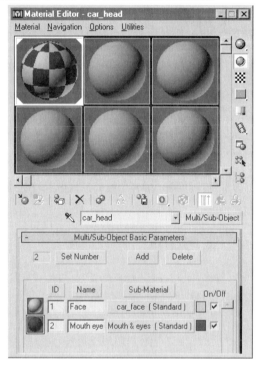

result in the smearing of the texture on the nose and ears. To compensate for this, the UVW coordinates must be "unwrapped" so that a bitmap can be projected onto it more evenly.

3ds max 6's new Relax feature, built in to the Unwrap UVW modifier, can make this process much easier. Continue with Carlo's head model by following these steps:

1 Select the polygons of the nose and ears (see Figure 9-3) and turn on Soft Selection with these settings. These are the polygons that will be spread out using the Unwrap modifier's Relax feature later.

FIGURE 9-3   The selection set for the nose and ears

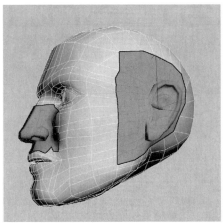

2   Apply a UVW map modifier and click the radio buttons in the Modify panel to give it a cylindrical mapping and a Y-axis alignment. Switch to Gizmo Sub Object mode by clicking the Gizmo entry in the stack, and then scale the cylindrical gizmo (the yellow cage) so that it is just a little bit larger than the head. Rotate the gizmo in the local Z-axis so that the green vertical line representing where the edges of the texture's map come together is in the back of the head.

3   Add an Unwrap UVW modifier to the top of the stack. This modifier now takes control of the mapping coordinates.

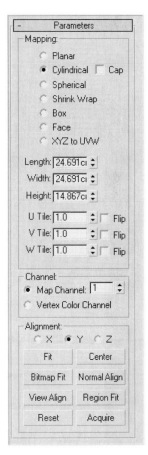

» TIP   *Once the UV coordinates are "baked" in the Unwrap UVW modifier, you can no longer change the topology of the mesh. Adding or deleting vertices, edges, or polygons at this point will probably scramble the UV coordinates. However, you can do minor sculpting by moving vertices, edges, or polygons.*

NOTE   *On the CD-ROM, the file ...\3dsmax6_CD\Carlo\ Carlo_texture_01.max contains the completed tutorial to this point.*

4   In the Parameters rollout of the Modify panel, click the Edit button to access the Edit UVW window (see Figure 9-4). Here you can see a diagram of the polygons of the mesh flattened out to lie on a rectangular bitmap.

5   At the bottom right of the window, change the drop-down box from "ALL IDs" to 1. This will hide the edges of the mouth and eyes.

The red vertices indicate the nose and ears selection set from the Editable Poly entry at the bottom of the modifier stack. If you zoom in on any of these areas, you'll see that these polygons have overlapping UVW coordinates. This is because the cylindrical projection of the UVW map modifier projects straight on to the nose regardless of the fact that some of the nostril polygons face backward.

FIGURE 9-4   The Edit UVW window shows the Carlo head mesh as though it were unwrapped onto a rectangular bitmap. This way, you can tell that the polygons in the upper-left corner will eventually receive the pixels located in the upper-left corner of whatever bitmap is used.

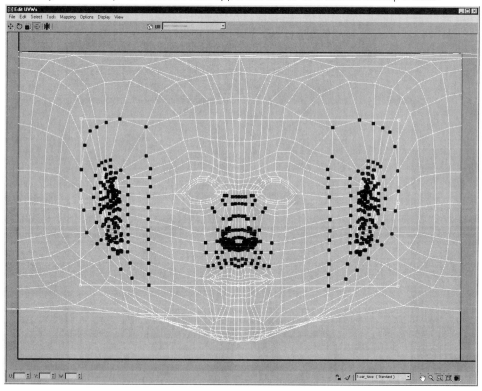

6 Correct this by using the Relax tool found in the main menu of the Edit UVW window under Tools/Relax dialog. Set the Amounts spinner to 1.0. Then move the Iterations spinner up to 120 while watching the projection. This evenly spreads out the mapping coordinates for the selected areas (see Figure 9-5).

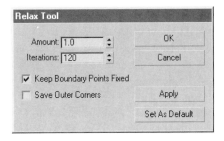

Creating a UV Template

Now you can use the projection of the unwrap UVW modifier as a template in Photoshop to create your facial texture. By taking a "snapshot" of the unwrapped mesh in the Edit UVW's window, you have an excellent reference for creating the texture. This image can be used as a base template layer for your facial texture map in Photoshop. For example, you can make the nose of your texture image lineup with the polygons of the nose in the mesh.

FIGURE 9-5   The vertices of the nose and ears have been relaxed using 3ds max 6's new Relax UVW's tool. Now the vertices are spread out so there's no overlapping.

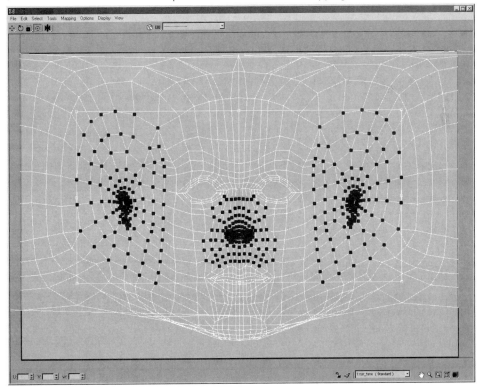

Continuing with the Carlo head, here are the steps to follow:

1 Open the Edit UVW window.

2 Use the pan and zoom tools to size the UV projection to fill the screen, as shown in Figure 9-6.

3 Now you can create a template for your texture either by capturing this window with the screen capture utility or by using your computer's built-in CTRL-PRT SCR function.

4 In Photoshop, crop this image to the edges of the blue rectangle and then resize the image, with Constrained Proportions unchecked, to 1024 by 512 pixels. Save this image in a TIF format and name it unwrap.tif. Save it in a subfolder called Working within the folder that contains the .max files for your character.

FIGURE 9-6 This is the UVW projection for the car_head mesh object. Because the head has been cylindrically mapped, this shows the UVW coordinates once they have been "unwrapped" and flattened into the two-dimensional space of a bitmap.

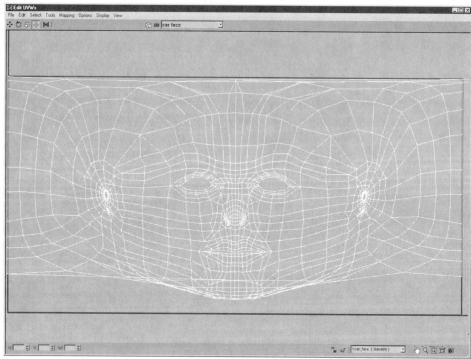

Creating the Face Texture Map in Photoshop

Of course, there are numerous ways to approach painting texture maps. To be sure, today's best character artists paint them by hand. But in the case of my film, I'm using photographs as the basis for the textures. This is first and foremost for expediency, to provide a fairly realistic result relatively quickly. However, I also chose this method because my film is supposed to represent a massively multiplayer videogame. In this case, this method fits the aesthetic of characters customized with personal photos by the players of the game.

Acquiring Source Images

To create facial texture maps using this method, you'll need front and side photographs of someone who looks something like your character (see Figure 9-7). You'll need to pay attention to several details to get photos that are usable for texturing, including the following:

▶ Make the focal length of your camera as long as possible to avoid any fisheye distortion. You can usually do this by backing away from your subject and zooming in.

▶ Shoot your subject in an evenly lit environment. Avoid as many shadows as possible because you want the lighting to come from your 3-D scene, not from the photographic textures.

▶ Make your photos as high resolution as possible and make sure the head and neck fill the frame.

FIGURE 9-7   For the source images, I chose someone sharing Carlo's approximate age, skin color, and facial build (but not Carlo's irritating personality!).

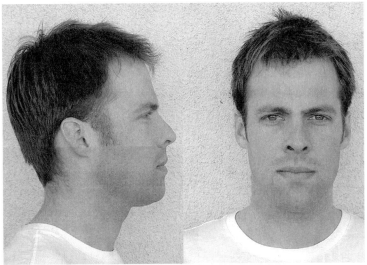

Creating the Rough Texture

Creating textures requires a strong knowledge of Adobe Photoshop or Procreate's Painter. Specifically, you'll need to be familiar with creating and manipulating layers as well as cloning and erasing so that you can take the relatively limited source material of your photos and create skin texture for the entire face. Here are the steps for creating a facial texture map for Carlo in Photoshop. You can follow along using the example files provided on the CD or create a different facial texture from your own source photographs.

1 Create a new file that's 1024 by 512 pixels. Save it in the Working folder as a Photoshop PSD file named car_face_00.psd.

2 From the …\3dsmax6_CD\Carlo\ Working\folder, open the unwrap.tif, source_profile.tif, and source_portrait .tif files. Using the Move tool, click in each of these images and drag them, one by one, onto the Face_00.psd window. This puts all three images onto new layers that you can see in the layers pallet. You can rename these layers by double-clicking the layer name next to the thumbnail. Call them unwrap, portrait, and profile.

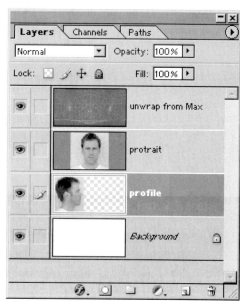

3 Click the thumbnail for the unwrap layer to select it. From the drop-down list above the thumbnails, choose Lighten so that you can see the UV projection superimposed over the images.

4 Turn off all the layers except for the profile layer by clicking the eye icons to the left of each layer in the Layers palette. Use the Lasso tool to select the usable portions of the profile image—that is, excluding the edges. Leave out the area around the eyes because it's better to use the eyes from the portrait image. Invert and feather this selection about five pixels and clear it using the DELETE key (Figure 9-8). Feathering this selection will form a semitransparent edge that can be blended with the other layers to form seamless boundaries for a continuous skin texture.

FIGURE 9-8   All unusable areas have been deleted from this profile layer. The eyes and mouth have been removed so that the texture will feature the eyes and mouth from the front image.

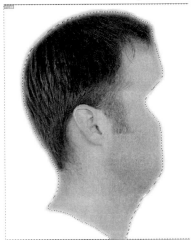

5   Now the portrait and profile layers can be moved and scaled to align roughly with the unwrap layer. Duplicate and flip the profile layer and align it with the opposite side, as shown in Figure 9-9.

FIGURE 9-9   The images have been trimmed, flipped, and then positioned as close as possible to the UVW projection template.

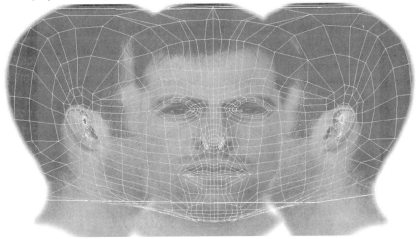

6 Once the profile images are next to the portrait image, color variations will become obvious. These can be corrected with the Color Balance adjustment. With the layer you want to correct selected, select Image | Adjustments | Color Balance from the menu.

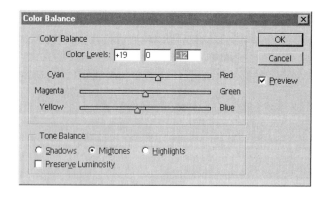

Adjust the sliders in the resulting dialog box until the colors match.

7 To quickly save a flattened version of this image to use as the texture map in 3ds max while preserving the layers in the PSD file, you can use Photoshop's Save for Web feature in the File menu. You can save a JPEG image to a folder specifically for your finished maps that's also in the same folder as your .max files. Name this folder Car_Maps. Placing only finished maps here will help control the clutter of numerous bitmap files. Name the JPEG file car_face.jpg.

NOTE *On the CD-ROM, the file ...\3dsmax6_CD\Carlo\Working\car_face_01.psd contains the Photoshop file of the completed Photoshop portion of the tutorial to this point.*

Editing the Unwrapped Projection

Although we are still at the very early stages of creating the texture, we can now view the rough texture on the model in 3ds max and continue the process of unwrapping. These steps will take you through the process of testing the preliminary facial texture map on the model to see how it is lining up:

1 In the Material Editor, access the car_face sub material of the car_head Multi/Sub Object material. Click the small blank button next to the diffuse color setting. Choose Bitmap from the Material/Map Browser, and then choose the car_face.jpg bitmap file. Click the Show Map in Viewport button to see the bitmap on the mesh.

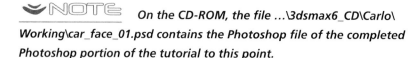

2 With car_head selected, go to the Modify panel and click the Unwrap UVW modifier's Edit button to bring up the Edit UVW window.

3 From the drop-down list at the top of the window, choose Pick Texture and then choose the car_face.jpg bitmap file.

4 You can now use this window's Move and Scale tools to align the vertices' UV projection more precisely to the texture image.

This phase of the unwrapping process can be both time consuming and challenging, and it requires an understanding of how to use max's Edit UVW window. To avoid stretching and smearing of the texture, the UV coordinates need to be distributed across the texture map space similarly to the way they are distributed across the mesh. That is, if a particular polygon is small or large on the mesh it should be similarly small or large on the UVW projection in the Edit UVW window.

This is done through using the Edit UVW window's Soft Selection feature to move vertices on the projection. These Soft Selection settings work similarly to those within the Editable Polygon tools.

5 Select the UVW vertices of one of the main facial features, such as the mouth, and set the Soft Selection falloff so that it encompasses the surrounding area, as shown in Figure 9-10a and Figure 9-10b.

FIGURE 9-10 This image shows the mouth UVW vertices being selected in the Edit UVW window (a) and the texture map for the mouth being out of place on the mesh (b).

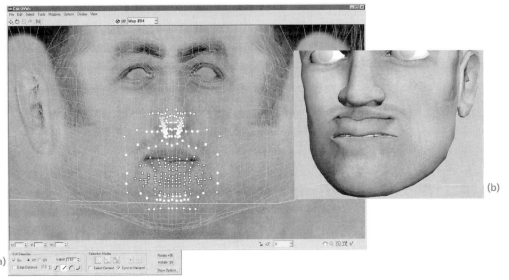

FIGURE 9-11   Here, the UVW vertices for the mouth have been moved into position over the mouth on the texture map in the Edit UVW window (a). In the viewport (b), the texture is now in place.

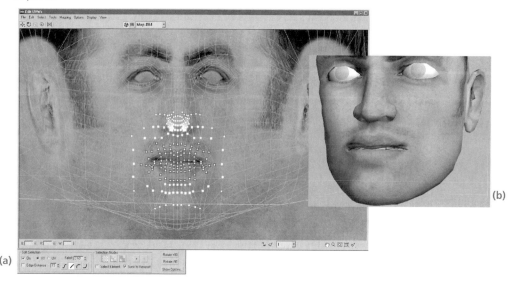

(a)

(b)

6   Use the Move tool to position vertices over the corresponding feature of the texture map, as shown in Figure 9-11a and Figure 9-11b. At this stage, your texture map is only partially completed, so getting the UV projection generally aligned with the rough texture is fine.

> **>> TIP**   *The Soft Selection tools for the Edit UVW window appear at the bottom of the window. However, they are hidden if the Edit UVW window is maximized. Leaving the window unmaximized avoids this caveat.*

The two most difficult areas to deal with are around the ears and around the nose. The polygons in these areas of the mesh were relaxed to spread them out and to keep those areas from overlapping in the UV projection. But as you spread out the vertices of the nose and ears again in the UV projection, this can cause the texture in the surrounding areas of the mesh to stretch in toward the nose and ears. This can be compensated for through careful use of Soft Selection. By selecting the nose, for example, and setting a generous falloff, you can scale up the UV coordinates of the nose, and the falloff of the Soft Selection will lessen the effect of this scaling on the surrounding UVs.

>>TIP   *An excellent feature added to the latest versions of 3ds max allows you to select faces on the mesh in the viewport and see the corresponding vertices selected in the Edit UVW window, and vice versa. This is invaluable for determining where particular vertices in the UVW projection occur on the mesh. You can access this feature by having the Sub Object mode of the Unwrap UVW modifier activated.*

NOTE   *On the CD-ROM, the file ...\3dsmax6_CD\Carlo\Carlo_texture_ 02.max contains the completed 3ds max portion of the tutorial to this point.*

Finishing the Texture in Photoshop

The next part of the process is iterative. Returning to Photoshop, you can proceed with filling in the blank areas of the texture map, and then you can use the Save for Web feature to save over the car_face.jpg bitmap file. When you return to 3ds max, the file updates automatically. Because you are changing the UV coordinates, you may occasionally want to create a new UV template to replace the old one in your PSD file. It is typical to repeat this process, adjusting the UV projection and modifying the texture in Photoshop, several times during the course of finishing the texture.

The facial texture map is completed by selecting various patches of skin with feathered selections and copying and pasting to fill in gaps in the map. Pasting the selections automatically creates new layers that can be easily positioned and scaled. Coverage and blending can also be achieved through using the Clone and Eraser tools, both with a soft brush and reduced opacity. Create all this skin coverage as layers above the source images. This way, they are always available for cloning, and mistakes can be easily undone by simply deleting layers.

Of particular note are the nostrils and eyes. Because the model will have its own eyeballs and nostril openings, you don't want the texture of these features. Create layers of cloned skin, blended at the edges to cover these up.

Finally, back in 3ds max, you can fine-tune the UVW projection to match your finished texture. You'll want to pull the vertices of the eyelids together, as shown in Figure 9-12. Because the eyes of the texture have been covered up with skin, the eyelid vertices should be pulled over this. This will keep the texture on the eyelids from stretching when the mesh is animated blinking.

The finished projection is shown alongside the finished texture in Figure 9-13a and Figure 9-13b. The polygons at the top and bottom of the UVW projection are extremely stretched by the nature of the cylindrical unwrapping. This is unavoidable. Fortunately,

FIGURE 9-12 The UVW vertices of the eyes have been scaled shut. This aligns the UVW vertices for the eyelids with the eyelid areas of the texture map.

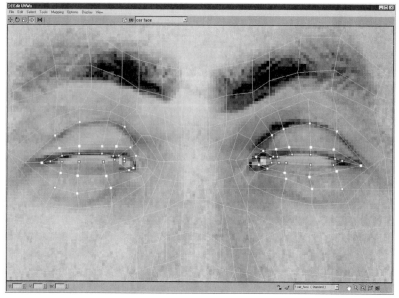

these polygons are only at the centers of the base and top of the head. These will be covered by the neck and by the hair so they are not seen.

Once the texture mapping is complete, you can collapse the stack by right-clicking the top entry in the stack and selecting Collapse All from the pop-up menu. This "bakes" the UV coordinates into the mesh. If needed, however, you can edit the UVW projection again by adding a new Unwrap UVW modifier. Also, all your unwrapping work will be preserved.

> **NOTE** *On the CD-ROM, the file ...\3dsmax6_CD\Carlo\Working\car_face_02.psd is the Photoshop file of the completed Photoshop portion of the tutorial to this point. Also, ...Ch9\Carlo_texture_03.max contains the completed 3ds max portion of the tutorial to this point.*

Modeling and Texturing the Teeth and Tongue

For my characters, modeling the teeth is fairly simple. Because I won't be rendering any high-resolution close-ups in the film, I'm not modeling individual teeth. Instead, I can model simple shapes and then texture them with an image of teeth. Figure 9-14 shows the construction of the teeth and tongue as separate objects.

First, a spline is drawn for a cross-section of one half of one set of teeth with the Line tool Figure 9-14 (a). This line is then used to create the geometry by adding a Bevel modifier to it (b).

FIGURE 9-13   The finished UVW projection (a) and the finished texture map (b).

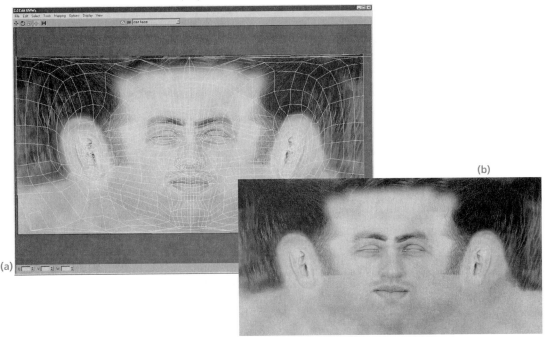

(b)

(a)

An Edit Mesh modifier is then added so that the geometry can be mirrored and welded to form a full set. A cylindrical UVW Map modifier is added, and a material containing the teeth texture is assigned (c). The other set of teeth is created by mirroring this object and sculpting the vertices by accessing the new object's Edit Mesh modifier (d). The tongue is created by adding an Edit Mesh modifier to a simple cylinder primitive. The vertices are scaled down at the Sub Object level, and the vertices at the top of the cylinder are welded together to form the tip of the tongue (e). Mapping is a simple planar UVW Map modifier.

FIGURE 9-14   Here is the step-by-step construction of the teeth and tongue.

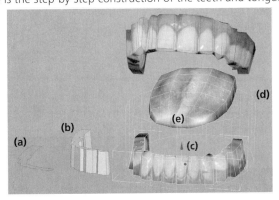

(d)

(b)

(a)

(e)

(c)

FIGURE 9-15   This image was created by starting with a photo of teeth, taken from the front. The sides were copied and stretched so that the image could be wrapped cylindrically around the teeth mesh objects.

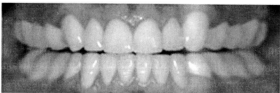

The texture for the teeth, shown in Figure 9-15, is a digital photo of my wife's teeth with the sides of the image stretched in Photoshop to accommodate for the cylindrical mapping. Because the texture contains both the top and bottom sets of teeth, both teeth objects can share the same material. The map can be aligned on the mesh by scaling and positioning the UVW map gizmo to show one set of teeth or the other. The texture of the tongue is a digital photograph of my lovely tongue. The edges of the tongue have been faded to pink so that the streaking on the edges of the mesh caused by the planar mapping will not be apparent.

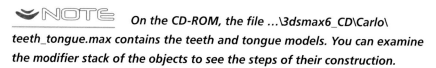

NOTE   *On the CD-ROM, the file ...\3dsmax6_CD\Carlo\ teeth_tongue.max contains the teeth and tongue models. You can examine the modifier stack of the objects to see the steps of their construction.*

Once the teeth and tongue objects are positioned and scaled inside the head mesh, as shown in Figure 9-16, they can be attached to the head mesh object. This is done the same way that the two halves of the head were attached—with the Attach button in the Modify panel. This will also cause the car_head Multi/Sub Object material to have two new entries for the teeth and tongue materials.

Creating the Eyeballs

Modeling eyeballs that exhibit convincing reflections and specular highlights is more complex than simply creating a sphere and texture mapping it, but the heart of the approach is simple: Imitate the major physical components of an actual eyeball. You can do this by creating separate pieces of geometry for the different components of the eye, cornea, iris, lens, and the back of the pupil. These can then be attached to each other at the sub object level and assigned separate material IDs for a Multi/Sub Object eyeball material. Since we covered modeling in the previous two chapters, here are the broad steps to follow:

1   Near the head model, create a sphere with the poles facing forward. Name it Car_Eye_L and convert it to an Editable Poly.

FIGURE 9-16   The teeth and tongue objects positioned inside the mesh

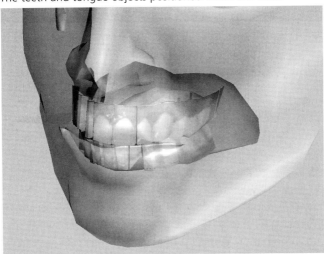

2 Select the two innermost rings of polygons. In the
Modify Panel, go to the Edit Geometry rollout, click
the Detach button, and then detach the polygons
as both a clone and an element. This will become
the lens. Assign these new polygons material ID 2.
Then temporarily hide these polygons by clicking
the Hide button in the Edit Geometry rollout.

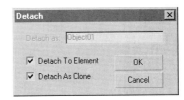

3 Select the original innermost ring of polygons and detach this as an element. Move
this new circular element behind the hole and scale it up. This leaves a hole for what
will be the iris, and the circle of polygons behind the iris will keep you from seeing
through the eye. I'll refer to that circle of polygons as the pupil. Give the pupil element
a material ID of 3.

4 Create a Multi/Sub Object material with three sub materials named Car_iris_and_white,
car_lens, and car_pupil.

5 The main texture map for the Car_iris_and_white sub material is shown in Figure 9-17a
and is placed in that sub material's Diffuse map channel. It was created from scratch in
Photoshop. The veins were created using Procreate's KPT Effects Lightning plug-in to create
the red veins. The iris is painted using standard brush tools in a feathered circular selection.

FIGURE 9-17 The Diffuse (a) and Reflection (b) texture maps for Carlo's eye

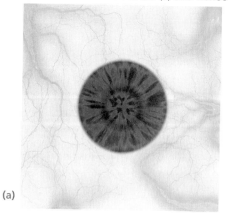

(a)

(b)

6 Give both the Car_iris_and_white and the car_lens sub materials a high Specular Level setting to make them very shiny. Use the same bitmap, shown in Figure 9-17b, in both the sub materials' Reflection map channel. This is a simple image of city lights at night.

7 Make the car_pupil material completely black with no specularity.

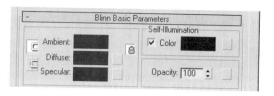

8 Finally, select Car_Eye_L and choose Edit/Clone from the main menu to make Car_Eye_R, and then use the Align tool to position the new eyes over the stand-in eyes created earlier. Then delete the old stand-in eye objects.

 **On the CD-ROM, the file …\3dsmax6_CD\Carlo\ Carlo_texture_04.max contains the completed tutorial to this point.**

Creating the Material for the Face

Now we'll create the rest of the maps and material settings for Carlo's face. Although materials, also known as *shaders*, can become very complex, we'll keep this topic fairly simple. Because the texture map for the diffuse color channel has already been created, we can use it as a starting point for a bump map to help add some surface detail and for a specular map to help define the shininess of the skin.

Bump Map

A *bump map* translates brightness information from a bitmap image into depth information at render time (see Figure 9-18). Although a bump map does not change the geometry itself, and therefore cannot change the *contour* of a mesh, it does affect shading. The dark areas of a bump map are translated into indentations, whereas the light areas are translated into protrusions. This can speed the rendering time of your scene over creating the effect with actual geometry.

To create a bump map, start with a grayscale Photoshop file that's the same resolution as the diffuse texture map and name it car_face_bump.psd. Fill the entire map with 50 percent gray. This way, the map can contain both indentations and protrusions (50 percent gray adds no bump to the surface). The closer to black, the deeper the surface indents, and the closer to whiter, the higher off the surface an area will appear. It will be helpful to have the diffuse texture map as a reference layer with 30 percent opacity within this file.

You can then use a fine, soft-edged brush set to a dark gray to paint the lines of negative bump to provide more surface detail in the lips, and you can give more definition to the eyelids by outlining them. You can trace the diffuse map in many cases to make this process go faster. When using a diffuse texture built from photographs, adding detail in the bump can accentuate details already in the diffuse texture.

Because Carlo's eyebrows are in the diffuse texture as opposed to being modeled, it is helpful to copy the eyebrows from the diffuse reference layer to the bump layer and make them a light

FIGURE 9-18   Carlo's bump map

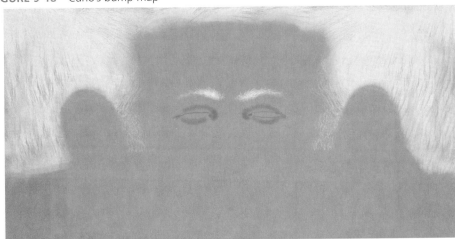

gray to give them more surface definition. This can also be done with the hairline. To create stubble bumpiness, you can make a custom brush that scatters one or two pixel dots.

Save a JPEG named car_face_bump.jpg to the maps folder for the Carlo model. Then in max, place the bump map in the Bump channel of the car_face sub material and leave the setting at the default (100).

Specular Map

The procedure for creating a specular map is similar to creating a bump map, except the grayscale image controls shininess instead of depth (see Figure 9-19). This is a powerful way break up the unnatural evenness typical of computer shading. Again, starting with a grayscale Photoshop file filled with a neutral tone, use a large soft-edged brush with a light gray color to define areas of the skin you want to be shinier. You'll typically want to make these patches correspond to areas of the face that are naturally oilier, such as the area around the nose, and areas you want to pick up more specular highlights, such as the apple of the cheeks.

Save a JPEG named car_spec_bump.jpg to the maps folder for the Carlo model, and then in 3ds max, place the specular map in the Specular Level channel of the car_face sub material and set the amount spinner to 50. In the Basic Parameters section of the sub material, set the Specular Level to 5 and Glossiness to 8. Keeping Specular Level set to 50, combined with the settings in Basic Parameters, will help make the effect of the map more subtle (see Figure 9-20).

 **NOTE** *On the CD-ROM, the file ...\3dsmax6_CD\Carlo*
Carlo_texture_05.max contains the completed tutorial to this point.

FIGURE 9-19 Carlo's specular map

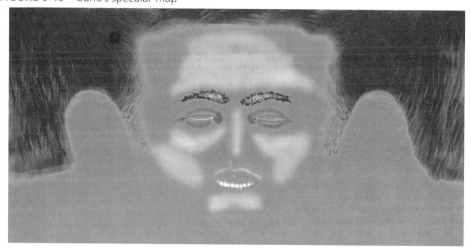

FIGURE 9-20   Here is the completed head rendered to show the effects of the shader.

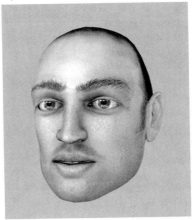

Texture Mapping the Body

To create and apply textures for the body, we'll use procedures similar to those we used for the head. Because we've made the body a single object, we will again use a Multi/Sub Object material to hold and organize the various materials the body requires. Within this context, texture mapping the individual sections of the body will be simpler than texture mapping the head.

Source Photos

To acquire the various source images for the body, follow the same procedures used to acquire photos for the face. As you take the images, you'll want to consider what type of UVW mapping coordinates you'll be using to map a particular image onto the mesh (see the next section, "Preparing the Body Mesh"). For example, if you'll be mapping the pants with planar mapping coordinates projected from the side, you should shoot images of the pants from the side as well.

The way clothing wrinkles is also an issue to address. If you are creating full-blown photorealistic models like those in *Final Fantasy* or using a cloth simulator, all the wrinkles in the clothing should come from actual wrinkles in the polygonal mesh of the object. On the other hand, if you are creating a very low polygon model, you'll want source images with wrinkles in them to provide added detail, though you will want the wrinkles to be subtle.

For the source images for Carlo's clothes, I photographed myself wearing the clothing I intended Carlo to wear when I designed and modeled him.

Preparing the Body Mesh

Like the head object, the body object will have a Multi/Sub Object material with sub materials for each part of the body mesh. This allows each different body part or piece of clothing to have different texture maps. However, each section of the body will need specific UVW mapping coordinates and a specific material ID that corresponds with the proper material slot in the Multi/Sub Object material.

Applying UVW Coordinates

Mapping coordinates for each specific section of the body can be provided by selecting a group of polygons in the Sub Object level of the car_body object and applying a UVW map modifier. This limits the effect of the gizmo to only the selected polygons. This way, the forearm can be mapped cylindrically, whereas the hand is mapped with a planar projection. After each new application of a new UVW Map modifier, collapse the stack. This again "bakes" the UVW coordinates into the mesh, and then the process can be repeated. Figure 9-21 shows the gizmos of Carlo's various UVW projections.

Certain areas, such as the front and back of the shirt, the left and right side of the pants leg, and the top and palm of the hand can all share a planar mapped gizmo. The front and back

FIGURE 9-21   The gizmos in this diagram illustrate how each section of the body mesh was UVW mapped individually. Also, the labels show the name of the sub object material and the material ID number that has been assigned to each region of the mesh. For the arms, hands, legs and feet, the right side receives the same sub materials and material IDs as the left.

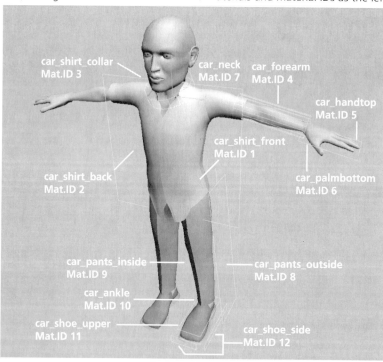

of the shirt will have different texture maps because they will have different material IDs (see Figure 9-21), but both of these texture maps can be projected similarly.

Material IDs
Figure 9-21 shows the different material IDs assigned to the various sections of the car_body object. Each material ID number will correspond to a material slot in the Multi/Sub Object material assigned to the mesh. Notice that symmetrical sections can share the same material ID. This way, one texture map can do double duty. For example, the map for the top of the hand can be used on both hands.

Creating a Top-level Multi/Sub Object Material
In a Material Editor, select an open slot and make it a Multi/Sub Object material. Name this material car_body. Set the number of Sub Object materials to 12 to correspond with the material IDs that have been assigned to the car_body mesh object (see Figure 9-22), and then assign this material to the car_body object.

FIGURE 9-22   This is the top level of the car_body Multi/Sub Object material in the Material Editor. The list shows the sub materials and their material IDs that corresponds to the material IDs assigned to the polygons in the car_body mesh object.

 **On the CD-ROM, the file ...\3dsmax6_CD\Carlo\ Carlo_texture_06.max contains the completed tutorial to this point.**

Hands

The hands are mapped simply with two photos that correspond to the planar mapping projections from above and below (Figure 9-23). The main challenge is positioning the UVW vertices of the fingers properly on the projected texture and then blending the seams where the top hand map meets the palm map.

Preparing the Photos

If you want to follow along, you can open ...\3dsmax6_CD\Carlo\Working\source_hand.tif and source_palm.tif. Work on both maps simultaneously so that you can see how well they match and blend. First, crop both maps and name them car_hand.psd and car_palm.psd. The maps will need to be color balanced to match each other as closely as possible. Then they should be color balanced to match the texture of the face as well.

Use the Lasso tool to make a selection along the edge of the hand and invert this selection so that everything but the hand is selected, and then feather the selection about ten pixels and create a new layer named Cover. Use the Paint Bucket to fill it with a neutral flesh color (see Figure 9-24).

FIGURE 9-23 The source photos for the hands

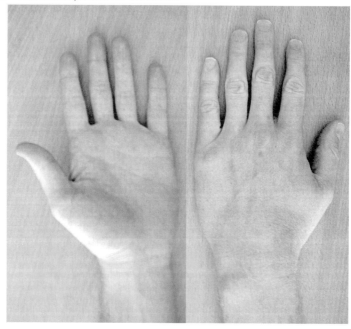

FIGURE 9-24   This breakdown shows the source file with the outline selected (left), the Cover layer filling the feathered selection with the paint bucket (middle), and the final texture map with both layers combined (right).

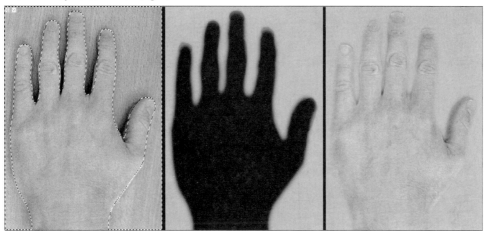

Apply this same procedure to the palm map as well, filling the cover selection layer with the same color as the top map. This way, the sides of the fingers and the edges of the hand will blend into a seamless solid color. Save the JPEGs of these maps as car_hand.jpg and car_palm.jpg in the \Car_Maps folder.

Creating a Sub Material

In a Material Editor, access the slot for material ID 5 and name this sub material car_hand. Assign car_hand.jpg (either the one you have created or the one from the …\3dsmax6_CD\Carlo\ Car_Maps folder) to the Diffuse map channel and use the Show Map in Viewport button to make it visible. Repeat this, making a sub material called car_palm in the Material ID 6 slot using car_palm.jpg in the Diffuse channel.

Unwrapping
The hands are now texture mapped, but the UVW coordinates will need adjusting. Apply a UVW Unwrap modifier to the car_body object. When you click the Edit button to access the Edit UVW window, you'll be confronted with an incomprehensible hodgepodge of UVW projections. But by selecting material ID 5 from the Material ID drop-down list, you'll see the UVW coordinates for the top of the hand isolated. You can then position the UVW vertices to match the texture map. Be sure that the edge vertices of the fingers are positioned over the areas where the map blends to the neutral color.

>> CAUTION << *Because both arms and hands share the same material IDs, the IDs for the hand tops, palms, and forearms will display a double set of vertices in the Edit UVW window. You can tell this by clicking a UVW vertex and moving it to see the duplicate vertex behind it. This problem can be corrected by temporarily deleting one arm/hand Sub Object element from the car_body mesh object. Once the remaining arm is fully textured, that element can be cloned and mirrored.*

Also, do not use Soft Selection when positioning the UVW's fingers, because the Soft Selection falloff will "bleed" over to the other material IDs. This will result in the unwanted moving of other UVW vertices, particularly those in the palm (ID 6) if you're working in the hand (ID 5).

Arms

You can use a procedure similar to texturing the face for the forearm. Start with images from several sides of the arm to form several layers (see Figure 9-25). Create a new Photoshop file, named car_arm.psd, with a resolution of 512 by 1024 pixels. Drag all your source images (…\3dsmax6_CD\Carlo\Working\ source_arm1-3.tif) into this new file and crop the usable parts of each layer. Make duplicates of the layers you have until your map is mostly filled (see Figure 9-26a). Then save a JPEG named car_arm.jpg and put it in the sub material for material ID 4, named car_arms, to check alignment. This way, you can see whether the elbow of your map is aligning with the elbow of your mesh, and you can move the layers in the Photoshop PSD file accordingly.

To make the texture seamless when it is cylindrically wrapped, copy the layer at the left edge of the map and flip it horizontally. Position this layer at the opposite edge of the map to create a seamless border when the map is wrapped cylindrically. Then fill in the gaps in the layers through cloning and erasing, in the same manner as you did for the face texture (see Figure 9-26b).

➷ NOTE *Mapping in this method will create seams at the wrist where the textures of the arm and hands join. Normally, you'll want to make these joints seamless. This can be done through a process of copying pieces from the edge of one map (say, the wrist part of the hand map), flipping them, and placing them on the wrist edge of the arm map, where they meet the hand, and then blending. Beyond this, you can use an external 3-D paint package.*

FIGURE 9-25   The source images for the arm textures

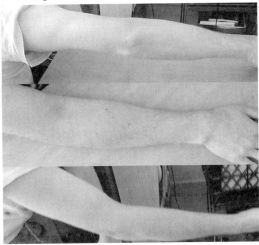

Carlo's Shirt

The shirt is easier to texture than other parts of the body because this type of shirt has seams that fall on the boundaries of the material IDs. Start with images for the front, back, and collar, as shown in Figure 9-27a and Figure 9-27b (...\3dsmax6_CD\Carlo\Working\source_shirt_front.tif, source_shirt_back.tif, and source_shirt_collar.tif), making three separate Photoshop files, car_shirt_front.psd, car_shirt_back .psd, and car_shirt_collar.psd. Color-correct the front

FIGURE 9-26   The source images have been cut and pasted together to form the preliminary texture (a), and then through cloning, erasing and color balancing the textures completed (b).

(a)   (b)

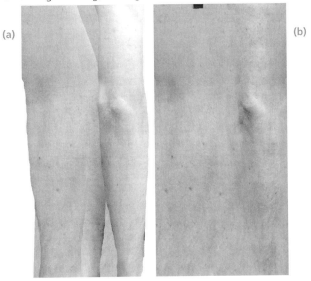

and back and collar images. Then, in the same manner as the hand textures, add blend layers of a matching neutral color sampled from the shirt (see Figure 9-28a through Figure 9-28c).

Place JPEGs of each texture in the diffuse slot of the corresponding sub material in max— 1 for the shirt front, 2 for the shirt back, and 3 for the shirt collar, and then use the Edit UVW window in the Unwrap UVW modifier to adjust the position of the maps.

Pants

The pants are the easiest to texture map because creases in the front and back of the pants hide the seams between the virtually identical texture maps. The source images for

FIGURE 9-27 Here are the front (a), back (b), and collar (c) source images for the shirt.

FIGURE 9-28   Here are the front (a), back (b), and collar (c) final shirt textures.

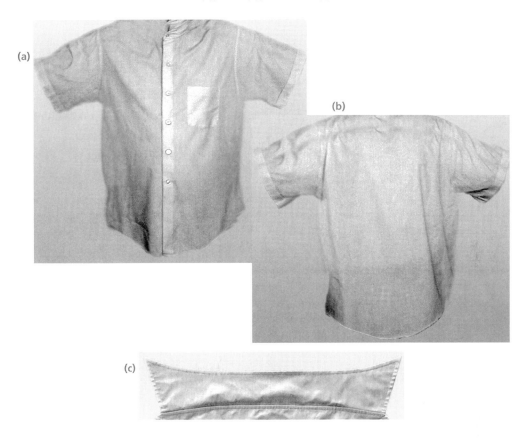

the inside and outside of the pants leg, shown in Figure 9-29 (…\3dsmax6_CD\Carlo\Working\ source_pants_outside.tif and source_pants_inside.tif), need very little modification. Simply crop them and name them car_pants_in.psd and car_pants_out.psd. Color-balance the maps with each other and add blend layers as before.

Once the JPEGs (see Figure 9-30a and Figure 9-30b) are in the diffuse slots for sub materials of car_pants_ inside (ID 9) and car_pants_outside (ID 8), use the Edit UVW window in the Unwrap UVW modifier to adjust the position of the maps.

Shoes

The source for the shoes, shown in Figure 9-31a, was created by placing one of my shoes on a scanner (…\3dsmax6_CD\Carlo\Working\source_shoe.tif). An even piece of texture was simply

FIGURE 9-29   Source photos for the pants

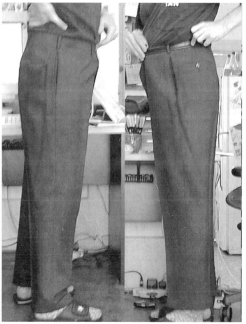

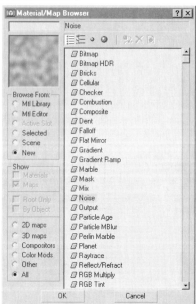

cropped out and saved as car_blueshoe.jpg (see Figure 9-31b) and placed in the car_shoe_upper sub material (ID 11).

For the soles of the shoes, bitmap texture mapping isn't really necessary because they will be so small onscreen. A quick way to keep nontextured materials from looking like computer plastic is to use procedural noise maps. Procedural maps generate textures programmatically instead of from bitmaps. In this case, noise maps in both the Specular Level and Bump channels can break up the even surface of a standard material. To assign a noise map, assign a map to the map channel as usual, but choose Noise

FIGURE 9-30   The final pants textures (a and b)

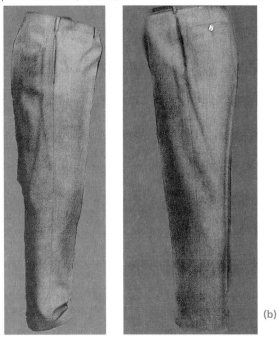

(a)   (b)

FIGURE 9-31   The source scan for the shoe texture (a) and the finished shoe texture (b)

(a)   (b)

A Few Words on Hair

For the characters in my film, I have created their hair with a 3ds max plug-in—Digimation's Shag: Hair. This is one of the few plug-ins I used to make this film. Because it would require you, the reader, to own the plug-in to be able to follow along, I have not included tutorials about Shag: Hair in this book. If you choose to use this plug-in, you should know that it comes with tutorials, and tutorials are available on the Net as well. These will help to get you started.

If you don't want to use a plug-in, you have other ways to create your characters' hairstyles. A common way is to create multiple polygon mesh objects, not unlike the petals of a flower, and then texture map these with textures of hair and opacity maps to make the edges invisible.

from the window's Material/Map Browser pop-up menu instead of Bitmap. See Figure 9-32a and Figure 9-32b for settings for the two noise maps.

FIGURE 9-32 The settings for the procedural noise maps in the Specular Level channel (a) and the Bump channel (b) for the car_shoe_sole sub material.

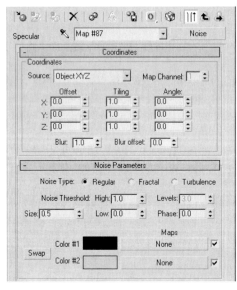
(a)

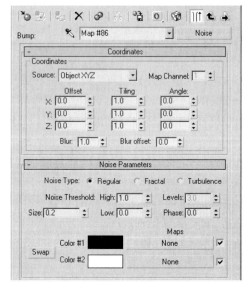
(b)

 **NOTE** *On the CD-ROM, the file ...\3dsmax6_CD\Carlo\ Carlo_texture_07.max contains the completed tutorial to this point.*

Carlo Is Ready to Rig

Now that all the final texture maps for Carlo are in one folder and the mesh consists simply of head, body, and eyeball objects, the Carlo model can be easily copied to other folders and merged into other scenes without confusion. Carlo is now ready for the next step in the production pipeline. We'll cover rigging in Chapter 10. Because this chapter is only a simple introduction to the deep pursuit of texture mapping, it's not hard to realize why larger studios have people who do nothing but texture map full-time. I recommend exploring a few different methods for creating textures, such as painting them by hand or using procedural textures (we'll cover these in Chapter 11) before choosing a method for your film.

Chapter 10

Rigging: Preparing the Characters for Animation

Once you have sculpted the outer shell

for your characters, the first step in bringing

them to life is to craft the mechanism for their

movement. Articulating a 3-D mesh with

bones and creating handles by which to grab

and manipulate a character is one of the more

technically challenging pursuits that CG animators

face. But by applying some forethought and

ingenuity to the skeleton of your character, and some thorough attention to detail when attaching the skin, you can make your subsequent animation process vastly more fluid and intuitive. Also, you can enable ranges and types of motion for your character that will allow you to make it express and emote in ways that would be otherwise impossible.

Quality rigging is essential for quality animation because a simple mesh cannot be bent or twisted. Creating an anatomically correct skeleton, connecting the mesh to it in a fluid, facile way, and providing handles and controls that allow for action figure–like posing is a practice that has been steadily maturing (see Figure 10-1). Through constant use in professional animation situations, the standard tools within 3ds max not only allow for flexible, deeply customizable rigging solutions, but they also allow you to draw upon methodologies tested in demanding production environments. The system of bones, inverse kinematics, skin, helper objects, and MAXScripts have even allowed for a cross-pollination of techniques between 3ds max and Maya.

The range of possible character-rigging solutions spans simply linked hierarchies and the Skin modifier to sophisticated plug-in muscular systems and extensive MAXScripting. To be sure, the study of character rigging could easily fill this entire book, and then some. Contemporary professional character riggers, often known as *technical directors*, are fluent not only in

FIGURE 10-1　Characters in 3ds max are rigged using a variety of max features, including bones, inverse kinematics, and helper objects. These elements are, in turn, controlled by shape objects. This way, the character can be controlled almost entirely by moving and rotating shape objects alone, which act as handles.

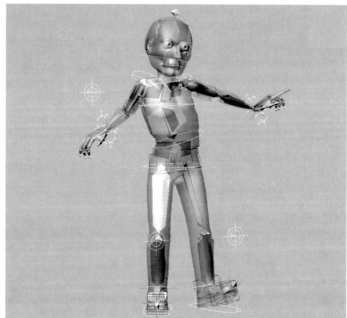

character modeling and animation techniques, but often possess respectable mathematics and programming skills as well. Nevertheless, in this chapter, we'll strike a balance between a very pared-down approach to rigging and creating a character armature that will allow for some solid human character animation.

Approaching Rigging: What You'll Need to Know

Character rigging is done through a combination of max bones, inverse kinematics, hierarchical linkages, wire parameters, the Skin modifier, and in many cases MAXScript. But before you start building a rig, it is important to know what you'll be demanding of your character as you animate.

A Series of Questions

To give yourself an underlying strategy for creating your rig, it is necessary to understand a number of issues pertaining to your character's movement and to how you will be animating later.

How Will the Character Move?

First, allow your story and storyboards to inform you about what type of movements your character will be required to perform. A martial arts action story may require different types of articulation and more attention to joint flexibility and range of motion, whereas an intense emotional drama may warrant more attention to subtle expressiveness. Characters that engage in heavy interaction with their environment, such as climbing rocks and cliffs, or grapple with other characters have different requirements than characters that fly or swim.

Get into the specifics of what types of gestures and mannerisms as well as the style of walking, running, and any other type of locomotion your character needs to exhibit. It will be difficult to answer this question unless you have created rigs already, but it is good to have it in mind even as you build your first rig.

What's Your Character's Anatomy?

Whether you need to understand actual bone structure and human musculature or are creating a fantasy creature's anatomy based on real-world animals, at least a cursory knowledge of anatomy is required to make character movements believable. Convincing animation requires an understanding of weight, balance, and joint structures. Even if you're not planning to give your characters an elaborate muscular system, understanding where the pivot points of joints should go in relation to your mesh is critical.

How Do You Animate?

Next, your animation habits should play a role in the design of your character rigs. If you want to animate as quickly as possible, you may want to automate certain movements, such as the direction of a shoulder turn or the bending of the spine. On the other hand, if you are intending to create the richest and most expressive animation possible, you may want fine, manual control over virtually every joint.

To be sure, this question is also difficult to answer unless you have done some animation first. But answers to this and other more specific details related to your animation habits will become more evident once you start the animation process. I recommend actually animating with a thoroughly articulated rig (several of which are freely available on the Net) before attempting to design your own. However, by building a rudimentary yet thorough rig in this chapter, you'll not only gain a firm grounding in rigging, but also a better understand of how to animate with a fully rigged character like the ones we'll be using in later chapters.

Key Concepts

As with most of this book, key rigging concepts are presented within the context of the examples and exercises. However, a few concepts are pervasive and important enough to be covered at the start—namely, coordinate systems, pivot points, and axes.

Coordinate Systems, Pivot Points, and Axes

When it comes to rigging, a firm understanding of an object's transform axes is necessary. Here is a very simple exercise. To begin, open the file …\3dsmax6_CD\Felix\axes_example.max on the CD-ROM and then follow these steps:

1 Choose the Move tool from the main toolbar and select the box on the left.

2 Use the Reference Coordinate System drop-down list to change the display of the axis tripod to Local. Observe how the orientation of the tripod now follows the box. The local coordinate system defines the direction of the X-, Y-, and Z-axes of the object itself (see Figure 10-2a).

3 Change the Reference Coordinate System setting to World and observe how the axis tripod aligns itself with the viewport grid (see Figure 10-2b).

4 Now change the Reference Coordinate System setting to Parent. Because the box is not linked to anything, this coordinate system reflects the World coordinate system.

5 Now click the Link tool Select and Link button in the main toolbar. Click the box on the left and drag over to the box on the right while observing the orientation of the tripod. When the first box is linked to the second, its Parent coordinate system is changed to reflect its new parent, the other box (see Figure 10-2c).

6 Change back to the Move tool and to the Local axis coordinate system and go to the Hierarchy panel. Click the Affect Pivot Only button and notice the larger tripod

Affect Pivot Only

that appears in the viewport. In Affect Pivot Only mode, you can move an object's pivot point (see Figure 10-3).

7 Move the pivot point tripod to another point on the box and then switch to the Rotate tool and to the Local axis coordinate system. You can see that the box now moves around the new position of the pivot.

FIGURE 10-2 These figures show the same object selected with different Reference Coordinate Systems settings and how the transform gizmo (the Move gizmo is shown here) changes orientation to reflect this. The Local coordinate system is the object's own coordinate system defined by its pivot point (a). The World coordinate system is aligned to the overall max scene (b). The Parent coordinate system is aligned to the object that the selected object is hierarchically linked to (c).

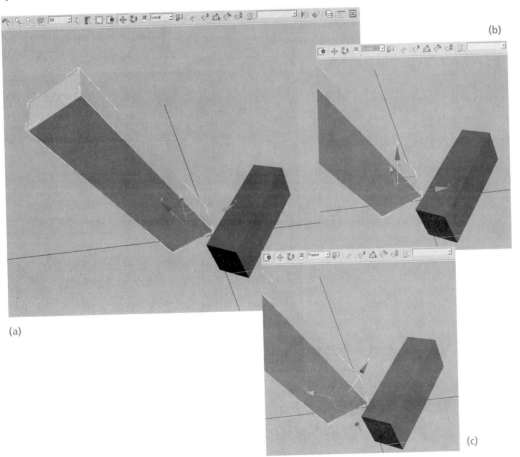

(a)

(b)

(c)

FIGURE 10-3   The larger, wireframe gizmo shown here indicates that Affect Pivot Only mode is on. Moving this wireframe gizmo moves the object's pivot point. The object will rotate, scale, and move in relation to the position and orientation of this pivot point.

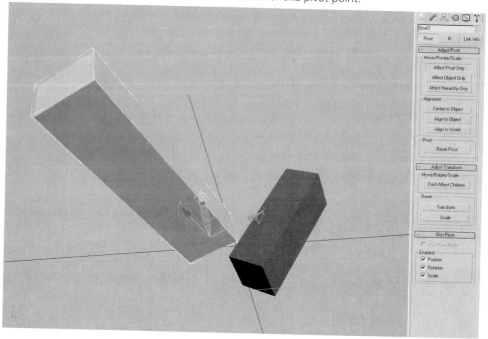

Understanding whether a particular object is rotating around the Local, Parent, or World coordinate system and where its pivot point or the pivot point of its parent is located will both be critical as we proceed.

A Simple Rig for a Human Character

In this chapter's main exercise, we'll go through the process of creating a simple human character rig. The character Felix from the example film will make a good test bed for rigging because he is a straightforward human character. We'll try to achieve as much sophistication as possible without resorting to heavy MAXScripting or plug-ins. This approach will be a good launching point for more ambitious rigging on your own.

Making a Skeleton from Standard Max Bones

3ds max bones are, at their heart, very simple objects made specifically for the purpose of character rigging. Although the Bone object does have its own geometry, consisting of the tapered shaft and fins, this geometry is typically not rendered. A bone is essentially a transform—that is, its main components are the orientation of its local coordinate system and its length along its main axis (usually the X-axis).

Knowledge of which direction the axes of your bones face will be important as you build your skeletal structure and then rig it. Besides changing to Local coordinate system and viewing the axis tripod of a given bone, you can turn on a bone's fins to see which way the bone is oriented as well. The local X-axis of a bone will point down the length of its shaft, and its Z-axis will be parallel to its side fins (see Figure 10-4).

An important thing to note about creating bones is that their initial orientation depends on which viewport they are created in. Although they can be rotated after creation, you can save yourself both time and confusion by knowing this.

Open the file …\3dsmax6_CD\Felix\felix_geometry.max. This file contains the modeled and textured Felix character geometry scaled to the size of the Cloud10 environment. If you prefer, you can create a rig for your own character geometry. Note that it is important to have your character geometry at the scale needed to fit into the environment. Once the character is rigged, it can be difficult to rescale the character.

Instead of creating the skeleton from a single hierarchy of bones, we will create several separate hierarchical bone chains that can be linked together later. This will allow us to more discreetly work on separate portions of the skeleton when it comes to rigging controls.

FIGURE 10-4   Here is a typical max bone with its X-axis running down its length, its side fins indicating the Z-axis, and its front and back fins indicating the Y-axis.

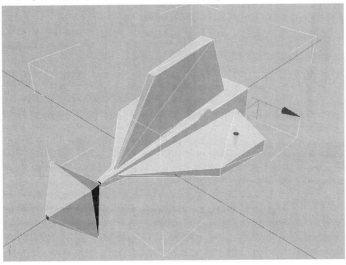

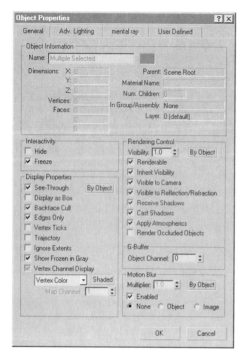

Creating the Leg Bones

A basic human character that wears shoes will need joints at the hip, knee, ankle, and one for the toes (the individual toes are covered by shoes). We'll therefore make a simple bone hierarchy chain to accommodate this:

1 Select all the geometry and right-click it to access its Properties dialog box. Click the See Through check box and the Freeze check box and then close the dialog box.

2 From the main menu, choose Character | Bone Tools to pop up the floating Bone Tools window. This window can be kept open throughout the bone-creation process so that you have quick access to the bone-related tools.

3 Switch to a left viewport and zoom in on Felix's leg.

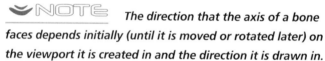 *The direction that the axis of a bone faces depends initially (until it is moved or rotated later) on the viewport it is created in and the direction it is drawn in.*

By creating bones in the left viewport, you make the rear fins face to the rear of the character when they are turned on.

4 In the Bone Tools window, click the Create Bones button located in the Bone Editing Tools rollout. Not only does this put you in Bones Creation mode, it also brings up the Bones Creation rollouts in that Create panel. In the Bone Parameters rollout, enter a width of 5 cm and a height of 5 cm so that the bones you create will have these dimensions.

5 To create the bones of the leg (see Figure 10-5), left-click in the center of the hip area, then click close to the front of the knee, the center of the ankle, down to the center of the ball of the foot, and then straight to the right at the tip of the toe. Then right click twice—once to create a tip bone for the chain and again to cancel out of Bones Creation mode.

FIGURE 10-5   Here are the bones of the leg created in a left viewport.

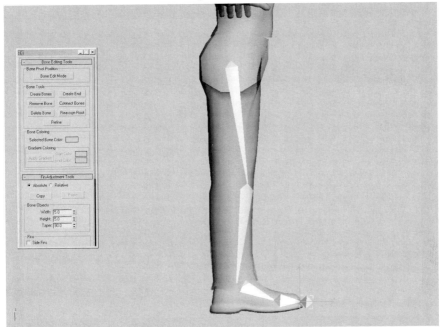

🌊NOTE   *By placing the knee joint closer to the front of the knee, a slight bend is built into the knee. Later, when we setup inverse kinematics (IK) linkages for the leg, this will help the knee bend in the proper direction more easily.*

6 Starting from the first bone in the chain, select each bone separately and rename it. Name the first bone Bone_UpLeg_R. Name the second Bone_LoLeg_R. Name the third Bone_Foot_R. Name the fourth Bone_Toes_R, and name the last bone Bone_ToesTip_R.

This will be one of the most critical naming systems in your film project for several reasons. Making sure all the bones begin with the prefix "bone" (adding a prefix for your character's name) will allow you to quickly select bones from the name-selection dialog boxes. More importantly, having the bones named logically for their position in the skeleton will greatly simplify the process of adding wire parameters and script controllers later on.

7 Switch to a front viewport and zoom in on the legs. Notice that the bones have been created over the origin of the X-axis so that they run down the center of the character (see Figure 10-6a). Select the Bone_UpLeg_R bone and move it to the left so that its pivot point is in the center of the top of Felix's right leg.

8 Select the Bone_LoLeg_R bone and move it to the left to be in the center of the knee.

9 Select the Bone_Foot_R bone and rotate it in the local Z-axis so that the bones of the foot are aligned vertically (see Figure 10-6b). The geometry for Felix's foot has been modeled so that the foot is flat on the ground plane.

10 Switch to a perspective view and select the Bone_UpLeg_R and Bone_LoLeg_R bones. In the Bone Tools window, open the Fin Adjustment Tools rollout. Click the Back Fin check box to turn on the back fins for these bones. Then give the fins a size of 8.

FIGURE 10-6 In the front viewport, the bones of the leg (a) have been moved and rotated into position inside the geometry of the leg (b).

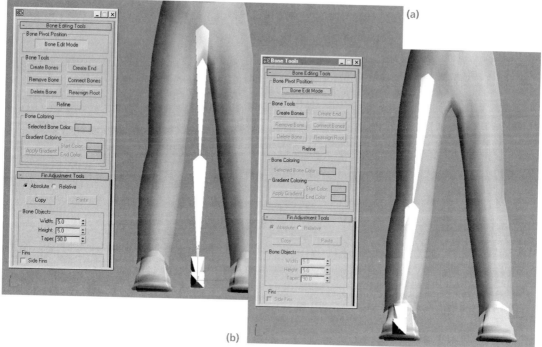

(a)

(b)

FIGURE 10-7   This image indicates that the back fins have been turned on for the upper and lower leg bones and that the side fins have been turned on for the bones of the foot.

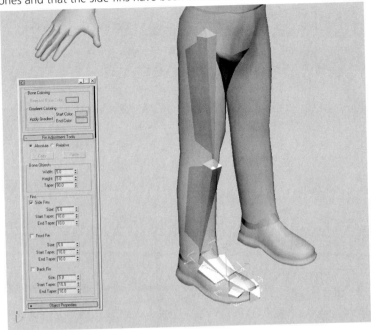

11   Select the Bone_Foot_R and Bone_Toes_R bones and click the Side Fins check box. Give these fins a size of 5 (see Figure 10-7).

These fins will not only show the orientation of the bones, revealing the alignment of their axes, they also give a quick visual idea of the character's volume, even when the geometry is hidden. Fins also affect the initial envelope size when the Skin modifier is applied, as you'll see later in this chapter.

12   Though not strictly necessary, you can give the bones color by using the Bone Coloring tool in the Bone Editing Tools rollout of the Bone Tools window. The most common rigging convention is to make the right leg green.

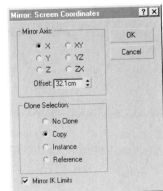

13   In a front view, select all the bones for the right leg and mirror them along the X-axis. Click the Copy radio button and use the Offset spinner to position the new set of bones (see Figure 10-8).

FIGURE 10-8   Here, the bones of the right leg have been mirrored to create the bones of the left leg.

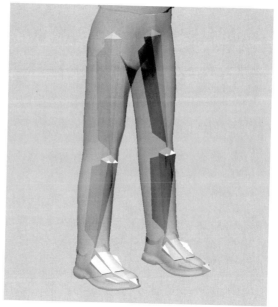

14 Mirroring the original right leg bone hierarchy will cause the new bones to have the same names with a "01" appended. Rename all the new bones so that their names correspond to the left leg. For example, rename the Bone_UpLeg_R01 bone object Bone_UpLeg_L, and so on, down the hierarchy.

15 Again, the bones of the left leg can be colored. The most common convention is to make the left leg blue.

Creating the Spine Bones

For added simplicity when rigging and animating the spine, we'll create a spine with a minimal number of bones. This means fewer bones to animate as well as fewer bones to connect to the mesh with the Skin modifier. We mainly need the spine to bend at its base near the hips, at the lower back, and the upper back in the neck. Here are the steps to follow:

1 Change to a right viewport and zoom in on the character's torso area. Click the Create Bones tool in the Bones Tools window.

2 Create the bones of the spine starting at the tailbone and working up toward the neck. Click just behind the tops of the upper leg bones to make the first bone. If you click too close to the existing leg bones, the new bone will be automatically connected to these. If this happens, right-click to cancel and start the bone further away. Make the second bone at the curve of the lower back. Make the third bone at the top center of the shoulders (the base of the neck), and make the last bone at the top of the neck. Right-click twice to create a fifth, tip bone and then cancel out of the tool. Figure 10-9 shows the spine bones from two different vantage points so that you can see their position within the torso.

3 Starting at the bottom of the chain, name the objects Bone_Spine01, Bone_Spine02, Bone_Spine03, Bone_Neck, and Bone_NeckTip.

4 Turn on front and side fins for the spine bones and adjust them so that the fins occupy most of the volume of the torso.

5 The spine bones can be given a yellow color.

FIGURE 10-9   The bones of the spine are created near the back of the geometry in keeping with human anatomy. This is a very simplified skeleton for easier rigging and animation.

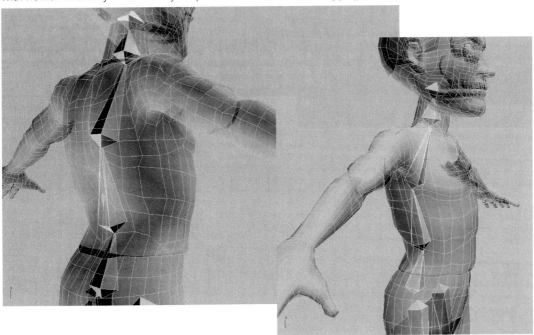

Creating the Arm Bones

For the arm bones, we need simply a clavicle, upper arm, and forearm. Creating these bones in the top view and drawing from right to left will cause the rear fins to face backward like we want. Follow these steps:

1   In a top view, zoom in to focus on the torso and right arm. Using the Create Bones tool, click near the center of the spine to establish the base of the clavicle bone. Next, click near the base of the arm, then toward the rear of the elbow, and then in the center of the wrist. Finally, right-click twice to establish a tip bone and cancel out of the Create Bones tool (see Figure 10-10a).

Initial placement of these bones is not crucial because they are being created on the ground plane anyway (see Figure 10-10b). Now they will need to be moved into their final positions from a front viewport. Normally, if a bone is moved or rotated, its children bones are moved or rotated along with it. This can make it hard to adjust bone positions once they are created. In Bone Edit mode, however, individual bones within a hierarchy can be adjusted without affecting their children.

2   In a front viewport, select the first bone in the arm chain and move it up near the base of the neck, as shown in Figure 10-11. Zoom in on the torso and right arm.

3   In the Bone Tools window, click the Bone Edit Mode button. In the viewport, use the Move tool and select the third bone in the chain (what will be the forearm). Move this

FIGURE 10-10   The bones of the arm are created in a top view (a) so that the back fins of the bones will be facing to the rear of the character. By creating the bones in a top view, they are initially on the ground plane (b).

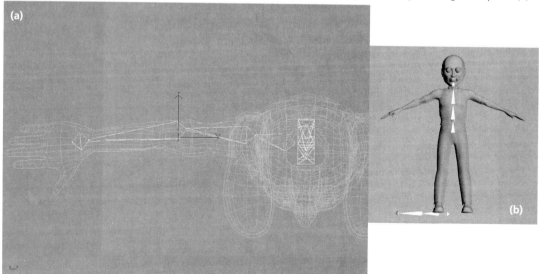

FIGURE 10-11 The bones of the arm are moved by selecting the first bone and moving it up to the shoulder.

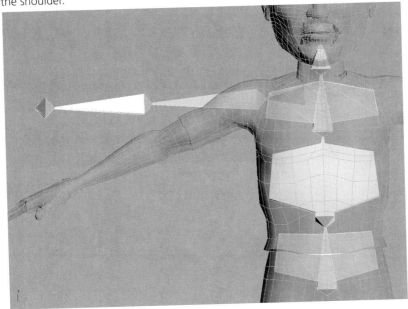

bone so that its base (which is also its pivot point) is in the center of the elbow. Select the last bone in the chain, the tip, and move it until its pivot point is in the center of the wrist. Then rotate this bone until it points down the hand geometry in the same direction as the fingers (see Figure 10-12).

4 Starting at the base of the hierarchy, name the bones Bone_Clav_R, Bone_UpArm_R, Bone_LoArm_R, and Bone_ArmTip_R

5 Assign the right arm bones a green color.

6 Adjust the side and front fins of the upper and lower arm bones so that they occupy the volume of the arm mesh.

Creating the Hand Bones

The bones of the hand will consist of several chains—one for the hand as well as one each for the fingers and for the thumb. The bones of the hand will remain separate from the bones in the arm and connected in the rigging process later. Here are the steps to follow for this exercise:

1 Set the default bone size to 3×3 cm.

FIGURE 10-12   The bones of the arm are put in their final positions by moving the forearm bone in Bone Edit mode.

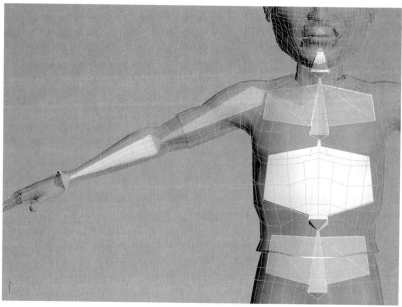

2 In a top view, zoom in on the right hand. With the Create Bones tool, click near the end of the Bone_LoArm_R bone so that the new hand hierarchy will start at the wrist. Then click just past the base of the fingers and right-click twice to create a tip bone and cancel out of the Create Bones tool (see Figure 10-13a).

3 Use the Align tool to align the pivot point of the new hand bone to the position and orientation of the pivot point of the Bone_ArmTip_R bone.

4 In a front viewport, move the new tip bone down so that the hand bone follows the direction of the hand mesh (see Figure 10-13b).

5 Name these new bones Bone_Hand_R and Bone_HandTip_R and assign them a green color.

6 Turn on the side fins for the Bone_Hand_R bone. Because it is aligned vertically, rotate this bone –90 degrees along its local X-axis (see Figure 10-14).

7 Set the default bone size to 1.5×1.5 cm.

FIGURE 10-13   The bones of the hand are created in a top viewport (a) and moved into position in the front viewport (b).

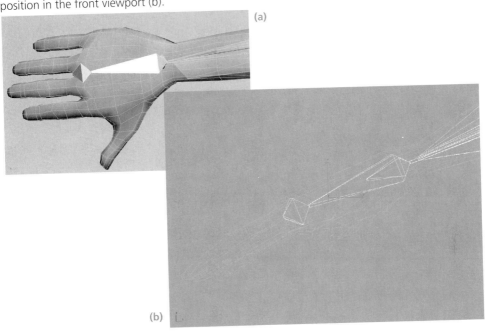

(a)

(b)

FIGURE 10-14   The hand bone has its side fins turned on and is rotated 90 degrees.

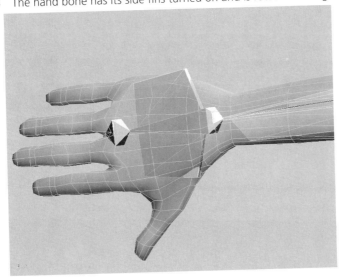

8 Create the first finger bones in a front view. Their placement can be loose at this point. With the Create Bones tool, click at the base of the fingers, then at the first knuckle, the second knuckle, and then at the very tip of the finger. Right-click twice to create a tip bone and cancel out of the Create Bones tool (see Figure 10-15).

9 In a top viewport, select the first bone in the finger hierarchy (see Figure 10-16a) and move it to the base of the index finger geometry. Rotate it in the Z-axis to align the finger bones with the direction of the index finger geometry (see Figure 10-16b).

10 In Bone Edit mode, you can move each finger bone pivot between the double edge loops of each knuckle of the index finger geometry. You will want to check the position of the finger bones from different angles using a perspective view (see Figure 10-17). Move the tip bone so that it rests on the end of the finger.

11 Starting with the base of the hierarchy, name the finger bones Bone_Fin1_1_R, Bone_Fin1_2_R, Bone_Fin1_3_R, and Bone_Fin1_Tip_R.

12 In a top view, select all the finger bones and move them while holding down the SHIFT key to clone them. Move them up roughly into the position of the middle finger.

13 Rename these new bones Bone_Fin2_1_R, Bone_Fin2_2_R, Bone_Fin2_3_R, and Bone_Fin2_Tip_R.

FIGURE 10-15 The bones of the initial finger are created in a front viewport.

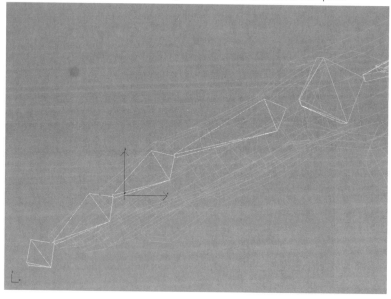

FIGURE 10-16　The bones of the initial finger (a) are moved into place in the top viewport to become the index finger (b).

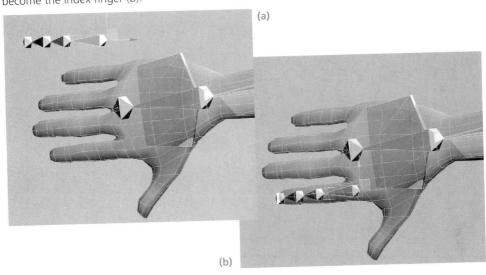

(a)

(b)

14　Use Bone Edit mode to reposition these bones to align with the geometry of the middle finger.

FIGURE 10-17　It will be necessary to check the positions of the finger bones from different angles, preferably in a perspective view. This way, the bones can be precisely positioned between the edge loops that make the bending points in the geometry.

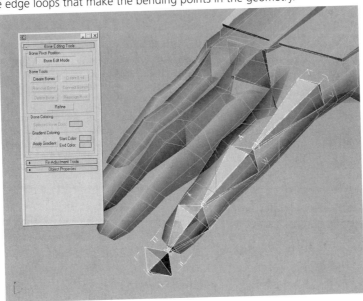

15 Repeat this procedure for the third and fourth fingers (see Figure 10-18).

16 In a top view, create the bones for the thumb by clicking near the base of the thumb geometry, then at the first thumb knuckle, at the second knuckle, and then at the very tip of the thumb geometry. Then double-right-click to create a tip bone and cancel out of the Create Bones tool (see Figure 10-19).

17 In a front viewport, select the root bone of the thumb hierarchy and move it up near the geometry of the hand. Rotate this bone on its local X-axis so that its Z-axis will swivel in the direction of the thumb geometry.

18 Switch to Bone Edit mode and move the thumb bones into position in a perspective viewport (see Figure 10-20).

19 Select the first bone of all four fingers and the thumb and link them to the Bone_Hand_R bone.

20 Now you can mirror the arm and hand bones in a front viewport in the same way you mirrored the leg bones. The position of the new bones for the left arm needs to be precise so that all the finger bones match the geometry. To do this, select all the arm

FIGURE 10-18 Here, the bones of the fingers have been duplicated and positioned within the geometry of the hand.

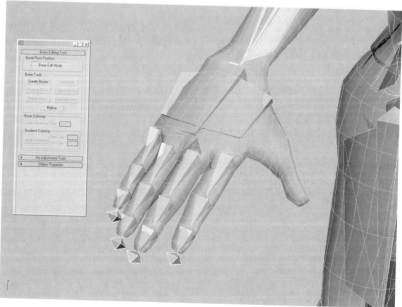

FIGURE 10-19   The bones of the thumb are created in a top viewport.

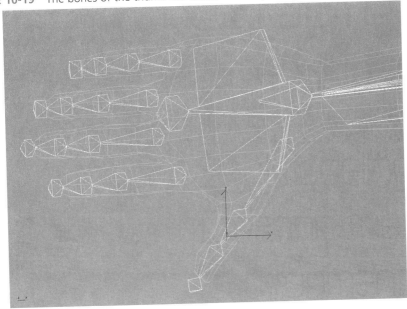

and hand bones. Then zoom in on the clavicle and spine bones before clicking the Mirror tool and using the Offset spinner in the Mirror dialog box (see Figure 10-21). Once you've mirrored the arm and hand, zoom in on the left fingers to make sure the bones are positioned properly. If they are not, select the entire left arm and hand and move them slightly in the X-axis.

FIGURE 10-20   Here, the bones of the thumb have been moved into position using Bone Edit mode.

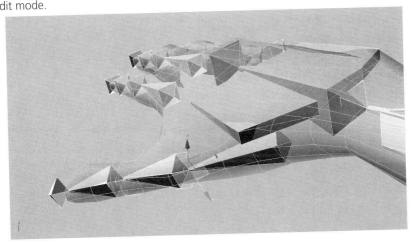

FIGURE 10-21   Even though all the bones of the arm and hand are being mirrored, it is helpful to zoom in on the clavicle bone so that the new hierarchical chain of bones can be placed exactly opposite the other chain.

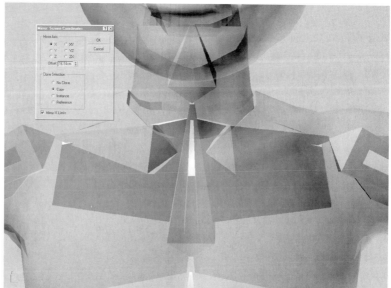

21 Use the Rename Objects tool to change the names of these bones so that they refer to the left side. You'll do this for all the bones at the same time. Select all the bones of the left arm and hand and choose Tool | Rename Objects from the main menu. Use the settings shown here in the dialog box. When the bones were copied and mirrored, the new bones were, by default, given the same names as the originals with a "01" tacked onto the end, so removing the last three characters removes this and the "R," which you'll replace with "L."

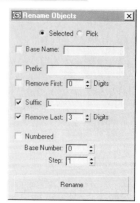

Creating the Head Bones

Similar to the bones in the hand, the head bone and its terminator will be on a separate chain from the spine so that they can be rigged independently later. Here are the steps:

1 In a right viewport, create the bones for the head. Start the head bone close to the neck tip bone but just far enough away so that it is not automatically connected. Click again at the top of the head and then right-click twice to create the tip bone. Name these bones Bone_Head and Bone_HeadTip (see Figure 10-22a).

2 Select the Bone_Head bone and align it with the position of the Bone_NeckTip bone. You can then turn on the fins for this bone (see Figure 10-22b).

FIGURE 10-22   The bones for the head are created near the neck tip bone in a right viewport (a), and then the head bone is aligned exactly with the neck tip bone (b).

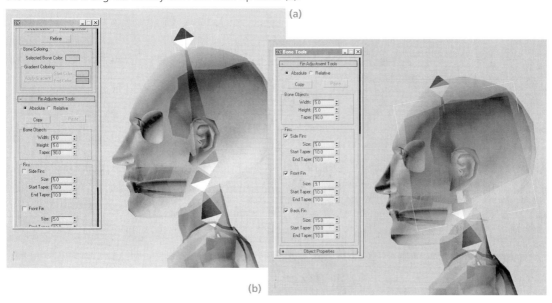

(a)

(b)

You can look at the completed skeleton in the file …\3dsmax6_CD\Felix\felix_bones.max.

Rigging the Skeleton: Giving Your Character Handles

Although the term *rigging* often refers to the entire practice of creating skeletons, character controls, and skinning of characters, it's also used more specifically to refer to creating systems of linkage and control for the character's skeletal structure.

We'll now take advantage of 3ds max's inverse kinematics, helper objects, custom attributes, and wire parameter capabilities to establish a system of handles for our example character.

Merging Control Shape Objects

Most character riggers will create control handles for their characters made out of simple spline shape objects. Then they will rig their characters so that these control shapes are the only objects that need to be touched to animate their characters. This way, animators can turn on the Shapes selection filter to simplify animating.

To be sure, simple circles, ellipses, and rectangles can suffice for these purposes, but riggers will often create custom spline shapes to help visually indicate what their function is. Because building these control shapes is a very simple modeling exercise, I won't take up space in this chapter with building them. The file …/3dsmax6_CD/Felix/felix_controls_only.max contains shape objects that we'll use to control the Felix character. These objects, shown in Figure 10-23, are all simple shapes that will be rigged to the bones. They serve the simple purpose of being

FIGURE 10-23   These shape objects have been created simply from line primitives such as Circle and Ellipse and then converted to Editable Spline objects for further modeling. Their design is only to visually indicate their function. The shapes act as handles for the character once the rigging is completed.

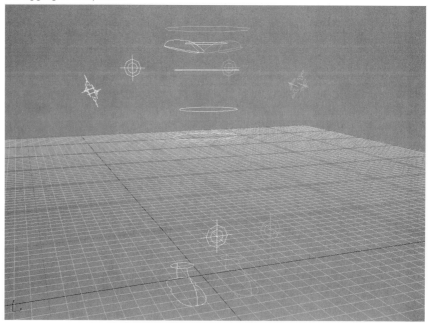

"handles" that are selected and rotated or moved. The pivot points of each shape object are aligned exactly in both position and orientation with the pivot points of the bones they are intended to control.

Forward Kinematics and Inverse Kinematics

A key rigging concept centers on the way the transforms of bones are manipulated. In a typical hierarchy, forward kinematics (FK) is used, meaning all transforms are translated down the hierarchy from parent to child. This method requires the top bones in the hierarchy to be rotated and then their children rotated separately down the chain of the hierarchy. On the other hand, when inverse kinematics (IK) is used, the rotations of the hierarchy are controlled automatically to follow an inverse kinematic goal helper object at the end of the chain. When IK is used, transforms are translated backward up the chain of the hierarchy from child to parent. For example, with forward kinematics, if you want a hand bone to move to a target, the upper arm must be rotated to get the hand as close as possible to the target. Then the forearm must be rotated to place the hand in the desired position. To make the same hierarchy rigged with inverse kinematics point to the target, the goal, represented by a blue cross, is simply moved to the target in a one-step operation. To make this exercise simpler, Figure 10-24 provides a comparison of these two methods.

FIGURE 10-24   This comparison shows the difference between a simple arm bone hierarchy reaching for a target with forward kinematics and then inverse kinematics. With forward kinematics, the first bone must be rotated (a) and then the second bone (b). With inverse kinematics, the last bone in the chain is simply moved to the target in a one-step operation (c).

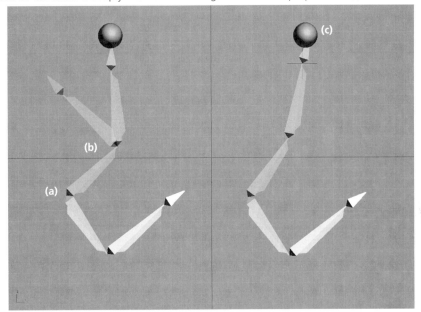

Both of these methods have strengths and weaknesses, and one or the other can be useful in different areas of a character rig, depending on the preferences of the animator. Furthermore, both methods can be controlled procedurally. For example, an IK goal can be linked to other objects so that they can be controlled from different pivot points, and a forward kinematics chain can be driven by wire parameters. You'll see examples of both as we proceed.

Rigging the Legs and Feet
To rig the legs and feet, we'll use a series of inverse kinematics chains whose IK goals will be linked to dummy helper objects and, in turn, to the control shape objects for the feet.

Adding IK to Bones   The actual rigging process begins with adding inverse kinematics to the bones. The IK goals become control points affecting several bones at once. These will, in turn, be controlled by shape objects that will be added later. Continue working on the file in which you have created the bones or open the file …\3dsmax6_CD\Felix\felix_bones.max. Here are the steps to follow:

1   Hide everything except the bones of the right leg and right foot and the Foot_CTRL_R shape object.

2 Create an IK chain for the leg. Select the Bone_UpLeg_R bone object and from the main menu, choose Animation | IK Solver | HI Solver. A dashed rubber band line will appear. Click the Fel_Bone_Foot_R bone object. A blue cross will appear at the ankle joint (see Figure 10-25). This is the IK goal. Select it and name it IK_Ankle_R.

3 In the Motion panel, in the IK Display Options rollout, set the Goal Display size to 25 cm.

Now you can move the IK_Ankle_R object around in the viewport and see the bones of the leg follow it. But note that rotating this IK goal does nothing. We'll rig controls to move this goal shortly. Make sure to undo any movements to the IK_Ankle_R goal object before moving on.

4 Now select the foot bone, Bone_Foot_R, and again choose HI Solver from the main menu. Then click the Bone_Toe_R bone. This creates a second IK chain between the ankle and the ball of the foot. Name the new IK goal IK_Ball_R. Moving it in the viewport will only move the foot because the leg is being controlled by the IK_Ankle_R goal.

5 Set the size of this IK goal to 20 cm.

FIGURE 10-25   The blue cross, or goal, at the ankle indicates the end of the inverse kinematics chain. When this target is moved, the bones in the leg will follow while maintaining their pivot points.

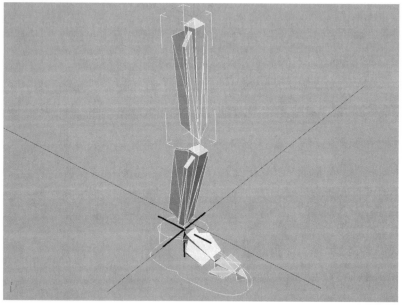

6 Select the Bone_Toes_R bone object and choose HI Solver from the main menu. Then click the Bone_ToesTip_R bone object to create the third and last IK chain for the leg. Name this IK goal IK_Toes_R. Moving this goal will move only the toes now.

7 Set the size of this IK goal to 15 cm (see Figure 10-26).

Making Foot Controls   As you've noticed, although we want to rotate the different parts of the foot independently, rotating the IK goals has no effect. However, moving them does. It would be awkward to animate the foot and leg by moving the IK goals. But if the IK goals are linked to dummy objects that rotate, then the goals will rotate around the pivot points of their parent dummy objects. Follow these steps to create the foot controls:

1 From the main menu, choose Create | Helpers | Dummy. Then click and drag on the ground plane next to the foot assembly, to create a dummy object roughly the size shown in Figure 10-27. Use the Align tool to align the dummy's pivot point to both the position and orientation of the IK_Ankle_R goal object. Name this dummy object Ankle_Helper_R.

2 Create another dummy roughly the same size and align its pivot point with the position and orientation of the IK_Ball_R goal object. Name this dummy object BallRoll_Helper_R.

FIGURE 10-26   Here, the other IK chains have been created for the foot and for the toes.

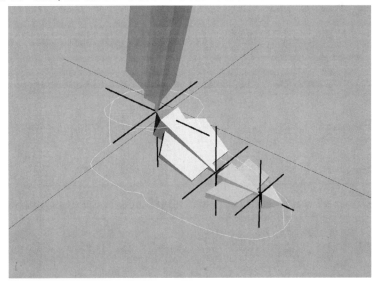

FIGURE 10-27   This dummy object is aligned exactly with the foot bone and will eventually control the rotation of the ankle.

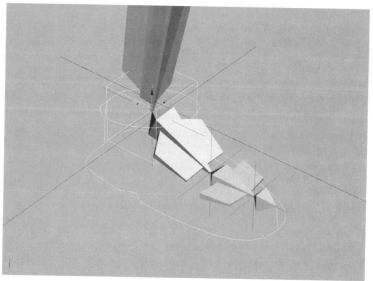

3   Create a third dummy object somewhat smaller than the other two and align this one to the IK_Ball_R goal object as well. Name this dummy object Toe_Helper_R (see Figure 10-28).

Linking Helpers and Goals   The next steps are deceptively simple, consisting of linking the IK goals and dummy objects together. However, this system of basic hierarchical links is what will provide us with the complex control for the foot. Follow these steps:

1   Using the Select and Link tool, select the IK_Ball_R goal object and drag to the Ankle_Helper_R dummy object. Now rotating the Ankle_Helper_R dummy object will control the ball of the foot to roll the foot back on its ankle.

2   Link the IK_Toes_R goal to the Toe_Helper_R dummy object. Now rotating Toe_Helper_R will control the toes.

3   Link the IK_Ankle_R goal object to the BallRoll_Helper_R dummy object. Now rotating BallRoll_Helper_R will control the ankle lifting the back of the foot and rolling it on the ball.

FIGURE 10-28   These two new dummy objects are aligned exactly with the bone of the toes. The smaller one will control the rotation of the toes, and the larger one will control the rotation of the foot at the ball.

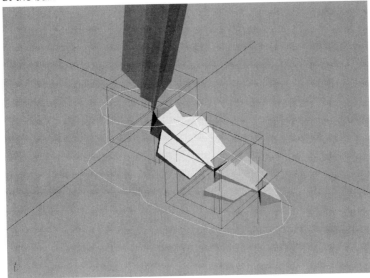

4 Select both the BallRoll_Helper_R and Toe_Helper_R dummy objects and drag to the Ankle_Helper_R dummy object. Now the entire foot will lift when Ankle_Helper_R is rotated.

5 Link the Ankle_Helper_R dummy object to the Foot_CTRL_R shape object. The pivot point for the Foot_CTRL_R is located at the tip of the toe so that the whole foot can be rotated from that point.

6 You can visualize this hierarchy by using the Schematic view. Select the dummy objects and the IK goal objects in the viewport. Click the Schematic View button in the main toolbar. In the Schematic View menu, choose View | Zoom Extends Selected (see Figure 10-29).

Here, you can see the hierarchical relationships between the objects in the foot assembly. The Schematic view is not only a tool in which you can view the relationships of objects, but you can manipulate them as well. You can link objects in the Schematic view as well as establish wire parameter connections and other types of connections.

Now the placement of the foot and the entire leg can be animated by moving the Foot_CTRL_R object. Then the various rotations of the foot can be animated by rotating the dummy objects.

FIGURE 10-29   The Schematic view shows iconic representations of objects, modifiers, controllers, and many other aspects of a max scene. This view shows the hierarchical arrangement of the foot's dummy objects and the IK goals. The lines between the icons show how the objects are parented.

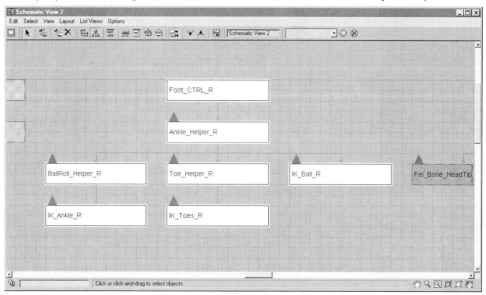

When the knee is bent, the inverse kinematics calculations automatically decide which way the knee should point. You can give the knee joint a target so that you can animate this orientation.

7 Select the IK_Ankle_R goal object and go to the Motion panel. In the IK Solver Properties rollout, click the button labeled None and then click the target-shaped Knee_CTRL_R object in the viewport. Now this Knee_CTRL_R object can be animated to swivel the position of the knee.

The same rigging procedure can be repeated for the left leg. To take this method a step further in sophistication and make it so the leg can be animated without selecting helper objects, you can use wire parameters to control the dummy objects from the Foot_Control object. We'll explore wire parameters when rigging the hand.

🖐 NOTE   *You can continue working on the same file as you continue this tutorial, or you can open the file …\3dsmax6_CD\Felix\felix_legs_rigged.max to see the Felix rig completed to this point.*

3ds max 6 Animation:
CG Filmmaking from Concept to Completion

FIGURE 1

This is a scene from this book's example CG film, *The Game to Save the World*, which uses the setting of a fictitious online videogame. Here, Zoey and Felix's game characters tell each other a joke, while Carlo looks on.

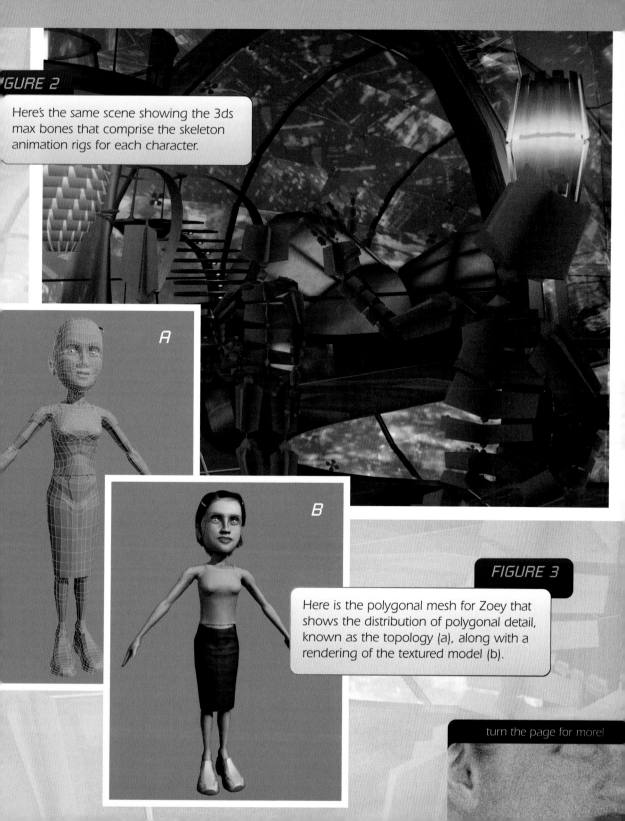

turn the page for more!

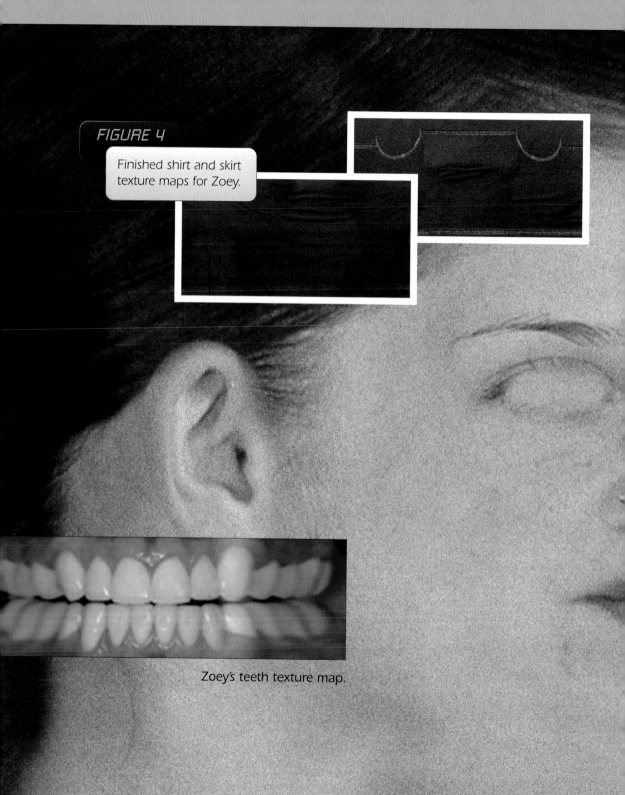

FIGURE 4

Finished shirt and skirt texture maps for Zoey.

Zoey's teeth texture map.

FIGURE 5

This is the finished facial texture map for Zoe
It was created in Photoshop starting with fro
and side photographs and is cylindrically
projected onto the Zoey head model.

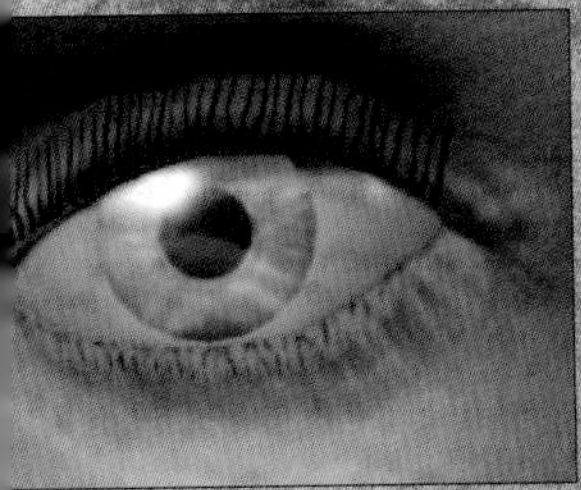

FIGURE 6

Here is the polygonal mesh for Zoey's
head showing the topology of the
face in detail and the textured head
with procedural hair applied.

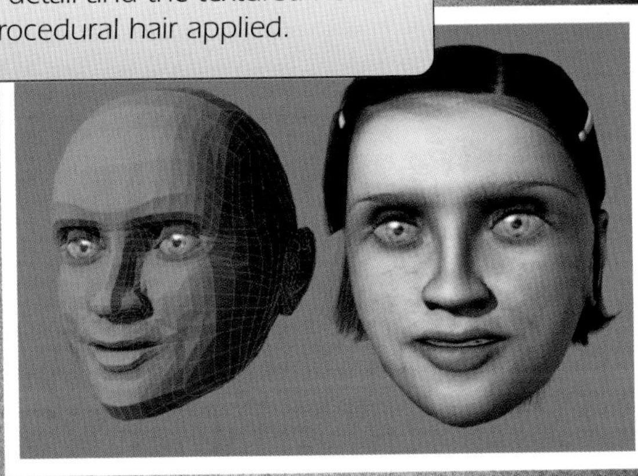

Zoey's morph targets. Each can be blended in varying degrees on its own and in combination with other targets. This way, an endless variety of facial expressions can be created even with this minimal set of morph targets.

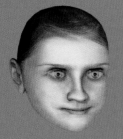

**M B & P
Close**

**A & I
Open**

**Brow
Up Left**

**Brow
Up Right**

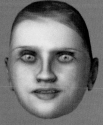

**Brow
Down L**

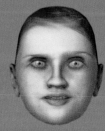

**Brow
Down R**

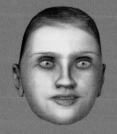

Furrow

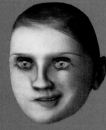

Mouth L

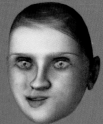

Mouth R

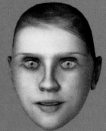

Stretch

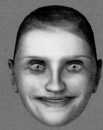

Smile

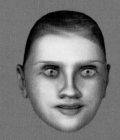

Nostrils

**EE
Sneer**

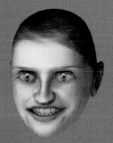

**EE
Wide**

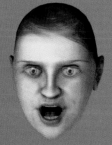

O

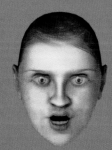

U & OO

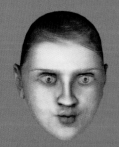

**W & Q
Pucker**

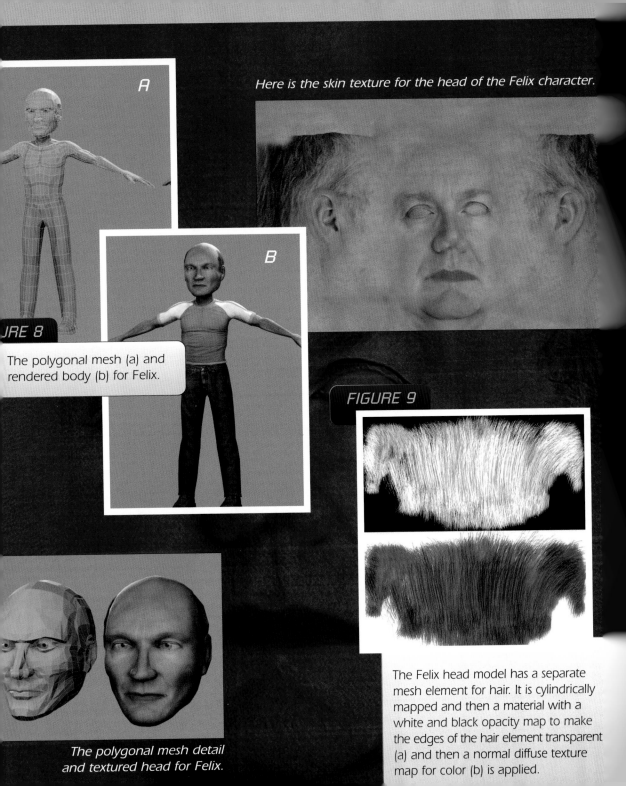

A

Here is the skin texture for the head of the Felix character.

B

JRE 8

The polygonal mesh (a) and rendered body (b) for Felix.

FIGURE 9

The polygonal mesh detail and textured head for Felix.

The Felix head model has a separate mesh element for hair. It is cylindrically mapped and then a material with a white and black opacity map to make the edges of the hair element transparent (a) and then a normal diffuse texture map for color (b) is applied.

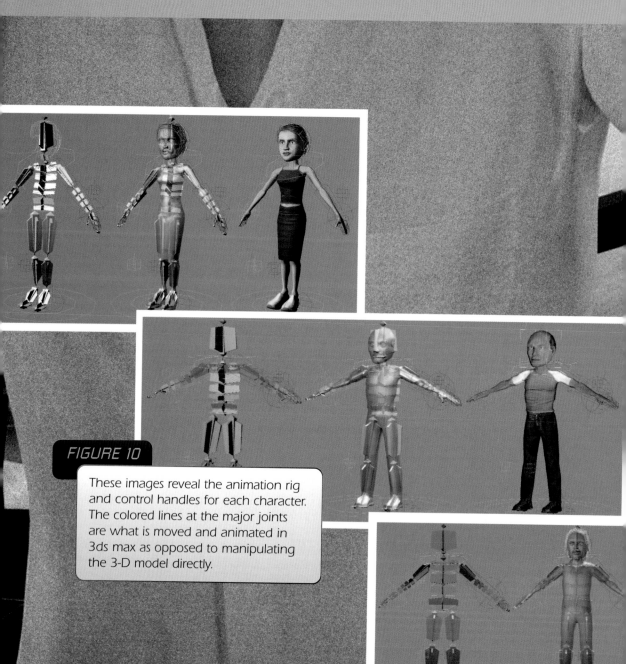

FIGURE 10

These images reveal the animation rig and control handles for each character. The colored lines at the major joints are what is moved and animated in 3ds max as opposed to manipulating the 3-D model directly.

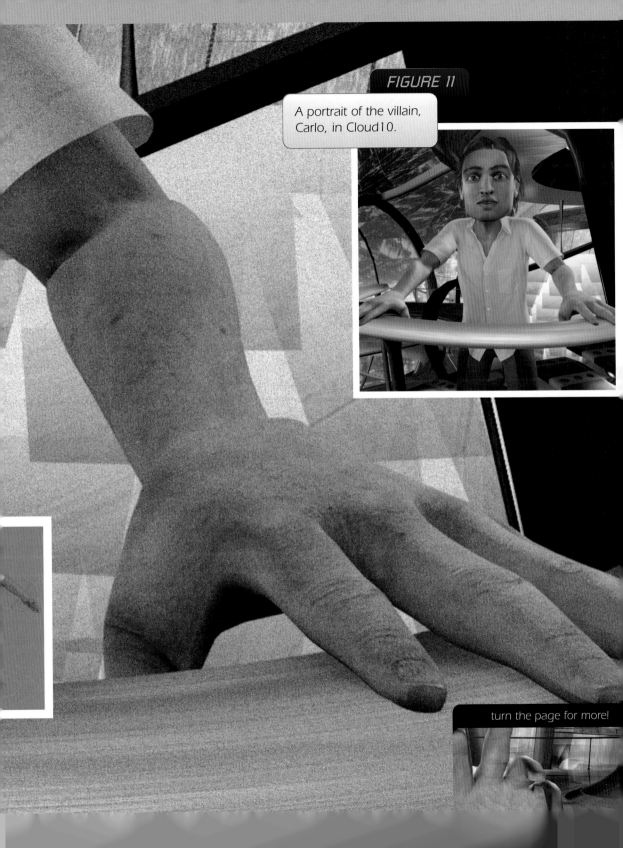

FIGURE 11

A portrait of the villain, Carlo, in Cloud10.

turn the page for more!

A portrait of Felix in Cloud10.

FIGURE 12

A portrait of Zoey showing her aura.
In the example film, she grows her aura
by playing the fictitious videogame that
is the film's setting. Her aura is created
using 3ds max's Particle Flow and the
Scatter compound object.

FIGURE 13

Felix's aura was constructed and animated using 3ds max particle systems and space warps.

The concept sketch for Felix's aura called for glassy green bubbles billowing out in a flame-like pattern.

FIGURE 14

The title of the film, *The Game to Save the World*, refers to the CG film's setting in a fictitious online videogame. The game interface was created using Adobe Illustrator and then composited with the rendered 3-D video using Discreet's Combustion. This is the videogame as seen through the eyes of Felix. The icons at the bottom of the screen are for controlling the gestures and expressions of his game character.

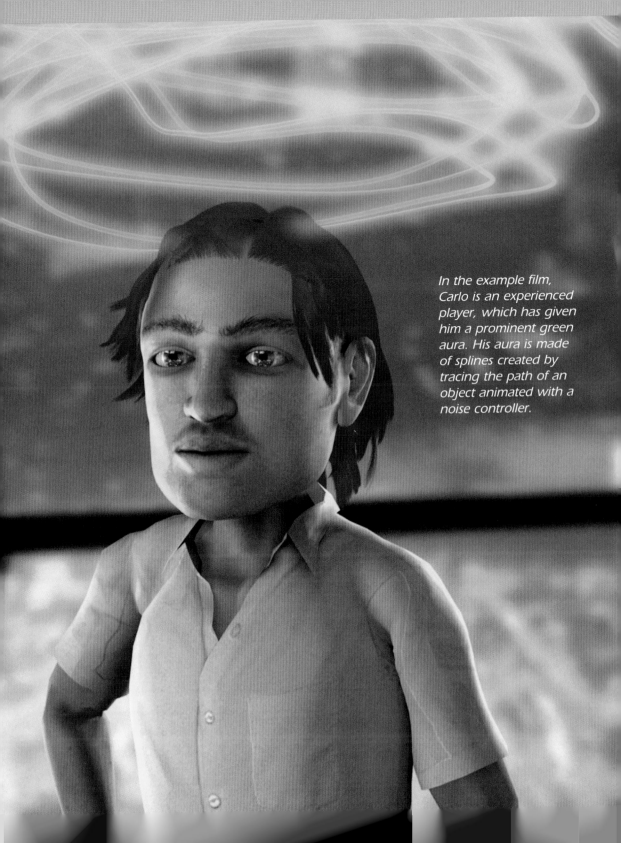

In the example film, Carlo is an experienced player, which has given him a prominent green aura. His aura is made of splines created by tracing the path of an object animated with a noise controller.

FIGURE 15

A bird's-eye view of Cloud10, the videogame environment that is the setting for *The Game to Save the World*.

The booths in Cloud10 take advantage of 3ds max's translucency shader. The shadow of the person inside is cast with a simple polygonal cutout instead of needing an entire 3-D character model.

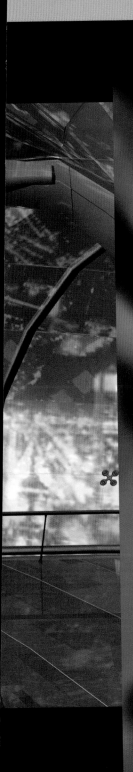

Character sketches are invaluable, not just for character design, but throughout the animating process. They are a valuable tool to help CG filmmakers work out the acting that they must animate their characters performing.

In this still from the example film, Zoey's game character tentatively and curiously enters Cloud10 for the first time. Her 3-D model has been posed and animated using 3ds max's bones which drive the Skin modifier.

Zoey wonders what the game has in store for her as she begins exploring Cloud10. As her character model moves through the 3-D environment from shot to shot, the lights that illuminate the Zoey model exclusively are changed in color and intensity to match the lighting of the scene.

Zoey is looking for her game-playing friend Felix as she looks off the balcony of Cloud10. A rendering of this scene without Zoey has been used as a reflection map on the glass material for the balcony's railing.

Zoey scans the scene of Cloud10 before she enters the thick of the socializing going on in the videogame. The lighting fixtures and Carlo's electric green aura have been given a glow post-rendering effect using 3ds max's Lens Effects.

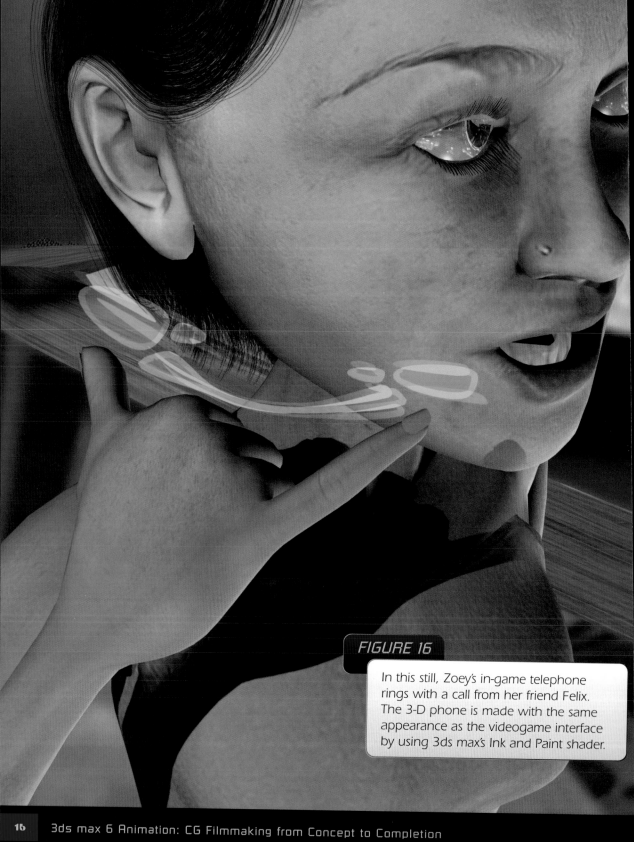

Rigging the Spine and Neck with Forward Kinematics

Because the spine was created simply with just a few bones, we can also take a simpler approach to rigging it. The spine and hips will be animated by simply rotating the yellow shape control objects. Follow these steps to complete this exercise:

1 Create a dummy object named Hip_Helper_R and align its pivot point with the position and orientation of the Bone_UpLeg_R bone object. Link the Bone_UpLeg_R bone object to this dummy object (see Figure 10-30).

2 Repeat this procedure for the left hip.

3 Link the two hip dummy objects to the Hips_CTRL_Rotate shape object (the smaller pink ellipse around the hips). The Hips_CTRL_Rotate shape object can now be rotated to control the hips.

The spine and neck are composed of a simple, single hierarchy of bones. Although it would be possible to animate the spine by manipulating these bone objects directly, to keep consistent with our plan to control only shape objects, all that is required is to simply put control shape

FIGURE 10-30   Dummy objects are created and aligned to the upper leg bones. The leg bones are linked to the dummy objects, and the dummy objects will be linked to the shape control object for the hips.

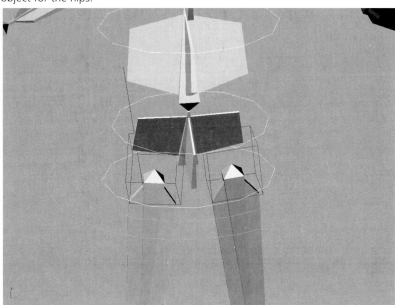

objects below each bone in the hierarchical order. As long as these control objects have their pivot points aligned to the position and orientation of the bone that is linked to them, these shapes can be rotated to animate the spine. The yellow ellipse control shapes have already been aligned, so you only need to relink the spine bones to them. Follow these steps:

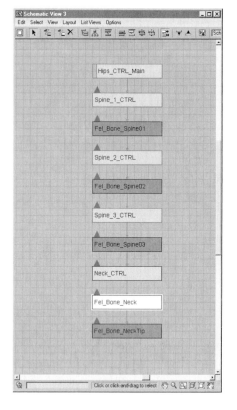

1 Link the Bone_Spine01 bone object to the Spine_1_CTRL shape object.

2 Link the Spine_2_CTRL shape object to the Bone_Spine01 bone object.

3 Link the Bone_Spine02 bone object to the Spine_2_CTRL shape object.

4 Link the Spine_3_CTRL shape object to the Bone_Spine02 bone object.

5 Link the Bone_Spine03 bone object to the Spine_3_CTRL shape object.

6 Link the Neck_CTRL shape object to the Bone_Spine03 bone object.

7 Link the Bone_Neck bone object to the Neck_CTRL shape object.

8 Now link both the Hips_CTRL_Rotate and Spine_1_CTRL shape objects to the Hips_CTRL_Move shape object.

With this arrangement, the hips and spine can be rotated independently. The Hips_CTRL_Move object can be moved to move the entire center of the character. However, if the Hips_CTRL_Rotate and Spine_1_CTRL objects are moved, the character will be split in half. This can be avoided by placing transform locks on these two objects.

9 To make it so that the spine and hips cannot be moved away from one another, select both the Hips_CTRL_Rotate and Spine_1_CTRL shape objects. Go to the Hierarchy panel and click all three Move locks. Now each of these control objects can be rotated but not moved directly. They can be moved simultaneously by moving the Hips_CTRL_Move object.

Rigging the Arms and Shoulders

To rig the arm, we need an IK chain at the wrist connected to the hand-control shape object and a simple forward kinematics rotation control for the shoulder-control shape object. Here are the steps to follow to for this exercise:

1 To create the main arm control at the wrist, select the Bone_UpArm_R bone and choose HI Solver from the main menu. Then click the Bone_ArmTip_R bone to create the IK chain. In the Motion panel, set the size of this IK goal display to 15. Name this new IK goal IK_Arm_R (see Figure 10-31).

2 Link the IK_Arm_R goal to the Hand_CTRL_R shape object that is aligned to the wrist bones. The Hand_CTRL_R can now be moved to control the arm.

3 Link the Bone_Clav_R bone object to the Clav_CTRL_R shape object. Now the Clav_CTRL_R object can be rotated to control the shoulder.

Rigging the Hands

Rigging the hands is complex for several reasons. The hands need to follow the position of the wrists as the arm moves, but it is easier to animate them if they have their own independent rotation controlled by the Hand_CTRL_R object. Also, we need to give the Hand_CTRL_R object some built-in controls so that we can animate the fingers automatically.

FIGURE 10-31   The IK goal of the wrist will control the bones for the upper and lower arm.

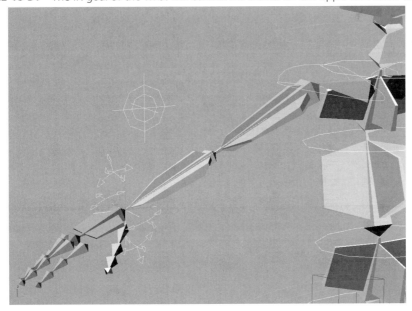

Rigging the Wrist   For the hand bone to move along with the bones of the arm while maintaining its own rotation, a more flexible hierarchical arrangement is needed than simple linking. To do this, we need to use animation constraints. The hand bone can be given a Position Constraint that locks it to the Bone_ArmTip_R bone object and then a separate Rotation Constraint to lock its orientation only to the Hand_CTRL_R shape object. Here are the steps to follow:

1   Select the Bone_Hand_R bone and from the main menu, choose Animation | Constraints | Position Constraint. Press the H key and select Bone_ArmTip_R from the object list (it is difficult to click this object in the viewport because it is hidden by the Bone_Hand_R object).

2   Choose Animation | Constraints | Orientation Constraint from the main menu and click the Hand_CTRL_R object in the viewport. This will cause the hand bone to flip as its orientation is made to match the Hand_CTRL_R object. However, this can be corrected in the Motion panel by first clicking the Rotation button in the PRS Parameters rollout and then clicking the Keep Initial Offset check box in the Orientation Constraint rollout.

Rigging the Fingers   We'll make the controls for the fingers associated with the Hand_CTRL_R object so that all the animation tracks for the hand and fingers will be contained within one object. This is done by creating custom attributes for the Hand_CTRL_R object and then using wire parameters to connect the custom attributes to individual rotation axes in each finger bone. This way, the fingers can be animated by adjusting spinners in the Modify Panel when the Hand_CTRL_R object is selected.

Adding Custom Attributes to the Hand_CTRL_R Object   Adding Custom Attributes for the editable spline Hand_CTRL_R Object will cause new spinners to show up in the Modify panel. Once these Custom Attributes are wired, values can be entered setting keyframes for whatever they control.

1   If needed, copy the MAXScript file from the max installation, …\3dsmax6\scripts\ PluginScripts\Modifier-AttributeHolder.ms to the folder \3dsmax6\stdplugs\stdscripts\. Save the file you are working on and restart max.

2   Zoom in on the hand in a perspective viewport and select the Hand_CTRL_R object. In the Modify panel, click the Modifier List drop-down menu and choose Attribute Holder to assign it. Using this modifier will cause any custom attributes added to be the only thing visible in the Modify panel for this object because it is now the top modifier in the stack.

3 From the main menu, choose Animation | Add Custom Attribute. In the Add Parameters dialog box, fill in the fields, as shown here. At the bottom, you can see a test version of the attribute that will be added to the Hand_CTRL_R object. The Name field at the top of the dialog box provides a name for the custom attribute. Name this first CA "Index." The Width field defines how many pixels wide the input field will be. Make this 85. The Range values define the numerical values that the spinner will output. Give them values of –10 and 80. Also, choosing Object's Current Modifier from the Add Attribute to Type drop-down list causes the custom attribute to be added to the Attribute Holder modifier.

4 Click the Add button and see the Index custom attribute appear in the Modify panel.

5 Repeat this procedure, creating four other identical custom attributes named Middle, Ring, Pinkie, and Thumb.

6 Create one last custom attribute named Spread, with Range values of –10 and 20.

Using Wire Parameters to Connect the Finger Bones   These next steps are somewhat tedious because they require both a fair amount of repetition and attention to detail. We'll wire the numeric values from the Custom Attribute spinners to the rotation axes in the finger bones. If this is done directly, each bone will snap its rotation to match the current value of the custom attribute. To avoid this, we'll add a list controller to any rotational axis that will be connected to a custom attribute. A list controller allows there to be several inputs into the transform of an object and blends between them. Here are the steps to follow:

1 Check to see which axis you need to use to rotate the finger bones up and down. Using the Move tool, set to Local Axis, select one of the finger bones. You can see from its tripod that the Z-axis will be the one that needs to rotate (see Figure 10-32).

FIGURE 10-32   With the Reference Coordinate System set to Local, you can select the bones in the fingers and see that the Z-axis will rotate them in the proper direction.

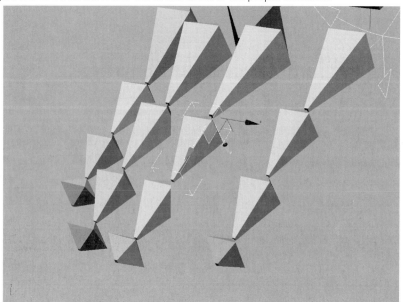

2   For each finger and thumb bone (except for the tip bones), go to the Motion panel and click the Assign Controller rollout. Use the plus signs in the tree view to navigate down to the Z Rotation Bezier controller. Then click the Assign Controller button and choose Float List from the dialog box.

3   For each of the root bones of the finger chains (Bone_Fin1_1_R, Bone_Fin2_1_R, Bone_Fin3_1_R, Bone_Fin4_1_R, and Bone_Thumb_1_R) assign a List controller to its Y-axis as well. This will be for the Spread custom attribute.

4   Now select the Hand_CTRL_R object. From the main menu, choose Animation | Wire Parameters and navigate to the Index custom attribute, as shown in Figure 10-33a. Then, with the dashed rubber band active, click the first bone of the index finger (Bone_Fin1_1_R) and navigate its pop-up menus, as shown in Figure 10-33b.

5   This will pop up the Parameter Wiring dialog box with the Index custom attribute in the left tree view and the Z Rotation List controller for Bone_Fin1_1_R in the right tree view. In the right tree view, click the plus sign (+) next to the Z Rotation: Float List track and then select the Available track. In the top center are direction buttons that dictate

FIGURE 10-33   The process of wiring the Index custom attribute of the hand-control object to the Z-rotation of the finger bones is done by selecting and right-clicking the Hand_CTRL_R object, navigating in the menus to the Index custom attribute (a) and then clicking a finger bone and navigating the pop-up menus again to its Available track in its Z-rotation list controller (b).

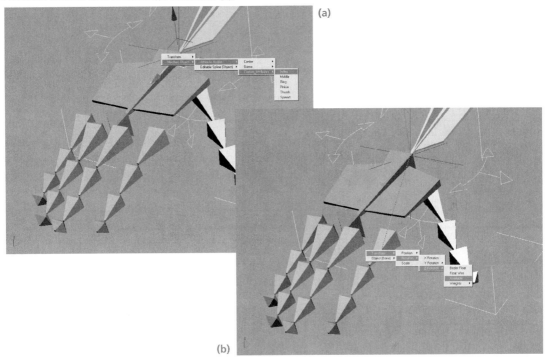

which field will control the other. Click the right arrow so that the Index custom attribute will control the rotation, and then click the Connect button (see Figure 10-34).

Without closing the Parameter Wiring dialog box, go to the Modify panel and move the Index spinner. You'll see that the index finger bone rotates around many times when it should simply bend downward. This is because the custom attribute is outputting a numerical value between −10 and 80, but the rotations for max bone objects are measured in radians. A *radian* is a numerical value that expresses an angle in relation to *pi*.

Luckily, max has a built-in math function, DegToRad, that converts numerical values into radians automatically. This is done in the expression field at the bottom right of the Parameter Wiring dialog box. This expression window is where you can write extensive mathematical expressions to control how one parameter is wired to another. This is a powerful capability of 3ds max that anyone with a modicum of mathematical skill can exploit to great effect.

6   In the expression field, change the expression "Index" (signifying a straight one-to-one wiring) to "DegToRad(Index)" and then click the Update button. Now if you move the

FIGURE 10-34   The Parameter Wiring dialog box shows the parameter of one object in the left hierarchical tree view and the parameter of another object in the right hierarchical tree view. The connection between these two parameters is shown with the arrow buttons in the center. Also, the fields at the bottom can be used to define the relationship between the wired parameters with mathematical and logical expressions.

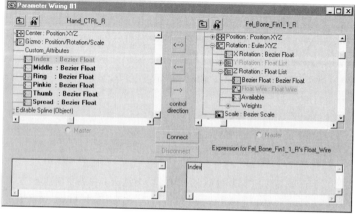

spinner for the Index custom attribute in the Modify panel, the finger bone should rotate a reasonable amount.

7 Now the other finger bones need to be wired in the same manner. Wire the Index custom attribute to the other two index finger bones (Bone_Fin1_2_R and Bone_Fin1_3_R) in the same way, and then wire the Middle custom attribute to the middle finger bones in the same manner, testing the appropriate spinner as you go.

Now you can experiment with the character rig. Move or rotate the various control shape objects to see how the skeleton moves. Be sure to undo any transforms when you're done.

Analyzing the Entire Rig with Schematic View   A new feature in 3ds max 6 expands the capabilities of the Schematic View by allowing you to use a screenshot or a rendering as a background image for the Schematic View and automatically synchronizing the Schematic View's icons with this image. This allows you to see the icons and connections of many different relationships like axes constraints and hierarchical parenting related visually to the 3-D objects they signify. This is done taking a screenshot from your viewport and then using a utility called Project into Schematic View. This MAXScript utility is added to the right-click menu of the Schematic View. Here's how to do it:

1 The Project into Schematic View MAXScript utility comes with max. Copy the file \3dsmax6\scripts\maxscripttools\macro_schematicviewtools.mcr to the folder \3dsmax6\ui\macroscripts and then restart max.

2 From the main menu, choose Customize | Customize User Interface, and then choose the Quads tab. From the drop-down menu on the right, choose Schematic View. Scroll down the list on the left to find the Project into Schematic View command and drag it into the menu list on the right, and then close the Customize User Interface window.

3 Hide everything but the objects you want to visualize, select them and then frame them in your viewport. Use a screen capture utility to create an image of the viewport. Click the Open Schematic View button and then choose Option | Preferences from the Schematic View's main menu. In the background map slot, choose your screenshot file.

4 Right-click and choose Project into Schematic View from the quad menu. This will arrange the icons for your selected objects according to your viewport. You may need to move the icons manually to arrange them according to your background image.

5 Now you can save your Schematic View by entering a name for it in the blank Schematic View name field (it is the left of the two name fields at the top of the Schematic View). Later this named Schematic View can be called up by choosing Graph Editors | Saved Schematic View from the main max menu.

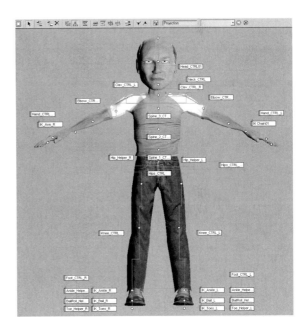

You can see an example Schematic View of Felix's character rig if you open the file …\3dsmax6_CD\Felix\Felix_Rigged.max and choose Graph Editors | Saved Schematic View | Felix Rig Projection from the main menu. The icons have been arranged according to the organization of the rig, but you can select them and move them around to further examine their relationships.

Exploring Character Rigging Further

From here, you can build upon the techniques and methodologies used to create this rig for more sophisticated rigging. As a start, you can create custom attributes in the foot-control objects that can drive the rotation of the foot dummy helper objects. Alternatively, you can add bones to the forearms with script-driven rotations to simulate the twisting of the radius and ulna bones.

For further study, I recommend the character rigging tutorials in the 3ds max documentation under "Tutorials for Animation Professionals." These tutorials are written by Michael Comet, one of the best 3ds max character riggers. Also, examining some of the rigged characters available on the Internet can be helpful as well.

Turning the Mesh into a Skin

Now the character geometry must be stitched to the rig so that the bone transformations transform the mesh as well. The Skin modifier provides this function in 3ds max and contains an extensive toolset for controlling the way the bones deform the mesh. Setting up the Skin modifier so that the mesh deforms the way you desire can be an exacting and time-consuming task, requiring extensive and recursive testing and adjustment. However, the more thorough you test the rig at this point, the fewer problems that will crop up when you're attempting to focus on character animation.

For the next exercise, open the …\3dsmax6_CD\Felix\Felix_Rigged.max file from the CD-ROM.

Applying the Skin Modifier

Now the actual Skin modifier is added to the stack of the Fel_body geometry object. Here are the steps to follow:

1 Right-click anywhere in a viewport and choose Unfreeze All from the right-click menu. Select the Fel_body geometry object, go to the Modify panel, and assign a Skin modifier.

2 Near the top of the Parameters rollout in the Modify panel, click the Add button. Click the None button on the right side of the Select Bones dialog box and then click the Bone Objects check box. Click the All button on the left side of the Select Bones dialog box. Then CTRL-click, one by one, any name in the list that has the word "Tip" in it to remove these items from your selection. Then click the Select button. The list of bones will appear in the envelope list in the Parameters rollout.

This creates an envelope of influence around each bone that is added to the Skin modifier's list (see Figure 10-35). Any vertices that fall inside a given envelope will be moved when the bone associated with that envelope moves. Each envelope consists of an inner and an outer envelope and is accessed in Sub Object mode of the Skin modifier. Both inner and outer envelopes are represented by cross-sections at each end, which can be adjusted with handles manipulated with the Move tool. Another handle at the center of each end of the envelope can be moved to position the entire envelope.

FIGURE 10-35   Once all the bones are referenced by the Skin modifier, envelopes are created for each bone.

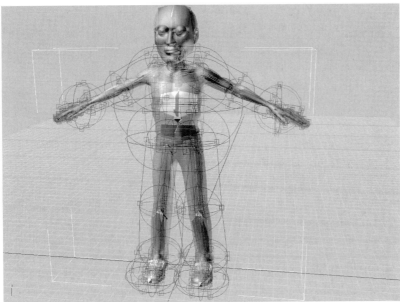

The vertices that fall within the inner envelope are affected at the full strength of that envelope. Vertices that fall between the inner and outer envelopes are affected stronger or weaker, depending on their proximity to the inner envelope. Vertices that are close to the edge of the outer envelope will only be moved slightly when the envelope moves.

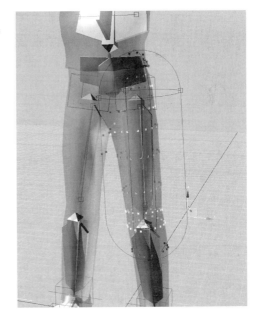

The default positions and sizes of the envelopes are based on the position and length of the bones as well as the bones' size and the size of their fins. If the bones and fins are sized carefully, the default envelopes may be reasonably close to what is needed to animate the character. However, most envelopes will need at least some fine-tuning, if not massive readjustment. Otherwise, you'll see all manner of kinks and creases in the character geometry as it animates. You can see quick evidence of this by grabbing one of the hand-control shapes and moving it around in the viewport while looking at the shoulder area.

FIGURE 10-36   The Skin modifier will likely require envelope adjustments to begin to control the deformations at trouble spots such as the ankles (a), shoulders (b), and chest (c), to name a few.

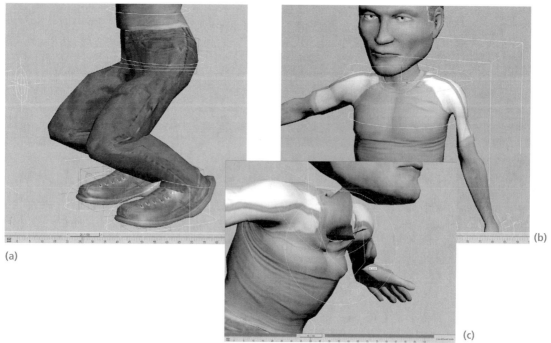

(a)

(b)

(c)

Character Stress Test: Creating Poses

Because it is impossible to see all the potential trouble spots at once, it is helpful to put the character through a systematic series of poses to help reveal them. You can do this by turning on Auto Key mode, moving the Time slider forward 10 or 20 frames, and then moving one or two of the control shape objects. Put the character into different poses every 10 frames are so.

Because we haven't covered much animation yet (this topic is covered in Chapters 12 through 15), I've already done this for the file you are working on. You can scrub the Time slider to see the character move through a series of very basic movements to highlight different difficult joints. Because the envelopes will need quite a bit of readjustment, it will be helpful to be able to scrub the Time slider to see how well the adjustments are working. Figures 10-36a through 10-36c show a few of the trouble spots that this process reveals.

Adjusting Envelopes

The first phase of tuning the character skin involves adjusting the positions of the envelopes with their end handles and the size of the envelopes with their cross-section handles. Because of 3ds max 6's new envelope and vertex weight-mirroring feature, it is only necessary to adjust one side of the character. This cuts the time and effort of this, a lengthy task, in half. Here are the steps to follow:

1 With the Time slider on frame 10, zoom in on the right shoulder area. Select the body object and under the Skin modifier, go to Envelopes Sub Object mode. In the viewport, select the middle spine bone by clicking the gray line (see Figure 10-37a). The cross-sections for this envelope are too large, so it is having an effect way out onto the arm vertices where it shouldn't. Correct this by moving the handles on the right hand's outer cross-section inward, toward the center of the envelope (see Figure 10-37b). Notice that the colored vertices disappear and the arm geometry regains some of its volume as the cross-sections become smaller.

NOTE ***The envelope's effect is based on its relationship to the geometry in the skin pose, which in this case is at frame zero. The skin pose is whatever pose the rig is in when the Skin modifier is applied. So in the case of Figure 10-37b, the envelope appears to be covering vertices in the arm. But in the original position of the mesh, the arm is raised higher away from this adjusted envelope.***

FIGURE 10-37 The envelopes on the chest will often expand at their ends into the vertices of the arm, making the arm form incorrectly as it bends (a). Adjusting the cross-sections and endpoints on the envelopes of the chest can begin to correct this (b).

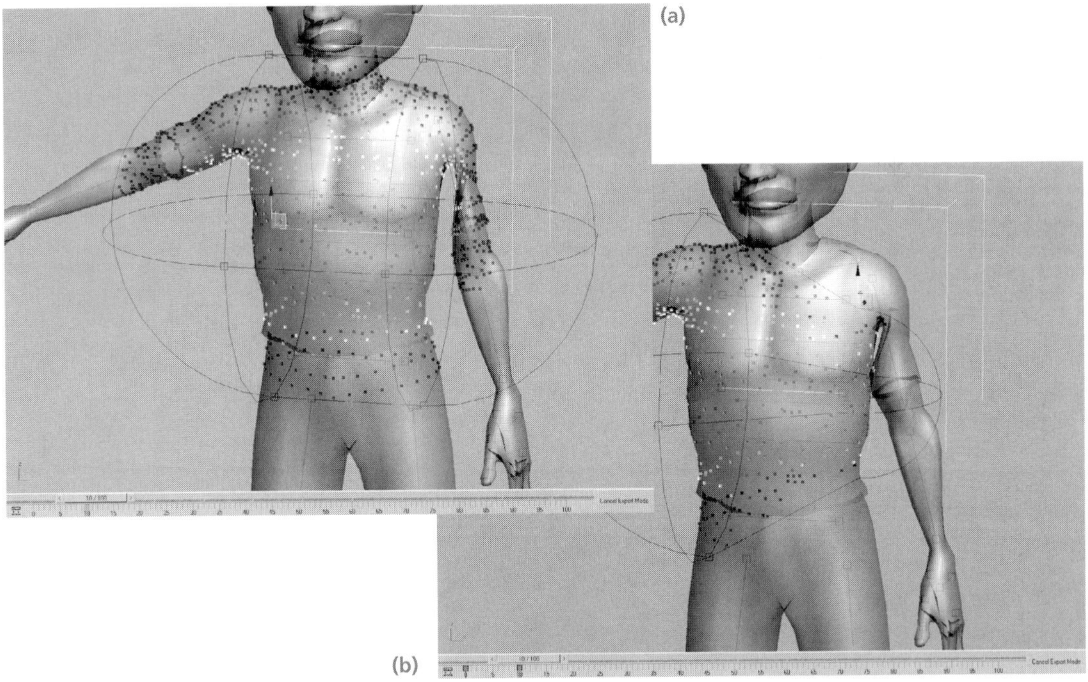
(a)
(b)

2 Repeat this procedure for the other spine bones, making sure that the cross-sections of the envelopes are small enough not to effect the arm but large enough to enclose the torso.

3 Another area that will need adjusting is the ankle (see Figure 10-38a). Because the foot bones take a diagonal path between the ankle and toes, the envelopes for these bones have the same diagonal direction. Move the Time slider to frame 25. Select the end handle of the left foot bone envelope. Move this handle downward and to the rear until the envelope is parallel with the ground plane and the rear end handle is in the center of the heel. You can watch the vertices of the heel move as you change the envelope position (see Figure 10-38b).

Continue adjusting envelopes in this manner for all of the character. Identify trouble spots by scrubbing the Time slider or by manipulating the character-control objects. It will usually be impossible to get perfect results from this method alone, so once you have adjusted the envelopes to get the deformations as good as possible, move onto the methods discussed next.

Excluding Specific Vertices from an Envelope's Influence

In areas such as the fingers, where vertices that need to be on different envelopes are in close proximity to one another, it can be difficult to adjust the envelopes so that they do not affect the vertices of other fingers while still affecting the vertices they need to. To correct for this, you

FIGURE 10-38 Because the endpoint of the envelope for the foot bone is at the ankle joint, the default envelope is not influenced by the vertices in the heel (a). To correct this, the endpoint of the envelope is moved down to the heel (b).

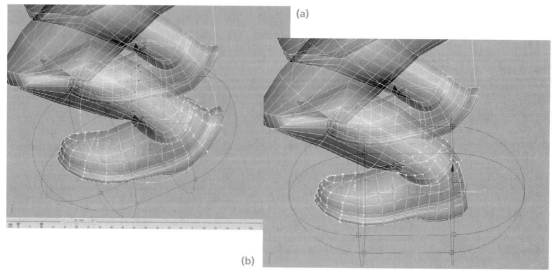

(a)

(b)

can use the Skin modifier's Exclude Vertices function found in the Weight Properties section of the Parameters rollout. Here are the steps to follow for this exercise:

1 Select the Hand_CTRL_L shape objects and adjust the Spread custom attribute spinner to its maximum value of 20. As the fingers spread out, some of the vertices on the sides of the fingers bulge out. This is because they are being influenced by envelopes on the other fingers.

2 Select the body object and go to Envelopes Sub Object mode. Select the first ring finger envelope and notice the vertices on the middle finger that become highlighted along with those on the ring finger (see Figure 10-39a).

3 Select the vertices on the middle finger that become highlighted. It can be helpful to first check the Vertices check box and uncheck the Envelopes and Cross Sections check boxes in the Selection section of the Parameters rollout. Then click the Exclude Vertices button (see Figure 10-39b).

4 Repeat this for the other finger envelopes as needed. Select an envelope and then select and exclude any vertices it is affecting that it should not be.

5 Remember to set the Spread spinner back to zero. This can be done by right-clicking the arrows of the spinner.

FIGURE 10-39   When the envelope for the first bone of the ring finger is selected, vertices in the middle finger become highlighted because they are influenced by this envelope (a). Once they are excluded from the other fingers envelope, they pop back into place (b).

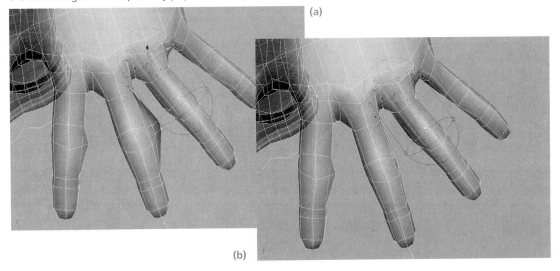

(a)

(b)

This technique is helpful when you need to remove vertices completely from certain envelopes. However, in areas where vertices need to blend smoothly between the influences of two or more envelopes, simply excluding vertices can cause abrupt creases in the mesh when deformed.

Hand Editing Vertex Weights

Each vertex has what is known as a *weight*, which refers to the influence placed on it by the envelopes. The total weight for each vertex is a value of 1. If two envelopes are equally influencing a vertex, each envelope will have a weight for that vertex of 0.5 so that the total influence is 1. If three envelopes equally weigh a vertex, the individual weights from those envelopes will be 0.333.

The next (and one of the most powerful) method for controlling the influence of the bones is adjusting the weights for the individual vertices. This is done by using the Weight Table, which is accessed in the Weight Properties section of the Parameters rollout in the Skin modifier. Follow these steps:

1 Move the Time slider to frame 25 and zoom in on the character's waist. The mesh is badly creased here and can be a difficult area to control by adjusting envelopes alone. Select the eight vertices along the crease in the geometry, as shown in Figure 10-40.

FIGURE 10-40   Vertices are selected where a crease forms at the top of the leg.

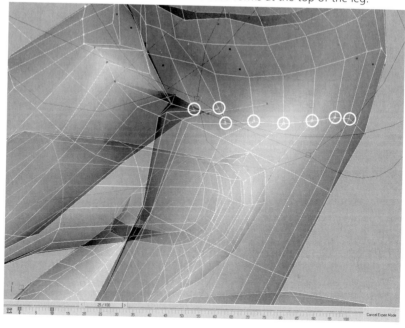

Weight Table

2 Click the Weight Table button to bring up the Skin Weight Table window. In the bottom-left corner of the window, choose Selected Vertices from the drop-down list so that only those vertices that are selected in the viewport will be visible in the Weight Table. Use the horizontal scrollbar at the bottom to locate the entries for the two envelopes that influence these vertices, Bone_UpLeg_L and Bone_Spine01 (see Figure 10-41).

3 Click the bottom entry in the left column and drag to the right while watching in the viewport. One of the vertices will move as you do this. Drag until the vertex is in a position that smoothes out the crease in the geometry. Continue this process, moving up the left column until the crease in the leg is as smooth as possible.

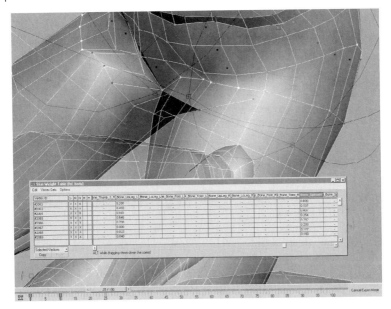

It is advisable that you take a very methodical approach to editing vertex weights. Keep track of the areas in the mesh where you have done hand editing. It may even be helpful to keep notes

FIGURE 10-41   As the weights for the selected vertices are balanced out between the two envelopes that influence them, the creased area at the top of the leg becomes smoother.

Vertex ID	S	M	N	R	H	ne_Thumb_3_R	Bone_UpLeg_L	Bone_LoLeg_L	el_Bone_Foot_L	H_Bone_Toes_L	Bone_UpLeg_R	Bone_LoLeg_R	H_Bone_Foot_R	H_Bone_Toes_R	Bone_Spine01	Bone_Sp
#2062	X	X				-		-	-	-	-	-	-	-	1.000	-
#2063	X	X				-	0.003	-	-	-	-	-	-	-	0.997	-
#2064	X	X				-	0.153	-	-	-	-	-	-	-	0.847	-
#2065	X	X				-	0.136	-	-	-	-	-	-	-	0.864	-
#2066	X	X				-	0.288	-	-	-	-	-	-	-	0.712	-
#2067	X	X				-	0.330	-	-	-	-	-	-	-	0.670	-
#2068	X	X				-	0.433	-	-	-	-	-	-	-	0.567	-
#2069	X	X				-	0.610	-	-	-	-	-	-	-	0.390	-

Selected Vertices
Copy   Paste

Use the middle mouse button to pan the window

on this. Although this is an extremely detailed and painstaking process, most professional character riggers understand its necessity and become proficient at it. And again, thanks to the Skin modifier's mirroring feature, it is only necessary to do this for one side of the mesh.

Mirroring Vertex Weights

Once you have thoroughly adjusted the envelopes and weights for one side of your character, you can mirror both the envelopes and the weights from the side you have adjusted to the other. This is, of course, is dependent on your having created a symmetrical character. If you have, this can be a great timesaver.

Here are the steps to follow for this exercise:

1 Zoom out so that you can see the entire character mesh. In Envelopes Sub Object mode of the Skin modifier, open the Mirror Parameters rollout. Click the Mirror Mode button.

2 If some of the vertices are red, raise the threshold spinner until all the vertices are displayed as either blue or green.

3 Click the Paste Blue to Green Bones button and then the Paste Blue to Green Vertices button.

Now you can exit Sub Object mode and scrub the Time slider or manipulate the control objects to see that the right side of the character is now weighted properly.

Adding Angle Deformers

Even after envelopes have been adjusted and vertices weighted as well as possible, some joints like the shoulder, for example, may still not deform as you want them to. Angle deformers are another built-in feature of the Skin modifier that can be used to control the behavior of the mesh when joints are rotated. The three flavors of Angle Deformers allow you to sculpt the mesh as a joint rotates. The Joint and Bulge Angle Deformers place a lattice around a portion of the mesh similar to an FFD modifier. The vertices of the lattice can then be moved to different positions when a joint reaches specific angles.

The more powerful of the three Angle Deformers is the Morph Angle Deformer. It allows you to sculpt the vertices of the mesh directly creating morph targets that are triggered automatically as joints reach specific rotation angles. Here's how to create a Morph Angle deformer for Felix's left shoulder:

1 First, you need to assess which positions of the shoulder joint cause unwanted creasing and set keyframes for the Hand_Ctrl_L object so the shoulder is in that position. A bad crease happens on the top of the shoulder when Felix raises his arm above his head. Set a keyframe for the Hand_Ctrl_L object at frame 24 (see Figure 10-42).

2 Select the Fel_body object and add an Edit Mesh modifier to the top of the stack. You can then sculpt the vertices of the shoulder (see Figure 10-43a) to give the shoulder the proper shape when the arm is in this position (see Figure 10-43b).

3 Back in Envelope sub object mode of the Skin modifier, select the vertices of the upper shoulder area and then CTRL-select the envelope for the left upper arm. In the Gizmos rollout choose Morph Angle Deformer from the drop-down list and click the Add Gizmo button. This will create a new entry called Base Morph in the Deformer Parameters rollout. The number next to the entry indicates the angle of the joint in its neutral position.

4 In the field at the top of the Deformer Parameters rollout, rename the Gizmo M A D – Bone_Clav_L. This will help maintain clarity as you add other Angle Deformer gizmos to other parts of the body.

FIGURE 10-42 This image shows a trouble spot in Felix's shoulder when his arm is raised.

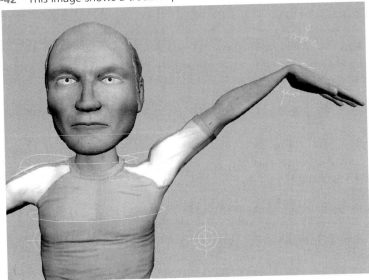

FIGURE 10-43 Here the vertices of the top of the shoulder (a) have been sculpted within an Edit Mesh modifier at the top of the stack so that the shoulder is shaped in this position (b).

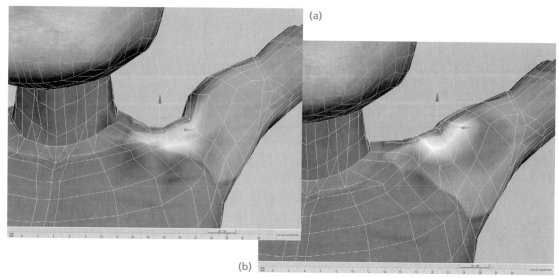

(a)

(b)

5 Move the Time slider to frame 24 and click the Add from Stack button to create a new angle-based morph using the Edit Mesh modifier at the top of the stack as the target. This will add a new entry in the Deformer Parameters rollout.

6 This will cause the shoulder to temporarily bulge twice as much as what you sculpt (see Figure 10-44). This is because deformation is not only happening from the Morph Angle Deformer in the Skin modifier but also from the Edit Mesh modifier. This is easily corrected by deleting the Edit Mesh modifier.

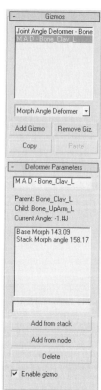

Now you can test the deformation by moving the Hand_Ctrl_L object or by moving the Time Slider. You can add other angle-based morph targets to this same gizmo by creating other Edit Mesh modifiers with the shoulder at different angles. Since the Angle Deformers are not highly sophisticated when blending the effects of multiple angle-based morph targets, I recommend keeping the number of targets for each Morph Angle Deformer gizmo to a minimum. Angle Deformers are still a powerful tool that allows you to be creative and artistic about the way the mesh deforms as the character moves. You can use them to simulate bulging muscles, flexing tendons and other dynamic anatomical features.

FIGURE 10-44   Here, the vertices of the shoulder are bulging upwards twice as far as they were moved in the Edit Mesh modifier. This is corrected by deleting the Edit Mesh modifier from the stack.

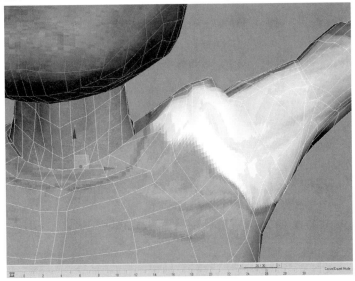

 NOTE   *The file …\3dsmax6_CD\Felix\felix_morph_angle_*
deformer.max shows the Felix character with two example Angle Deformers.

Character Node Setup

Before you begin to animate your character, you need to be sure that you can easily return the character back to its default pose. This means putting every control object, helper object, and bone object back to its original state. This is necessary if you need to adjust the rig or the Skin modifier. This is often referred to as "zeroing out" the character. One way to do this is using 3ds max Character node.

1   Open the finished, rigged character (…\3dsmax6_CD\Felix\Felix_All_Deformers.max) and select everything in the file except for the lights.

2   From the main menu, choose Character | Create Character. You will see a Character node icon appear between the character's feet (see Figure 10-45).

3   Scrub the Time slider to a frame where the character is posing and choose Character | Skin Pose Mode from the main menu. The character will then be in its default pose position for easier adjustments to the rig or skin.

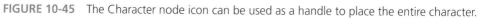
FIGURE 10-45   The Character node icon can be used as a handle to place the entire character.

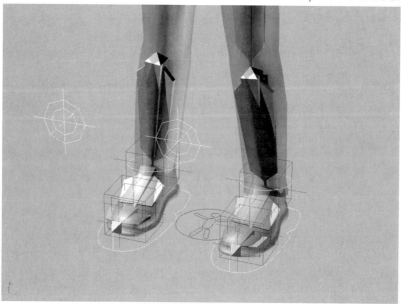

The Character node also has other built-in functionality. Any character encapsulated in a Character node can be saved as a character file (.chr) for easy merging into other files.

> **NOTE**   *You can see the completed Felix rig in the file ...\3dsmax6_CD\Felix\felix_final.max. You can then see the rig in animated action in the file ...\3dsmax6_CD\Felix\felix_final_walk.max. We'll cover character animation in Chapter 13, and then we'll cover rigging facial expressions with morph targets and rigging the eyes with Look-at constraints in Chapter 14.*

The Character Rigs for the Example Film

The characters for the example film in the animation chapters utilize highly flexible and sophisticated character rigs. The rigs were created automatically using a character-rigging script, by Michael Comet, freely available on the Internet, and then the Skin modifier was used to stitch the mesh to these rigs in the same manner shown earlier. Several excellent scripts are available that can be used to build custom rigs with all the animation controls built into them. These rigs leverage extensive MAXScripts and custom attributes to create a flexible and powerful rig that is easier to animate. This will be helpful in the chapters on animation.

Chapter 11

Set Modeling: Creating the Environment

Now that you have cast your production with virtual actors, you can move on to creating the virtual stage on which they will perform. To some, modeling environments may conjure up analogies to being an architect, but it is more appropriate to compare this part of production to the work of set designers working in film or the theater.

While modeling a 3-D environment, CG filmmakers are confronted with a seductive, godlike feeling of being able to create an entire world for their characters to inhabit. Although CG technology excels at portraying hyper-detailed visual richness, this richness must be balanced with your time constraints and what your computer can handle.

A good approach to environment building is to take cues from real-world set designers. Movie sets for Westerns commonly have façades for buildings with nothing behind them because the camera doesn't see the backs of the buildings. As you create your environment, be sure not to waste any time or polygons on things the camera does not see. Figure 11-1a shows the Cloud10 environment for the example movie, and Figure 11-1b shows the back of the set.

Animation environments can take an infinite variety of forms—from the surreal, organic expanse of a planetary landscape to the cramped interior of a chicken coop. So attempting to describe how to model all possible environments would be folly, and having you re-create the entire environment for my film would not be helpful because it is so specific. Therefore, in this chapter, we'll cover a more general array of 3ds max's procedural modeling techniques. I'll show you how they were used to create my environment. Then you can readily use these techniques to create your own. We'll also get into more complex materials and begin to create lighting. As in other chapters, this chapter starts out with a couple detailed examples to show you some key tools and techniques, and then we'll move through the rest of the Cloud10 scene so you have a sense of what goes into a finished environment.

FIGURE 11-1   The Cloud10 environment, while fairly complex (a) is built like a Hollywood façade (b).

(a)

(b)

Building the Cloud10 Glass Bubbles and Dome

In contrast to the organic, freeform modeling of the characters, more geometric architectural spaces can still start from primitives. To create the main form of my environment, I used modified primitives combined with Boolean operations. Here's an exercise based on my environment that will show you how to use these techniques for your own projects.

Creating a Space

To start with, create a new max file with the same units set up as your character files (in our case, centimeters). Save the file in a folder called Cloud10 that has subfolders for finished images and for working files. To create the main dome, start with a Chamfer Cylinder primitive and then follow these steps:

1 From the Create panel's drop-down menu, choose Extended Primitives and then click the Chamfer Cylinder button. Set the parameters for the Chamfer Cylinder as shown in the illustration to the right. Make sure that the center of the Chamfer Cylinder is placed at the origin. Name this object Glass_Dome.

2 To form the first glass bubble, create a Sphere primitive with a radius of 750 centimeters and 24 segments. Set the Sphere primitive's Hemisphere parameter to .5 and click the Squash radio button. Nonuniformly scale the Sphere primitive up by 275 percent along its local Z-axis. Then position the now bullet-shaped bubble object so that its base is just within the outer perimeter of the Glass_Dome object (see Figure 11-2).

3 Make two clones of the glass bubble object, rotating one 45 degrees and the other –45 degrees in the world's Z-axis (see Figure 11-3). Knowing the angles in which the bubble objects are rotated from one another will make it easier to clone and rotate other objects into place. This way, objects that need to be duplicated for each of the glass bubbles can be easily aligned.

FIGURE 11-2 Here, the hemispherical Sphere primitive has been positioned with its base just within the Chamfer Cylinder.

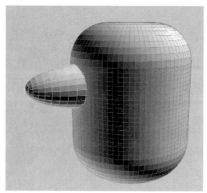

4 To partially flatten the top of the Glass_Dome object (so the ceiling of the space will not be too high), add a cylindrical FFD Cylinder modifier. Click the Set Number of Points button and give the FFD lattice the settings shown here in the Set FFD Dimensions dialog box. Then, in Control Points Sub Object mode, move the top two rows of control points down to flatten the top of the Glass_Dome object, as shown in Figure 11-4. Click the top entry in the stack for the Glass_Dome object to leave Sub Object mode.

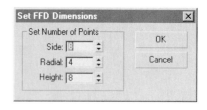

NOTE *On the CD-ROM, the file ...\3dsmax6_CD\Cloud10\ Cloud10_00.max contains the completed tutorial to this point.*

FIGURE 11-3 The glass bubble objects have been cloned and rotated. These glass bubbles will become the rooms of the environment where the character conversations take place.

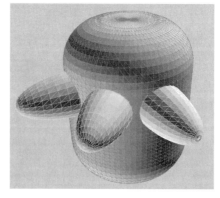

FIGURE 11-4   A cylindrical FFD modifier has been added to the Glass_Dome object to lower what will become the ceiling of the interior.

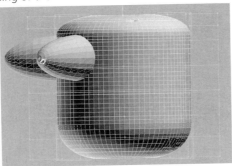

5 Right-click one of the glass bubble objects and choose Convert To | Editable Poly from the pop-up menu. In the Modify panel, click the Attach button and click the other two glass bubble objects to make all three glass bubbles a single object. Click the Attach button again to cancel out of that tool.

6 With the Glass_Dome object selected, choose Compound Objects from the drop-down list at the top of the Create panel. Click the Boolean button to make the Glass_Dome object a Boolean object. Click the Pick Operand B button and choose the glass bubble object by clicking it in the viewport, and then click the Union radio button in the Parameters section of the Modify panel to complete the Boolean operation.

Pick Operand B

7 Right-click the combined Boolean object and convert it to an Editable Poly object. In the Modify panel, click the Elements button to change to Elements Sub Object mode. The three glass bubble elements should already be selected. Make these a separate object by clicking the Detach button, naming it Glass_Bubbles.

Now the Glass_Dome object can be "shrink-wrapped" with a Relax modifier to make the curves of the interior form more sculpturally interesting.

8 Delete the polygons of the bottom half of the Glass_Dome object.

9 Add the Relax modifier and set the Iterations parameter to 100. This sucks in the mesh while preserving its edges, which will protect the joint between the Glass_Dome and Glass_Bubbles objects.

10 Right-click the Glass_Dome object and convert it to any Editable Poly object again, and then delete the polygons for the rear half (see Figure 11-5).

FIGURE 11-5   Here, the Relax modifier has been added to the Glass_Dome object to make the eventual interior form more expressive.

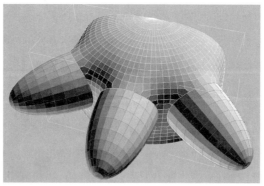

Turning Polygons into Glass

Now that the basic form of the interior has been defined, it needs to be turned into glass with a little bit of polygon modeling and a material. Many effective techniques can be used for creating convincing glass in 3-D. For this environment, I chose to actually create polygons for the edges of the panes of glass. Although this does add a lot of polygons to the scene, I made the tradeoff because the modeling is quick and easy, and other methods, such as displacement mapping, would add more render time. By taking the following steps, you can give each polygon some depth by extruding them:

1 Because you're creating an interior space, the polygon normals on all the glass objects need to be flipped to face inward. For both of the Glass_Dome and Glass_Bubbles objects, go to the Modify panel and switch to Polygon Sub Object mode. Then, under the Edit Polygons section, click the Flip button. If you turn the viewport so that your vantage point is from inside the glass objects, you can see the interior surfaces (see Figure 11-6).

FIGURE 11-6   With the polygon normals flipped, you can see the general form of the interior space.

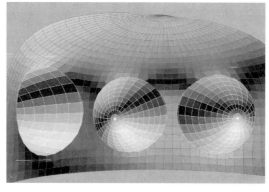

2 Select the Glass_Bubbles object and switch to Polygons Sub Object mode. Select all polygons and click the button located next to the Bevel button and enter the settings shown here in the Bevel Polygons dialog box. By beveling with the By Polygon radio button checked, you create new polygons along the borders of each polygon. This turns all the original polygons into boxes so that each can serve as a pane of glass. Repeat this procedure for the Glass_Dome object (see Figure 11-7).

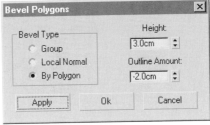

Creating a Glass Material

For creating prerendered imagery (as opposed to real-time models), it is more common to use raytracing to obtain a realistic effect. However, raytracing creates notoriously long render times, which I want to avoid for the example film. So instead of a raytraced material, I chose to use a standard material with a simple falloff map for transparency and a basic bitmap for reflection. By following these steps, you can create a simple, yet artistic, glass material that renders quickly.

1 In the Material Editor, select an open material sample slot and name it Glass_Outer. Assign the material to both the Glass_Dome and Glass_Bubbles objects using the Assign Material to Selection button.

2 Click the 2-sided check box to automatically give these objects back faces (though these will only show up in renderings, not in the viewports).

3 Assign both objects Ambient and Diffuse colors using RGB values of R: 143, G: 183, B: 182.

FIGURE 11-7   This close-up of the wireframe for the Glass_Bubbles object shows how beveling the polygons individually gives each polygon four sides.

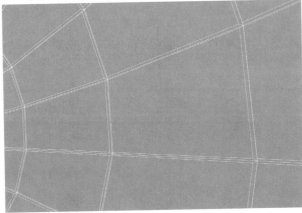

4 In the Maps rollout of the Material Editor, click the open slot next to the Opacity map channel and choose Falloff from the Material/Map Browser that pops up. You can leave the falloff map with its default settings.

The falloff map is a versatile map type. It is essentially a gradient between white and black (or whatever colors or maps you choose). However, the gradient is applied based on the angle of a surface to the camera. When the falloff map is used in the Opacity channel, if the glass is facing the camera directly, it will be mostly transparent. If it is angled sharply away from the camera, it will be mostly opaque.

 5 Use the Go to Parent button to navigate back to the top level of the material. In the Maps rollout, click the open slot next to the Reflection channel. Choose Bitmap from the Material/Map browser and assign the bitmap reflect.jpg, found in \3dsmax6_CD\ Cloud10\C10_Maps\.

This file was created using the same source file as the background image for the environment (see the section "Backgrounds"). The sky has been cropped out and certain colors have been selected and brightened using Photoshop's Levels function. This was done to achieve more dramatic reflections in the glass.

6 In the Reflection Map settings, set the UV Tiling, as shown next. (As I place different cameras around the scene to set up different shots, I change the UV Tiling settings to make the reflections look as good as possible for each shot.)

◡ NOTE *On the CD-ROM, the file ...\3dsmax6_CD\Cloud10\ Cloud10_01.max contains the completed tutorial to this point.*

Floor and Railings

Creating the floor for the environment is a little bit tricky. I want the tiles of my floor to be arranged in a pattern that radiates from what would be the center of this building. To do this with normal UV mapping coordinates, I would have to create a bitmap texture with the curved pattern, which means the bitmap pattern will not tile easily. However, because the cameras will be so close to the floor in so many different areas, the bitmap would have to be gigantic in resolution.

To get around this problem, we'll build the floor straight by simply beveling an outline. We'll then add a Bend modifier to the floor to bring it into alignment with the glass bubbles and dome. This will bend the mapping coordinates along with the mesh, allowing us to use a simpler, square tiling texture. You can follow along with these steps to see how this is done.

1 In the Create panel, click the Shapes button and then the Line tool. In a top viewport, draw an outline that matches the contour of the center glass bubble (see Figure 11-8). This is easily done by placing the five points, as shown, and then in Vertices Sub Object mode, adjusting the Bezier handles. Name this object Floor.

The floor's outcroppings will be suspended within the glass bubbles, leaving a gap around the edges. Therefore, the outline should be smaller than the glass bubble. Also, because we'll be adding a Bend modifier to the floor, that outline should be sharper than the bubble as well. Adding a Bend modifier will bow it out to the proper form.

2 In Spline Sub Object mode, hold down the SHIFT key while moving the spline to the right. Align the leftmost vertex of the new spline with the rightmost vertex of the old spline. Repeat this procedure to create the outline for the left bubble as well.

3 Select the four vertices at the two joints between the outline splines and weld them together to form a single spline.

4 In Vertices Sub Object mode, click the Create Line button in the Geometry section of the Modify panel. Then click the rightmost vertex to start drawing a line down, across to the left, and up to connect to the leftmost vertex of the outline, as shown in Figure 11-9.

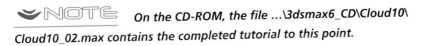 **On the CD-ROM, the file ...\3dsmax6_CD\Cloud10\ Cloud10_02.max contains the completed tutorial to this point.**

FIGURE 11-8   The outline for the first bubble

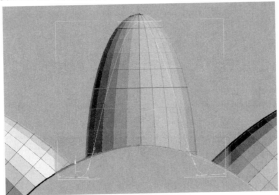

FIGURE 11-9   The finished floor outline

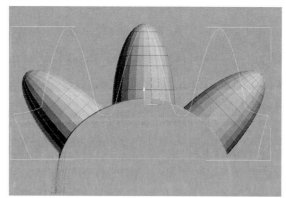

5   Exit Sub Object mode, and then clone a copy of the Floor object and name it Floor Outline. This will be the basis for other objects.

6   Select the original Floor object again and add a Bevel modifier with the settings shown in this illustration. This gives the floor thickness and rounded edges.

7   Add a Bend modifier to the Floor object with the settings shown here:

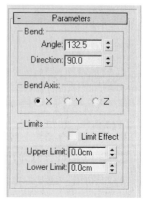

It's likely that your initial outline will need to be adjusted so that the floor shape fits neatly within the glass bubbles. To do this, you can traverse down the stack back to the Sub Object level of the outline and adjust the vertices while watching how the finished floor will look.

8   In the stack for the Floor object, click the Vertex Sub Object level for the base Line object at the bottom of the stack. Make sure the Show End Result button, shown left, is toggled on.

9   Now you can move vertices with the Move tool while watching the shape of the final floor (see Figure 11-10).

Creating the Floor Material   The material for the Floor object is a Multi/Sub Object material. Thanks to the Bevel modifier, the sides of the floor are automatically assigned a different material ID than the top of the floor. This is preferable because assigning the same sub material to the sides

FIGURE 11-10   Moving a vertex in the base outline changes the shape of the Floor object. Because the Bend modifier at the top of the stack is in effect—thanks to the Show End Result button—the actual Floor object exhibits the final shape.

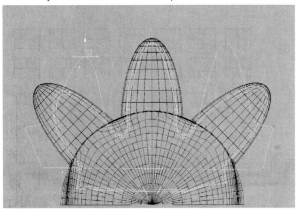

that is mapped with a planar map to the top of the floor would cause streaking. The Bevel modifier also assigns different mapping coordinates for the sides.

1   In the Material Editor, select an open material slot and name it Floor. Click the button labeled Standard and change the material from Standard to Multi/Sub Object. Set the number of Sub Object materials to 3. Assign the bitmap …\3dsmax6_CD\Cloud10\C10_Maps\floor.jpg to the Diffuse channel of the first sub material and give it these UV coordinates settings.

	Offset	Tiling	Mirror	Tile
U:	0.02	1.7	☐	☑
V:	0.0	3.3	☐	☑

2   Navigate back to the top level of the Floor Texture sub material with the Go to Parent button (not all the way to the top of the Multi/Sub Object material). In the Maps list, drag the map in the Diffuse channel onto the Specular Level channel and choose Instance from the resulting dialog box (see Figure 11-11). Set the Specular Level spinner to 137.

3   Drag the map from the Specular Level channel into the Glossiness channel, this time choosing Copy from the dialog box. Set the Glossiness spinner to 34.

4   Access the settings for the Glossiness map by clicking it in the Maps list. Scroll to the bottom of the Material Editor to the Output section and then click the Invert check box.

5   Back at the top level of this sub material, click the empty Bump channel and assign the texture …\3dsmax6_CD\ Cloud10\C10_Maps\floorgrid_ bump.jpg. Set the Bump spinner to −10. Give this map the same UV tile settings as the map for the Diffuse channel, shown here:

	Offset	Tiling	Mirror	Tile
U:	0.02	1.7	☐	☑
V:	0.0	3.3	☐	☑

FIGURE 11-11   To copy a texture map from one material channel to another, you can drag and drop in the Maps list.

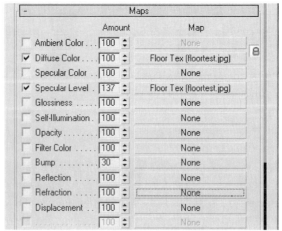

6   On the empty Reflection channel, choose Flat Mirror from the pop-up Material/Map Browser. This creates the fairly complex Floor Texture sub material that uses multiple Map channels. The original texture is used to control the shininess; you use it in the Specular Level and Glossiness channels. The Flat Mirror map in the Reflection channel will create an automatic reflection from other objects in the scene. Calculating these reflections can add a significant amount to render times, but the effect is rich, and flat surfaces are difficult to get reflections on in other ways.

7   For a sub material for the sides of the floor, go to the top level of the Floor Multi/Sub Object material in the Material Editor. Drag the Floor Textured material from material ID slot 1 to slot 3, making it a copy. Name this new sub material Floor Side.

8   In the Floor Side sub material, click the check boxes to turn off the Diffuse channel and the Reflection channel.

Railings   To model the glass balustrade and handrail that follows the contour of the floor, copies of the floor outline can be used to make the process go faster. The glass balustrade requires only a simple Bevel modifier. These objects are excellent examples of creating complex models procedurally. Here are the steps to use the Bevel modifier and the Loft compound object to create the railings for the environment:

1 Select the Floor Outline object and clone another copy named Floor Glass. Add a Bevel modifier to the Floor Glass object with the settings shown here:

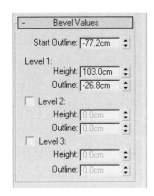

2 Select the Floor object and right-click the Bend modifier in the stack and copy it. Reselect the Floor Glass object and right-click the top of the stack and paste the Bend modifier.

3 Move the Floor Glass object up in the Z-axis until the bottom is sitting on the top of the Floor object.

4 In the Material Editor, make a copy of the Glass Outer material by clicking its sample window and dragging to an empty sample window. Rename this new material Glass Railing and assign it to the Floor Glass object.

To make the handrail, you'll create a shape to become a cross-section for a Loft object. Lofting is a powerful modeling technique that I used many times throughout this environment in many different ways. It allows you to create an infinite variety of shapes quickly, and the resulting forms are also highly editable, making Loft objects easy to modify. What's more, UVW coordinates are automatically created, thus making texturing easier as well.

5 Using the Line tool, create a simple triangle outline in the top viewport, as shown in Figure 11-12. Make the long horizontal dimension around 20 cm and the shorter vertical dimension around 7 cm. Name this object Floor Rail Cross-section.

FIGURE 11-12   The cross-section outline for the handrail

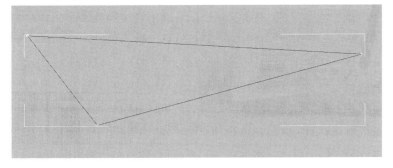

6 Clone another copy of the Floor Outline object, naming it Floor Rail Path. Move the Floor Rail Path object up in the Z-axis until it is even with the top of the Floor Glass object.

7 Copy the Bend modifier from the Floor object again and paste it on to the Floor Outline object's stack.

The outline for the Floor Rail Loft object needs to be adjusted to fit on top of the Floor Glass object, which was shrunk inward by the Bevel modifier. Simple scaling will not work here. The Outline function within the Edit Spline modifier affects a shape similarly to the Outline parameter within the Bevel modifier.

8 Add an Edit Spline modifier to the Floor Outline object and switch to Spline Sub Object mode. In a perspective viewport, zoom in close to the Floor Glass object near

| Outline |

one of the tightly curved areas between the glass bubbles. Adjust the spinner next to the Outline button until the outline is aligned with the top of the Floor Glass object. Because this action creates a duplicate, delete the original spline and exit Sub Object mode.

9 In the Create panel, make sure the Geometry button is clicked and select Compound Objects from the drop-down list. With the Floor Rail Loft object already selected, click the Loft button in the Create panel.

10 Click the Get Shape button and select the Floor Rail Cross-section object in the viewport. Creating the loft makes a new object named Loft01 by default. Rename this object Floor Rail.

11 Choose an empty material slot in the Material Editor and name it Railing. Make the Diffuse and Ambient colors a dark gray.

12 In the Specular Level channel, assign the map …\3dsmax6_CD\Cloud10\C10_maps\ rail_spec.tif and set the Specular Level spinner to 100. Set the Bump channel spinner to 50 and assign the map …\3dsmax6_CD\Cloud10\C10_maps\railing_bump.tif. Then assign this material to the Floor Rail object.

➤ NOTE   **On the CD-ROM, the file …\3dsmax6_CD\Cloud10\
Cloud10_03.max contains the completed tutorial to this point.**

Now the environment is starting to take form, as shown in Figure 11-13. The pieces that we have built in this tutorial serve as a foundation for the rest of the elements in the scene.

Modeling the Rest of the Scene

Most of the objects in the scene are created with simple combinations of primitives, Booleans, lofts, and other basic max modeling tools. In the following sections, I'll point out some of the other objects and explain briefly how they were created.

Balusters

The balusters for the glass railings on the floor and balcony were created by lofting a simple oval shape along a straight path. Two different loft deformations were used. The editing windows for these deformations are accessed in the Deformations section of the Modify panel. The Scale deformation changes the size of the shape as it traverses the path, and the Teeter deformation changes the orientation of the shape as it traverses the path (see Figure 11-14).

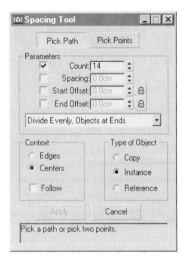

The balusters are duplicated as instances and automatically placed along the paths used for the railings using the Spacing tool (shown here), which is found in the main menu under Tools | Spacing Tool. Using the Path button in the Spacing Tool dialog box, you can basically array the objects along the path. This saves an enormous amount of time that you would otherwise have to spend placing each baluster by hand.

FIGURE 11-13 The environment rendered so far from the view of the Cam_Interior_View camera

FIGURE 11-14   The baluster is modeled by lofting a simple ellipse along a single segment path (a). A low-detail version (b) or a higher-detail version (c) can be created by changing the Path Steps and Shape Steps parameters in the Loft object. The Scale Deformation window (d) controls the size of the shape at each step in the path. The Teeter Deformation window (e) controls the orientation of the shape at each step in the path.

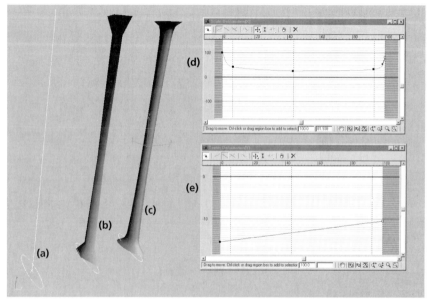

Rear Wall

The main rear wall is created by adding an Extrude modifier to a Line object. Setting the Amount spinner determines the thickness of the extrusion. The large outside line was created by tracing the Glass_Dome object in a front viewport. The smaller outlines are made from duplicates of the outline used to create the elevator. The lines are combined using the Attach tool in the Modify panel (see Figure 11-15).

Center Lathe

The sculpted part of the rear wall is modeled by drawing a simple curve with the Line tool and adding a Lathe modifier. This modifier works similarly to a loft, but it revolves a shape around a center point instead of lofting it along the path. The resulting Lathe object is sculpted further with a cylindrical FFD Cylinder modifier (see Figure 11-16).

Balcony

The balcony and its railings are modeled using exactly the same procedure as the floor, except they start with a different outline (see Figure 11-17). The position and shape of the balcony

FIGURE 11-15   The rear wall is a simple extrusion of a multiple-segment line shape.

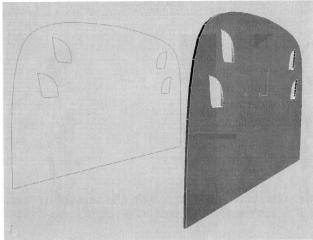

were determined as much by the script as by aesthetics. The script calls for Zoey to look out off the balcony immediately after exiting the elevator and for her to have a commanding view of the entire environment.

Beams

Lofts are again used to make the structural elements of the space, the beams at the joints between the glass bubbles and glass dome, and the beams supporting the ceiling (see Figure 11-18).

FIGURE 11-16   This image shows the initial Lathe object (a), the curve that was used to create it (b), and then the deformation lattice of the cylindrical FFD is used to sculpt the final form (c).

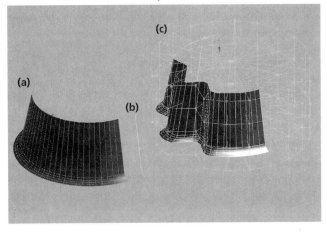

FIGURE 11-17   The placement and shape of the balcony were largely defined by the dictates of the story.

The Line tool is used to trace contours of the glass dome and the glass bubbles, and then a simple trapezoidal shape is lofted along them (see Figure 11-19).

For the circular beams, the joint between the glass bubbles and the glass dome is a complex shape. But only a quarter of a circle is traced. Once the cross-section is lofted along this path, the resulting Loft object is mirrored and then this pair of Loft objects is mirrored again to create an entire circle. A path for the ceiling beam is created by tracing the glass dome with the Line tool in the left viewport.

FIGURE 11-18   The beams supporting the roof and glass bubbles are created by lofting a simple trapezoidal shape along paths that follow the contours of the glass dome and glass bubbles.

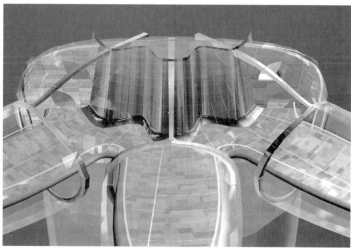

Begin Cameras Early

In some larger animation productions, set builders will have floor plans to build from with measurements and dimensions. However, I derived many of my dimensions from the mockups I built in Chapter 4. I often place a 200-cm-high Cylinder primitive in my scene and frame it with a camera to give myself a sense of scale as I build the different components of the scene.

These are very early renderings from test cameras used to help determine scale. The cylinders are 200 cm high to provide human scale.

Because the Glass_Bubble objects were rotated 45 degrees on the world axis, beams only needed to be created for the center roof beam and the center glass bubble joint. These objects are then cloned and rotated 45 degrees on the world Z-axis to align automatically with the other glass bubbles.

FIGURE 11-19   This image shows the paths and cross-sections and the lofted beams. Tapering along the path is achieved through use of Scale Loft Deformation. The "T" at the end of the roof beam was created by converting the Loft object to an Editable Poly object and beveling.

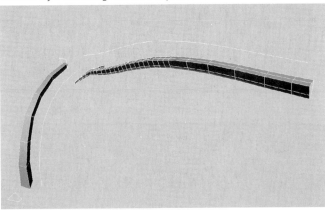

Bubble Frames and Fasteners

Other architectural details include frames and fasteners for the glass bubbles (see Figure 11-20). To create the bubble frames, edge loops are selected on the Glass Bubble object in Edge Sub Object mode. The Create Shape From Selection button is then used to automatically make these edge loops a separate Editable Spline object. This Editable Spline object is then given thickness by clicking the Renderable check box in the Rendering section of the Modify panel and giving the object the settings shown here.

Create Shape From Selection

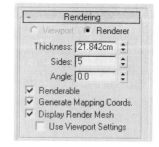

The architectural glass fasteners for the glass bubbles would create an enormous amount of geometry if they were all modeled with polygons. Borrowing a trick from real-time video games, I used a rendering of a detailed polygonal model as a texture map for a simple polygonal "card." To populate the glass bubble with these cards, I copied and placed individually one row of card instances (see Figure 11-21a and Figure 11-21b). I then copied and rotated this row of cards simultaneously as instances using the Array tool (see Figure 11-22).

Lamps

Lamps were modeled so that they would appear complex while actually being low detail and very quick and easy to model. A simple plane was tapered by scaling the bottom vertices in Vertex Sub Object mode. The plane was given a simple material consisting of a simple crisscrossed texture for the Diffuse channel and a white-to-black gradient for the Self Illumination channel.

FIGURE 11-20   Each glass bubble has a frame consisting of the Shape object that has been made renderable and given a thickness. Then, the two-dimensional fasteners are arrayed.

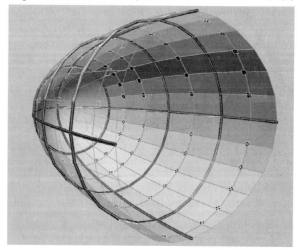

FIGURE 11-21 A rendering of the geometry on the left (a) has been used as a texture map for the simple polygonal square on the right (b).

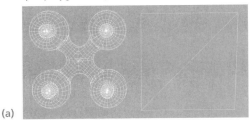
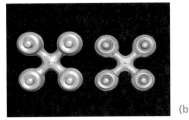

(a)   (b)

This single plane was copied and rotated using the Array tool to form a ring, as shown in Figure 11-23 (a). This ring was arrayed vertically and slightly rotated again using the Array tool (b). The resulting cylindrical assembly was then tapered with a Taper modifier and finally collapsed into a single object (c).

Booth and Furniture

Modeling the furniture and private booths once again combined very simple modeling techniques. The booth itself was sculpted from a Sphere primitive with the front and bottom polygons removed. The frame for the booth was created in the same way as the frames for the glass bubbles.

The seat cushions were created from Chamfer Cylinder primitives, and the seat bases were sculpted from Boxed primitives. These objects were arrayed to form the row of seats. A Bend modifier and a Stretch modifier were then added to the assembly to fit it into the booth (see Figure 11-24).

FIGURE 11-22 Here is the dialog box for the Array tool. This shows that the initial row of fasteners will be duplicated 24 times and each duplicate will be rotated 15 degrees in the Z axis.

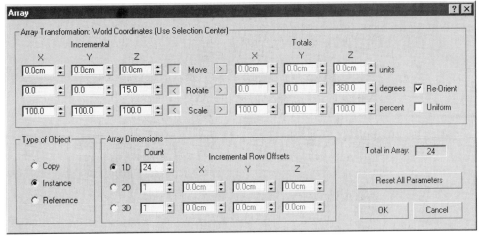

FIGURE 11-23 The lamp is formed by creating a simple plane object (a) and duplicating it with a radial array. Then the circular assembly is duplicated vertically (b) and a Taper modifier (c) is added. The left set of images shows the geometry in the viewport while the right set of images shows the models rendered with a material.

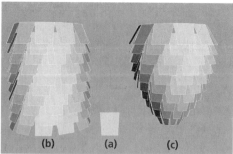 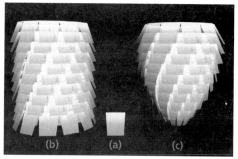

The material for the booths is very basic, except that it features a Translucent shader. A Translucent shader can be assigned to a material by choosing it from the drop-down list in the Shader Basic Parameters section of the Material Editor. This shader allows shadows to be cast by lights shining on the back of an object.

This translucency is a key way to imply that much more is going on in the background of the film. This way, a simple "cutout" or silhouette shape of a person can be placed between the light inside the booth and the booth wall. And thanks to the Translucent shader, the shadow this cutout casts can be seen on the outside of the booth. This makes it appear as though there are other characters within the booths, without all the added polygons, textures, and complexity of creating those other characters (see Figure 11-25a and Figure 11-25b).

FIGURE 11-24 To create the seats in the booth, a boxed primitive (a) has been slightly modified to serve as the base. Two Chamfer Boxed primitives (b) have been arrayed to form the seats (c). A Bend modifier is added (d), and finally a Stretch modifier is added to fit the seats into the booth (e).

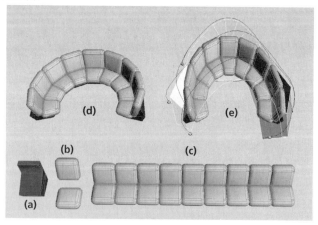

FIGURE 11-25 The booth assembly (a) shows the shadow cast by the cutout (b) thanks to the Translucent shader.

(a)   (b)

Elevator

The elevator frame and car are beveled and extruded, respectively, from the initial elevator outline shape. The door is made of three chamfer boxes, and the hinge is made of two chamfer cylinders (see Figure 11-26).

Stairs

The stairs start with a chamfer box for the first step. A material for the steps is created in a similar manner to the fastener material. A detailed model of the step is made using Boolean operations to cut sections, and then cylinders are used to cut holes in those sections. Next, a long, thin cylinder is arrayed across the top of the step to form the tread. A blue Omni light is

FIGURE 11-26 This exploded view of the elevator shows how all the components are very simply modeled.

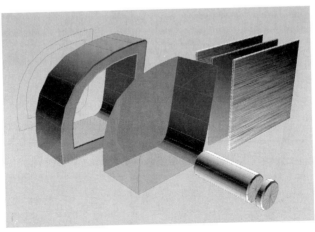

placed in the scene to create the light cast from the tread light on the front of each step. When the step is rendered directly from above, not only is a detailed texture created for the original chamfer box, but the light is "baked in." This way, the scene does not need to have actual lights placed for each step. Because lights add to render times, this is a significant reduction (see Figure 11-27).

Laying out the stairs is done much like in the real world. The height of the balcony is measured and divided by the height of each rise (16 cm) to determine how many steps are required (in this case, 24 steps). The Array tool is then used to copy and move each step up 16 cm in the Z-axis and 35 cm (the length of the run) in the Y-axis. The stairs are then split up into two groups, each with its own Bend modifier. A landing is placed in between the two groups that's beveled from a simple shape. Railings and balusters for the stairs are made in exactly the same way as those for the floor and balcony (see Figure 11-28).

Backgrounds

Creating the background for this environment starts with taking photographs of a night skyline from a high vantage point to approximate the height of the building that this environment is on top of. The images are cropped and blended together in Photoshop. The resulting image is used as the Diffuse channel in a simple, self-illuminated material that is mapped cylindrically to a Cylinder primitive (see Figure 11-29). Using this image in the Reflection channel of the Glass material helps tie the scene visually together.

FIGURE 11-27 The high detail stair model is lit with a blue Omni light (a). A top view rendering (b) is used for the texture of the original step.

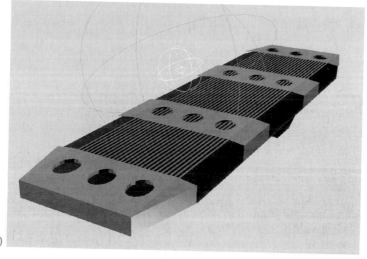

(a)

(b)

FIGURE 11-28 "Baking" the surface detail and the lighting into each step greatly reduces the lighting and polygonal detail needed in the scene.

⌣NOTE   *On the CD-ROM, the file ...\3dsmax6_CD\Cloud10\ Cloud10_04.max contains the completed scene to this point. This file will allow you to examine the stacks of most of the objects to see how they were created. Using the Material Editor, you can examine how each material has been constructed. Cameras have been placed in the scene to demonstrate what shots from the film will look like.*

FIGURE 11-29 Here is the background texture map (a). It is composed of several photographs shot from a high vantage point to match the vantage point of the virtual skyscraper, and then the image is texture mapped onto a cylinder with its normals reversed to be used as the background (b).

(a)

(b)

Lighting the Environment

Just as in real-world cinematography, lighting is all-important for setting mood and atmosphere. However, lighting a complex environment could lead one to add numerous lights, which could quickly become cumbersome to manage and make render times impractical. Therefore, I recommend a very simple approach to lighting that mimics real-world lighting where possible.

Mimicking the Light from the Night Skyline

For the simple approach, I add two Targeted Directional lights to roughly mimic the ambient light that would be coming from the skyline (see Figure 11-30). One is a very light yellow color (R: 223, G: 238, B: 197), and the other is a light green color (R: 138, G: 173, B: 168). I set the Hotspot/Beam spinner very high (4000 cm) in each light so that it covers the entire environment. The lights are initially positioned above and outside the environment, and their positions are occasionally adjusted on a shot-by-shot basis.

Architectural Lighting

For my environment, I wanted to have pools of light in contrasting colors. It adds to the drama and helps underscore the cinematic pacing to have the lighting on the characters change as they move through the environment and traverse the storyline. The main lighting of the environment consists of three blue lamps above the balcony, four orange lamps on the main floor, and a row

FIGURE 11-30   Two Targeted Directional lights serve to roughly mimic the light of the surrounding skyline.

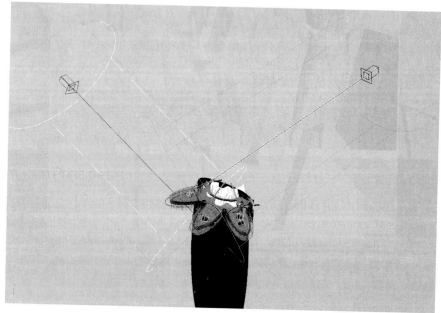

of small green lights on the underside of the balcony. Other specific lighting consists of the large blue chandelier next to the stairs and smaller blue lamps within the booths (see Figure 11-31).

Omni lights are placed inside all the 3-D lamp fixtures—orange Omni lights (R: 251, G: 138, B: 47) in the orange lamps and blue Omni lights (R: 106, G: 127, B: 216) in the blue lamps. This combination of Omni lights and fixtures helps make the light more believable by giving it a visible source. The blue Omni lights are instances of each other, and the orange Omni lights are instances of each other for easier adjusting. The green spotlights (R: 133, G: 221, B: 129) are instances along a path drawn under the balcony using the Spacing tool.

Mini Lighting Primer

To have control over lighting in your scene, you'll have to be thoroughly familiar with both Omni lights and spotlights. The illustration to the right shows some of the key parameters found in the Modify panel that were used extensively throughout this environment.

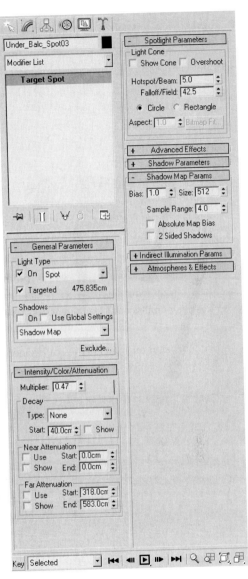

Color and Multiplier   The color setting and Multiplier value work in combination with each other to define the intensity of the light as well as, obviously, the color.

Attenuation   The Attenuation settings define where the light starts to trail off based on a distance from the light source. Without an attenuation set, lights will illuminate objects infinitely far away, which is unnatural. Clicking the Use check box will turn on attenuation, and clicking the Show check box will cause the attenuation to be displayed in the viewports as a circle surrounding the lights, which can be a helpful visualization tool.

Falloff   Spotlights have extra parameters to define the cone of light they cast. The Hotspot/Beam and Falloff/Field parameters work together to define the size and softness of the light they cast.

FIGURE 11-31 This image shows the various lights placed around the scene within the 3-D models of the light fixtures. Three blue lamp models appear above the balcony with three blue Omni lights. Four orange lamps with orange Omni lights appear on the floor at the edges of the glass bubbles. A row of green spotlights shines down from underneath the balcony.

Shadows   A number of parameters are used to define the quality of shadows, and there are some specific ones to pay attention to. They can be turned on and off through the Shadows On check box. The light can cast several types of shadows, and these are chosen from a drop-down list in the General Parameters section of the Modify panel. Although it is possible to get highly accurate shadows with Raytraced and Advanced Raytraced shadows, these add significantly to render times. For this environment, the default Shadow Mapped shadows are adequate. The amount of detail in the shadows of a given light is determined by the Size parameter in the Shadow Map Parameters section of the Modify panel. Typically the default size of 512 is sufficient, but this can be raised higher if more detailed shadows are necessary.

Exclude and Include Lists   Unlike in the real world, in CG animation you have the ability to determine whether or not a given object is illuminated by a particular light. This is done with the Exclude/Include dialog box, shown right. It is accessed in the General Parameters section of the Modify panel. This dialog box gives you powerful control in your scene.

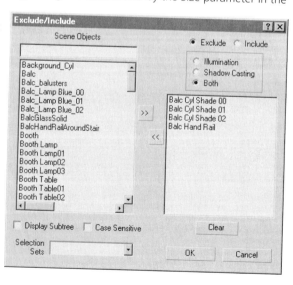

For example, if you need to light some objects with a certain color or intensity to color those objects with specific highlights, other objects do not need to be affected. Objects from the scene are selected from the lists on the left, and the arrow buttons are used to place them in a specific light's list. The list can contain either the objects that are excluded from the light or objects that are included in the light, depending on the radio button selected.

Balancing and Render Testing

During the placing of lights, and once all of the lights are in place, you will need to do many test renders while tweaking the light parameters listed earlier, particularly the parameters in the Intensity/Color/Attenuation section of the Modify panel. This will often need to be done in conjunction with adjusting the various Specular parameters in the materials of the scene.

A tool that can help you enormously in this process is the Light Lister (see Figure 11-32). This tool is found in the main menu under Tools | Light Lister. It presents all the lights in your scene, with access to many of the most important parameters all in one window. This alleviates the need to navigate the scene, find the light you need, and tweak it individually. This console can greatly speed the process of balancing the lighting in your scene.

FIGURE 11-32   This is the Light Lister for Cloud10. It provides easy access to light parameters and allows you to compare values between lights.

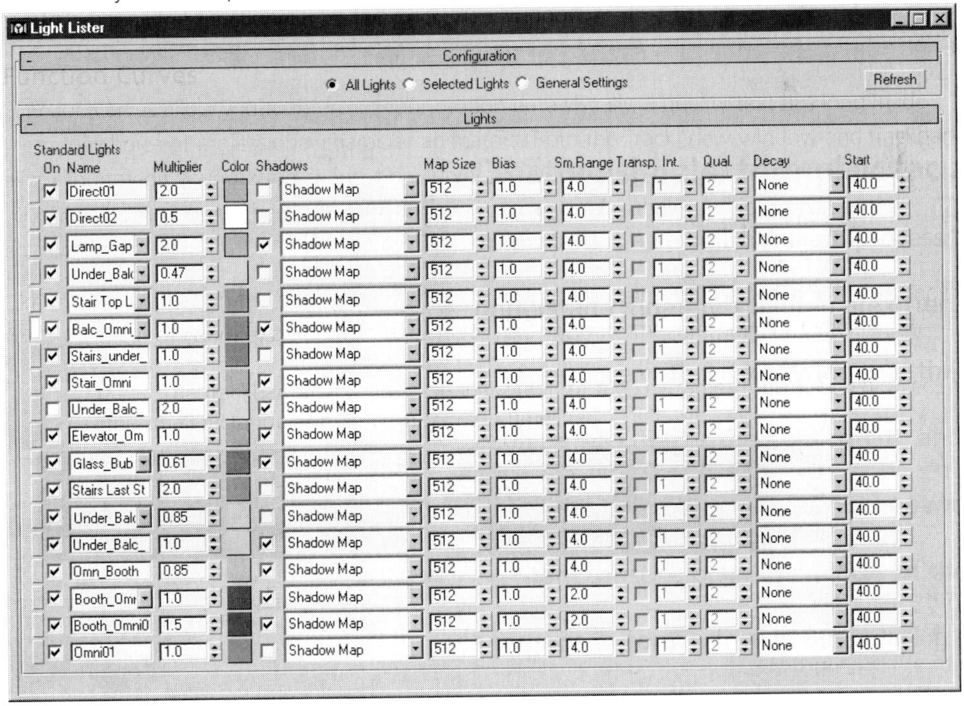

 **NOTE** *On the CD-ROM, the file ...\3dsmax6_CD\Cloud10* *Cloud10_05.max contains the completed scene.*

Organizing Your Scene(s)

From here, it is recommended that you spend some time preparing your scene for heavy usage during the animation process. This entails both organization for easy usage and optimization for render times that are as short as possible. Here is a list of some of the things you can do to keep complex scene files organized:

▶ Remove any unseen polygons from objects. This may require converting the object to an Editable Mesh or Editable Poly object.

▶ Delete any shapes that were used in the construction process that are no longer needed. These can be merged back from an older file if needed.

▶ In most cases, you'll want to collapse the stacks of objects and convert them to Editable Poly objects for simplicity in your file. If you have very high polygon objects created procedurally, you may not want to do this because your file size may grow when converting them to raw geometry. If you need to edit objects afterward, you can always merge in the uncollapsed versions of specific objects from a previous file.

▶ As mentioned in Chapter 2, make sure your objects are named as logically as possible. This aids not only in finding an object but also in selecting and hiding groups of objects. For example, if the balcony in this environment needs to be hidden, all objects related to the balcony can be selected by typing "balc" in the Select Objects dialog box.

▶ Make sure all textures being used in the scene are in the same folder so that they can easily be copied along with the file.

If your project calls for multiple scenes, you will need an extra level of organization. It may be helpful in this case to use external references (which we'll explore in the next chapter) for objects that are in more than one scene. Also, make sure that wherever possible your different scene files reference texture maps located in one central repository folder. Having multiple scenes will require you to be careful about the naming of your folders and files as well as the objects within them.

Part III

The Second Production Phase: Animating

Chapter 12

Layout: Preparing the max Scene

Scene layout is a relatively tiny undertaking in terms of time and effort, but it stands tall in its effect on the rest of the animation process. A few focused organizational tasks with an eye toward the animation workflow can have a great impact on how smoothly your animating, arguably the largest filmmaking task, proceeds.

Back to the Producer's Job

3-D animation scene files can become highly complicated, sometimes consisting of almost all the assets produced for a short film. Once a scene consists of the character models and their rigs, environment models, lights, and other scene components, viewports can become confusing and interactivity performance may bog down. Therefore, scene organization is critical to being able to animate at all.

Additionally, initial staging and timing of the various shots required by the storyboards also require organization and preparation. A scene file may need to accommodate several sequential shots presenting logistical issues of basic filmmaking, such as character and camera placements, shot composition, timing, and so on.

The organization and layout of scene files may have many valid approaches. It all boils down to what is the most effective, streamlined workflow for you. In this chapter, we'll prepare to animate the first scene of *The Game to Save the World*, according to the script and storyboards. This will start with the opening credits and include the character Zoey entering, answering her phone, talking, and then starting down the stairs.

Scene Breakdown and File Creation

First, we'll construct a scene-encompassing max file by breaking down the film into discrete, manageable segments and then merging together the environment, characters, and the audio file. It is usually impractical to make one max file that contains the entire animation. As the many animated objects start to contain more and more keyframes, and as audio files get longer, memory quickly becomes full and the file becomes unwieldy to work with. As a rule of thumb, the more complex the animation, the shorter each file should be.

Creating a Max File

This first max scene file will encompass the first scene, which ends when Zoey begins to descend the stairs. This mark comes at one minute and 22 seconds into the animation. At 30 frames per second, the 1:22 mark translates into 2,460 frames. Start by creating a new file and populating it with the character and environment with these steps:

1 Create a folder called Scenes and create a new max file named Scene_01_00.max. Save it in the root folder, …\3dsmax6_CD\.

 2 In the bottom right of the max interface, use the Time Configuration button to access the Time Configuration dialog box, shown here, and set End Time to 2460 frames.

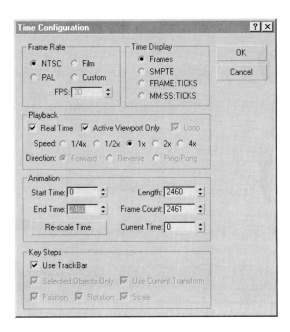

Making XRefs for the Environment

XRefs are external references to objects contained in another file. By bringing the environment models into the scene as XRefs, several advantages are gained over including the actual geometry. XRefs allow you to modify objects in their original file and have those modifications automatically propagate to all scene files that reference the original file. And because you'll be creating many scene files in which to animate, it will be helpful not to have to make modifications in multiple files if you need to change something about the environment. Another advantage to using XRefs is that they help save disk space. The sizes of the scene files will be smaller because they do not need to contain the environment geometry. Also, because you'll be making multiple iterations of each scene file as you work, using XRefs can save you significant disk space.

To make XRefs work properly, you need to maintain the original source file in its designated folder and make sure that the names of all the objects that get externally referenced do not change in either your scene files or the original environment file. Make sure that you have copied the folders from the CD-ROM to your hard drive so that the folder structure from the CD-ROM is duplicated, and then you can create the external references for the Cloud10 geometry.

1   Copy the folder …\3dsmax6_CD\Cloud10\ into the \3dsmax6_CD\ folder on your hard drive if necessary. This folder contains the file Cloud10_Final.max and the subfolder C10 maps.

2 In max, choose File/XRef Objects from the main menu. Click the Add button and choose the Cloud10_Final.max file. The XRef Merge dialog box, shown next, appears. In the List Types section of the dialog box, click the Lights and Cameras check boxes to remove all Light and Camera objects from the objects list. Click the All button under the objects list (not the All button in the List Types section) to select all the listed objects. Then click OK.

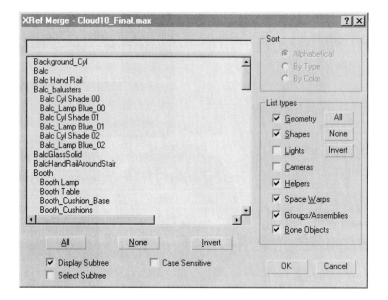

This adds all the selected objects in the list to the scene as XRefs. They are then listed in the bottom of the XRef Objects window (see Figure 12-1).

Merging Environment Lights and Cameras

Because you will have to modify some lights for specific scenes, the environment lights should be merged into the scene completely instead of XRef'ed. We'll merge the camera from the original source file to use it in this tutorial. Follow these steps to continue to assemble the scene file:

1 Choose File | Merge from the main menu and choose the Cloud10_Final.max file again.

2 In the Merge dialog box, click the Lights and Cameras check boxes again and then click the Invert button in the List Types section of the dialog box. Then click the All button under the objects list and click OK.

FIGURE 12-1   The XRef Objects window provides control over adding and removing objects in the scene that are externally referenced.

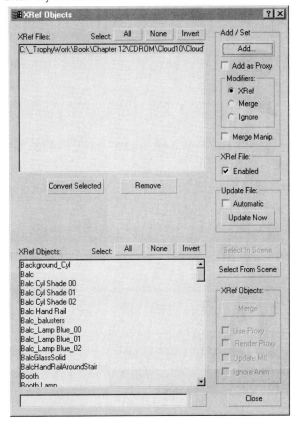

Merging and Placing the Character

In Chapter 10, we prepared characters by rigging and organizing them for animation. Now we can bring an entire rigged character file into the scene by merging it. Continue to assemble the scene file by following these steps:

1 Copy the …\3dsmax6_CD\Zoey\ folder to \3dsmax6_CD\ folder on your hard drive if necessary. Then in max, choose File | Merge from the main menu and choose the Zoey_Rigged.max file. Use the All button to select all objects within this file and click OK.

The Zoey character objects will appear at the origin because this is where they are in the Zoey_Rigged.max file. Because the scene is large, hunting around the viewports with the Pan and Zoom tools can be tedious. By using the Select by Name and Align tools together, you can place the Zoey character quickly.

2 Click the Select button and then the Select by Name button at the top of the max interface. Scroll down to choose Zoe_placementCTRL from the list and then click Select. Click the Lock Selection button at the bottom of the interface.

3 Change to a camera viewport (Camera_Elevator) and click the Maximize Viewport button at the bottom right of the max interface.

4 Click the Align Tool button. Then click the Select by Name button, select ElevDoor Hinge Front from the list, and click Pick. Click the Align Position X, Y, and Z check boxes and click OK.

5 Select the ElevDoor object (either by clicking the object itself or by using the Select by Name button), right-click it, and choose Hide Selection. Now that the elevator door is out of the way, select the Zoe_placementCTRL object again and use the Move tool to move it into the elevator. Move it up in the Z-axis until it is even with the floor of the elevator.

6 Because Zoey is facing the wrong way, select both the Zoe_placementCTRL and Zoe_headCTRL objects (because the head is rigged to rotate independently from the rest of the character) and rotate them 180 degrees in the Z-axis (see Figure 12-2).

Organizing with Selection Sets and Filters

To make the scene easier to work in, you can create selection sets that allow you to quickly hide and unhide specific groups of objects. This will improve the frame rate in the viewports, making interactivity more responsive and animation playback smoother. It will also make the viewports less cluttered and therefore more informative. Follow the steps to do this:

1 Click the Select by Name button and turn off all check boxes in the List Types section except for Geometry and XRefs. Select all the objects in the object list except for the Zoey objects and then click the Select button.

2 Click inside the blank drop-down list in max's main toolbar and name this selection set Cloud10 Geometry. This selection set will allow you to isolate characters easily.

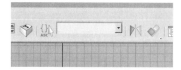

FIGURE 12-2   Here is Zoey in position in the elevator.

3   Create another selection set that includes the balcony XRef objects (names beginning with {balc...), the elevator XRef objects (names beginning with {elev...), and the {Wall_rear} object. All names of XRef'd objects begin with a "{". This selection set isolates the objects needed to work specifically on this scene. Name this selection set Balc Elev & Wall.

4   Create another selection set that includes all objects (geometry, shapes, helpers, bones and lights) that begin with Z.... This will, of course, allow you to hide and unhide the character as needed. Name this selection set Zoey.

Further streamlining of the workflow can be achieved by controlling object categories. Using the check boxes in the Hide by Category section of the Display panel, you can hide and unhide categories to unclutter the viewports. Also, the Filters drop-down list near the left of the main toolbar allows you to arrange for only a particular category of objects to be selected in the viewports.

It is particularly helpful to choose Shapes from the drop-down list. This allows for much easier selection of the character's various control objects.

The use of filters and selection sets also makes it easier to change from a setup for animating, where bones may need to be visible and portions of the environment need to be hidden, to a setup for rendering, where mostly geometry objects need to be visible.

>> TIP *Layers are another powerful 3ds max organizational feature. Objects can be placed on separate layers to quickly control many properties across groups. Layers can control both viewport and render visibility and many other object properties. Particularly if your scenes contain many objects or complicated rendering setups, layers can further streamline workflow.*

Dialogue Audio Placement

Once the scene has been broken down so that you know how long the section of film you will be working on is, the corresponding portion of the soundtrack can be separated as a scratch WAV audio file. You can save memory by using only the amount of audio that is needed for the scene you're working on. Here's how to add the audio file to this scene:

1 Copy the …\3dsmax6_CD\Audio\folder from the CDROM to your \3dsmax6_CD\ folder if necessary.

2 Load the audio file into the scene by first opening the Graph Editors | Track View window. At the top of the Controller window, in the hierarchical tree view on the left side of the track view, click the Sound entry to select it. Then right-click and choose Properties from the pop-up menu.

3 Click the Choose Sound button and select the file roughdialogue_scene1.wav from the \3dsmax6_CD\ Audio folder. Then click OK.

Now when you play animation in the scene or scrub the Time slider back and forth, you will hear the audio.

NOTE *On the CD-ROM, the file …\3dsmax6_CD\Scene1_00_CH12.max contains the completed tutorial to this point.*

Blocking Movement

Now we can move on to blocking the movement of the Zoey character and setting up cameras to frame that movement according to the script and storyboards. By keyframing the gross movement of the character, we can quickly determine timing and pacing by plotting the entire scene—and the scene is also separated into smaller discrete sections. Then, during the actual character animation phase, we can focus on these shorter, more digestible sections.

To start, we'll create a camera for the opening shot of the film. This shot looks off of the balcony and slowly turns while the titles for the film roll. This makes the reflected glass of the environment a nice abstract backdrop for the titles sequence. Also, as the turning camera comes to rest on the elevator, the door will open to reveal Zoey.

Opening the Door

To get the timing right for our scene, we'll keyframe the door opening just before the "elevator voice" greets Zoey. This will give us a queue for when the camera should finish its turn. We'll add some simple keyframes to the door to make it open.

1 Hide the named selection set Cloud10 Geometry and unhide the Balc Elev & Wall selection set. In the Hide by Category section of the Display panel, click the Lights and Helpers check boxes.

2 To provide finer control when scrubbing the Time slider, click the Time Configuration button and set End Time to 1200 frames. The start time and end time, which make up the active time segment, can be changed as needed so you can work on different sections of the animation.

3 In a camera viewport (Cam_Elevator), select the {Elev_Door} XRef object and move the Time slider to frame 1000. Turn on Set Key mode by clicking the Set Key button. Click the Key Filters button and uncheck everything except Rotation. Then click the Set Keys button to set a rotation key for the door.

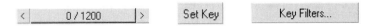

This key establishes the door's initial rotation angle at frame 1000 so that any rotation keys set afterward will cause the door to rotate starting from this frame.

4   Move the Time slider to frame 1040. Rotate the door –100 degrees in the Y-axis and click the Set Key button. Then turn off Set Key mode by clicking the Set Key Mode button again.

This sets the key for the door to rotate into the open position. You can scrub the Time slider back and forth to see the animation. For each key that is set, a marker appears in the trackbar below the Time slider. These markers can be moved to the right or the left in the trackbar to make an action happen earlier or later (see Figure 12-3).

Setting Up the First Shot

Now you can begin to the set up cameras and timing for the shots for this scene according to the storyboards. The first shot starts with the camera pointing off the balcony and gradually rotating around to the elevator just in time to see Zoey enter Cloud10.

1   Click the Maximize button to return to the standard four-window viewport layout. Right-click the word (for example "Top" or "Perspective") at the upper-left corner of one of the viewports and choose Configure from the pop-up menu. Then click the Layout tab.

2   Click the icon for the vertical two-window layout, as shown in Figure 12-4. Click in the left panel and make it a top view. Leave the right viewport for now.

3   Use the Pan and Zoom tools in the left viewport to frame the area of the balcony around the elevator. Make this viewport a wireframe view (see Figure 12-5).

4   Select and freeze the Balc Elev & Wall selection set.

5   Select and delete the Cam_Elevator object—it was just a temporary camera used to get a good view of the elevator.

6   In the Create panel, click the Cameras button. Then click the Free button. Create a free camera in the left viewport in the hole in the balcony floor where the stairs descend. Name this camera Cam_01_.

FIGURE 12-3   The markers below the Time slider are the keyframes for the door's rotation. They can be moved right or left to change when the door rotation happens in time.

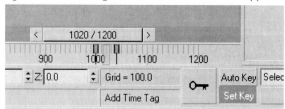

FIGURE 12-4   The viewport layout window

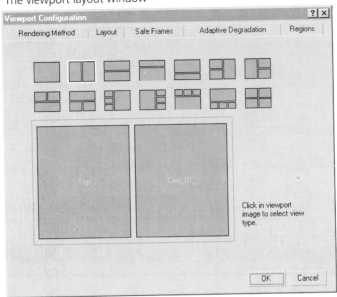

FIGURE 12-5   The left top viewport is set up as a plan view so that cameras can be selected, moved, and animated. The right viewport can be used as a camera view to show what the camera is framing.

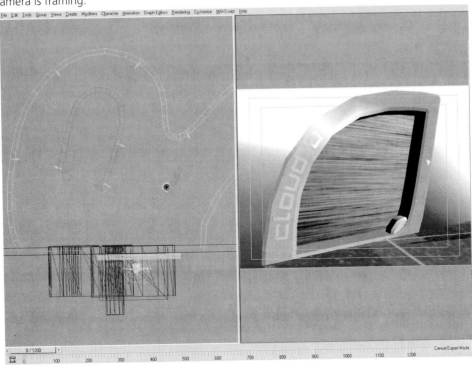

7 Change the right viewport to the camera view of Cam_01_. Select and rotate the camera in the top-left viewport first 90 degrees in the X-axis. Then temporarily change the top viewport to a left viewport and move the camera up until it is roughly level with Zoey's head. Then change the viewport back to a top view.

8 You can use the Camera Rotate tools on the right-side camera viewport to frame the shot like the first storyboard (see Figure 12-6a through Figure 12-6c). You'll want to unhide the selection set named Cloud10 Geometry temporarily to be able to frame the scene properly. To show only what the camera frames, right-click the camera name in the upper left of the camera viewport and choose Show Safe Frame from the pop-up menu. Once the shot is framed, hide everything but Zoey and the balcony again.

9 Set Key Filters to include rotation and position and then turn on Set Key mode. With the Cam_01_ object selected, set a key at frame 0.

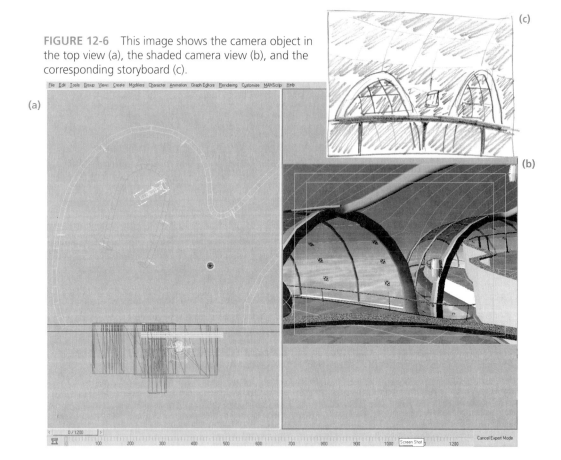

FIGURE 12-6 This image shows the camera object in the top view (a), the shaded camera view (b), and the corresponding storyboard (c).

10 Move to frame 1001. In the top view, move the camera to the right in the Y-axis and then rotate the camera 220 degrees in the Z-axis, as shown in Figure 12-7a. You may need to do some minor adjustments to the shot by using the Pan tool in the camera view (see Figure 12-7b) to frame the shot like the second storyboard (see Figure 12-7c). Set a key for the camera's position and rotation here at frame 1001.

11 Rename this camera Cam_01_0-1001 to indicate which frames of the animation will need to be rendered from this camera.

You can save yourself many headaches by creating simple camera movements wherever possible. Through economical use of keys, the animation of the cameras can remain easy to change. Simpler camera movements also lend themselves to camera shots that are more familiar to viewers because real-world camera movements are often simple due to the physical constraints of camera rigs, unless you want a specific effect such as a handheld camera shake.

FIGURE 12-7   This image shows the camera object in the top view (a), the shaded camera view (b), and the corresponding storyboard (c).

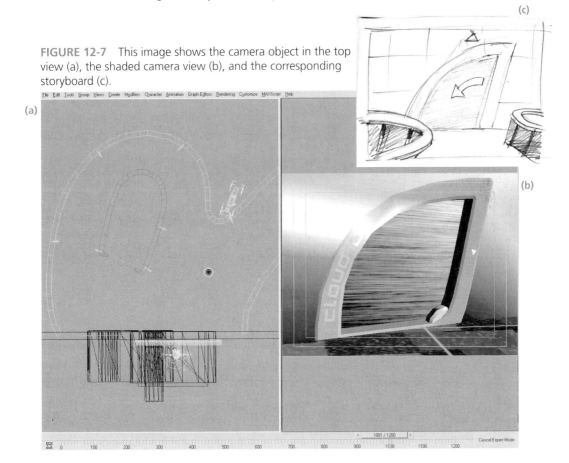

Now you can move the Time slider to frame 0 and play the animation in the Cam_01_0-1001 viewport. This gives you a sense of the time available for the film's titles to appear as the camera slowly rotates. By the time the titles are done, the camera will come to rest at the elevator just before it opens to reveal Zoey.

> **≫TIP** *When playing back animation in the viewports, you may get better real-time performance by maximizing the viewport. Real-time performance can vary greatly from system to system. Also, in my experience, frame rate is much better when the video card is driving only one viewport.*

Keyframing Zoey

Now we have a starting point for Zoey to begin moving through the scene. We only need to create position and rotation keys for the hips and feet control objects at key points in the animation, as dictated by the script and storyboards.

In this scene, Zoey pauses very briefly after the elevator door opens to hear the recorded voice. She exits the elevator, walking to the nearest railing, around the stairs, and pauses as her phone rings. She begins to talk and continues walking toward the balcony railing that overlooks the main space. She slides along the railing briefly while she continues to talk. Then she finally turns and walks toward the stairs, where the scene ends as she starts to descend.

We'll set keys for Zoey's various stage marks. Specific moments in the dialogue will help determine what frames to place keys on. Specific frame numbers are included in the following exercise, but you can also scrub through the animation in a particular section with the Time slider to hear the corresponding passage.

Figure 12-8 shows the different positions that Zoey will be in at different points in time. You can use this diagram as a guide as you create keyframes. Here are the steps to follow:

1 In the Time Configuration window, make the Active Time Segment stretch between frame 1000 and 2460 by setting these values in Start Time and End Time, respectively.

2 Select Zoe_footRCTRL, Zoe_footLCTRL, and Zoe_hipCTRL. I'll refer to this selection set as the hips and feet. With Set Keys mode on, move the Time slider to frame 1109 and set keys for the position and rotation of the hips and feet.

This keyframe establishes Zoey's position in the elevator right up until the time that the recorded voice in the elevator begins.

FIGURE 12-8   This is a diagram of Zoey's keyframes.

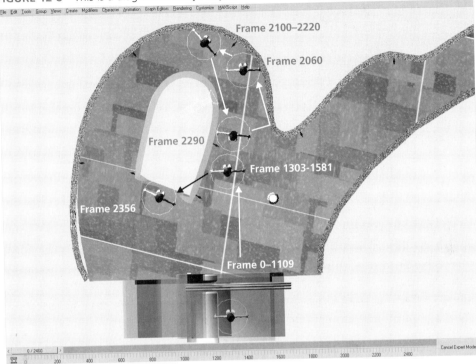

3   Move the Time slider to frame 1303 and then move the hips and feet in the Y-axis to be near the right side of the stair railing between the two balusters.

This keyframe obviously moves Zoey to the railing. This is where Zoey, when animated, will hit the pose of storyboard 4.

4   Set another key to hold the position at frame 1581. This is where Zoey will pause to answer the phone.

Zoey needs to hold her position here long enough to look around briefly, answer her phone, and start talking.

5   Move the Time slider to frame 2060 and move the hips and feet to Zoey's next stage mark at the balcony railing. Set a key.

When Zoey realizes it's her friend Felix, she begins walking toward the balcony railing as she talks on her telephone. This starts her walking right about when Felix says, "Welcome to the upper-middle class…."

6 Move the Time slider to frame 2100 and move the hips and feet to Zoey's next stage mark to the left, along the railing. Rotate the hips and feet together so that her body roughly faces the farthest glass bubble. You'll have to reposition the feet so they are not crossing. Then set a key.

Just as Zoey's voice changes intensity to say, "Are you here? Where are you?" she will slide abruptly along the railing as though looking for her friend. The abruptness comes from moving her a relatively longer distance in a fewer number of frames.

7 Move the Time slider to frame 2220 and make keys for the hips and feet to hold her position.

She'll continue to pause at the railing as she talks to Felix until he says, "Just go straight on through…."

8 Move the Time slider to frame 2356 and move the hips and feet to the start of the stairs. Rotate the hips and feet so that Zoey faces the stairs and then set keys for rotation and position.

This last keyframe causes Zoey to take a direct line from the balcony railing straight through the stairs. To correct this, you can move the Time slider halfway back toward the previous keyframe and move the hips and feet back outside of the railing that rings the stair opening.

9 Move the Time slider to frame 2290 and move the hips and feet to the right, along the X-axis, until Zoey is outside the railing. Rotate the hips and feet so that Zoey is still facing her destination and then set position and rotation keys.

Play back the animation to watch Zoey hit her marks at key points in the dialogue.

NOTE *Because Zoey's head rotates independently from the character, she will be doing her* Exorcist *impersonation as she moves through the scene. If this is disconcerting to you, you can add rotation keys for the Zoe_headCTRL object. However, this is not necessary because you'll be creating keys to control the head and the rest of the character in great detail during the character-animation phase.*

Creating Cameras and Framing Shots

As Zoey moves through the scene, cameras will be stationed in spots that frame her movement and the background. Now that Zoey's movement is blocked in, cameras can be placed according to the storyboards.

The rest of the cameras we'll use are targeted cameras. Having the camera's target (that is, what the camera is pointing at) as an independent object allows you to align or even link the target to other objects so that the camera can track them automatically. While you're working with cameras, you may want to turn on the cameras' selection filter so that only cameras can be selected in the viewports.

Camera 2   Camera 2 is a close-up camera of Zoey as she exits the elevator. The camera target is keyframed to briefly follow her as she moves forward. The purpose of this shot is to highlight Zoey's facial expression as she glimpses Cloud10 for the first time. Figure 12-9a through Figure 12-9c can

FIGURE 12-9   This image shows the Camera 2 object in the top view (a), the shaded camera view (b), and the corresponding storyboard (c).

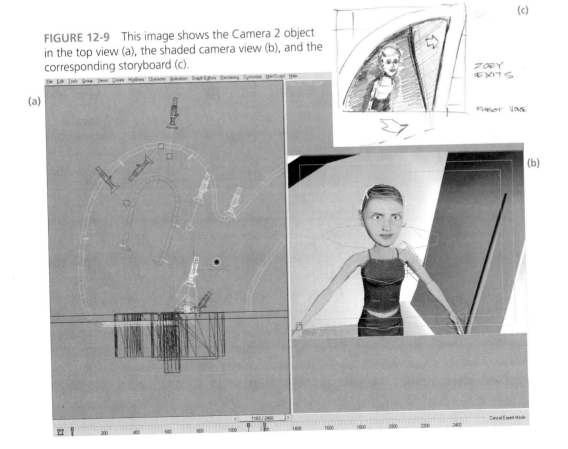

be used as a guide to frame this shot. Continue setting up camera shots for this scene file with these steps:

1 Move the Time slider to frame 1101.

2 Return to the dual-viewport layout used earlier. Click the Target button in the Cameras menu and drag in the top view, starting where the camera will be placed and dragging to Zoey's head. Name this camera Cam_02_1101-1300.

3 In a left view, move the camera and target up to be level with Zoey's head. In the camera view, use the camera-navigation tools to frame the shot according to the second storyboard. Move the target to be right at Zoey's nose. Create position and rotation keys for both the camera and its target.

FIGURE 12-10   This image shows the Camera 3 object in the top view (a), the shaded camera view (b), and the corresponding storyboard (c).

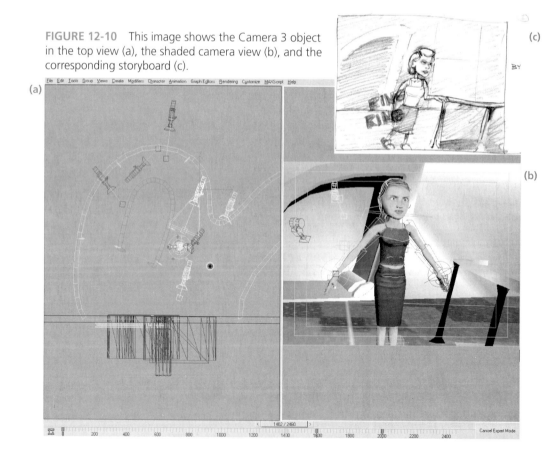

4   Move the Time slider to frame 1300. Use the camera-panning tool in the camera viewport to frame Zoey again. Move the target to be at Zoey's nose again so that the camera will point directly at her. Set rotation and position keys for both the camera and its target.

Camera 3   The third camera will frame Zoey as she walks toward the stair railing, pauses, and then answers her phone. The camera for this shot will be farther away to frame Zoey's body language as she enters. This camera will cover frames 1301–1580. Create the camera and frame the shot according to the third storyboard (see Figure 12-10a through Figure 12-10c opposite page). Name the camera Cam_03_1301-1580.

Camera 4   The fourth shot focuses on Zoey's right hand as her phone materializes from thin air (see Figure 12-11a through Figure 12-11c below). It's impossible to frame the shot until the

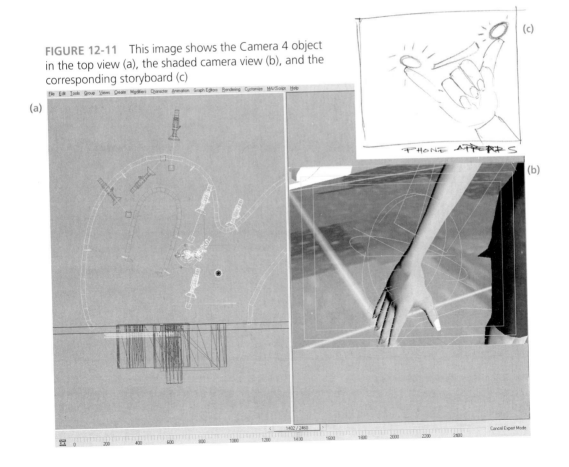

FIGURE 12-11   This image shows the Camera 4 object in the top view (a), the shaded camera view (b), and the corresponding storyboard (c)

scene has been animated. Therefore, you can simply create a camera and link it and its target to Zoey's Zoe_handRCTRL object for now. Name this camera Cam_04_1581-1615.

Back to Camera 3   If this were a real-world film production, the director would simply switch back to footage from Camera 3 during the editing process. We can do this by rendering frames 1616–2060 from Camera 3 in addition to the previous Camera 3 sequence. You may want to tack on "1561-2000" to the camera name to make it Cam_03_1201-1500_1616-2060. Because Zoey is moving forward during this sequence, the camera needs to be animated dollying back to keep Zoey in frame.

As before, create keyframes for the initial positions and rotations of the camera and target at the beginning of this sequence (Frame 1616). Then move the Time slider to the end of the sequence (Frame 2060) and use the camera-navigation tools to frame the shot again. Set keys for the rotation and position of the camera and target again (see Figure 12-12a through Figure 12-12c).

FIGURE 12-12   This image shows the Camera 3 object again in the top view (a), the shaded camera view for the second Camera 3 sequence (b), and the corresponding storyboard (c).

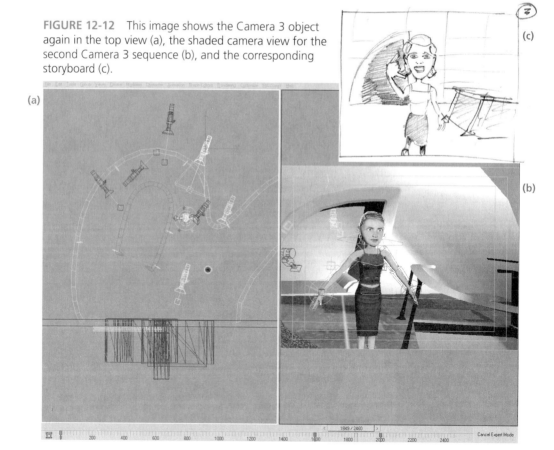

Camera 5   Camera 5 looks slightly upward at the balcony as Zoey slides into frame when she says, "Are you here? Where are you?" Having Zoey slide into frame will help accentuate her motion. This camera is named Cam_05_2061-2100 and is not animated (see Figure 12-13a through Figure 12-13c).

Camera 6   Camera 6 looks over Zoey's shoulder to see what she is seeing while Felix describes Cloud10 to her. This camera is named Cam_06_2101-2220 and is not animated (see Figure 12-14a through Figure 12-14c).

Camera 7   Camera 7 frames Zoey as she walks back to the start of the staircase. This camera is named Cam_07_2221-2430 and is not animated (see Figure 12-15a through Figure 12-15c).

⌣ NOTE   *On the CD-ROM, the file …\3dsmax6_CD\Scene1_01_CH12.max contains the completed tutorial to this point. Later in production, during the animation process, camera 7 was split into three shots. This file includes these cameras as well.*

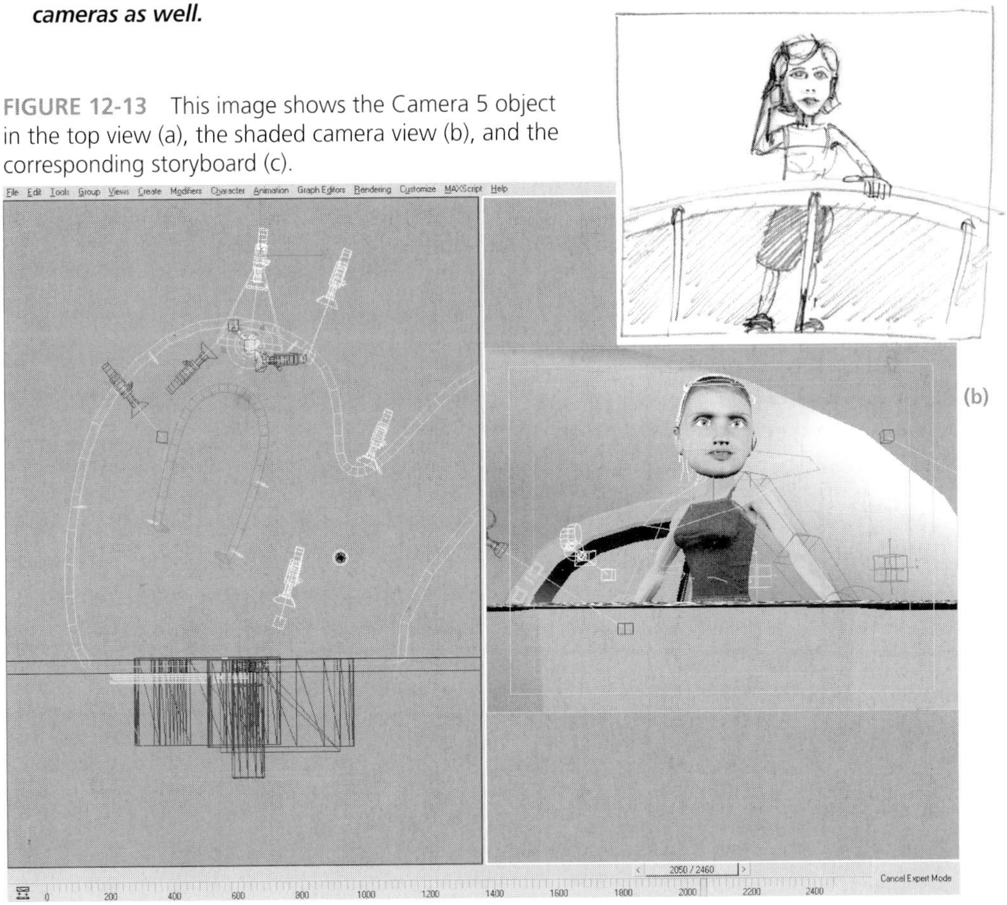

(c)

FIGURE 12-13   This image shows the Camera 5 object in the top view (a), the shaded camera view (b), and the corresponding storyboard (c).

(a)

(b)

FIGURE 12-14 This image shows the Camera 6 object in the top view (a), the shaded camera view (b), and the corresponding storyboard (c).

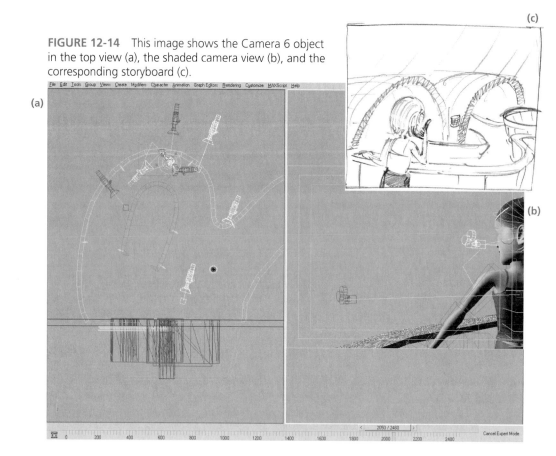

Either camera placement or character blocking can come first in your process, according to the dictates of specific shots. For the first shot, it was helpful to know when the camera would finish its rotation and when the door would open before Zoey exited the elevator. For the other shots, it was helpful to have Zoey's movement through the scene blocked and then frame that movement.

Shot compositions and timing will undoubtedly change as the animation is fleshed out. However, blocking the scene in this manner, according to the storyboards, should allow you to create your animation with the context of where it will be viewed from. Then, only minor changes to the cameras may be required once the animation is done. Camera shots can be composed further by adjusting the cameras' position, field of view and focal length once the scenes are animated.

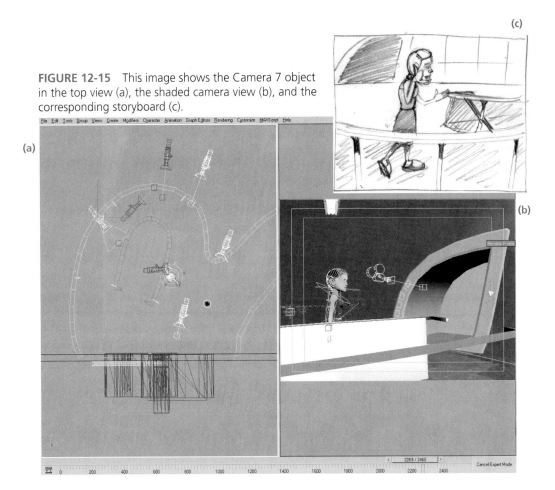

FIGURE 12-15   This image shows the Camera 7 object in the top view (a), the shaded camera view (b), and the corresponding storyboard (c).

Previsualization Revisited

Once you have blocked the character and camera movements for a series of shots, you can quickly create an animatic using 3ds max's preview feature. This is a powerful way to provide insight into your film's pacing and overall cinematic qualities. It can also tell you a lot about whether your story is being communicated. Follow the steps to create a preview:

1   Make the camera viewport for the camera whose animation you want to preview the active viewport by clicking in it.

2 In the main menu, choose Animation | Make Preview. In the Make Preview dialog box, click the Custom Range radio button and set the frames according to the sequence for that camera.

3 Set the image size to 100 percent and uncheck all the check boxes except Geometry and Shapes. Click the Create button.

4 When the preview is completed, the resulting AVI file will automatically run in the Windows Media Player (or whatever your default AVI player is). Close this, and in the max main menu choose Animation | Rename Preview and save the file.

5 Repeat this for each camera in the scene and give each file a unique name when you rename it.

6 The files can then be edited together in a video-editing program such as Premiere and then exported as a single file (see Chapter 17).

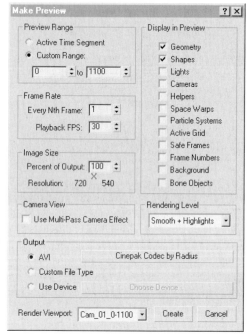

It is wise to leave yourself open to making this process of blocking shots and creating an animatic an iterative one. This way, you can consult the animatic and make changes before you commit to full animation. To be sure, camera timings and compositions may need to change as you animate. But there is no substitute for the structure that thorough shot set ups can give you during the animation process. Your best work will be done when you can strike a balance between gaining all the benefits of thoroughly planned shots while still allowing for some serendipity and improvisation as your animations take shape.

Chapter 13

Body Animation: Character Motion Through Keyframing

Animating objects and characters is much like painting with motion. Many falsely heralded the advent of photography as the death of painting, yet painting and illustration are still vibrant art forms. Likewise, many have predicted the death of keyframed animation with the arrival of motion capture technology, yet it still thrives. The painting-versus-photography analogy can provide us with a helpful insight. The motions created by animators can be as expressive and individual as the animators creating them. And just like a photograph cannot duplicate the expressiveness of a good cartoon illustration, motion-capturing actual movements can't compete with the artistry of a skilled animator.

The Basis for Animated Motion: Keyframing

In traditional animation studios, senior animators typically draw every few frames, known as *keyframes*. This allows them to focus on the critical poses of the character most important in telling the story. Then lower-level animators, known as *inbetweeners*, draw all the frames between these keyframes. As computer animators, we have a similar ability to focus on keyframes and can allow the computer to do the grunt work of inbetweening. Animation is a mature art form, full of history and tradition, so it is good to recognize the similarities between what traditional and computer animators do. This way, we can draw upon the larger world of animation for excellent reference, instruction, and inspiration.

Animation Principles

The cornerstone of almost any animation instruction today, whether for 2-D or 3-D animation, is some version of the 12 basic principles outlined by the early Disney animators. These principles cover the various qualities of adding believable and expressive motions to characters as you create keyframes. Although many educators present variations on this list of principles, it is most commonly presented as the following principles. There has been much written about them to draw upon for instruction, so I'll simply list them here:

▶ **Squash and stretch** Showing objects to be flexible while maintaining their volume.

▶ **Anticipation and follow-through** The windup before a baseball pitch and pulling a fist backward before a punch are anticipations that must be included in those actions for them to be believable. The knees of a character buckling upon landing after a jump is an example of follow-through.

▶ **Staging** Even the most expertly animated actions must be framed so they can be understood. If a camera is behind the back of a knife-wielding attacker, the assailant may as well be brandishing a flower as far as the audience is concerned. Viewers cannot see a character's facial expressions if its back is to the camera. Any action must be staged so that the story point is communicated, and scenes must be framed so that visual compositions are balanced and dynamic.

▶ **Pose-to-pose and straight-ahead keyframing** These are the two main approaches toward creating keyframes. The pose-to-pose method focuses the animator's attention on the crucial story moments, whereas the straight-ahead method is a one-frame-at-a-time approach, typically used by stop-motion animators.

▶ **Overlapping** There are usually many components to a character action made by the different parts of its body. These components are usually not in lock synchronization with one another but overlap in time to far richer more fluid motions. As a character walks, its arms may swing in a different cycle than its legs, making for overlapping motions.

▶ **Ease in and ease out** Except for machine and robot movements, most character actions involve at least some acceleration at the beginning and deceleration at the end. This principle is also known as *slow ins and slow outs*.

▶ **Arcs** Because characters are usually constructed from bones and joints, things such as hands and feet typically travel in curving arcs centered around elbows and shoulders, as opposed to moving in straight lines.

▶ **Secondary action** A whipping ponytail and a bouncing belly are examples of secondary actions that help accent the main motions of the character's body.

▶ **Timing** Devoting the proper number of frames to a particular action can help to determine whether that action is believable or exaggerated for dramatic or comedic intent.

▶ **Exaggeration** In much the same way that cartoonists and illustrators exaggerate poses and expressions for both dramatic and comedic intent, animators can exaggerate to provide caricature and emphasis to an action.

▶ **Solid drawing** In the original definitions of the 12 animation principles, solid drawing referred to drawing characters consistently from frame to frame. In his book *The Art of 3D Computer Animation and Effects*, Isaac Kerlow updates the idea, defining it as solid modeling and rigging.

▶ **Personality and appeal** All your animated actions should be assessed based on how well they communicate your character's unique personality traits. The most subjective element to consider is how appealing those actions will be to your audience.

We'll get into the practical applications of many of these principles as we proceed with the animation exercises. Indeed, there are more principles, but you can use these as a starting point for your own animation research and study.

Setting Keys with Set Keys Mode

Creating key positions for your characters' joints, guided by the animation principles, will be the heart and soul of your animated film. In 3ds max, keyframes for a given object are created by moving the timeline slider to a particular frame and positioning, rotating, or scaling the object or changing its parameters. For this project, we'll use max's Set Keys mode to do this. By turning on the Toggle Set Key Mode button, you can experiment with moving and rotating objects at a given frame and then commit to a pose using the Set Keys button, which will create keys at that frame. This allows you to be deliberate and avoid setting keyframes accidentally, which can wreck your animation.

Animating with the Track View Window and the Trackbar

It will be imperative that you are able to clearly visualize a number of aspects of your keys. This is done through the track bar and the Track View window. Both of these components of the 3ds max interface allow you to see *when* a key happens in time by showing a marker at the frame the key occurs on in a ruler-like timeline. These key markers can be selected and moved to change the *timing* of your animation. Also, their properties can be changed to affect their ease in and ease out.

Track View

The Track View window (see Figure 13-1) is composed of a list of the animated components of your scene (called the controller window) on the left and a timeline-based diagram of each component's motion (the edit window) on the right. The Track View window can be used in either Dope Sheet mode, which displays markers for the keys in your scene, or in Curve Editor mode, which displays function curves of the various motion components. For this project we'll work mostly in Curve Editor mode.

FIGURE 13-1   The Curve Editor mode of the Track View window is an essential tool for the animation process. Animators can use the graphical curves to visualize and manipulate the motions of objects in their scenes. The curves illustrate an object's behavior over time.

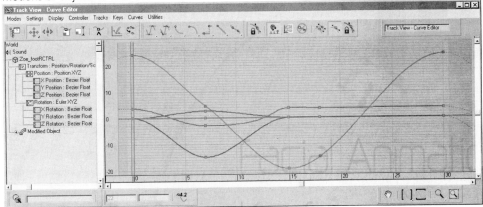

Trackbar

The trackbar, located just below the viewport windows, is a miniature version of the Track View window (see Figure 13-2). Here, you can see key markers for the objects that you have selected in the viewports. This provides a quick and uncluttered way to perform many animation-editing tasks. The trackbar can also be expanded with the Open Mini Curve Editor button, which gives the trackbar all the functionality of the Track View window.

Function Curves

Function curves allow you to interpret your motion data visually, a quality that has long made them the choice of professional character animators. Both the Track View window and trackbar allow you to edit your motion as function curves. By highlighting the specific controllers that you want to work on in the controller window, you can display their function curves in the edit window.

Like the key markers in the dope sheet and the trackbar, the points on the function curves show you the timing of your keys. However, the curves also illustrate the interpolation between the

FIGURE 13-2   The trackbar provides quick visualization of the keyframes for a selected object, shown as the small rectangular markers along the timeline.

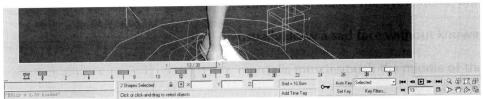

keys, that is, the way an object moves from one state (or *pose*) to another. By moving the handles on the points of a function curve, you can change the motion from robotic, computer-like, straight interpolation to the fluid, expressive movements of a character.

In the simplest of examples, the motion of a ball can be changed from floating weightlessly up and down (see Figure 13-3a and Figure 13-3b) to bouncing realistically by changing the trajectories between the keys on its Z-position function curve (see Figure 13-3c and Figure 13-3d).

Notice how the spacing of the in-between balls change even though the keyframes for both balls are the same. They both pass through the same apex positions at the same times. Easing into and out of keys is important in character animation to avoid stiff and unnatural movements.

Function curves for other components of the animation, such as rotation, scaling, and parameter changing, may not have the visual one-to-one relation of this example, but the interaction remains similar. Sharper bends in the curves mean snappier motions, whereas more rounded curves mean more flowing transitions. Steep curves mean rapid change, whereas flat curves mean no change it all. Learning to interpret the function curves through experimentation and experience will allow you to make the most of this powerful animation tool and dramatically improve the speed at which you can animate.

Getting Zoey Walking

Today, a typical CG animation class will start with lessons on making a ball bounce believably and giving simple objects, such as a block, characterized movements. Making a character walk is also usually among the first tasks given to new animators. Creating a walk cycle is a good, focused exercise for getting to know the character controls. And, more importantly, the way in which a character walks reveals much about that character's personality.

Just about every character will have a walk that is distinctive to them from a combination of their unique physical features and their own personality. A cocky, big-chested, short, middle-aged man will walk very differently than a tall, lanky, insecure 15-year-old girl. This is then combined with the myriad of moods a character may be in. A sleepy boy walks very differently than an excited boy.

For this exercise, we'll give Zoey a basic walk that fits her character and in an even, upbeat mood at a medium pace.

Locomotion

We can approach creating a walk by starting simply with the basic mechanical locomotion that Zoey's body dictates and build in complexity and personality afterward. We'll start with the core

FIGURE 13-3   Here, the trajectory of the ball through space and through time is shown with straight interpolation (a and b), making the ball float robotically up and down. Then the ball is shown with curved interpolations (c and d), which give the ball weight and anticipation as it rises up in the air and slowly falls and bounces sharply on the ground.

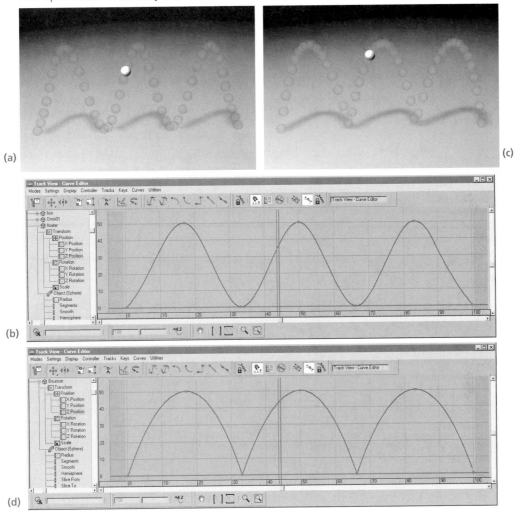

(a)

(c)

(b)

(d)

elements of any walk, by keyframing footsteps, spine counterbalance, and arm swings. Here are the steps to follow:

1   Upon opening the rigged Zoey model (…\3dsmax6_CD\Zoey\ zoe_walk_rigged.max), click the Time Configuration button and set the animation length to 30 frames. This is for a typical one-second walk cycle.

2 In a front viewport, rotate the Zoe_upArmRCTRL and the Zoe_upArmLCTRL objects (the box-shaped controls around Zoey's upper arms) down so that her arms are by her sides (see right). These box-shaped controls use forward kinematics to control the arm bones.

3 For all of the exercises in this chapter, turn on Set Keys mode by clicking near the bottom right of the interface and switch to a left viewport. Set the key filters as shown here to avoid creating unwanted keys.

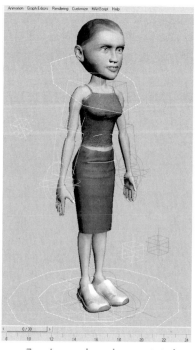

Zoey's arms have been rotated downward to hang by her sides. The box-shaped arm controls can be used to move the arms using forward kinematics, whereas the circular hand controls can be used to move the arms using inverse kinematics.

4 Set the Selection Filter to Shapes.

The Contact Positions

Start by creating what are called the *contact positions*. These are the extreme positions for the legs where the feet first touch the ground on their heels. For Zoey, although these are the farthest positions of her steps, they will be relatively close together because of her skirt. You can combine the consideration that a skirt would actually keep her steps short with the consideration of the rig's limitations. The polygons of the mesh around the legs will start to come apart when the foot controls are moved past a certain point.

1 With the Time slider at frame 0, move the Zoe_footLCTRL object forward (that would be to the right in the left viewport) and click the Set Keys button to set a key for that foot. Position the Zoe_footRCTRL object about the same distance toward Zoey's rear and set a key for that foot. Markers will appear on the left side of the trackbar at frame 0.

2   Move the Zoe_hipCTRL object slightly downward, just far enough so that Zoey's knees are slightly bent, and set a key.

3   Use the Custom Attribute spinners within the foot-control objects to roll the feet so that the left foot is striking on its heel and the right foot is leaving off its toe. Select the Zoe_footLCTRL shape object and in the Modify panel, move the Roll spinner down to about –10 and the toeRotate spinner to 9 and set a key. Select the Zoe_footRCTRL object, move its Roll spinner to around 13 and its toeRotate spinner to –16, and then set a key. With the key filters set, as shown earlier, keys are set for the custom attributes along with position and rotation.

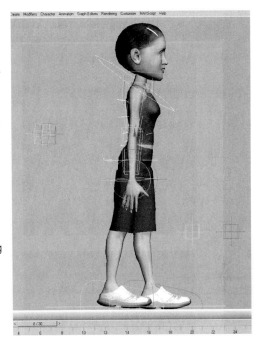

Here, the Zoe_footLCTRL object has been moved forward.

The custom attributes contained within the foot-control objects have been adjusted to roll the ankles and bend the toes.

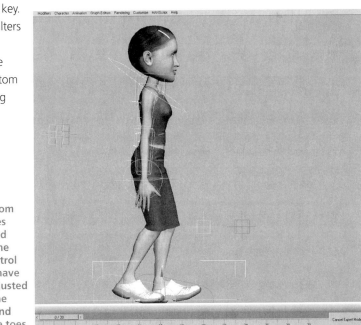

4 Now select the Zoe_footLCTRL, Zoe_footRCTRL, and Zoe_hipCTRL objects. Drag the Time slider with the right mouse button to frame 30 and click the Set Keys button.

By dragging the Time slider with the right mouse button, you cause objects to be, in effect, frozen. This makes it easy to copy a pose from one frame to another. This initial pose of the left foot forward and right foot back is copied to frame 30. Because the beginning pose at frame 1 and the ending pose at frame 30 will be identical, the animation can cycle. When we render the animation, we'll render frames 0 through 29. By leaving out frame 30, frame 29 will loop into frame 0 seamlessly.

5 Use the left mouse button to move the Time slider to frame 15. Create a pose for the feet and hips that is opposite of the pose at frames 0 and 30. This can be done easily by moving the right foot forward and adjusting its custom attributes to match the left foot. Again, set a key. Now you can move the Time slider to frame 0 and right-drag back to frame 15. This way, you can use the previous position of the right foot to line up the left. When you set a key for the left foot, you will see the right foot snap into its forward, frame-15 position again.

6 Although it is not changing positions, set a key for the Zoe_hipCTRL object because the hips will be changing position between frame 15 and the other keys.

Now you can play back the animation in the viewport to see the legs shuffle back and forth.

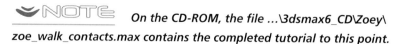 **NOTE** *On the CD-ROM, the file ...\3dsmax6_CD\Zoey\ zoe_walk_contacts.max contains the completed tutorial to this point.*

Passing Positions

The next positions to keyframe are the passing positions where the foot moving forward must be lifted to keep the character from tripping (or in this case from having their feet pass through the virtual ground plane). Zoey has been modeled wearing open-heeled sandal-sneaker hybrid shoes. For this reason, she will not be picking her feet up very much but rather walking with a bit of a shuffle. Think of a girl walking in flip-flops. Here are the steps to follow to keyframe the passing positions:

1 Move the Time slider to frame 7 and in a left viewport move the Zoe_footRCTRL object up until the geometry of the foot is just above the ground plane. Adjust the Custom Attributes spinners to around −7 for the Roll and around 13 for the toeRotate so that the toes are pointing up slightly as the foot moves forward. Then set a key.

2 Move the Zoe_hipCTRL object up until the left leg straightens out somewhat and then set a key. Do not make the leg completely straight because this will cause the legs to pop unnaturally when animated.

3 Go to frame 22 and repeat this process for the left foot. Raise the hips again and set keys for both.

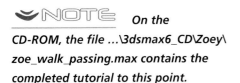 **On the CD-ROM, the file ...\3dsmax6_CD\Zoey\ zoe_walk_passing.max contains the completed tutorial to this point.**

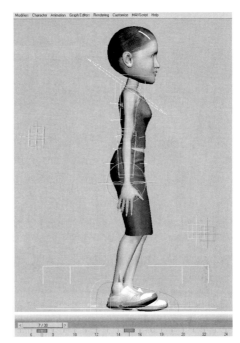

The hip-control object has been moved upward so that the left leg stretches out, pushing the character off the ground.

Maintaining Balance

Maintaining a sense of a character's balance is an element that many experienced animators highlight as important and one that beginning animators often get wrong. Without keeping the apparent center of mass of the character over their feet, the character will appear as though they are about to fall over, and any animation will appear awkward. As a character hits the passing positions, one leg will straighten, bearing all the character's weight, and cause the hips to rotate upward on that side. This hip rotation causes the spine to bend in the opposite direction so that the horizontal line of the shoulders rotates in the opposite direction of the hips. This way, the right shoulder will point down when the right hip points up. Here's how to keyframe these movements:

1 Select the Zoe_body object by name (you can't click it in the viewport because the selection filters have been set to Shapes). Then right-click the body object and choose Properties from the pop-up menu. Click the See-Through check box. This will make the body object transparent so that the spine-controller shape objects will be more visible.

2 In a front viewport, rotate the independent hip-controller and spine-controller object to form a curve in the spine. Rotate the Zoe_hipIndiCTRL object–10 degrees in its local Y-axis so that the hips are higher over the left leg, which is planted. Rotate the Zoe_spine01CTRL and Zoe_spine02CTRL objects a few degrees in the local Y-axis so that Zoey leans to her right. Then rotate the upper three spine controllers in the opposite direction so that Zoey's shoulders eventually tilt slightly to her left. Set keys for the spine and independent hip controls.

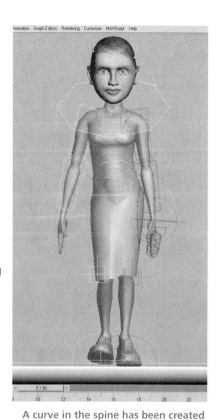

3 Go to frame 22 and repeat this procedure for the opposite passing position.

The local Y-axis rotations for the spine and independent hip controllers will be at 0 at frame 15 because this is the halfway point between the opposite rotations of the passing positions at frame 7 and 22. However, the animation will not loop because there is no connection between the rotations of the spine and hips at frame 22 and their opposite rotation at frame 7. You'll correct this in the following steps.

4 Set keys for the independent spine and spine-controllers so their Y rotations are at 0 degrees for frames 0 and 30.

5 The head and neck will counterbalance the shoulders, completing an *S* shape from the hips

A curve in the spine has been created by rotating the spine-controller objects. The See-Through property for the Zoe_body object has temporarily been turned on so that the spine-control objects can be seen more easily.

to the head. However, the head and neck will also anticipate the weight shift of the body to help kick-start the momentum. At frame 0, rotate the local Y-axis of the Zoe_neck1CTRL and the Zoe_headCTRL objects just slightly to Zoey's right and set a key for both. Drag the Time slider to frame 30 with the right mouse button and set keys for both the head and neck to copy the position.

6 Move the Time slider to frame 15 and rotate the head- and neck-control objects to the opposite angles in their local Y-axes. Set keys for both control objects.

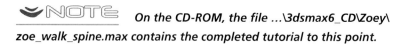

NOTE *On the CD-ROM, the file ...\3dsmax6_CD\Zoey\ zoe_walk_spine.max contains the completed tutorial to this point.*

Swinging the arms not only helps to counterbalance the opposite leg but also helps to start the momentum for that side of the body and ready the leg on that side to step forward. The arm swings can be easily created by rotating the box-shaped controllers around the arms.

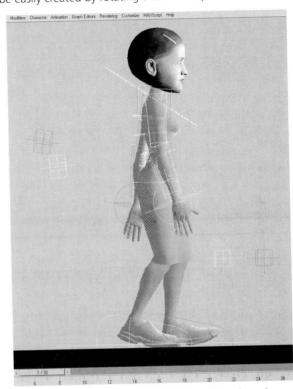

7 At frame 0, rotate the Zoe_upArmRCTRL object and then the Zoe_loArmRCTRL object forward and rotate the Zoe_upArmLCTRL object and then the Zoe_loArmLCTRL object forward, as shown in this illustration. The forward swinging right arm should have a little more bend in the elbow. However, you should maintain a slight bend in the elbow even when the arm is swinging backward so that the arm does not pop when animated. Set keys for all four arm objects and copy those keys to frame 30.

The arm-control objects have been rotated to swing the right arm forward and the left arm backward.

8 At frame 15, rotate all four arm objects to their opposite positions and set keys for all four.

✎ NOTE   *On the CD-ROM, the file ...\3dsmax6_CD\Zoey\ zoe_walk_arms.max contains the completed tutorial to this point.*

We now have a very rudimentary walk for Zoey. In a perspective viewport, make a preview of frames 0 through 29 to see the looping animation.

Adding Character and Personality to the Walk

Now we can begin to add details to our motions. And with these details we can begin to define motion that is more unique to the Zoey character and make the character seem more alive. Also, certain parts of her personality should define her walk. For example, she is a casual and energetic young woman interested in what she is doing. Physically, her stretchy skirt, slip-on shoes, and oversized hands and feet can also provide other details about her motion.

You can also create motions that take place on more than one axis of movement at a time. For example, by having Zoey cross her feet as she walks instead of simply moving each foot directly ahead of itself, you can add more visual interest.

Adding a Hand Flourish

Even as Zoey's arm swings forward and back, her right hand swings from side to side in front of her waist. Her fingers curl in a relaxed manner as she raises her hand, and the fingers flare out as her arm extends backward. This is a walking hand gesture I observed in several of the people I watched walking in flip-flop-type shoes, and I thought that fit Zoey's personality. Here's how to animate the gesture:

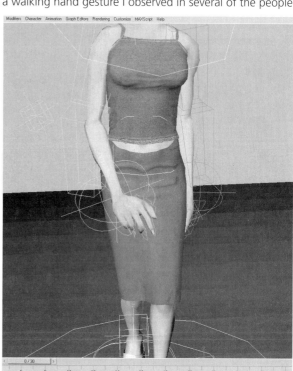

1 At frame 0, move the Zoe_handRCTRL object forward and to Zoey's left across the front of her hips. Rotate the Zoe_handRCTRL object so that the wrist tilts upward slightly, almost horizontal to the ground, as shown right. Set a key for this position at frame 0 and frame 30.

The custom attributes contained in the Zoe_fingerRCTRL object have been set to give the right hand a lifelike gesture as the right arm swings forward.

2 Back at frame 0, select the Zoe_fingerRCTRL object and set the custom attributes, as shown left. Set a key for this position at frame 0 and frame 30.

3 At frame 15, rotate the hand backward slightly on its local Z-axis and upward on its Y-axis. Rotate the X-axis so that the palm faces the thigh, as shown right. Set a key.

4 Select the Zoe_fingerRCTRL object and set the custom attributes as shown below, and then set a key. This will make the fingers flare out.

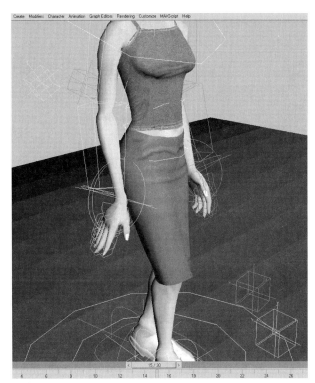

Now, the custom attributes contained in the Zoe_fingerRCTRL object have been set to make the right hand extended with a flourish as the right arm swings backward.

5 The right hand will be passing through her hips because the computer will try to interpolate between the position of her hand at the side of her hips and the position in the front of her waist. Correct this by going to frame 22 and moving the hand out of her hip to the right and then set a key.

Because the left hand is not making such a pronounced gesture, it can be given some life by making the fingers curl slightly more when the arm extends backward. It's also helpful to rotate the palm outward as the arm swings back and inward as the arm swings forward.

Crossing Zoey's Feet

Having Zoey cross her feet slightly as she walks will make her walk more expressively. Also, this helps her center of mass stay over the foot with weight on it to maintain her balance. By having each foot cross in toward the center for the contact positions and by flaring out the raised foot in the passing positions, you can make her walk more dynamic by creating movement across more axes.

First, you need to make Zoey's feet make solid contact with the ground.

1 Upon the heel making contact with the ground, the foot very quickly rotates down to stand flat on the ground. Select the Zoe_footLCTRL object and go to frame 4. Adjust the Roll and toeRotate custom attributes so that the foot comes in solid contact with the ground, and then set a key.

2 Repeat this for the Zoe_footRCTRL object at frame 18 and set a key.

3 On frame 15, select the Zoe_footRCTRL object and open the Curve Editor with the Curve Editor button or by selecting Graph Editors | Track View – Curve Editor from the main menu.

4 In the controller window on the left side of the Curve Editor, select the X-Position track for the Position Transform controller, as shown right, to see the function curve for the foot position's X-axis. Select all the keys on the function curve and use the Move Keys Vertical button to move the keys upward. If you position the Track View window so that you can see Zoey's feet in the viewport, you can see her foot move as you move the keys on the function curve. Move the keys upward until the inner edge of her shoe is close to her center (see Figure 13-4).

5 Scrub the Time slider to watch the animation. You'll see that her right foot is now passing through her left foot when it is planted. Move the Time slider to frame 7 and select the key on the function curve at that frame. Move this key downward until the right foot moves outward and clears the planted left foot (see Figure 13-5).

6 For added flair, rotate the foot so that the toes slightly point outward at this frame. You can do this either by rotating the Zoe_footRCTRL object in the viewport and setting a key or by changing the Z Rotation function curve in the Curve Editor.

FIGURE 13-4   The keys in the X-Position track are moved upward in the Curve Editor window to make Zoey's right foot move to her left so that her feet will cross as she walks.

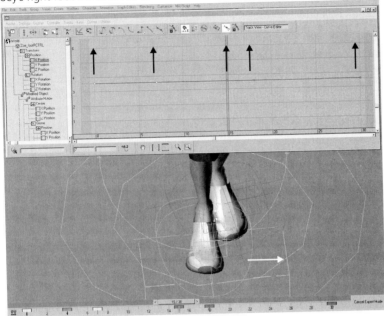

FIGURE 13-5   The key at frame 7 for the X-Position track has been moved downward so that Zoey's right foot will go around her left ankle as her right foot moves forward.

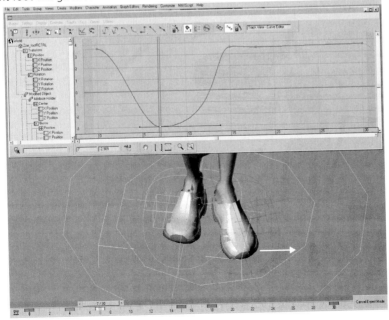

Ins and Outs: Fine-tuning Interpolation

Most of the keys for the walk are in place, so we can now fine-tune and place finishing touches. Now is the time to pay attention to the ease ins and ease outs of the keys. We'll focus on the hips and the arms.

Because the hips are at their lowest point as the feet make contact on frames 0, 15, and 30, the hips can act like a bouncing ball with the "ball" being Zoey's center of mass. This will literally put some "bounce" in her step.

1 Select the Zoe_hipCTRL object, open the Curve Editor, and select the Z-Position controller in the controller window. On the function curve, select the keys at the base of the arcs on frames 0, 15, and 30. Use the Set Tangents to Linear button to make the ease ins and ease outs of these keys straight (see Figure 13-6).

2 To make the arm swings a little snappier, go through each rotation controller for both upper and both lower arm-control objects and for both hand-control objects and change the function curves, as shown in Figure 13-7a and Figure 13-7b.

⌣ＮＯＴＥ   ***On the CD-ROM, the file …\3dsmax6_CD\Zoey***
zoe_walk_final.max contains the completed tutorial to this point.

Offsetting Timing

The walk cycle is complete now, but because most of the action falls on frames 0, 7, 15, 22, and 30, the motion is still a bit more robotic than it needs to be. Realistically, the individual motions that comprise walking don't all happen at the same time. It is good animation practice to keep keys for poses on as few frames as possible for clarity. However, once the motion is nearly

FIGURE 13-6   The curve for the Z-Position track of the Zoe_hipCTRL object shows the bouncing motion of her hips as she walks.

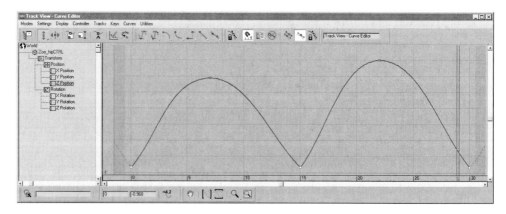

Body Animation: Character Motion Through Keyframing

FIGURE 13-7   Here, the curve for the Z-Rotation of the Zoe_LoArmRCTRL object has been changed from a smooth back and forth rotation (a) to a snappier rotation (b).

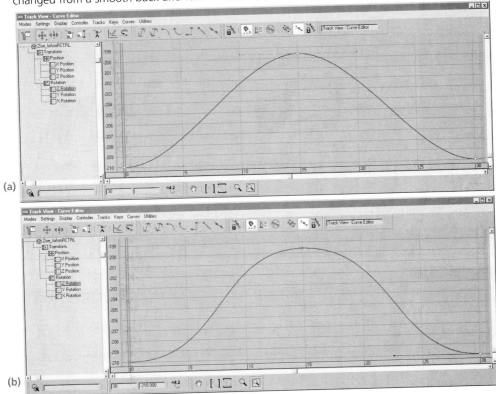

(a)

(b)

complete, offsetting the keys of certain objects to create overlapping can provide a more fluid, lifelike motion.

The arms and the head not only counterbalance the legs but also help kick-start the momentum on that side of the body. We can account for this by making the arm motions a few frames earlier than the rest of the body.

1 Select all four arm controls, both hand controls, both finger controls, and the head and neck controls.

2 In the trackbar at the bottom of the interface, select all the key markers and move them two frames to the right.

Offsetting motions, also known as *overlapping*, is another one of the key principles of animation. As we proceed into actual character animation within a scene, we'll be offsetting often to keep the animation from being in lockstep.

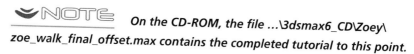

NOTE *On the CD-ROM, the file …\3dsmax6_CD\Zoey\ zoe_walk_final_offset.max contains the completed tutorial to this point.*

Once again, you can make a preview of frames 0 through 29 to see the walk in action.

I recommend experimenting with this walk cycle by changing the timings of various keys, creating different poses, and playing with the function curves. Then, for further study, I recommend creating entirely different walks. Make a walk cycle for Zoey in a tired state (start with a longer cycle, such as 45 frames). Make an angry walk, a sad walk, a sultry walk, and so on. Seeing what types of poses, key timings, and curves create these different emotions is good practice for the next step of character animation in a scene.

Animating Scene 1

Now we'll get into the character animation for a portion of the scene that we blocked out camera shots for in Chapter 12. To keep from getting lost and overwhelmed as you begin animating, it's best that you approach the scene armed, of course, with your storyboards, but more importantly, you should approach the scene in the way an actor would. Getting past technical constraints and the nuts and bolts of setting keyframes and creating natural motions is crucial to getting to the heart of animation artistry. Character animators are essentially actors in the slowest of slow motion. Ed Hooks' excellent book, *Acting for Animators* (Heinemann Press, 2000), is a great resource for training in this approach.

Another approach to conceiving your actions is to re-create them physically with your body. It's no accident that you'll almost undoubtedly find mirrors wherever you find character animators. Once you have a sense of your character's personality, motivation, and demeanor, physically acting out the animation that you are about to keyframe is a must. This will allow you to have an intuitive sense of the motions you will put your character through and determine whether they are natural, expressive, and communicative. Being shy and self-conscious is not a good thing when pantomiming your motions. Pixar animators actually have an entire room in their studio covered with mirrors on all four walls specifically for this purpose. I recommend having a full-length mirror near your workstation.

Because we've gone into keyframing in great detail in the previous exercise, for the upcoming exercises, we'll focus more on the creative decisions that go into choosing and crafting poses for each story point and less on the technical issues.

Readying the Interface for Animation

Open the ...\3dsmax6_CD\ Scene1_02_CH13.max. This is essentially the same file we ended with 3in Chapter 12. To streamline the interface, bone and helper objects have been hidden as well as all the geometry, except what Zoey will interact with for these first few camera shots. Shapes have been left visible. Make sure to set Selection Filters to Shapes. Selection sets have been added to the scene to make various groups of objects easier to select.

The active time segment of the scene has been set to frames 1000 through 1200 to allow us to focus on the segment of the timeline we'll start animating in. Keeping the active time segment focused on the area of interest spreads out the keys in the trackbar so they are easier to select and move. Finally, make sure Set Key mode is on with the same filter settings as for the previous exercise.

Pose-to-Pose Method

A tiny handful of time-tested, successful methods to character keyframing have evolved over the years. One of the most common is the pose-to-pose method. This method is one of the best ways to avoid confusion of an indecipherable mess of keys in your scene. By breaking down the action of your scene into the critical poses needed to tell your story, you get a ready-made starting point for keyframing your scene. In the pose-to-pose method, you keyframe these main poses much like a traditional animator would draw them and then go back and focus on the in-between interpolations. Then, overlapping motion is achieved by shifing keyframes on the timeline so that all body parts do not hit the pose at the same frame.

The first shot focuses on Zoey's brief reaction to the elevator door opening and then her first glimpse of her new videogame environment as she looks around briefly before exiting. Her demeanor is curious and interested and should reflect in her body language as she begins to explore. She will not be taut like a cat ready to pounce, or slouching deeply like someone tired or bored, but the positions of her hands, arms, head, shoulders, spine, hips, legs and feet all contribute to communicating what mood the character is in. This type of attention to the emotional attitude of the character is paramount to almost all good quality character animation. The emotions of the character, in this situation—anticipation—will in most cases (unless the character is deliberately trying to hide their emotions) help dictate the body language needed to effectively convey the story. Follow these steps to create the initial poses:

1. Switch to the camera view for camera 1 to center the view on the elevator. Then switch to a perspective view and zoom in on the elevator. Temporarily hide the elevator door so that you can see Zoey standing inside.

The first pose is the most basic of standing positions. But even for this simple stance, we need to give Zoey's body some asymmetry and life. Simply putting her hands down to her sides would leave her stiff and straight like a robot (see Figure 13-8a). A relaxed standing position, like one might have during an elevator ride, would leave the spine bent and the weight shifted over one foot. The arms would appear slack but not locked straight, and the fingers slightly curled.

2 Create this first pose at frame 1000. Move and rotate the various control objects and the custom attributes for the fingers to match Figure 13-8b. To set keys for this pose, you can wait until the pose is completed, select the selection set named Controls from the Selection Sets drop-down list, and then set keys for the entire group. If you work this way, you must be careful not to move the Time slider before you set keys with the Set Key button or the pose will be lost. Otherwise, you can set the key for each individual control object as you move it.

Looking Around

In the next pose, Zoey will shift her weight to the opposite foot, turn her body slightly, and tilt her head left and up. As with the walk cycle, when the weight shifts, the hips move and the back curves in counterbalance. This movement will be a bit of a reflexive move for Zoey as she idly reacts to the opening door.

1 Move the Time slider to frame 1028 and create a pose similar to this illustration and set keys for the objects in the Controls selection set. The hips (Zoe_hipCTRL) are moved from being over the left foot to being over the right foot to shift Zoey's weight. The independent hip control (Zoe_hipIndiCTRL) is rotated so that the right hip is slightly higher. The spine controls are rotated so that the back and shoulders counterbalance the hips. The head is turned to look roughly toward the top of the elevator door.

Zoey's next pose, at frame 1028, has her looking in another direction. Her hips and spine have been curved a bit further so that her weight is shifted over her right leg. The hips are tilted up over the right leg so that it straightens out.

FIGURE 13-8   Here, various control objects have been moved and rotated to change Zoey's standing pose from a static, lifeless pose (a) to a more relaxed, lifelike pose (b). Her weight is fairly centered, but there's a slight curve in her spine and hips that shows natural relaxation.

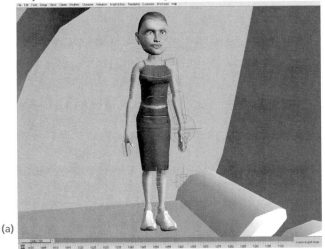

(a)   (b)

2   Move the Time slider to frame 1053 and create a pose similar to the one shown here and set keys for the objects in the Controls selection set. Zoey shifts her weight back to her left foot and puts her right foot out slightly in a casual pose.

3   Move the Time slider to frame 1075 and create a pose similar to the illustration on the next page and set keys for the objects in the Controls selection set. Here, Zoey turns her whole body as she scans across the room to her right. This time her weight not only shifts from her left to her right but also moves forward

Zoey's pose at frame 1053 has her weight shifted again, this time over her left foot. The hips have been moved, and both the spine and hips are rotated in the opposite direction. The right foot is moved slightly forward.

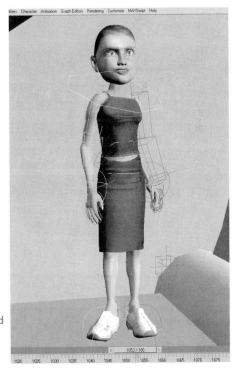

because her right foot moves forward in the previous pose. The turning is accomplished by rotating the Zoe_hipCTRL and the Zoe_headCTRL objects.

4 Allow Zoey to remain in this pose, holding this position for a brief moment. To do this, simply move the Time slider to frame 1099, select the Controls selection set, and set keys.

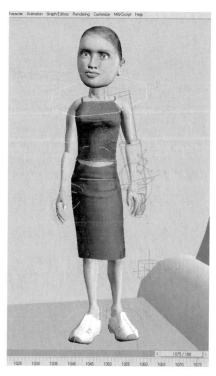

> At frame 1075, Zoey's weight not only shifts back to the right but her hips move forward because the right foot was moved forward in the previous pose.

Getting Set to Walk

Now Zoey will shift her weight into one last standing position in anticipation of propelling herself forward into a walking motion by throwing her weight forward.

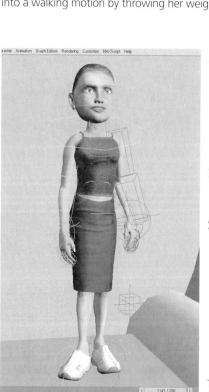

1 Move the Time slider to frame 1141 and create a pose similar to the one shown left and set keys for the objects in the Controls selection set. Zoey shifts her left foot backward and then her weight back onto that foot.

2 Hold this pose briefly by setting identical keys for the Controls selection set at frame 1147.

3 Move the Time Slider to frame 1160 and create a pose similar to Figure 13-9a and Figure 13-9b and then set keys for the objects in the Controls selection set. In this pose, Zoey is throwing her weight forward and well over her right foot to begin walking. She's leaning into her walk to get momentum going but is not in full stride yet.

> This pose, at frame 1141, is the final anticipation before Zoey begins to walk forward.

FIGURE 13-9 Zoey's pose at frame 1160 from the left view (a) and perspective view (b) shows her pushing her weight forward. Her left shoulder is rotated forward to help gain momentum for the left leg as it begins its swing forward.

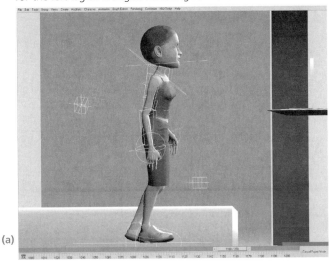

(a)   (b)

4 Move the Time slider to frame 1167 and create a pose similar to Figure 13-10 and set keys for the objects in the Controls selection set. This pose is similar to the passing position pose from Zoey's walk cycle.

5 Move the Time slider to frame 1175 and create a pose similar to Figure 13-11 and set keys for the objects in the Controls selection set. Here, Zoey is into the first contact pose for walking. This pose is very similar to the contact poses for the walk cycle in the previous exercise. Zoey's right hand is not gesturing as pronouncedly because she will get into full walking stride after a few steps.

Now you can play back the animation in the viewport, or for a smoother frame rate you can preview frames 1000 through 1200. Although the audio track is simply the elevator recording and not Zoey speaking, it is not important to synchronize her actions with the audio. Nevertheless it is helpful to avoid making the keyframes land exactly where sentences change because this can accidentally give the illusion that the recorded voice is somehow controlling Zoey. Timing of the poses can be easily adjusted at this point because all the keys for a given pose are still on the same frame. This also makes it easier to tweak poses for more expression or clarity because all the keys are easy to find.

FIGURE 13-10 At frame 1167, Zoey is in her first passing position. The left foot is lifting up and moving forward as the spine rotates to compensate.

Now that the essential poses for this first sequence have been laid out, we can begin fleshing out the animation by making some of the motions overlap and adjusting ease ins and ease outs.

> **NOTE** *On the CD-ROM, the file ...\3dsmax6_CD\Scene1_03_CH13.max contains the completed tutorial to this point.*

FIGURE 13-11 Zoey reaches her first contact position at frame 1175.

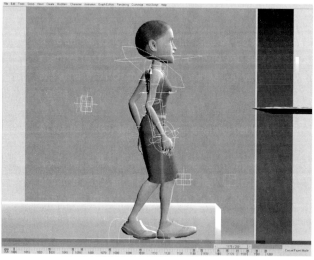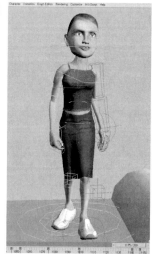

Offsets

Offsetting the motions of certain body parts will do a lot to make these idle movements appear more lifelike. One of the things we'll concentrate on is making the head turn before the rest of the body, which most people do. Also, in some instances, a foot will shift before weight shifts over that foot. Finally, we'll try to avoid the lifelessness caused by flat curves, particularly in places where the pose is being held.

The first head turn happens when Zoey looks up at the elevator door as it opens.

1 The body is shifting between frames 1028 and 1053. To make the head turn appear more natural, make its movement start earlier and finish earlier than the body. Copy the key for the Zoe_headCTRL object from frame 1000 to frame 1023. This is where the heads motion will start. Move the key for the Zoe_headCTRL object that you created at frame 1028 to frame 1033 to make the head land at its destination earlier.

2 The body shifts again between frames 1053 and 1075. Make the head's movement occur between frames 1046 and 1063. To do this, copy the key for the Zoe_headCTRL object from frame 1033 to 1046 to create a hold for the head. Then move the key for the Zoe_headCTRL object that was created with the rest of the pose at frame 1075 to frame 1063.

3 The pose at frame 1053 has Zoey's right foot forward from its original position at frame 1028, now that the weight has been shifted over the left foot. However, the foot movement would start only after the weight has been shifted off of it. Copy the key for the right foot from frame 1028 to frame 1046 to create a hold until just before the weight has finished shifting onto the left foot. Now the foot motion goes between frames 1046 and 1053.

4 The body shifts back to put weight over the left foot between frames 1099 and 1141. However, the left foot needs to get there sooner so that the weight can be shifted onto it. Make its backward movement go between frames 1111 and 1121. To do this, move the key for the left foot that was created at frame 1099 to frame 1111 and the key that was created at frame 1141 to frame 1121.

Easing

Now you can adjust the ease ins and ease outs between the different poses in the Curve Editor. Applying ease ins and ease outs to the keys on certain body parts (such as the head) will help us avoid some of the artificiality that comes from default interpolations. This can take some keen observation of your own and other's movements and, of course, practice with keyframing to get it right.

FIGURE 13-12   Here, the control curve for the Y-Position track (a) is adjusted to make the movement of the Zoe_footRCTRL object snappier (b).

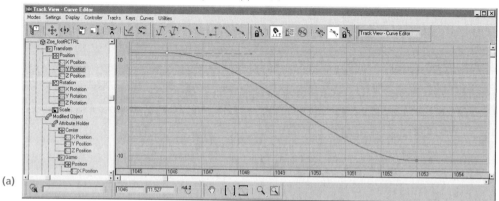

(a)

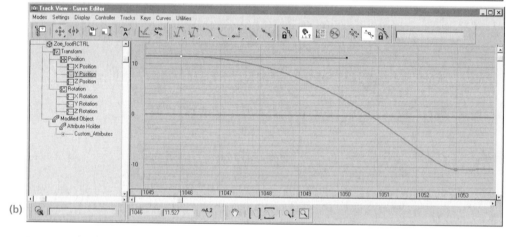

(b)

For example, the right foot motion that we offset to be between frames 1046 and 1053 should end fairly abruptly. Most of that motion happens in the left foot's Y-axis, so changing its curve will affect the snappiness of that motion.

1   Select the Zoe_footRCTRL object and open the Track View – Curve Editor window. Select the Y-axis position controller from the controller window and use the Track View window's Zoom Region button to zoom in on the keys between frames 1046 and 1053, as shown in Figure 13-12a. Use the Track View window's Move tool to adjust the handles of both of these keys so that the curve looks like Figure 13-12b. This will make the foot's movement snappier.

In another example, the body is in a hold between frames 1075 and 1099, and Zoey pauses briefly. But if the interpolations between the keys of these two poses are too flat, as shown in Figure 13-13a, the body will appear to freeze during those frames. To avoid this, you can adjust the handles in the curves for those keys.

2   Use the drop-down Selection Set list to select the Spine and Independent Hip selection set. In the Track View – Curve Editor window, select the Y-axis rotation controllers for all six objects and zoom in on the keys between frames 1046 and 1053. Use the Track View window's Move tool to adjust the curves at these keyframes, as shown in Figure 13-13b, so that there will be subtle movement while that pose is held.

Although all control objects in the body can benefit from close attention to ease ins and ease outs, the main objects to pay attention to for easing at this stage are the shifting feet, the turning head, and the moving hips.

Layering Method to Get Zoey Walking

To make Zoey walk out of the elevator, we'll use another method of keyframing besides the traditional pose-to-pose and straight-ahead methods. CG animation allows a layered approach to adding keyframes that is not possible in traditional animation. This way, we can quickly lay out keys for footsteps and hip movements to take Zoey out of the elevator and to the railing where she will pause. Then we can create the contact and passing poses for the rest of the body and copy the keys of everything but the hips and feet along the timeline at each foot step.

FIGURE 13-13   Here, the curves for the spine and independent hip controllers are adjusted to smooth out interpolations between two held positions. The flat sections of the curves (a) show that the spine will freeze and look unnatural between the keyframes. Once the handles in the curves are adjusted for a rounder interpolation (b), there will be a slight movement in the spine instead.

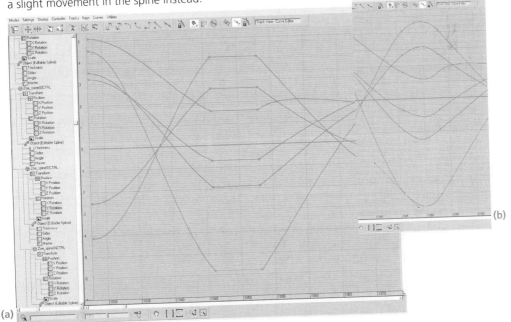

The keys for the hips and feet themselves need to be placed in context with the environment for the walk between the elevator and the railing. Therefore, the feet need to be moved into place and keys need to be created individually for each footstep. However, all the other control objects' positions and rotations are children of the hips. Therefore, arm, back, head, hand, and spine rotations as well as the custom attribute keys for the fingers and feet can all be created once. Poses for these objects can be created at the left foot contact position, the right foot passing position, the right foot contact position, and the left foot passing position. Then these four poses can be copied along the timeline to the appropriate point in each footstep.

Creating the walking animation can follow the same sequence of procedures used to create the walk cycle. You can start by laying out the contact positions for the feet and hips. For a consistent walk, I recommend measuring the distance in scene units (in our case, centimeters) between the feet at their farthest, the contact position (in this case, a short 25 centimeters). Also, remember that each footstep takes about 15 frames.

1. Starting at frame 1175, where the left foot is in the extended, contact position, move the Time slider 15 frames ahead to frame 1190. Move the Zoe_hipCTRL object forward 25 centimeters in its local Y-axis and set a key. Then move the right foot forward 50 centimeters in its local Y-axis and set a key. Then set a key for the left foot to keep it planted while the right foot moves forward.

2. Repeat these 15 frames ahead at frame 1205, this time moving the left foot 50 centimeters forward and hips 25 centimeters forward again. Continue in this manner until Zoey reaches the railing next to the stairs. It should take her about 15 or 16 steps and get her there around frame 1400 (see Figure 13-14).

3. Create the keys for the passing positions for the feet and Zoe_hipCTRL objects for all the footsteps you created. Remember to raise the hips for each passing position (see Figure 13-15).

4. Create the right foot-passing pose for all the other control objects of the body at frame 1183 (halfway between contact frames 1175 and 1190).

5. Create the right foot contact pose at frame 1190.

6. Create the left foot passing pose at frame 1197.

7. Create the left foot contact pose at frame 1205.

FIGURE 13-14 At this point in laying out the footsteps, only the contact positions for the feet are keyframed.

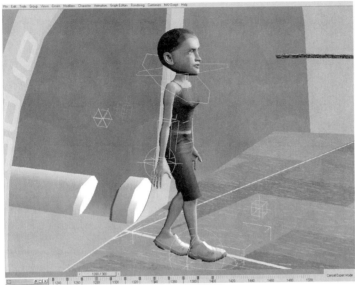

Copying the keys for the walking poses down the timeline requires some care because you'll be copying keys for many objects and many tracks at the same time. To be sure, you can copy the tracks individually or in smaller groups, but this method is faster.

FIGURE 13-15 The passing positions for the feet are keyframed in-between all the contact positions.

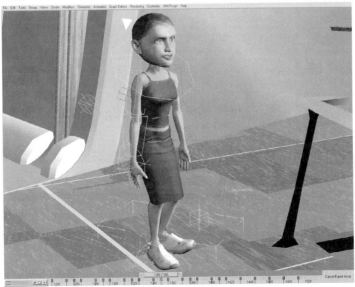

8 Select all the character control objects except for the Zoe_hipCTRL, Zoe_placementCTRL, and Zoe_groundCTRL objects. Open the Track View dope sheet and use the Track View window's Filters button to make sure to show only selected objects and animated tracks, as shown left.

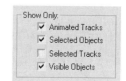

9 In the controller window, select the first controller at the top of the list, scroll to the bottom of the controller window, and SHIFT-select the last controller in the list.

≫CAUTION≪ **The tracks for the custom attributes in the hand-, finger-, and foot-controller objects do not always auto-expand in the Track View window's controller window. Make sure that the plus signs next to the custom attributes have been expanded. Then you can CTRL-select those tracks as well.**

10 ALT-select the position and rotation tracks for the Zoe_footLCTRL and Zoe_footRCTRL objects to remove them from the controller selection set. These are the tracks containing the keys already in place for all the footsteps.

11 In the edit window, you can select all the keys at a given frame and copy them to the other footsteps. For example, you can select all the keys for the right contact position at frame 1190 and copy them to the other right contact positions at frames 1220, 1250, 1280, and so on.

You'll probably want to have Selection Lock on in the Track View window as you copy poses from one frame to another. Also, I recommend expanding the Track View window as large as possible and zooming in to the edit window to show only the range of frames you need (that is, the frame you want to copy and its destination). This way, when you SHIFT-drag the keys, you'll have better accuracy and it will be easier to place them on their intended destination frame.

Once all the footsteps have been created, you can edit function curves to fine-tune Zoey's walking animation as she leaves the elevator and walks to the railing. For example, Zoey's right hand swinging should start out fairly gradual. To dampen it for the first few steps, select the tracks for its position controllers in the Curve Editor and lower the first few peaks of those curves, as shown in Figure 13-16.

FIGURE 13-14   The curves for the movements and rotations of Zoey's hands can be dampened at the beginning so that she gradually hits full stride.

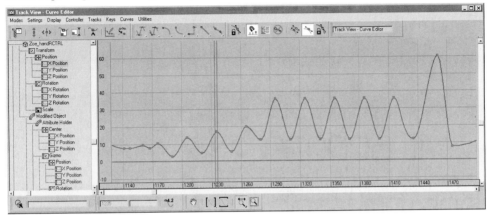

More Pose to Pose

Once Zoey reaches the railing, she places her left hand on it and slows down her walking to look around her environment. Then her phone rings, she answers it and begins talking to her friend Felix as she continues to explore. The rest of this animated sequence was done in the same manner as the preceding exercises. The critical creative decisions involve giving Zoey poses during the key story moments that enable her to act out the scene expressively and communicatively. Then the keys that make up the poses are edited for timing, ease ins and ease outs, and overlapping. Here are some examples of some of the main acting poses.

Figure 13-17 shows Zoey's key pose at frame 1435. Zoey is placing her hand on the railing, and she takes her final steps before pausing to stand by the railing.

Figure 13-18 shows Zoey at frame 1460 leaning back as she takes slower steps. The poses for these steps are similar to the regular walking steps, but they are 25 frames along instead of 15.

Figure 13-19a shows Zoey at frame 1490 with her hand trailing behind her. The hand has been keyed to stay at its original position on the railing and remain in place as she slowly walks by. This gives her demeanor an air of idleness and wistfulness.

Figure 13-19b shows Zoey at frame 1515 being a bit startled by the sound of her phone ringing. Her hands and shoulders have gone up while her hips have gone down and her knees together. This pose is just a few frames after the previous, more relaxed pose so that she reaches this position abruptly.

FIGURE 13-15 At frame 1435, Zoey arrives at the railing and reaches out to rest her hand on the railing.

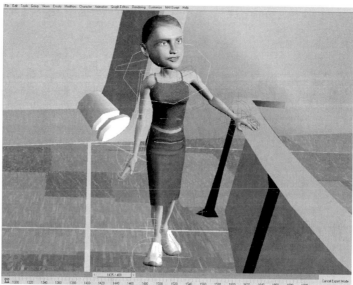

FIGURE 13-16 Continuing to rest her hand on the railing, Zoey now takes slower steps forward and leans away from the railing.

FIGURE 13-17   With Zoey's hand keyed to hold its position on the railing (a), her hips continue to move forward as she stretches her arm out behind her. When Zoey hears her phone ring at frame 1515, she is slightly startled (b). She raises her hands and hunches slightly.

(a)

(b)

Figure 13-20a shows Zoey at frame 1555 answering her phone. The script and storyboards call for Zoey to answer the phone by extending her hand in this gesture. The phone then magically appears.

Figure 13-20b shows Zoey at the frame where she puts the phone to her ear and begins talking in a typical telephone conversation pose.

As before, the keys that make up the poses are edited for timing, ease ins and ease outs, and overlapping.

This is now a completed sequence of animation for Zoey's body and is now ready for facial animation of expressions, lip-sync, and eye movements, which we will do in the next chapter.

> ⌄NOTE   *On the CD-ROM, the file …\3dsmax6_CD\Scene1_03_CH13.max contains the completed tutorial to this point.*

FIGURE 13-18 At frame 1555, Zoey looks down at her phone as she turns it on (a). At frame 1645, Zoey puts her phone to her ear and her hand on her hip (b). She adopts a casual pose, shifting her weight once again.

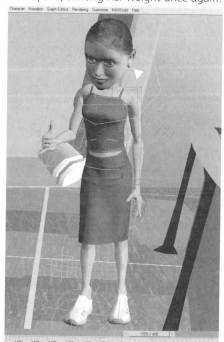

(a)

(b)

Adding Keyframes, Tweaking, and Repeating

The rest of the film is animated in this manner and is probably the single largest task of the entire film project. Further into the film are scenes with more characters acting and interacting with one another. Although this scene is not an action sequence, creating that type of animation is done by following essentially the same procedures and adhering to the same animation principles.

The process of learning to keyframe emotionally expressive character motion is not unlike that of learning to draw. Practice and repetition in animating, combined with keen observation of the way humans and animals move, are the keys to this art form.

Chapter 14

Facial Animation: Keyframing Expressions

Creating simple, formulaic facial animation is a straightforward process that many understand innately. Children are often able to draw a happy face without knowing that the orbicularis oculi muscle makes the eyes squint, and they can usually draw a sad face without knowing that the mentalis muscles push the middle of the bottom lip upwards to form a frown. But creating subtle and expressive facial animation is infinitely complex, and capturing the full range of human emotions can be a lifelong pursuit for actors, illustrators, and animators.

In this chapter, we'll explore rigging the face to strike a balance between simplicity and range of expression. We'll animate the face to go along with the acting we started with the body animation, and then we we'll create lip sync to match the dialogue.

Rigging the Face with Morph Targets

Even within just 3ds max, there are many workable approaches to rigging and animating the face—from using max bones and the Skin modifier, to Free-form Deformation lattices, to several available commercial plug-ins. However, the most common and arguably the simplest approach is through keyframed morphing with the Morpher modifier.

Although creating morph targets requires artistic skill to achieve good results, the process is a simple one. A copy of the head mesh is made and sculpted to form a particular expression or component of an expression with the same modeling tools used to create the head. This target mesh is then referenced by the Morpher modifier, which is added to the original head mesh.

Defining a Set of Morph Targets

Your choices of which facial positions to sculpt and add to your set of morph targets will play a major role both in how fast and efficiently you can animate and in the range of emotions you can convey through your character. Simply animated characters may have as few as 10 or 20 morph targets, whereas Weta Digital's Gollum character from *The Lord of the Rings* movies has several thousand for an endless variety of facial expressions.

Morph targets can be created for each individual facial expression you want the character to exhibit. This allows you great control in sculpting subtle and distinctive facial expressions. However, this approach can quickly result in a very large set of morph targets, which takes both time to create and can result in larger, more memory-intensive max files. It also means you'll have that many animation tracks to create keyframes for.

Another approach is to create morph targets based on the underlying muscles of your character's face. Each of the muscles of the face pull or constrict a portion of the face in combination with other muscles to form facial expressions. Morph targets can be sculpted to duplicate the contortions of individual muscles or of groups and then keyframed in combination to form facial expressions.

Additionally, animators typically create morph targets for the different phonetic shapes the mouth forms when speaking. The mouth's phonetic shapes can be achieved through the use of muscle-based morph targets, but the lip-syncing process can go faster and more intuitively by keying, for example, *M* and then *EE* morph targets to make a character say "me" instead of the combination of several muscles for each phonetic sound.

Morph target sets will differ from character to character and from animation to animation, depending on what the acting requirements of the character may be. The basic rule of thumb when defining a set of morph targets to animate with is to achieve the widest range of expressions with the fewest morph targets. This will not only help keep your file sizes manageable but will keep you from being overwhelmed by too many morph channels to animate.

For Zoey, I've created a very minimal set of morph targets that combines morph targets to control the eyes and eyebrows with a set of phoneme-based targets for lip sync. Because many of the phoneme targets are loosely based on simple muscle movements, these can be used to create many different facial expressions as well.

Modeling

Making facial morph targets that move in a believable way requires an understanding of the structure of the head and muscles of the face. The more realistic you want your face to be, the more facial anatomy reference becomes a requirement. Even for nonhuman characters this can be helpful. For the movie *Stuart Little*, the special effects team at Sony Pictures Imageworks created reference illustrations of human musculature stretched over a mouse skull to aid in visualizing how they would make their morph targets.

The main thing to bear in mind while sculpting morph targets is that the muscles of the face are stretched over the skull. As a muscle contracts, it bulges and pulls the skin across the surface of the various bones of the skull. For example, when a character smiles, the zygomatic major muscles of the cheeks pull upward toward the eyes and outward toward the ears around the cheekbones. But this contraction makes those muscles bulge, causing the cheeks to puff up.

Because we went into detail on the modeling process in Chapters 7 and 8, we won't go into step-by-step detail to create all the morph targets. The process of creating morph targets is simpler than for modeling the head because the topology of the morph targets cannot be altered. For the Morpher modifier to be able to reference a morph target, the morph target's vertices must be numbered internally by max exactly the same as the original head mesh. This means that no vertices can be deleted or added because this causes all vertices in the mesh to be renumbered. A morph target is created by simply cloning the original mesh, and then vertices in the morph target can only be moved, rotated, or scaled into new positions (usually with Soft Selection turned on) using the now familiar sub object modeling tools. Although this does limit your morph targets by making them depend on the topology of the original mesh, it makes the process of creating them more straightforward.

The morph targets can be modeled in your rigged character file. Because the order of the chapters in this book have led us to create character animation in our scene files already, the morph targets can be merged into the scene files when you're ready to keyframe the facial animation.

The *A* and *I* Target: The Open Mouth

The first morph target to start with is the target for the open mouth, which is also the target used when a character makes the sounds *A* and *I*. To create this morph target, make a clone of your original head mesh and name it head_A_I. The mouth is opened by rotating the jaw on its hinge next to the ear. This means that the chin does not move straight down and slightly backward when the mouth opens.

In Polygon Sub Object mode, the polygons of the jaw, chin, and center of the lower lip are selected with Soft Selection (see Figure 14-1a and Figure 14-1b). Edge Distance is turned on, as shown here, so the Selection falloff does not bleed over to the teeth and tongue. If you turn on Snap and set the snap options to Vertex, you can rotate the selection around a vertex just in front of the top of the ear lobe (where the hinge of the jaw connects) to get a fairly realistic jaw rotation (see Figure 14-1c and Figure 14-1d).

The corners of the lips can then be sculpted so that they stretch evenly to form the open mouth. The teeth and mouth can be selected in Element Sub Object mode and rotated around the same vertex to match the rotation of the jaw.

Each morph target should be sculpted at the extreme position for that target so that each facial motion has as much freedom of movement as possible when animating. In this case, sculpt the mouth area of the open-mouth target open a little farther than you ever want to go.

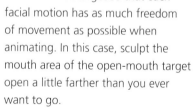

As you build each morph target, you can test it by adding the Morpher modifier to the original head mesh, clicking an empty morph channel, and then clicking the Pick Object from Scene button under the Create Morph Target. You can then select the morph target in the viewport. Move the spinner for this channel back and forth from 0 to 100 to see the morph target in action.

FIGURE 14-1   The polygons of the jaw area have been selected with Soft Selection (a and b) and then rotated around one of the vertices below the ear (c and d).

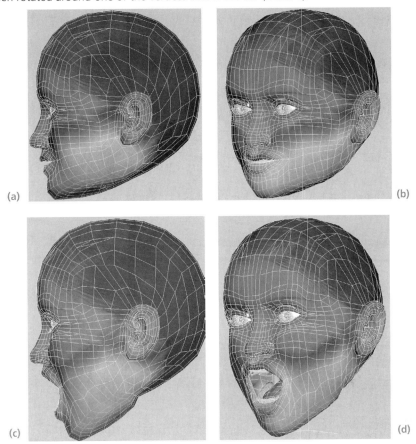

(a)

(b)

(c)

(d)

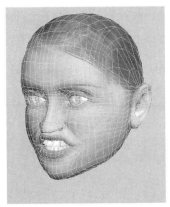

The *EE* Sound: Grimacing

The target for the *EE* sound is created by moving the upper lip along with the nostrils upward using Soft Selection. The vertices of the nasolabial fold are pulled backward slightly to accentuate this crease. This target can be used not only for lip sync but for grimacing in pain or disgust.

EE_wide

For Zoey, I created a second *EE* morph target (shown on the next page) as an extra variation. This is not strictly necessary for lip sync, but I wanted her to have this added expression possibility. Considering the expressions you want your character to make throughout your animation should guide you in what morph targets to create.

The *O* Sound

The target for the mouth making the sound *O* (shown below) can be created by using the open-mouth target as a starting point. With the Morpher modifier on the base head mesh containing the open-mouth target, you can adjust the spinner until the mouth is partially open, as it is when making the *O* sound. You can then clone the original head in this state and collapse it to an editable poly. You can then sculpt the lips to

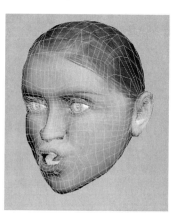

form the *O* sound without having to worry about opening the jaw first. As you create more morph targets, it becomes slightly easier to make subsequent targets by starting with combinations of existing targets.

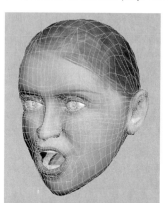

The *U* and *OO* Sound

This target can start with the *O* target, shown right. The lips are then moved forward and scaled smaller using Soft Selection.

The *W* and *Q* Sound: The Pucker

This target can start with the U_OO target (shown left), but the lips are scaled to be even narrower and

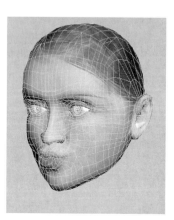

the inside areas of the lips are brought together, making the lips fuller vertically. The area of the cheeks around the mouth is also pulled slightly inward and forward.

The *M, B,* and *P* Sound: The Closed Mouth

For this sound (shown on the next page), the jaw is rotated similarly as was done for the open-mouth target but this

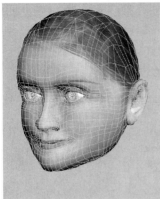

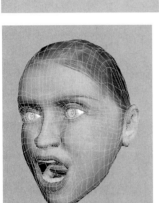

time slightly upward. The vertices around the lips are then sculpted to be thinner and pursed together. The lips are also stretched slightly.

The *F*, *V*, and *Th* Sound: Biting the Lower Lip

This target can start with the M_B_P target, at about 60 percent, combined with the EE target, also at about 60 percent. Then the bottom lip is moved backward to be behind the upper teeth.

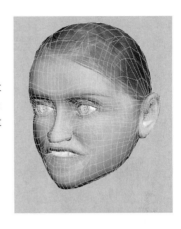

Tongue Up

For many phonetic sounds, such as *L*, *T*, and *Th*, the tongue travels upward to the roof of the mouth. This can be done with a morph target. You can select the tongue at the Element Sub Object level and then apply a Bend modifier to the tongue and collapse the stack once the tongue has been bent upward.

Mouth Right and Mouth Left

Real faces are asymmetrical, and real people talk asymmetrically. In other words, the mouth will often shift right or left as a person talks, as shown below. These targets also allow your character to talk out of the sides of their mouths. For each target, the corner of the mouth is moved to the side and backward as it moves around the head. The bottom of the nose is moved slightly in the same direction. Also, the cheek on that side of the mouth is bulged slightly.

Smile

The smile, shown on the next page, is created by stretching the corners of the mouth outward, upward, and backward. The cheeks are bulged and move upward to bunch up under the eyes. The nasolabial fold is deepened and accentuated. A character

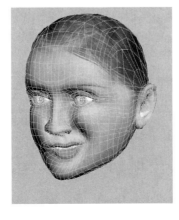

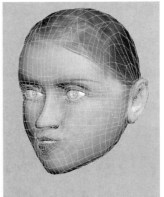

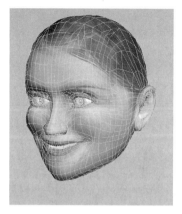

may need to exhibit many different smiles, and many variations on the smile can come from what percentage its morph channel is set at and how it is combined with morph targets for other parts of the face. For some characters, having several unique smile targets can be helpful.

Blink Left and Blink Right

Eye-blink morph targets are created by scaling the vertices of the eyelids together and moving them forward. Depending on how big the eyes of your characters are, you may need to use the Morpher modifier's Progressive Morph feature. When you're animating a head mesh between one morph target and another, this action is very simple. If a given vertex is in a different position in the morph target, then that vertex travels in a straight line between its original position and its position in the morph target. This means that vertices will not follow the contour of an eyeball. You can correct for this by creating an in-between morph target. In the case of the Zoey character, because her face is low polygon, relatively large gaps exist between the eyeballs and the eyelids. Therefore, progressive morphing is not necessary.

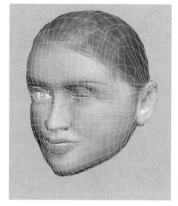
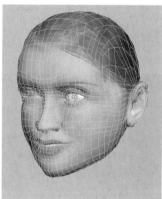
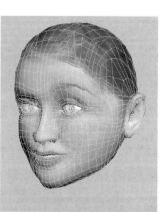
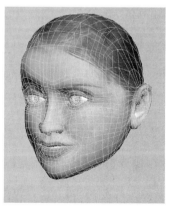
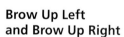

Brow Up Left and Brow Up Right

Anatomically speaking, eyebrows do not travel straight upward. The skull's superorbital ridge, which causes the brows' protuberance, does not move. However, the skin over the eyebrows, along with the short hairs of the eyebrows, is pulled upward along the contour of the brows and then the forehead by the frontalis muscle of the forehead. If your character's brows are pronounced and your models are detailed, this is another instance where progressive morphing may be helpful.

For expressiveness, it is helpful to make two separate morph targets so the eyebrows can be animated independently. However, this means that the effect of the morph target must trail off at the center of the face. The vertices at the center of the nose should move up only half as much as the rest of the brow (see Figure 14-2). This way, when both targets are combined, the center vertices will even out.

Brow Down Left and Brow Down Right

These morph targets are created similarly to the Brow Up morph targets except that the brows move slightly inward toward the center of the face when they are pulled down.

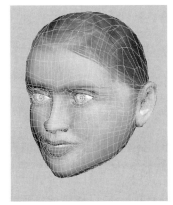 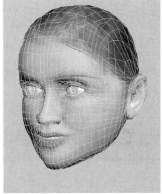

FIGURE 14-2   In the Right Brow Up morph target, the vertices in the center of the brow, above the ridge of the nose, are only moved up half as much as other vertices. This is so that when both Brow Up morph targets are set to 100 percent, the center of the brow will be even.

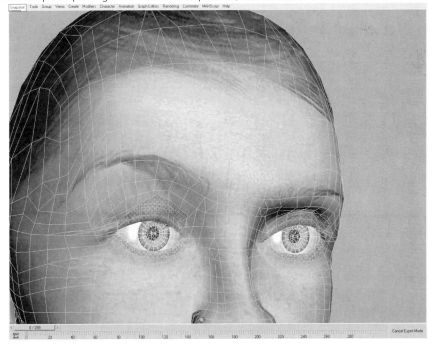

Furrow

The corrugator muscles in the center of the brow pull the eyebrows together and form short vertical bumps at the top of the bridge of the nose. This morph target is created by moving the vertices of both brows inward and sculpting the ridges above the nose.

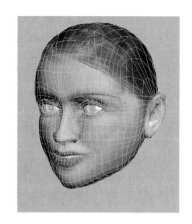

Nostrils Flare

It can be helpful to have a morph target specifically for flaring the nostrils. This can be created easily by scaling the outer vertices of the nostrils outward and moving them slightly upward.

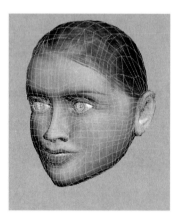

Face Stretch

Another facial expression target that I added for Zoey is a facial stretch. It is possible to move your jaw down slightly while keeping your lips closed. This target enables Zoey to do just that.

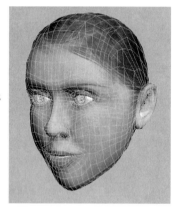

Fix

Once you have added morph targets, modeling for the head is essentially frozen because any changes in the topology of the base mesh will result in a disconnection with all the morph targets. However, one option remains: You can create a Fix morph target and do minor sculpting to this to change your base mesh, and then you can leave this fix morph target set at 100 percent to make the changes essentially permanent. This way, the effects of all the other morph targets will still work. In the case of Zoey, I felt that her eyes were too far apart in the base mesh so I made a Fix target to bring together slightly.

Setting Up the Morpher Modifier

Because you have probably been testing each morph target as you build it, you probably already have the Morpher modifier set up on the base head. It may be helpful to delete this modifier and set up a new one, and then you can arrange the morph channels in a logical order for easier animating.

It may also be useful to set specific limits or remove limits altogether for various morph channels. Morph channel limits can be set individually or globally. Certain morph targets may provide useful facial expressions when set at values greater than 100 or less than 0. For example, you can have the eye-blink morph targets make the eyes widen instead of blink by setting them to a value of –30. You can set the limits for those specific channels to enable this, as shown right.

Facial Animation

Now we can move ahead with keyframing eye movements and facial expressions to go along with our body animation. The basic approach toward animating the face is very similar to animating the body. All the same animation principles introduced in the previous chapter apply to creating facial animation as well. Creatively, the same cues taken from working through the adding of the scene can guide us in choosing which facial expressions will augment a given pose and help tell the story.

We'll create facial animation for frames 1600 through 1900 of our example film. In this sequence, Zoey answers her phone with a quick but curious "Hello." Upon recognizing the voice of her friend, Felix, she smiles and greets him with a playful, "Hey, girl." She then begins walking, smirks satisfactorily, and then smiles as Felix pays her a complement. We'll start by animating the eyes, then the facial expressions, and finally complete the animation with lip sync.

Animating the Eyes

When one person looks at another, the eyes are often the initial center of interest. They are packed with information about emotion, disposition, and intent. Taking time to carefully animate your characters' eyes allows you to pack a lot of story into your shots. Artfully keyframed eye movements can describe your characters' thought processes or direct the viewer's attention to a key story point, and most importantly, keeping the eyes moving believably helps enormously in keeping your character looking alive. People who are zombies, hypnotized, brain dead, and in any other vegetative state, are typified by frozen stares, which underline the importance of eye movements.

Traditional movie directors devote large amounts of time and effort into ensuring that the eye lines for their actors connect with what the actors are supposed to be looking at from one shot to another. That is, if the character is looking to their left in one shot and in the next shot you see that what they were looking at is actually on their right, the discontinuity is readily perceived. Our characters are rigged with an eye target control that allows you to keyframe the focus of the characters' gaze simply. Wherever the Zoe_Eye_CTRL is placed in the scene, Zoey eyes will point toward it.

Now we'll animate Zoey's eye movements. From the CD-ROM, open the file …\3dsmax6_CD\ Scene1_05_CH14.max, which contains the body animation for the opening shots of the example film. Be sure that Set Key Mode is toggled on, and set Selection Filters to Shapes.

As the sequence starts, Zoey is looking down at her hand (a phone geometry will be placed next to her spread-out fingers later in the animation production). A keyframe for the Zoe_Eye_CTRL object has already been placed earlier in the shot so that her eyes are looking down at her hand already. The first movement to key will coincide with her head tilting upward as she says, "Hello." As her head tilts back between frames 1630 and 1648, we want her eyes to look upward and to the side as though she's thinking about who is on the other end of the telephone. This will tell us *where* to place the eye target. For the timing, or *when* to place the keyframes, imagine that the gaze will linger briefly on her phone and then shift to its destination. The rule of thumb for eye movement is that the eyes will typically start sooner than the movement of the head when a character turns to look in another direction. This is a good example of the offsetting animation principle. In this case, we'll bend the rule because Zoey is not really looking at her environment but rather is thinking about who is on the phone. Here are the steps to follow:

1 Set an initial key for the Zoe_Eye_CTRL object at frame 1640. This holds the position of the Zoe_Eye_CTRL object from its previous key until this point (see Figure 14-3).

FIGURE 14-3   Here, the position of Zoe_Eye_CTRL determines the direction of Zoey's gaze. At frame 1640, she is looking slightly downward and in front of her as she answers her phone.

2 Move the Time slider to frame 1646, a couple frames before the end of the head turn. Move the Zoe_Eye_CTRL object so that Zoey is looking up and to her left. Make sure the Zoe_Eye_CTRL object is far enough away from Zoey and that it is rotated to face her. This will keep her eyes from crossing (see Figure 14-4).

3 Set another key for the Zoe_Eye_CTRL object at frame 1673. This will hold the eyes until that frame. Because there is some follow-through on the head's rotation, it has continued to turn. To compensate, move the Zoe_Eye_CTRL object slightly up and to Zoey's left and set this key.

Now we are at the spot where Felix greets Zoey by saying, "Hey, coffee achiever!" Zoey immediately recognizes Felix's voice, so we can signal this by having her eyes shift from one side to the other.

4 Move the Time slider to frame 1682 and move the Zoe_Eye_CTRL object so that Zoey's gaze is fixed slightly downward and to her right. Then set a key (see Figure 14-5).

FIGURE 14-4 At frame 1646, Zoe_Eye_CTRL is moved up and to Zoey's left. Her eyes look upward as though she is visualizing the person on the other end of the phone.

FIGURE 14-5   At frame 1682, Zoey looks back down again as she hears Felix's voice.

5 Zoey's head is turning (along with her entire body) to her left between frames 1698 and 1715. Set a key to hold the Zoe_Eye_CTRL object at frame 1694 (before the head starts). Then move the Time slider to frame 1707 (just before the head ends its turn) and move and rotate the Zoe_Eye_CTRL object so that Zoey is looking slightly downward and to her left (see Figure 14-6).

Because her head will continue turning until frame 1715, by having her gaze overshoot and look to her left at frame 1707, we cause her head to catch up, and she will wind up looking straight ahead. We'll then move onto the next head turn, which goes between frames 1786 and 1797.

6 Set a key for the Zoe_Eye_CTRL object at frame 1777 to hold its position and then move the Time slider to frame 1791. Move and rotate the Zoe_Eye_CTRL object until Zoey is looking forward and slightly downward. Set a key.

FIGURE 14-6   Here, Zoey is looking to her left, and her head rotates around to her left as well.

7   Move the Time slider to frame 1820 to set a hold key. Because Zoey has begun to walk forward, move the Zoe_Eye_CTRL object ahead of her, keeping her gaze in the same position, and then set the key.

8   Now Zoey is hearing Felix's compliment about her "finely honed conversational skills." Make Zoey react to this by shifting her gaze to her left at frame 1845. Move the Zoe_Eye_CTRL object forward as well to keep pace with Zoey's walking and then set a key (see Figure 14-7).

9   Hold this gaze until frame 1876 by setting a key. Then shift her gaze back forward at frame 1900 and set a key there.

Animating Facial Expressions

Now we'll create facial expressions to go along with Zoey's eye movements for the same sequence of animation. This time we'll be keyframing the Morpher modifier for Zoe_head_poly.

FIGURE 14-7 Zoey looks sideways as she receives a complement from Felix.

Because Set Key mode will set keys for all the channels in the Morpher modifier, it may be easier to use Auto Key mode. This way, you can set the keys by moving the Time slider and simply adjusting the spinner for a given Morpher channel. However, keep in mind that in Auto Key mode, each time you change an object's position, rotation, scale, attributes, or parameters, a key will be set at whatever frame the Time slider happens to be on. This way, you can set keys for the channels of the Morpher modifier individually by simply adjusting the spinners.

Eye Blinks
First we'll put in some eye blinks to go along with Zoey's eye movements. Another rule of thumb about eye movement is that the eyes typically blink when they turn and shift focus. I like to put the eye blinks in the middle of a move of the eyes so that not all of the eye movement is hidden by the closed eyelids. Here are the steps to follow for this exercise:

1   Select the Zoe_head_poly object and go to the Modify panel to access the Channel List of the Morpher modifier, and then move the Time slider to frame 1635. Move the spinner for blink_L up briefly and then back to 0 to automatically set a key. You can tell whether a key has been set for a given Morpher channel at this frame if the spinner becomes outlined in red. Repeat this for the blink_R channel.

2 Move the Time slider to frame 1639 and set the spinners for both the blink_L and blink_R channels to 100.

3 Move the Time slider to frame 1643 and set both blink channels back to 0.

This creates a blink while the Zoe_Eye_CTRL object is moving to a new position (see Figure 14-8a through Figure 14-8c). Now you can easily copy blinks to other spots in the animation where the Zoe_Eye_CTRL object is moving by using the Tract View window's Curve Editor.

4 Select the Zoe_Eye_CTRL object and scrub along the timeline to see when the eyes are moving and see the corresponding keys for the Zoe_Eye_CTRL object in the trackbar. Then in the Track View window's controller window, select the two blink tracks: blink_L and blink_R. This will show both curves in the Curve Editor. They are identical, so they will look like one curve (see Figure 14-9a).

FIGURE 14-8   The Morpher tracks for Zoey's blink_L and blink_R morph targets have been keyframed to blink while the eyes are in motion. The eyelids are open as the eyes start to move (a), closed at mid move (b) and open again just before the eyes stop moving (c).

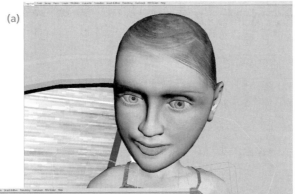
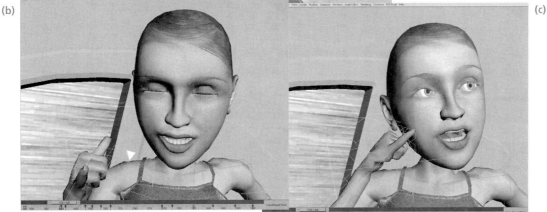

5 Window-select the three keys (actually six keys overlapping) that make the spike of the eye blink and use the Move Keys Horizontal button to SHIFT-move these keys to copy them to the other frames where eye blinks are needed. In this case, frames 1674, 1749, 1782, 1820, and 1876 (see Figure 14-9b).

Make the blink at frame 1820 last longer by using the Move Keys Horizontal button again. Move the second two keys of that blink forward so that it lasts 14 frames instead of eight. This is the spot where Felix pays Zoey a compliment about her "finely honed conversational skills." A longer blink will make her appear more demure.

Expressions

Next we'll add expressions to this same sequence, which begins with Zoey in a neutral expression as she is looking around Cloud10. Then as she answers the phone with "Hello," her expression will change to inquisitive. As she recognizes her friend Felix, a smile will cross her face. Finally, as she receives a compliment, her mouth will move to a smirk of self-satisfaction. Here are the steps to follow for this exercise:

1 Set hold keys for both BrowUp channels and the Furrow channel at frame 1629, and then move the Time slider to frame 1649 and set the BrowUp_L channel to 66 and the BrowUp_R channel to 53. Keying these channels with different settings gives the eyebrows

FIGURE 14-9 Here, the keyframes that create the peaks in the blink_L and blink_R tracks (a) are copied to create eye blinks at other points in the timeline (b).

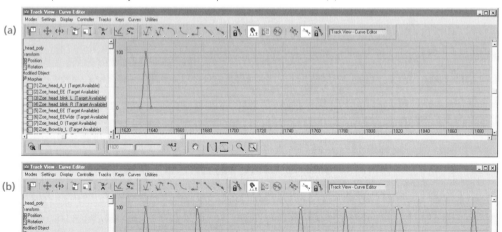

of little bit of asymmetry. Set the Furrow channel to 72. Pulling in the eyebrows with the Furrow channel will help make the expression more inquisitive to go along with her saying "Hello" (see Figure 14-10).

2. Now we'll make her brows unfurrow at the same time she starts to smile. At frame 1686, set a hold key of 0 for the Smile channel and a hold keys for the furrow in both BrowUp channels. Then move to frame 1707, where Zoey greets Felix by saying, "Hey, girl!" Set the Smile channel to 54, the BrowUp_L channel to 50, the BrowUp_R channel to 35, and the Furrow channel back to 0. This gives Zoey a happy expression, relaxing her eyebrows as she recognizes and greets Felix (see Figure 14-11).

3. At frame 1820, set hold keys for both BrowUp channels at their current settings and the Mouth_L channel at 0. To make her smirk, set the Mouth_L channel to 42, the BrowUp_L channel to 29, and the BrowUp_R channel to 0 (see Figure 14-12).

4. At frame 1885, Zoey will begin to smile brightly when Felix says, "…life of the party." Set hold keys for both BrowUp channels and the Smile and Mouth_L channels. Then at frame 1895, set the BrowUp_L channel to 61, the BrowUp_R channel to 72, the Smile channel to 79, and the Mouth_L channel to 0 (see Figure 14-13).

5. Now in the Track View window's Curve Editor, select the facial expression channels you've created keys for in the controller window so you can view the curves. The curves will have several sharp corners and flat segments that could result in snapping or frozen robotic movements in the face (see Figure 14-14a). To control easing, use the Move Keys tool to adjust the handles for the keys to round them out slightly (see Figure 14-14b).

FIGURE 14-10 At frame 1629, Zoey will be saying hello, so her eyebrows' morph targets are keyed up, as well as the furrow morph target, to give her a quizzical expression.

FIGURE 14-11   At frame 1707, the furrow target is keyed back down while the smile morph target is keyed up. The brows are also keyed back down so that her eyes relax.

FIGURE 14-12   At frame 1820, the brows are keyed up, along with the Mouth_L target. This, combined with her eyes shifting to the side, helps give her a self-conscious and pleased expression.

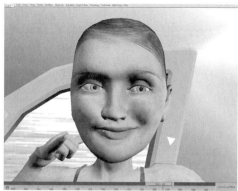

FIGURE 14-13   At frame 1895, after receiving her compliment, Zoey smiles to give her a gratified expression.

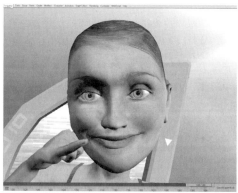

FIGURE 14-14   The curves for the Morpher channels (a) are smoothed out to avoid jerky motion and frozen sections (b).

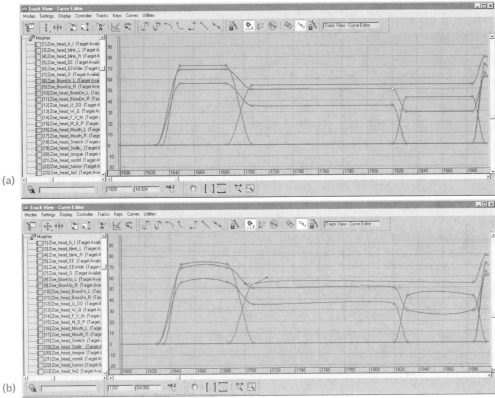

(a)

(b)

Lip-synching

Now we can finish this sequence of animation by adding keyframes to the phoneme-based Morpher channels in time with the spoken dialogue. Lip sync can be a very tedious and time-consuming task because there are many keyframes to create and edit for a passage of dialogue. It's also challenging to get animated mouth movements to re-create speech convincingly. Because people are so attuned to the way a mouth moves during speech, errors are very apparent. If the keyframe for a particular syllable is off by just to frame or two in either direction, a character's speech will not appear to be in sync.

Indeed, several different automated lip-sync tools can be handy if you have large quantities of lip-syncing to do. These tools typically create keys for your Morpher channels after analyzing the audio for the dialogue. Although you can edit the keyframes that these tools create, animating lip sync by hand provides you with another opportunity for adding distinct character to your animation. For example, physical comedian Jim Carrey's rubbery mouth moves very differently when speaking than Clint Eastwood's mouth.

You can enable your character to speak uniquely not only by the way you shape the morph targets but by the way you keyframe them.

For our sample sequence, we'll place the keys that make Zoey say the words "Hello" and "Hey, girl." Here are the steps to follow:

1 Right-click below the Time slider on the trackbar and select Configure/Show Soundtrack from the pop-up menu.

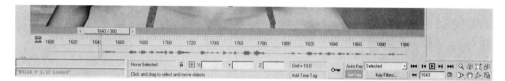

This will show the waveform of the audio track. The peaks and valleys of the waveform correspond to the sounds of the dialogue. By scrubbing the Time slider, you can hear when a particular syllable is being spoken. Then, by examining the waveform at that spot, you can see exactly when the syllable begins and ends.

2 Now you can scrub the Time slider over the first peak in the waveform, which will be Zoey saying "Hello." Move the Time slider back well before the sound starts and set a hold key for the A_I channel and set the M_B_P channel to 62. Because the neutral position for Zoey's face is modeled with her lips slightly parted, the M_B_P channel is given an initial value to close her mouth.

3 At frame 1643, just before the sound starts, set the M_B_P channel to 0 and set the A_I channel to 33 to create the "He…" syllable (see Figure 14-15).

4 To raise the tongue for the "LL" sound, go back at frame 1640 and set the tongue channel to 0. Then go to frame 1649 and set the tongue channel to 80. Hold this key at frame 1651 by moving the Spinner up temporarily and then back down to 80 (see Figure 14-16).

5 At frame 1660, set the tongue channel back to 0.

6 Now create the *O* syllable. At frame 1646, set a hold key for the U_OO channel. Then, at frame 1649, set a hold key for the W_Q channel. At frame 1655, set the U_OO channel to 57 and the W_Q channel to 21 (see Figure 14-17). Then at frame 1669, set both of these channels to 0.

FIGURE 14-15 At frame 1643, Zoey opens her mouth to begin to say the word *Hello*. This is done by keying up the A_I Morpher channel.

FIGURE 14-16 At frame 1649, the tongue is raised for the "LL" sound in "Hello".

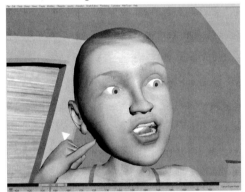

FIGURE 14-17 At frame 1646, Zoey finishes the word *Hello* by mouthing the *O* sound. This is done by keying up both the W_Q and U_OO Morpher channels.

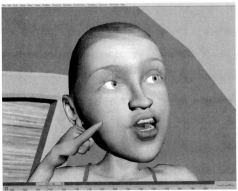

Although this is an *O* syllable, it is emphasized in Zoey's dialogue. Creating it by combining the W_Q and U_OO channels makes the lips protrude farther and pucker somewhat more than the O morph target. Sometimes experimentation with different channels is necessary to get just the right mouth shape.

Notice that most of these keys are set earlier than the actual sound in the waveform. This is because people usually form the shape of a syllable with their mouth before their breath and vocal cords actually create the sound. Therefore, it's a good rule of thumb to always keep the keys for lip sync two or three frames ahead of the actual audio. Also, make sure that the hold keys are set early enough so that the mouth has a chance to open and reach its peak in time for the syllable. Shape the curves of the sound as it trails off.

Now we'll move on to where Zoey says, "Hey, girl," and create the keys for those words. Here are the steps:

1 At frame 1700, set a hold key for the A_I channel. Then at frame 1703, set the A_I channel to 34. This will be the "Hey" syllable (see Figure 14-18).

2 At frame 1705, set hold keys for the EE and W_Q channels. To lip sync the word *girl*, you only need to keyframe one phonetic utterance. At frame 1708, set the A_I channel to 26, the EE channel to 25, and the W_Q channel to 54 (see Figure 14-19).

Many times in real speech, the mouth does not move much between syllables. To create believable lip sync, you need to be aware that sometimes syllables need to be left out.

3 Set the EE channel back to 0 at frame 1722 and the W_Q and A_I channels back to 0 at frame 1730.

FIGURE 14-18 At frame 1703, Zoey is mouthing the word *Hey* with the A_I channel.

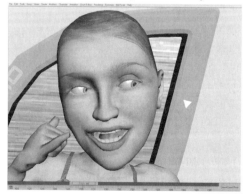

FIGURE 14-19   Here, at frame 1705, Zoey is mouthing the word *girl* with a combination of the EE and W_Q channels.

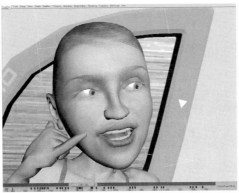

 **NOTE**   *On the CD-ROM, the file ...\3dsmax6_CD*
Scene1_06_CH14.max contains the completed tutorial to this point.

As you keyframe longer passages of dialogue, getting the timing right can become challenging. One methodology to follow is to quickly create keys for every syllable for a longer section of dialogue (several words, a short sentence's worth) exactly in sync with the audio waveform. Setting the values for these initial keys fairly high will make the animation easier to discern during playback. By matching the keys exactly with the waveform, you can be sure that the overall timing will be right. Then, when you have a passage completed, you can shift all the keys for that dialogue one, two, or even three frames earlier. You can then work on the nuances of toning down the keys, easing in and out, and removing keys for syllables that are not necessary.

Another Approach to Morphing: Muscles

In the movie *Stuart Little,* Sony Pictures Imageworks created a realistically animated CG mouse and incorporated it with live-action footage. Animators were confronted with the challenge of making a realistic mouse talk and emote like a human, but this is difficult since real mice do not have the teeth, tongues, eyes, and facial muscles needed for human facial expressions. To deal with this, the animators created a fictional anatomy for the mouse character. They created reference illustrations where human facial muscles were stretched over a mouse skull, and then animators created morph targets corresponding to these facial muscles. They were then able to animate Stuart Little delivering a convincing acting performance.

In the previous exercises, the head has been rigged as simply as possible for very straightforward animation, but for deeper control, on more detailed facial models, individual morph targets can be created to simulate the contraction of individual muscles in the face. This not only enables detailed control of the face but also provides it with realistic movement. In this method, morph targets are created in the same way as before, through copying the head and sculpting vertices for each new morph target.

Creating convincing facial movements is fairly straightforward with some knowledge of facial anatomy. As in all other areas of the body, the face features muscles that are attached to and pulled over the bones of the head, and, like all muscles, the facial muscles bulge when they contract. Therefore, once you have visualized where the facial muscles are on your character, you can create morph targets that correspond to their contractions. The skin around the muscle is pulled in the direction of the underlying muscle's contraction and pushes outward as the muscle bulges.

Figure 14-20 shows the morph targets and their corresponding muscles for the character Felix. This set is rudimentary, covering only the major muscles of the face. Furthermore, the morph targets for certain muscles should of course be broken down to right and left morph targets, but muscles like the frontalis can be broken up further into two sections on each side of the face. This way, each eyebrow can be lifted from the side toward the center of the face or from the outside enabling a wider range of expressions. Additional targets have been added for the rotational and side-to-side movements of the jaw.

Animating a face rigged in this way, by keying Morpher tracks that are named for the muscles, can be less intuitive. And while this may be preferable for some animators creating detailed facial animation, you can make a muscle-based facial rig simpler. You can rename certain muscle-based targets, for example, Levator Palbebrae can be named Blink. But beyond that, as explained earlier in this chapter, you can build more morph targets from the original muscle-based targets. For example, in the Morpher modifier, you can turn up the channels for Zygomatic Major and Orbicularis Oculi, and then if you copy and collapse the head, you can use this new head as a Smile morph target. The morph targets that correspond to emotional expressions, or phonetic utterances, can be created by combining the effects of the muscle-based morph targets in this manner.

NOTE *On the CD-ROM, the final models for both the Felix and Carlo characters have been rigged with muscle based facial morph targets. You can examine the files ...\3dsmax6_CD\Felix\felix_final_morphs_aura.max and ...\3dsmax6_CD\Carlo\Carlo_rigged_morphs_aura.max. You can adjust the spinners for the Morpher channels and you can unhide the morph targets to see how they have been modeled.*

Being able to identify with characters' emotions is what draws viewers into a story. Creating strong, believable emotions in your characters is a surefire way to make viewers remember your work. Keep this in mind as you create the facial animation for your projects.

FIGURE 14-20   The muscle based morph targets for Felix

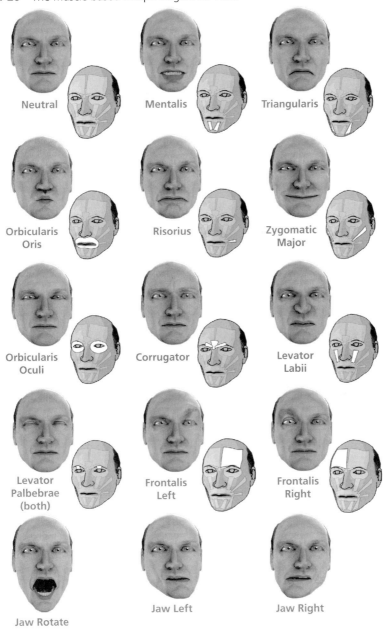

Neutral

Mentalis

Triangularis

Orbicularis
Oris

Risorius

Zygomatic
Major

Orbicularis
Oculi

Corrugator

Levator
Labii

Levator
Palbebrae
(both)

Frontalis
Left

Frontalis
Right

Jaw Rotate

Jaw Left

Jaw Right

Chapter 15

Secondary Animation and Effects: Bringing the Background to Life

Although character animation is undoubtedly the lifeblood of any evocative, emotional story, there are potentially many other things to animate. Characters can have more to them that move than simply limbs and faces, and the worlds they live in can be full of life and motion as well. It is good to keep in mind that anything that moves can be moved expressively, providing another opportunity to use animation skills for enriching your story. In this chapter we'll take a brief look at both secondary animation and effects animation.

Secondary Animation

Secondary animation is any character-related movement outside of the skeleton and face, and it's one of the 12 animation principles as defined in Chapter 13. This can mean a wide range of things—from the gravity-induced bouncing of a large belly to the flopping ears of a puppy to the springy flexibility of a bug-eyed alien's eye stalk. These motions can be rigged with extra bones or morph targets and keyframed along with or just after the main character animation. This can often be as straightforward as adding offset or follow-through to a ponytail.

And, as you'll see in this chapter, secondary animation can be created procedurally with modifiers such as Flex, plug-ins such as Reactor, or MAXScripts such as Michael Comet's Lag MAXScript. In these methods, the secondary animation is calculated automatically based on the movements that are keyframed into the body during character animation.

3-D Effects Animation

Beyond the characters themselves are the environments they navigate and inhabit, which can feature animated, moving elements to both set the scene and provide story points. Because this covers such a wide range of moving things, I usually refer to effects animation when describing the movement of anything not character related. These might include weather effects such as boiling clouds, rustling grass, and falling hailstones, man-made items such as factory machines, shattering glass, and careening missiles, and imaginary phenomena such as magic spells, psychic blasts, and black holes.

Because the subject matter is so vastly variegated, methods for animating effects differ greatly and can be very specific to a particular effect. Effects animation tends to involve more individual problem solving versus the slightly more consistent methods for building and animating characters. This harkens back to the work done in Chapter 2 when planning your film. There are so many powerful tools within 3ds max for animating an infinite variety of phenomena—from the versatile, event-driven particle systems of Particle Flow, to the deep physics simulation of Reactor, to the programmability of MAXScript. Therefore, it is best to focus on the tools specific to the exact demands of your animation task.

The Game to Save the World features both secondary animation and effects animation in the auras that float over the heads of the characters. These auras are made to show something more about the characters' personalities as well as what they have achieved in this fictitious online videogame. Each aura is constructed and animated in a completely different way, so we can explore a few of the many techniques for effects animation in 3ds max. These auras are good examples of the types of techniques used to simulate magic in a fantasy animation or physical phenomena in science-fiction animation. Also, we'll look at procedural secondary animation by having the auras move along with the characters using the Flex modifier.

Zoey's Aura: Swirling Information

Zoey's character biography says that she is a writer for a small newspaper. She is playing this online game partly for fun and partly for research. Her aura vaguely reflects this by being made of "information." In this case, it's a swirling headdress of transparent glowing folders orbited by more abstract-looking streams of geometric shapes. We'll construct her aura by using the Scatter compound object and particle systems.

Scatter Compound Objects

Scatter is a type of compound object in 3ds max that takes one object and multiplies it across the surface of another distribution object. We'll create the general headdress shape of Zoey's aura and then use Scatter to propagate a very simple folder-shaped polygon object across its surface.

Distribution Object for the Scatter Object

The Scatter compound object consists of a base object, or distribution object, over which another object is scattered. This distribution object can be used to define the overall shape of the scattered objects and can be an animated object. To create the general shape of Zoey's aura, follow these steps:

1 In an empty max file, start by giving the Active Time Segment a start time of 0 and an end time of 2000.

2 Create a cylinder at the origin sized relative to Zoey's head (name it Dist_Blue). This will determine the size and rough shape of the aura. Make the cylinder 60cm high with a radius of 16cm. Give it 8 height segments and 18 sides. Apply an Edit Mesh modifier and in Polygon Sub Object mode, and remove the top and bottom faces to leave the cylinder uncapped at both ends.

3 Apply an Xform modifier. Then, in the stack, go to Gizmo Sub Object mode and select the gizmo in the viewport. In Auto Key mode, animate one full, 360-degree rotation. Move the Time slider to frame 500 and rotate the gizmo 90 degrees in the Z-axis. Then rotate 90 degrees again and set keys on frames 1000, 1500, and 2000 to complete the rotation. Turn off Auto Key mode.

NOTE *It is good practice to create 360-degree rotations with four keys at 90-degree increments. Although the default rotation controller, the Euler XYZ, can handle higher rotation increments, other types of rotation controllers, such as Linear and TCB, will misinterpret a single rotation key of 360 degrees as a rotation of 0 degrees, leaving no rotation at all. Rotating at 90-degree increments avoids this problem altogether.*

4 In the Track View, select Z rotation track for the Xform gizmo of the Dist_Blue object and click the Parameter Curve Out-of-Range Type button. Set the Out-Of-Range types to Loop so the rotation animation will cycle.

5 Clone the Dist_Blue object three times to create Dist_Cyan, Dist_Gray, and Dist_Dark objects. Make the intervals for the rotation of each cylinder shorter by moving their keys to the left in the track bar. Make the rotation for Dist_Cyan 1,500 frames long, Dist_Gray 1,000 frames long, and Dist_Dark 750 frames long.

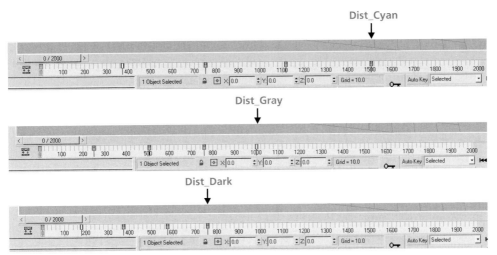

6 Hide the objects Dist_Cyan, Dist_Gray, and Dist_Dark. On the Dist_Blue object, apply a Taper modifier and then a Bend modifier with the settings shown in the following illustrations. Select these two modifiers in the stack and then right-click them. Choose Copy from the pop-up menu; then unhide and select the Dist_Cyan object in the viewport. Right-click the top entry in its stack and choose Paste Instanced to paste the two modifiers onto this object. Repeat this for Dist_Gray and Dist_Dark as well.

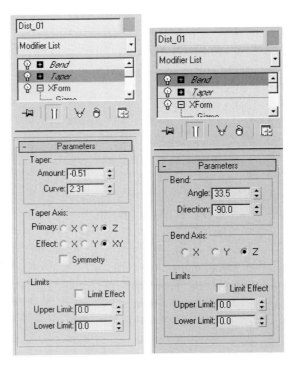

This will provide the general shape of Zoey's aura (see Figure 15-1). Because the Taper and Bend modifiers are instanced, you can change the aura's basic shape by accessing the modifiers in any of these cylinders. Also, because the rotation of the cylinder is below these modifiers in the stack, the surface of the shape will rotate while maintaining the form created by the Taper Bend modifiers.

FIGURE 15-1 A cylinder primitive is shaped with the Taper and Bend modifiers to form the general shape of Zoey's animated aura.

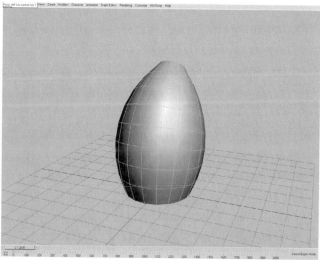

Base Particle—Folder Shape

Now you can create the object that will be scattered over the distribution object. In this case, a simple folder shape will convey the idea that Zoey is interested in collecting information. Here are the steps to follow:

1 In a top viewport, draw a simple folder shape by using the Line tool. Make it roughly 10cm long by 7cm high. Use only a few vertices to keep the

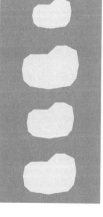

detail low because this folder object will be duplicated many times. Add an Edit Mesh modifier to automatically create a flat mesh from the two-dimensional Spline object. Name this object Folder_Blue.

2 Duplicate this folder object three times to create Folder_Cyan, Folder_Dark, and Folder_Gray. Scale these objects so that each one is slightly different in size.

3 Make a standard material named Zaura_Cyan. Check the 2-sided check box and set Opacity to 33%. Click the Color check box in the Self-Illumination section of the Blinn Basic

Parameters rollout and give the Self-Illumination color an RGB value of R:0, G:90, B:124. Assign this material to Folder_Cyan.

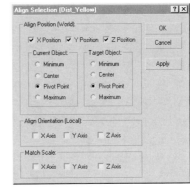

4 Create three more materials by SHIFT-dragging the first material into three other material slots. Name the second material Zaura_Blue and give its Self-Illumination color an RGB value of R:0, G:90, B:124. Name the third material Zaura_Dark and give its Self-Illumination color an RGB value of R:23, G:23, B:23. Name the fourth material Zaura_Gray and give its Self-Illumination color an RGB value of R:80, G:89, B:77. Assign each of the folder objects with the corresponding name.

5 Select all four folder objects and click the Align tool. Then click one of the distribution objects and align the pivot points of the folders with the pivot points of the distribution objects, as shown.

Scatter

Now the folder geometry object can be scattered across the distribution object and these folder objects can be given random motion by animating the parameters within the Scatter compound object. Here are the steps to follow:

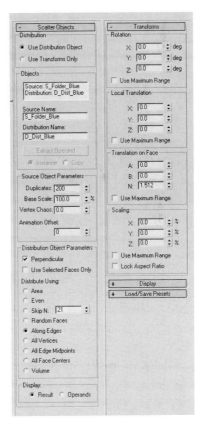

1 From the drop-down menu at the top of the Create panel, select Compound Objects from the list. In the viewport, select the Folder_Blue object and click the Scatter button in the Create panel. Click the Pick Distribution Object button with the Instanced radio button on and select the Dist_Blue object from the viewport. In the Modify panel, give the Folder_Blue object the settings shown here. In the Display rollout in the Modify panel, check the Hide Distribution Object check box.

2 Repeat step 1 three more times, pairing each folder object with its corresponding distribution object. Give the second, third, and fourth scatter objects the settings shown here:

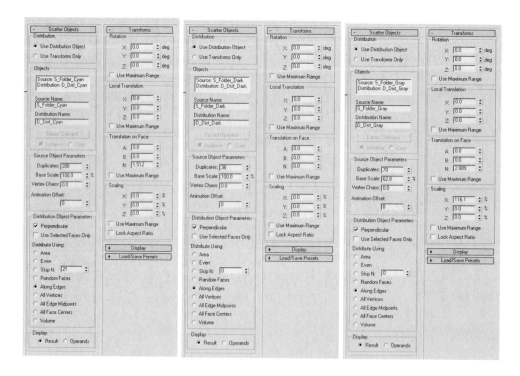

3 Hide the original distribution objects (Dist_Blue, Dist_Cyan, Dist_Gray, and Dist_Dark).

Now the aura is a collection of multicolored folders (see Figure 15-2). You can play the timeline to see the aura in motion. To add more motion, you can animate the values in the Transforms rollout of the each Scatter object. For an example of this, continue on with step 4.

4 Select the Folder_Blue object and turn on Auto Key mode. At frame 0, move the spinners for the A and B values in the Translation on Face section of the Transforms rollout of the Modify panel. Then right-click both spinners to set each to 0. Move halfway through the animated rotation interval for the Folder_Blue gizmo, to frame 1000, and give A: a value of 10 and B: a value of –8. At frame 2000, set them both back to 0. Now the positions of the blue folders will animate as they rotate around the aura.

FIGURE 15-2 Here, the original cylinder object has been used as a distribution sub object of a Scatter compound object. The folder shapes are scattered along the surface.

You can create this type of animation for other values in the Transforms rollout of the Scatter object for the Folder_Blue object and the other Scatter objects.

Orbiting Particle Systems

Now we'll delve into 3ds max's powerful new particle systems, called Particle Flow. Complex particle behaviors can be easily created in Particle Flow's flowchart approach. In the following steps, we'll make three particle emitters that orbit the aura leaving trails of blocks:

1 Create a dummy object at the origin named Anchor. Create a second dummy object, named Particle_Rotator, and move this one up in the Z-axis to the center of the aura. Link the Particle_Rotator dummy to the Anchor dummy.

2 Create 360-degree rotation animation for the Z-axis of the Particle_Rotator dummy, stretching between frames 0 and 200. In the Track View, set the Out-Of-Range curve type for the Z-axis track to Loop.

3 For the objects that will be used for particles, create two Box primitives anywhere in the viewport. Make the first a 2cm cube, named Cube_Particle. Make the second with a length of 4cm, a width of 0.5cm, and a height of 1cm and name it Box_Particle.

4 In the drop-down list at the top of the Create panel, choose Particle Systems. Click the PF Source button and drag in the viewport next to the aura to create a Particle Flow icon. In the Emission rollout, set both the Length and Width values to 4. Rotate the icon 90 degrees in the X-axis so that its arrow points toward the front of the aura, and move it until it is about a third of the way from the bottom of the aura on the right side, as shown in Figure 15-3. Link the PF Source 01 object to the Particle_Rotator dummy.

5 With the PF Source 01 object selected, click the Particle View button in the Setup rollout of the Modify panel.

This accesses the Particle View window, shown in Figure 15-4, which is where the appearance and behaviors of the particle systems are designed. The flowchart-like area at the upper left is the Event Display, and the boxes in it are known as *events*. To construct behaviors, you drag icons onto the Event Display from the list of available operators in the bottom left, known as the Depot. When a particular operator is selected within the Event Display, its parameters appear in rollouts in the upper right of the Particle Flow window.

FIGURE 15-3 A dummy object is placed within the aura and animated with rotation, and then the Particle Flow icon is linked to this dummy.

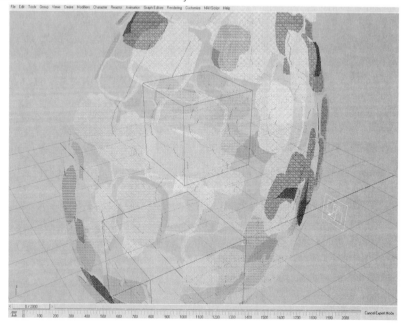

FIGURE 15-4   This is the Particle View window, where Particle Flow systems are designed and edited.

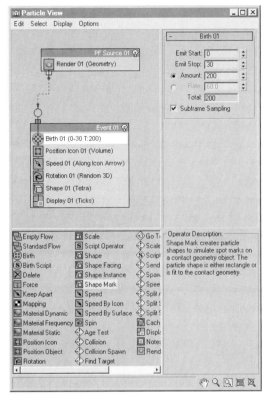

Creating Event Driven Behaviors with Particle Flow

While Particle Flow can be used to create highly complex particle systems and behaviors on its own and provide even more sophistication through MAXScript, it is best to start with a simple example. To create a simple particle system using Particle Flow events, follow these steps:

1 In the Event View, click the Birth operator to select it. In its Parameters rollout, give it the settings shown right. This defines how many particles there are and for how long they are emitted.

2 Select the Speed operator and set the Speed parameter in the Parameters rollout to 1.

3 Select the Rotation operator and choose World Space from the drop-down menu in its Parameters rollout.

4 From the Depot, drag a Shape Instance operator onto the existing Shape operator in the Event View. As you drag the new operator over the old one, a red line will appear to indicate that the old operator will be replaced when you release the mouse.

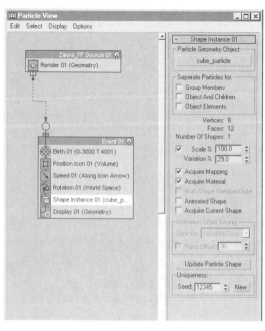

5 Click the button labeled None in the Parameters rollout for the Shape Instance operator and then click the Cube_Particle object in the viewport. This makes that object the particle that will be used by the particle system.

6 Select the Display operator. In its Parameters rollout, change the particle display type to Geometry by choosing it from the Type drop-down list.

Now if you play the animation in the viewport, you will see the stream of cubes being created by the particle emitter as it orbits the aura. But after the animation

plays for a while, the viewport will become bogged down because none of the particles are being removed. You can add new operators to make the particles shrink and delete them after the end of their lifespan.

7 Drag an Age Test operator onto the bottom of Event 01. As you drag the operator over the event box, you can see the line appear again, telling you at which point the new operator will be placed when you release the mouse button. In the Parameters rollout for the Age Test operator, set Test Value to 35.

8 Now drag a Scale operator to the empty area below the Event 01 box. This will create a new event based around the Scale operator with its own Display operator. Select the Display operator and set its display type to Geometry in the Parameters rollout. Select the Scale operator and set its type to Relative Successive. Set the Scale Factor to 93%. This will shrink the particle gradually.

9 Drag a Delete operator onto the bottom of Event 02. In its Parameters rollout, click the By Particle Age radio button and set Lifespan to 55. This removes each particle from the scene after it has been visible for 55 frames.

Now you must connect the events so that the Age Test operator flows into the Scale event. You can then duplicate these two event boxes so that the Box_Particle can be emitted as well.

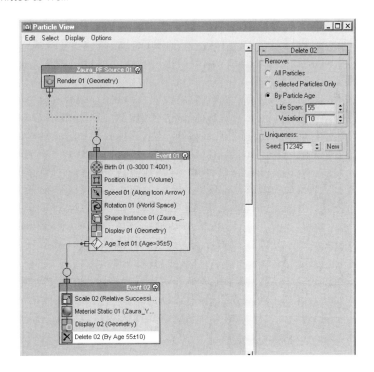

10 Click the small tab that sticks out to the left of the Age Test operator, called *test output*, and drag it on to the loop that sticks out to the top of the Event 02 box, called the *event input*. A wire appears connecting the two events showing the direction of the logic flow for the particle system.

11 Select the Event 01 and Event 02 boxes by clicking one of the title bars and then CTRL-clicking the other. Then SHIFT-drag the selection to the right in the Event View window to clone the two events. Drag from the output of the root event, PF Source 01 (which has the same name as the Particle Flow emitter object), to the input on the Event 03 box. Then drag from Event 03's Age Test operator to the newly cloned scale event, Event 04.

12 Select the new Shape Instance operator. In its parameters rollout, click the button currently named Cube_Particle and then click the Box_Particle object in the viewport.

This newly cloned set of events will cause the Box_Particle object to be emitted as well, but all the new particles will be in the exact same positions as the cube particles. Many of the various operators available in Particle Flow affect particles randomly. This randomness is generated by a base number called the *seed*. If two similar operators share the same seed, they will produce the same results.

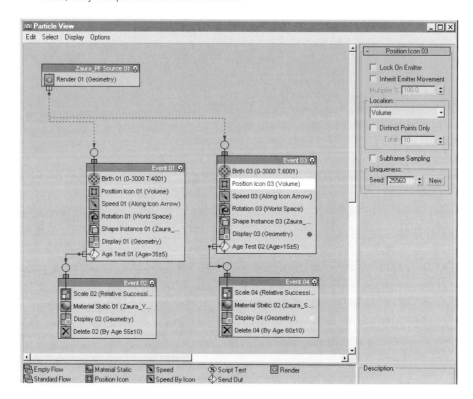

13 Select the new Position Icon operator in Event 03 and click the New button next to its seed value.

14 Clone the original Particle Emitter object in the viewport and move this new emitter up until it is about a third of the way from the top of the aura.

15 Clone this emitter and move the new emitter to the opposite side of the aura and about halfway down from the top of the aura. Rotate the new emitter 180 degrees in the Z-axis to face the opposite direction.

16 Create a new dummy named Particle_Rotator_ Parent somewhat larger than the Particle_Rotator dummy. Align the new dummy, center to center, with the Particle_Rotator and then link Particle_ Rotator to Particle_Rotator_ Parent. Now rotate Particle_Rotator_Parent –20 degrees in the X-axis to make the entire particle emitter assembly rotate in alignment with the curvature of the aura.

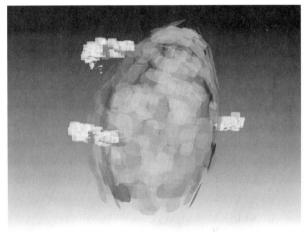

Secondary Animation with the Flex Modifier

The aura is now ready to be placed over Zoey's head and linked. However, if this is done with a simple hierarchical parenting, the position of the aura will be locked exactly to the movement of the head, which won't look very good. What is needed is some secondary animation that allows the aura to move more ethereally, bending and swaying as Zoey moves her head. This can be done procedurally with the Flex modifier.

Because applying the Flex modifier to the entire aura would be very demanding on the computer, a spline object can be created to be the "spine" of the aura. The simple object can be controlled with the Flex modifier, and the aura can be constrained to it with a path constraint. Here are the steps to follow:

1 In a right viewport, draw a three-vertex spline that roughly follows the curvature of the aura. Name this object Spine and link it to the Anchor dummy.

2 In Vertex Sub Object mode, select the top and bottom vertices and then the Flex modifier. Give it the settings shown here:

3 In the Create panel, click the Space Warps button and choose Forces from the drop-down menu. Click the Drag button and create a Drag icon in the viewport. Just to be organized, when the aura is merged into the Cloud10 animation scene, link the Drag icon to the Anchor dummy.

4 Select the Spine object and scroll down to the Forces and Deflectors rollout. Click the Add button in the Forces section and click the Drag icon in the viewport.

5 Select all four Folder objects and link them to the Anchor dummy object.

6 Select the Folder_Blue object and assign it a Path Deform World Space modifier and give it the settings shown here. Click the Pick Path button and select the Spine object from the viewport. Then copy this modifier to the three other folder Scatter objects.

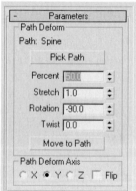

Now you can test the effect of the Flex modifier by temporarily animating the Anchor object. Move it around the scene with the Auto key button, setting keys every 50 frames or so. You can then play the animation back and watch the deformation of the objects controlled by the Flex modifier. You can see the finished Zoey aura by opening the file …\3dsmax6_CD\Auras\Aura_Zoey.max.

Final Linking, Naming, and Merging

Zoey's aura is now ready to be merged into the animation scene, and the Anchor dummy object can be linked to her head control object. To keep the naming organized, you can use the Rename Objects tool found in the Tools menu and modify the names of all the objects in one step. If everything related to the aura has the prefix "Zaura_," the aura will be easier to manage once it is merged into the scene. Once the Zoey aura objects are merged into the main animation scene, the cap Anchor object can be aligned with Zoey's head control object and linked to it. For longer scene files, it may be necessary to synchronize the duration of particle emissions with the animation within the Scatter objects.

Once the aura is in the main scene file, the emissions' start and end times and the particle emission rates of the particle systems need to be timed so that they emit particles during the correct frames of animation. It is best to have the particle system emitting particles only during the animation frames you will be rendering. For example, if you are rendering frames 1500 to 2000, your system can bog down if you have the particle systems emitting particles from frames 0 to 4000.

Carlo's Aura: Orbiting Light Trails

Carlo has an aura that's very different looking aura from Zoey's. To represent his character's status in the online videogame, his aura needed to be bigger, brighter, and more kinetic. In the film, his character is seeking followers to increase his standing and powers in the game. To represent this, his aura is composed of orbiting trails of light. The main challenges involved are getting the trails of light to have an interesting-enough pattern and creating an appearance that looks like a long-exposure photograph.

Creating Random Oscillations

To create the paths, a dummy object was given a spinning animation on its Z-axis. Then, in the Motion panel, the dummy object's rotation controller was converted to a new Rotation List controller, which preserved its original, spinning animation (shown left). A Noise controller was then added with a value only in its X strength (shown right). This caused the dummy object to oscillate randomly as it rotated.

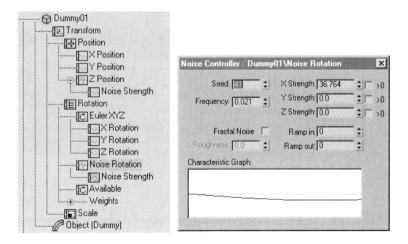

Two cone objects were then linked to this dummy object. With these two cone objects selected, the Trajectories button was turned on in the Motion panel. This made the paths of the two cones visible in the viewport. But more importantly, the tools in the Trajectories rollout could then be used to convert the paths into Spline objects. The paths could be sculpted indirectly by changing in the Noise controllers and the rotation keys of the dummy object.

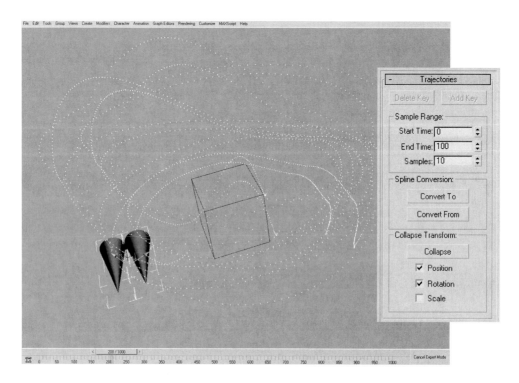

The Appearance of Light

To make the paths look like trails of light took two steps. First, a simple green, standard material was created using a falloff map for both the Opacity and Self-Illumination channels. This was applied to the path Spline objects, which had been set to be renderable (see Figure 15-5a). This is done in the Rendering rollout of the Editable Spline object.

A Glow post-rendering effect (see Figure 15-5b) was then added to the Editable Spline objects. The Glow effect is part of the Lens Effects plug-in, which has been a standard component of 3ds max for many years. This is accessed in the Effects tab of the Render Scene dialog box. This will be covered in slightly more detail in Chapter 16.

FIGURE 15-5 Here are the spline objects of Carlo's aura before the Glow rendering effect (a) and after (b).

(a) (b)

Once constructed, Carlo's aura is controlled using the Flex modifier in the same manner as Zoey's aura. You can see how his aura is constructed by opening the file …\3dsmax6_CD\ Auras\Aura_Carlo.max.

Felix's Aura: A Flame Made of Bubbling Glass

The creative directive for Felix's aura specifies glasslike, vaguely TV tube–shaped bubbles coming out in a flame-like movement. The base particle is simply a Chamfer Box primitive with a Relax modifier applied. This particle is then used by a relatively complex Particle Flow system. The particles are controlled by a Universal DynaFlector space warp. This space warp, in turn, references a Mesh object in the shape of a flame. This setup makes the particles follow the surface of the flame mesh shape as they billow out of the particle emitter. You can open the file…\3dsmax6_CD\Auras\Aura_Felix.max to see how the Particle Flow system is constructed. Select the PF Source 01 object and open the Particle View window to see the event flowchart. Also, you can see a rendering of Felix's aura on page 11 of the color insert.

To be sure, all these aura effects were created with a fair amount of experimentation and trial and error. This type of work's varied nature requires a broad knowledge of 3ds max's far-flung tool set. 3ds max has a myriad of tools and a myriad of additional plug-ins for creating all manner of animated effects. But taking a task-based, story-centric approach to learning these types of special effects animations can keep you from being overwhelmed and keep your efforts focused.

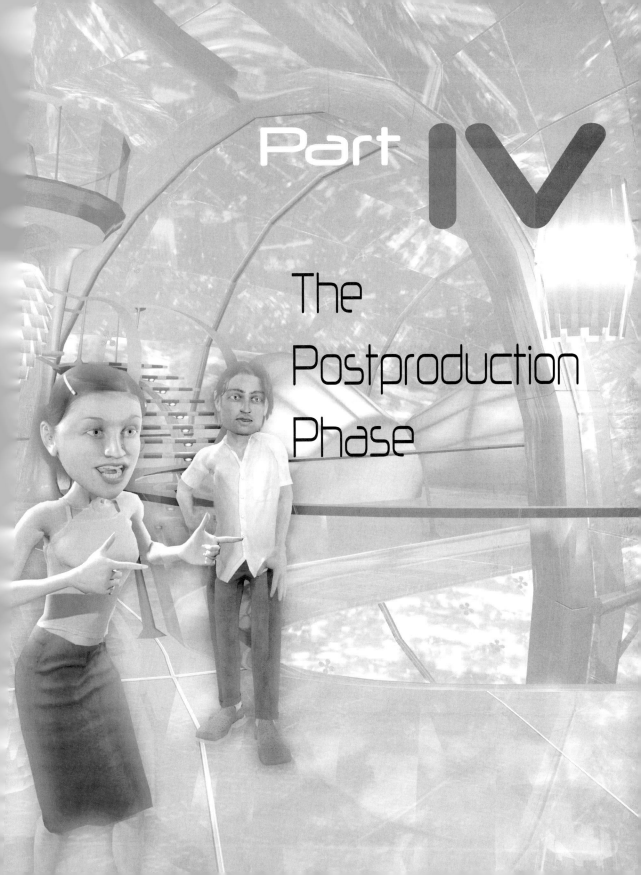

Part **IV**

The Postproduction Phase

Chapter 16

Lighting and Rendering: Crafting an Atmosphere

Now is the time to play the role of director of photography by setting up lighting and "shooting" our virtual scenes. In a traditional movie production, the director of photography is responsible for lighting a camera shot to evoke a mood, indicate a time of day, and accentuate the story points. As CG filmmakers, we can use virtual lights in much the same way a director of photography uses real lights, leveraging color, direction, intensity, and shadows to achieve the desired effect. The director of photography is also responsible for making sure that the combination of lighting, camera lenses, lens filters, and film stock give each frame of the movie the desired look. In Steven Spielberg's *Minority Report*, the director of photography, Janusz Kaminski, chose a grainy film stock to help provide that movie's distinctive texture.

In CG filmmaking, we construct our lighting solution and rendering strategies based on a combination of creative decisions and on the technical constraints of our rendering method. Global illumination played a prominent role in defining the look of Ruari Robinson's short 3ds max film *Fifty Percent Grey* while helping along the film's concept. The effects team, Shynola, created a video for the Queens of the Stone Age, used cartoon rendering to provide its distinctive, graphical treatment. In this chapter, we'll explore virtual lighting further and set up the lighting for our shots, and then we'll set up our rendering and create final rendered frames.

Choosing a Renderer

In addition to 3ds max's standard scanline renderer, several professional-grade renderers are available for 3ds max 6, including Cebas's finalRender, SplutterFish's Brazil r/s, and the now built-in Mental Ray. Each of these renderers has specific requirements for both lighting and materials that make it necessary to construct your scenes from the ground up with your chosen renderer in mind. Each has a fairly steep technical learning curve to climb before you can create exceptional renderings. Furthermore, being able to use the features of these renderers that make them stand out almost invariably increases render times dramatically. This means that having state-of-the-art rendering machines is critical. Two-hour render times are fine for creating one still image, but rendering thousands of images becomes prohibitive.

Although I encourage you to use one of these renderers to give your film project cutting-edge production values, there are distinct advantages to using 3ds max's standard rendering features. One is expediency, because a scene can be set up for the scanline renderer much more quickly. Also, because we can take advantage of 3ds max's global illumination (GI) and even High Dynamic Range Images (HDRI), we can still achieve rich, contemporary, quality renderings. And because we will be able to keep our per-frame render times to several minutes instead of several hours, we can keep our production feasible in the context of a one-person independent project. Furthermore, because most of the basic knowledge needed for this streamlined rendering solution is applicable to more powerful renderers, this becomes a good way for you to learn without being inundated by too many new features and concepts at once.

The Importance of Lighting in CG

Just like any traditional film, 3-D animated films depend on lighting for many cinematic aspects. Low-intensity blue lighting coming from a window can simulate nighttime illumination, whereas very-high-intensity yellow lighting can simulate the light cast from a single light bulb during an interrogation. Bright tubes of nearly white light can give a generic hallway feeling of an office building, whereas flickering orange candlelight can give the same hallway the feeling of an ancient basement. Lighting is a key tool for infusing your film with the color palettes defined by your art direction.

However, in CG animation, lighting serves another role. Even the most richly detailed 3-D models can look amateurish, unrealistic, and exhibit the telltale, lifeless look of computer animation when those models are cast in the wrong light. For the movie *Final Fantasy: The Spirits Within*, the state-of-the-art character model for the Aki Ross character had to have a pincushion of lights linked to her head object, following her at all times. In the wrong lighting, tests of these multimillion-dollar state-of-the-art character models didn't look much better than run-of-the-mill 3-D characters. But with the right lighting, they were some of the best 3-D characters to date. In real-world filmmaking, lighting alone can make the difference between a sickly pale, exhausted-looking actor and a beautiful, show-stopping movie star. And in CG, lighting can mean the difference between mediocre and lifelike images (see Figure 16-1a and 16-1b).

Because we've had a look at environmental lighting in Chapter 11, we'll focus more on lighting characters and then lighting the characters and scene together for final rendering.

Character Lighting: Three-Point Setup

In real-world filmmaking, the three-point lighting setup is a nuts-and-bolts technique for lighting an actor, and it's an excellent basis for lighting CG characters as well. Consisting of three spotlights, this approach is useful no matter what renderer you are using. The simplicity of the three-point light setup allows you to achieve rich lighting results without overcomplicating your scene with the interactions of too many lights.

FIGURE 16-1 Here is the same character model-lit with default lighting (a) and then lit with a basic, three-point light setup combined with global illumination (b).

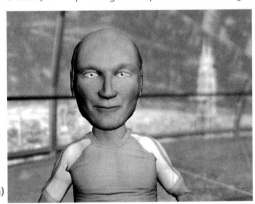

(a)   (b)

Main Light

The main light, often referred to as the *key light*, provides the dominant illumination and shadows. This will represent the main source of light in your scene. If your character is outside, the main light would represent the sun. Indoors, it would simulate the light coming from a window or a lamp (see Figure 16-2a and 16-2b).

Here are the key features of the Main light:

▶ **Color and Intensity**   The color and intensity of this light should mimic the brightness and color of the light source you are trying to simulate. This is done with a combination of the Multiplier setting and the light color.

▶ **Shadows**   The main light is the primary source of shadows. Therefore, shadow casting should be turned on. The default shadow type, Shadow Map, is typically adequate and is the fastest to render. Other types of shadows can be used for specific needs. For example, raytraced shadows can give more accurate, sharper shadows, and area shadows are affected by the shape of the light source. However, these types of shadows typically come at the cost of higher render times.

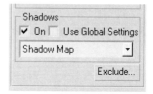

▶ **Placement**   In a generic lighting situation, the main light is typically placed at a 40- to 60-degree angle to the side of the subject and 30 to 50 degrees above the subject. However, this can change depending on the position of the simulated light source in relation to the character.

FIGURE 16-2   Here is Felix illuminated solely by the main light (a) along with a view from the top viewport to show the light placement and the parameters for the main light (b).

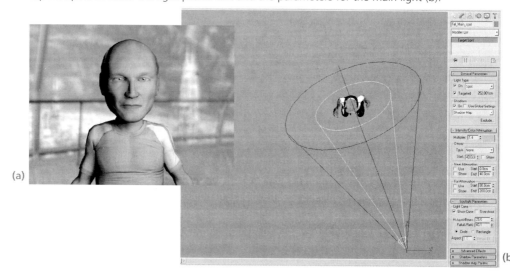

▶ **Falloff**   This setting defines how large the spotlight's circle of cast light is and how soft its edges are. This is displayed in the viewport as two cones connected to the spotlight. Everything within the area of the inner cone, or *hot spot*, is lit with the full intensity of the light. The area between the inner cone and the boundary of the outer cone defines the falloff or softness of the circle's edges. It is best to keep hot spot and falloff circles of light confined fairly closely to the size of the subject you are illuminating. This is because shadow maps have a certain resolution in making the cone of light higher and will cause shadows to have jagged, pixelated edges unless the resolution of the shadow map is increased. This also contributes to render times.

▶ **Attenuation**   To soften the shadows' effects, attenuation can be used. This sets distances from the spotlight at which the intensity of the light will begin to taper off. Otherwise, anything that falls within the light cone will be illuminated no matter how far away it is.

Fill Light

With only a single spotlight pointed at the character, the lighting will be very harsh. Because only one side of the character will be lit, the other side will be dark and indiscernible. To account for this, another lower-intensity light is placed to fill in the dark areas (see Figure 16-3a and Figure 16-3b).

FIGURE 16-3   Now Felix is illuminated by the fill light as well as the main light (a). The fill light illuminates the left side of the face while still leaving it darker than the areas lit by the main light. The top view shows the placement along with the light parameters for the fill light (b).

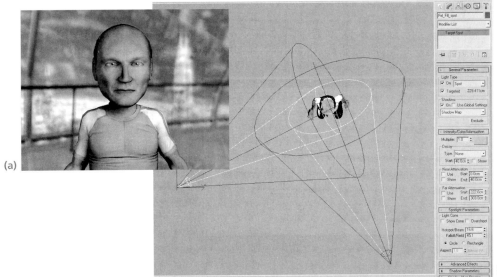

Here are the key features of the Fill light:

▶ **Placement**   The fill light is placed opposite of the main light, often at 90 degrees to the main light. This light is usually placed lower, closer to the level of the subject.

▶ **Color and Intensity**   The fill light should be somewhere between half and a quarter of the intensity of the main light. The brighter this light is, the less apparent the shadows of the main light will be. For darker, high-contrast environments that only appear to have one light source, the fill light should be dimmer still. Typically the color is set to contrast the color of the main light. For example, if the main light is bluish, the fill light will be reddish. This contrast helps add visual interest to the subject.

▶ **Shadows**   Typically, shadows are turned off in the fill light for a clear image. However, for more visual interest and to simulate more than one light source, shadows can be turned on.

Rim Light

A rim light, often referred to as a *back light*, is typically set behind and fairly high above the subject. This often very bright light helps to define the shape of the character with an accentuated outline of light and adds more visual interest to the scene. This light can also be used to simulate the glow from secondary light sources located behind the character (see Figure 16-4a and 16-4b).

FIGURE 16-4   In this image, a rim light, illuminating the right edge of Felix's head, has been added to complete the three-point lighting set up (a). The top view shows the rim light placement and light parameters (b).

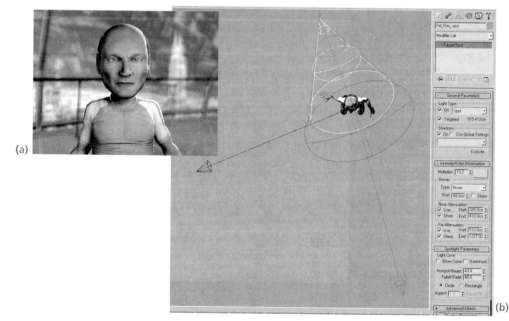

(a)

(b)

Here are the key features of the Rim light:

▶ **Placement**   A rim light is typically placed behind and at a fairly high angle above the character. Through experimentation and test rendering, the placement is finessed until the illumination of the rim light begins to peek around the edge of the character from above, to the side, or both.

▶ **Color and Intensity**   A rim light is typically a high-intensity light with a multiplier several times higher than the main light so that the border of light it creates is well defined.

▶ **Shadows**   Shadows are typically unnecessary for the rim light because their effect is usually not noticed.

The three-point lighting setup is very versatile and can be adjusted to simulate many types of lighting. Furthermore, it is not composed of a concrete set of rules that must be followed but rather is a rough scheme that can be adapted to the specific requirements of your shots. In real-world movies, artificial lights are often set up to simulate natural light sources, such as the sun, lamps, and other lighting that is actually seen by the viewer. In the same way, this lighting scheme can be rotated and positioned, intensified or dimmed, and colored to simulate what your viewers will see in your scenes.

Character Lighting Setup

In the files for each of your characters, you can set up a three-point lighting scheme. These lights can be merged into the main scene file along with the character. To maintain control over the lighting in your scene, I recommend making sure that the character lights illuminate only the character. This can be done with the Exclude button in the General Parameters rollout in the Modify panel for each light.

From the object list on the left, select only the geometry objects for the character, and then click the right arrow to place those objects in this light's Exclude/Include list. Click the radio button

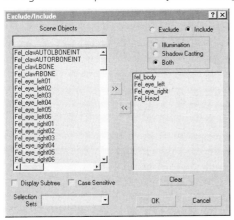

labeled Include and then click the OK button. This makes it so that each character's lights light only that character. If you want a light that is illuminating a character to cast shadows on your scene geometry but not to illuminate it, select all of the scene geometry in the list and click the Exclude radio button instead, along with the Illumination radio button.

To further organize the character lighting workflow, create a simple lighting rig to attach the lights to the character's root placement object. Construct a simple control object from splines in the same manner as the character-control objects and name it Light_rig. Link all the character's lights and their targets to the Light_rig object and then link the Light_rig object to the character's placementCTRL object or whatever the root node of your character is.

This way, the position of the Light_rig object can be animated independently of the character, moving from place to place as the character moves throughout the scene or even moving along with the character if needed.

Character Lighting Within a Scene

Although in previous chapters we already merged our characters into the scene and animated them, the lighting of the scene can now be integrated with the lighting we have created for the characters. The lighting can then be finalized on a shot-by-shot basis. If you have been following the exercises of the book as you create your own project, you can at this point merge the lighting rig itself from your character file into your scene and link it to the version of your character already in your scene.

Integrating Character and Environmental Lighting

To integrate the lighting of the character with the lighting of the scene, we can use the Exclude/Include lighting feature again. Because the character lighting has already been set to include only the character geometry, the environment lights can be set to exclude the character geometry.

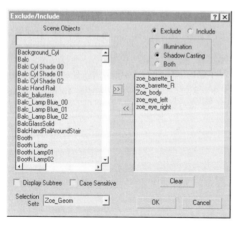

This can be done on a light-by-light basis (which has already been done in the sample scene files) but can be tedious if there are many lights. It can be helpful to use selection sets from within the Exclude/Include dialog box to more quickly add the character geometry to a light's Exclude/Include list. Occasionally, you may want to allow one or two specific lights to continue to illuminate the character. This can be particularly helpful when the character is walking by light sources in the environment. However, most of the time you'll be able to simulate scene lighting with your character's three-point light setup.

NOTE *This is one of many repetitive tasks for which there are helpful MAXScripts available. See the appendix for information on where to find MAXScripts online.*

By keeping the lighting for the environment and the characters separate, you will not have to change the numerous scene lights to ensure good lighting for the characters, or be concerned with character lights creating unwanted changes to your scene lighting. This greatly simplifies what can be a very complicated task of balancing the lighting. The environment is already lit, so only the lights of the character's three-point lighting rig need to be adjusted for their direction color and intensity.

To be sure, for the best renderings, sometimes it is necessary to light characters with the same lights that are lighting the environment. But even in those cases, this simplified approach is a wise starting point. Even if characters are excluded from environmental lighting, you can make specific environment lights illuminate characters on a light-by-light, shot-by-shot basis.

Once the character's lights are merged and integrated into the main scene file, they can be modified and, if necessary, animated to make it appear as though the scene's lighting is illuminating the character. But before we do that, we will add in some global illumination using 3ds max's Light Tracer advanced lighting solution to create more realistic ambient light for the characters.

Adding Global Illumination and High Dynamic Range Images

Traditionally, CG lighting and rendering solutions calculate only the light that comes directly from the virtual lights placed in your scene. Global illumination is a relatively new type of CG lighting that calculates the bouncing of light as it is scattered by the objects in the scene. Also, global illumination is a key rendering feature that has allowed 3-D renderings to go beyond the plastic, artificial surfaces and simple shadows most often associated with CG and attain the softly lit, subtly shadowed look of today's best CG.

Another new rendering advancement that works well in combination with Global Illumination is the High Dynamic Range Image (HDRI). This new image type, newly supported in 3ds max 6 as .hdr or .pic map types, goes beyond the capabilities of typical bitmap formats like JPEG or TIF. HDRI images not only store the color of a pixel but the luminance as well. This means that HDRI images of a particular environment provide an excellent head start towards realistically re-creating the light of that environment. These HDRI environmental images can act as lighting models that can be used by global illumination. Together, they provide the next evolutionary step in rendering realism.

Global illumination and HDRI have become requisite features for any contemporary renderer. Nevertheless, the steep learning curve and setup time as well as the added hardware requirements and increased render time brought on by state-of-the-art renderers such as Mental Ray, Brazil r/s, and finalRender can be prohibitive to a small production. But through the use of 3ds max's Light Tracer advanced lighting solution and a bit of careful setup and strategic compromises, it is possible to achieve some quality, globally illuminated renderings relatively quickly and easily. Furthermore, the knowledge you'll gain in this basic use of GI and HDRI will be of use when you move on to more powerful renderers.

Advanced Lighting with Light Tracer

Light Tracer is 3ds max's built-in global illumination solution. It uses either Skylight or max's physically based Photometric light types in your scene for its lighting calculations. When simply turned on, Light Tracer can cause render times to balloon exponentially, but through adjustments to a few settings and by including only important objects in the advanced lighting calculations, you can keep frame render times reasonable.

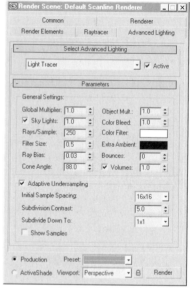

We'll set up global illumination with the Light Tracer for the opening shots of the example film and then set up standard max lights to look like the light coming from key lamps in Cloud10. Examine the scene file …\3dsmax6_CD\ Scene1_07_CH16.max. For a simple example, we'll look at the sequence of frames between frame 1500 and frame 1800. Here, Zoey is standing in one place, so we don't have to worry about animating the lights.

The first optimization to make is a compromise. Removing the environment geometry from the global illumination calculations will make render times a fraction of what they would be if Light Tracer were used to render the entire scene. Here are the steps to follow for this exercise:

1 Using the selection set's drop-down menu in the main toolbar, select the Cloud10 geometry and then right-click anywhere in the viewport and choose Properties from the context menu. Click the Exclude from Advanced Lighting Calculations check box. This way, the Cloud10 geometry will be lit only by its own standard lights and not by the Light Tracer.

2 Create a Skylight light object anywhere in the viewport. Its placement does not affect the lighting because it automatically places an invisible dome of lights over the entire scene. Organizationally, it is best to place the Skylight icon near the character. It can be left with the default name of Skylight01.

Using an HDRI Map for the Skylight

HDRI images are most often used to re-create the lighting of real world environments in CG scenes. They are usually created through a laborious process that involves taking 360-degree panoramic photographs at multiple exposures from the exact same vantage point. These series of panoramas are then combined to produce the final HDRI image. In images of a daytime landscape, for example, the low exposure images provide lighting information for the brighter areas such as the sun without "blowing out." The higher exposure images then provide lighting information for the darker, shadowed areas. When used as environment maps for a 3ds max scene by placing them in the Sky Color map channel of a Skylight, low-resolution versions of these images provide highly realistic lighting, and higher resolution versions of the same HDRI images provide highly realistic reflections when used within object materials.

Since creating these images currently requires special expertise and equipment, several vendors have begun selling collections of high-quality HDRI environmental images of a variety of real world locations (see the appendix). HDRI imaging is an area of much research and development both commercially and academically, so there is a lot of information on the Web for further study.

Our example film provides us with a different challenge than simply re-creating the illumination of a real-world environment. While the characters have omni and spotlights illuminating them, the Cloud10 scene that they are in features illumination from the background skyline as well. Regardless of realism, what we want creatively is for the characters to be illuminated by a combination of the evocative city background and the sculptural lamps of Cloud10. Since the background image and lamp geometry provides no actual illumination, re-creating this subtlety with simple omni and spotlights is next to impossible.

Running the global illumination on the entire environment instead of just the characters would take too long to render and require a much more complicated setup of the scene. Furthermore, this would not take into account the illumination of the background skyline, so I created a synthetic HDRI environment map of the Cloud10 scene to put in the Sky Color map channel of the Skylight for the Global Illumination of the Light Tracer.

Not only is this type of HDRI image useful for lighting the characters within the environment, but it is especially useful for scenes with a camera that doesn't move. You can make one rendering of the environment max scene to be used as a background image in a scene containing *only* the character. This scene can be lit with a skylight containing an HDRI file created in this manner and will of course render much faster. There are two example videos on the CD, …\3dsmax6_CD\Cloud10\teapotHDRI_.avi and teapotHDRI_noreflect.avi, that show a scene with only a teapot, a skylight, and the CL10_8exposure.hdr file.

How the HDRI Image for Cloud10 Was Created

To achieve the rich lighting results provided by HDRI images, the critical element is the extra luminance information provided by multiple exposures. It is then preferable for the HDRI image to be a 360-degree panorama. 3ds max 6 has several new features that can be used together to create an HDRI map from a 3ds max scene instead of from the real world.

First, 3ds max 6 has a new, easy-to-use Panoramic Exporter Utility, found in the main menu under Rendering/Panorama Exporter. It lets you choose any camera and render a single, spherically warped panoramic image from that camera's vantage point. This can be used with max's Exposure Control, Found in the Environment dialog. A series of panoramic renderings from a camera at the center of Cloud10 were created with a range of Exposure values. Additionally, as the exposure value was raised for each new rendering, the brightness of the background.jpg was raised, as was brightness of the Glow Effects on the omni lights within each lamp. This helped fake the light bloom scene in high exposure photographs of bright light sources.

These renderings, saved as normal bitmaps, were then combined using an external, HDRI assembly utility (several of which are freely available for non-commercial use) to create the final CL10_8exposure.hdr file.

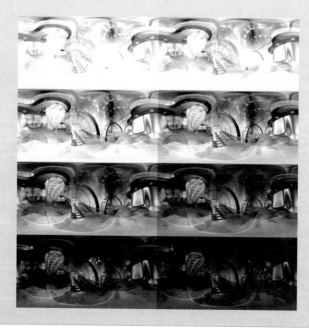

Now the HDRI panorama image can be added to the Skylight. Here are the steps to follow:

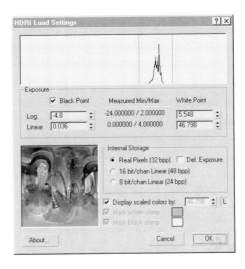

1 In the Modify panel, click the button labeled None and choose the file CL10_8exposure.hdr from the Cloud10 maps folder.

2 In the HDRI Load Settings dialog box, enter these settings. The two main settings you'll need to change are for the black point and white point. This is done by moving the bottom spinners for each until the vertical lines are near the left side peaks and valleys of the histogram for the black point and near the right side of the peaks and valleys for the white point.

3 Open the Material Editor and drag from the map slot in the Modify panel to one of the six material slots in the Material Editor. Click Instance from the dialog box. Then in the Material Editor, click the Environ radio button and choose Spherical Environment from the Mapping drop-down list.

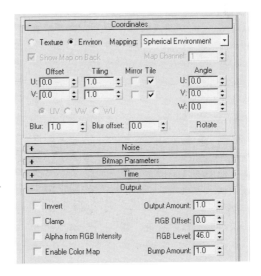

4 In Output rollout of the Material Editor, set the RGB Level close to the same value as the White Point setting for the HDRI map, in this case 46.

This HDRI image is low resolution (512x 256 pixels) which makes the calculations simpler for Light Tracer. Light maps with higher detail and contrast require the Light Tracer to make more calculations to avoid graininess in the shading it creates. Using this image as the Sky Color map for the skylight will give the global illumination the coloration of the city background plus the ambience of the Cloud10 lamps. The other colors from the blue, orange, and green lights within Cloud10 can be provided by the three-point lighting for the character.

Setting up Global Illumination and Scene Lighting

Now you can proceed with adjusting the settings in the Light Tracer to optimize the global illumination and setting up Zoey's spotlights. Here are the steps to follow:

1 Turn off all the Zoey character lights using the Light Lister. In the main menu, choose Tools | Light Lister and uncheck the check boxes to the left of the three Zoey lights.

2 Click the Render Scene button in the main toolbar and create a test render to see the effect of global illumination on Zoey. Render from the camera named Cam_03_1301-1580_1616-2060 at 320×240 pixels. Notice the time to render.

Note that the result is meant to be fairly dark because the Light Tracer will be used only for ambient illumination. Further lighting will come from the Zoey character lights.

3 To speed up the next test rendering, click the Render button to open the Render panel and then click the Advanced Lighting tab. Give the Light Tracer the settings shown in Figure 16-5. Test- render again and check the time to render.

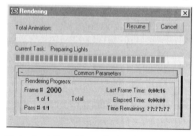

Note that Rays/Sample has been reduced from the default of 250 down to 100. This decreases the number of calculations per pixel, thus speeding up the render time. If Rays/Sample is set too low, the shading will appear grainy. This works in conjunction with the Filter Size setting, which is raised from .5 to 8 to help reduce graininess.

Next, make sure that Adaptive Undersampling is checked and ensure that both Initial Sample Spacing and Subdivide Down To are set to their maximum value of 32×32 subdivisions. These settings keep the light sampling calculations of the Light Tracer focused on areas with more acute curvature and shadows, such as the facial features and hands, and they optimize to

FIGURE 16-5   These are the Light Tracer settings for the sample scene. The settings to note here are Rays/Sample, Filter Size, Initial Sample Spacing, and Subdivide Down To.

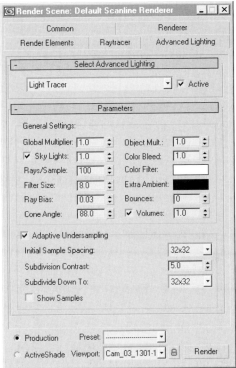

more broad calculations for larger, flatter surfaces, such as the torso. You can see a demonstration of this effect by rendering with Show Samples checked and observing the density of the red dots representing samples and where they are gathered. Lower values for these two settings will cause the samples to become very dense and render times to get longer.

All these settings balance with each other to affect render quality and render times. It is worth a fair amount of experimenting at this point to achieve optimum settings because saving seconds on an individual frame can translate to saving hours when you're rendering an entire series of frames (see Figure 16-6a and Figure 16-6b). The settings for your own projects will invariably be different. Furthermore, these particular settings may turn out to be too low to get a high-quality result. Nevertheless, they are good for doing test renderings to balance out lighting. Once this is done, Rays/Samples and Filter Size can both be set higher, and Adaptive Undersampling values can be set lower until you have the rendering quality you desire.

The skylight and Light Tracer can be left with the same settings for all shots in the film. Whereas the ambient light for the Cloud10 geometry is provided by the two directional

FIGURE 16-6 This is a comparison between global illumination rendering with low settings for sample rates (a) for faster rendering, and rendering with higher sample rates to get more smoothly rendered details (b).

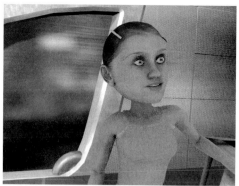 

(a)   (b)

lights (see Chapter 11), the skylight and Light Tracer provide much softer and more convincing shading for the more detailed character geometry.

Now you can turn on the three Zoey character lights and balance their illumination with that of the skylight so that the character lights can simulate the various lighting fixtures of the Cloud10 environment. It is best to do this in Set Key mode because Zoey's lighting rig has been animated to move through the scene with her from camera shot to camera shot. Keys are set for the position of the Zoe_Light_Rig object and the three character lights at the beginning and end of frames for each camera shot. Otherwise, the rig is animated to move along with Zoey's walking. Setting keys for the lights creates keys for its various parameters and color.

Turn on Set Key mode and move the Time slider to frame 1500. Make sure not to move the Time slider again until you have set keys for anything that you change in the following steps.

1 Move the Zoe_Main_Spot light close to the Balc_Omni_00 light, which illuminates this area of the environment. Then move the light forward in the Y-axis until it is somewhat in front of Zoey (see Figure 16-7a).

The position of the Zoe_Main_Spot light does not have to be in exactly the same position as the Cloud10 light for the illumination to look correct. In fact, because the balcony lighting fixture is now behind Zoey, the spotlight would illuminate her back, making it invisible from the angle of the camera. Moving it forward can simulate the light from all three balcony lighting fixtures.

2 Move the Zoe_Fill_Spot light to Zoey's left, slightly forward and below her to simulate the orange light and the city lights coming up through the staircase opening (see Figure 16-7b).

FIGURE 16-7 These images show the set up of the main light (a), the fill light (b) and the rim light (c) for Zoey's three-point lighting in the Cloud10 scene. The main light is simulating light from the blue lamp above Zoey. The fill light is simulating the orange light coming from downstairs, and the rim light is loosely simulating light from the blue lamp.

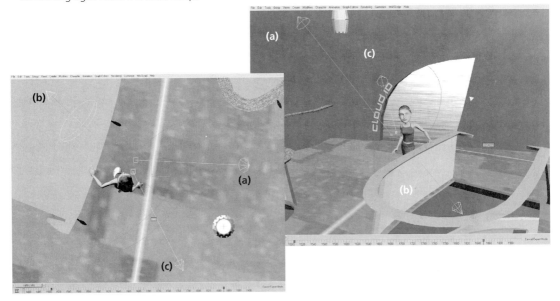

3 Move the Zoe_Rim_Spot light to be behind Zoey to her right and above her. This is a fairly arbitrary position to create a rim of bright lights to define Zoey's shape (see Figure 16-7c).

4 Create a test render.

In the Light Lister, you can quickly adjust the Color and Multiplier values for each of the three lights while adjusting their positions in the viewport. Balancing these colors and intensities with the global illumination of the Light Tracer will mean the multiplier values of these lights should be lower than if they were lighting Zoey only by themselves. Also, the saturation of the light color should be higher so that the color of that light will be apparent. The Zoe_Main_Spot and Zoe_Rim_Spot lights should be the same color as the Balc_Omni_00 light, but slightly more saturated. Also, the Zoe_Fill_Spot light should be orange to simulate the downstairs light shining upward. Follow these steps:

1 Give the three lights the following multiplier values and color settings:

Zoe_Main_Spot Multiplier: 1.33, RGB: 92, 129, 244

Zoe_Fill_Spot   Multiplier: 1.5, RGB: 182, 167, 95

Zoe_Rim_Spot   Multiplier: 9.675, RGB: 16, 75, 232

2 Select the three character lights and the Zoe_Light_Rig object and set keys for them. Move the Time slider to frame 1800 while holding down the right mouse button to freeze the lights and the lighting rig and then set keys. This way, the lights hold their positions in values between frames 1500 and 1800.

3 Test render.

NOTE *The file ...\3dsmax6_CD\Scene1_08_CH16.max contains the completed scene file ready for final rendering.*

Rendering

Now that the lighting is prepared, you can ready the scene for rendering. At this point, many different effects can be added to the images. Further realism can be attained by adding motion blur to fast-moving objects or depth of field to simulate camera focus.

Environment and Video Effects

Many different phenomena can be created and animated within 3ds max in the form of 3-D effects known in max as *environment effects*. Environment effects such as Fog and Fire come standard with max, and there are external plug-ins that show up as environment effects. Then, special effects in 3ds max can also take the form of 2-D post rendering processes, known in max as *effects*. These take the form of standard max effects such as Blur, Brightness and Contrast, Motion Blur, and others, in addition to the many available external plug-ins.

3ds max and Video Compositing

3ds max can create rendered frames in a number of file formats that can be used by video-compositing programs such as Discreet's combustion, and then a variety of post-rendering effects can be performed at the compositing stage. To further aid in this process, 3ds max scenes can be rendered in separate component layers, known as *elements*, that can be blended in many ways in a compositing package. Not only can different groups of geometry be separated and rendered in their own layer, but components of the image, such as shadows and highlights, can be rendered on separate layers to receive specific treatment at the compositing stage.

Controlling Effects

You have several ways to control exactly what an effect is applied to in 3ds max. Great control can be achieved by applying effects to specific objects or even specific sub objects.

G-Buffer   First, effects can be assigned at the object-level graphics buffer, or *G-buffer*. In the object's properties dialog box, an Object Channel ID number is assigned, and then the effect is, in turn, assigned to all objects with that Object Channel ID. This G-buffer data can be embedded in file formats that max can render to, such as the RPF format, which can be read by Discreet combustion. This means that even in the essentially 2-D compositing process, special effects can be added to what were individual objects in the 3-D scene.

Material Effects ID   Even finer control can be afforded to effects by assigning them using the Material Effects ID in the Material Editor. This ID can be assigned at either the material or sub material level or even at the level of individual map channels.

Atmospheric Gizmos   Some 3-D environment effects are assigned to gizmos, which can be placed and animated in the 3ds max scene. For example, a gizmo can be assigned a Fire effect and linked to a Torch object.

Effects in the Example Film

For the purposes of a streamlined production and for keeping the example film simple for instructional clarity, *The Game to Save the World* uses a minimum of effects and plug-ins. However, a few have been used so that you can see how various effects can be integrated into a scene.

Glowing Objects

Using 3ds max's built-in Lens effects, you can add a glow effect to the Cloud10 sign and the elevator (see Figure 16-8a and Figure 16-8b). This effect renders very quickly at the end of the each frame's rendering. Here are the steps to follow to add a glow effect to the Cloud10 sign:

1   Give the geometry for both objects unique G-buffer Object Channel IDs in their properties dialog box. Assign the Cloud10 text geometry object an Object Channel ID of 1 and the {Elev_button} object an ID of 2.

2   Add an instance of Lens Effects to the scene by clicking the Add button in the Effects rollout of the Environment dialog and selecting it from the list (see Figure 16-9a).

3   In the Lens Effects Parameters rollout, choose Glow from the list on the left and click the right-arrow button to add it to the active list (see Figure 16-9b).

FIGURE 16-8 These images show the Cloud10 sign without that Glow Lens effect (a) and with the Glow Lens effect added (b).

(a) (b)

FIGURE 16-9 These are the settings for the Glow Lens effect. Lens Effects has been added to the Effects list (a) and two separate glows have been added in the Lens Effects Parameters rollout (b).

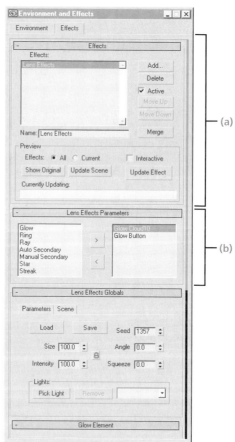

4 You can then click the Interactive check box in the Effects rollout. This will
    automatically render the scene from whatever camera is active and then update
    the image almost instantly as you change parameters.

5 In the Glow Element rollout, enter the settings shown here while watching the
    interactive update of the rendered image.

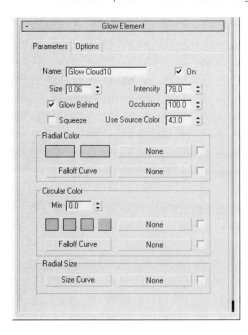
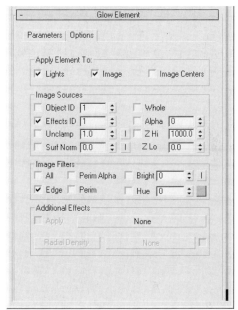

Compositing

For many shots in the example film, I used effects that were added in the compositing process.
This involved rendering the main shot, including background and characters, and then rendering
various objects separately. These moving images were then composited in Discreet's combustion,
sometimes with added effects such as transparency and glows. We'll cover this in the next chapter.

Final Rendering

Now you can render sequences of frames, with each frame becoming its own individual bitmap
file to be used directly in a video-editing program or first brought into a compositing package
to be used for effects, titles, or color correction. Each camera shot should be rendered as an
individually numbered sequence in an uncompressed bitmap format such as TGA or TIF, as
opposed to a compressed format such as JPEG. This is to ensure that no image quality is lost
before the compositing and editing stage.

Setting Up a Render

Even for 3ds max's scanline renderer, many settings can be tweaked. Fortunately, most of the default settings are adequate for most purposes. We'll set up a render as simply as possible.

Final Scene Optimization   Now is the time to be sure that your scene file is optimized to render as quickly as possible. This can entail many things, such as hiding all unnecessary geometry that is not in the camera shot you are currently rendering and making sure that all geometries are set to their rendering resolution. For example, objects using the Mesh Smooth modifier should be set to the higher resolution. Also, you need to make sure Light Tracer parameters are set as high as they need to be.

The Render Scene Dialogue

Change your viewport to a camera view of the camera shot that you want to render. Upon clicking the Render Scene button, you'll need to fill out the information in the Common Parameters rollout of the Common tab, shown in Figure 16-10, to render your sequence.

Frame Range   In this example, we are rendering Camera 5, which is for frames 2016 through 2100. This is entered next to the Range radio button in the Time Output section.

Video Formats and Frame Sizes   You'll need to know how you will deliver your final video so that you can decide at which pixel dimensions to render your frames. To render feature film, for example, you'll typically need to render frames at 2048×1556 or even 4096×3112 pixels. For typical NTSC D-1 video, use 720×486 pixels. Ideally, this decision should be made early in your production so you can have the proper aspect ratio in mind as you compose camera shots.

Options   Make sure that Atmospherics, Effects, Use Advanced Lighting, and Compute Advanced Lighting When Requested are all checked if you are using those features.

Naming Your Sequence   In the Render Output section, you'll need to click the Files button and create a folder for your frames as well as provide a frame name for the sequence. I recommend creating a parent folder for all your frames and then individual folders named after each camera, and then in that folder you can name the initial file of the sequence. For example, to render Camera 5, I created a folder called \Frames\Cam_05\ and have named the initial file Cam_05_.tga. This mean that the sequence will start with a file called Cam_05_2060.tga and end with a file called Cam_05_2100.tga. It will create 40 separate TGA files.

Letting Your Computer Work for You

Now is the time when you can sit back and let your computer calculate mightily, chugging along for hours on end while it renders your frames. It is best to prepare for these times in

FIGURE 16-10   These are the settings for rendering a typical shot in the Cloud10 scene. A frame range is given, near the top. Below that, the output sizes are chosen. Option check boxes can usually be left at their defaults, unless you want to turn off Effects and Atmospherics for faster test renders. Finally, a path is given for the rendered frames.

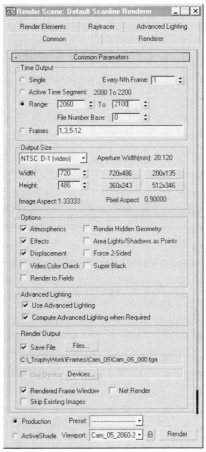

your schedule. Start long renders at the end of the day so that your computer can render through the night whenever possible. I also recommend taking a look at random images from a sequence as soon as possible (you can pause your rendering and look at a frame in Photoshop). This can help you find something you might have missed before you started the render and save you some time.

Chapter

Compositing and Video Editing: Finishing Touches

Now we can move on to putting a finish on our animation footage and turning it into playable video for delivery. With video compositing, CG filmmakers have new toolsets available that allow for deep creativity and powerful control over the final look and feel of their animation after it has been rendered in a 3-D package. Compositing tools can be used for many video-centric tasks, such as

color correction, layering, and adding two-dimensional effects, much like Photoshop for video. Compositing packages are also used to add all manner of graphical content to film and video, such as animated titles. However, CG filmmakers are finding that because today's video-compositing packages feature many new built-in 3-D capabilities, more and more tasks traditionally performed in a 3-D animation package can now be performed in video-compositing packages.

Compositing packages such as Discreet's combustion are now hybrids of 2-D and 3-D, with many varied capabilities, allowing artists to add many different effects to rendered 3-D animation footage. In some cases, even effects such as particle systems can be added more quickly and efficiently in a compositing package than they can be in a 3-D rendering environment. Furthering these capabilities is a new level of integration between the 3-D and video-compositing packages through the use of several new hybrid 3-D/2-D rendering formats. Not only can shots be composed of layered video elements, but these individual video layers can be arranged and animated in a 3-D space.

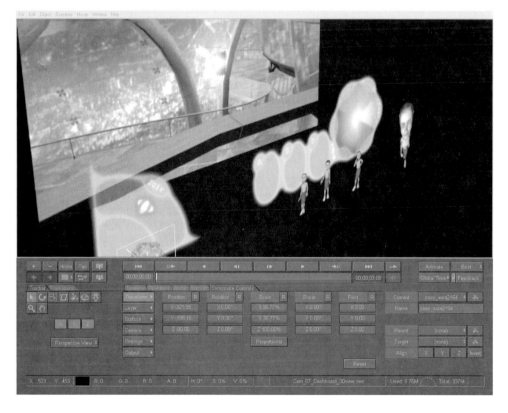

Furthermore, most state-of-the-art CG animation houses make compositing tools an integral part of their rendering pipeline. Today, packages such as 3ds max can render a scene and split the resulting images into component parts. An animation sequence can be rendered out as several files per frame instead of just one. These files may correspond to separate elements such as the specularity of the image, the diffuse lighting, the shadows, or the reflections. When the separate elements are composited back together in a compositing package, great control is afforded over the look of the final footage. This way, compositors can adjust only the specular highlights of a piece of footage or just the shadows as well as many other manipulations that would normally require a complete rerendering of the scene.

Compositing with combustion 3

At the risk of sounding like a marketing brochure, Discreet's combustion is a truly deep toolset, affording CG animators a host of creative possibilities. Besides all the requisite compositing features for blending various layers of video, combustion features a very powerful vector painting toolset much like an animated version of Adobe Illustrator. This is all combined with an extensive set of integrations that tie combustion and 3ds max together.

As thoroughly evidenced by the endless array of Hollywood blockbuster films featuring 3-D animated elements mixed in with live action footage, video compositing has long had the ability to match 3-D to 2-D. But now, through the use of 3ds max's RPF file format, 2-D video footage can now be integrated into 3-D animation. When 3-D scenes are rendered in this format, depth information is saved with each frame.

Combustion is easily deep enough to warrant its own series of books, but in this chapter we'll focus on a few key capabilities particularly relevant to CG filmmaking. We'll start by creating a straightforward, layered composite built up from separately rendered animations. This will introduce you to a simple combustion workflow and to its base capabilities.

Creating a Videogame Interface

The title of the example film, *The Game to Save the World,* refers to an online role-playing game that the characters in the film are playing. The videogame interface that we see in camera shots from one of the characters' point of view contains various pieces of animation that show what their videogame character is doing. The raw material for this videogame interface is created by rendering short clips of characters separately and at low resolutions. The small animation clips are layered together with the full-size background footage that is rendered from Zoey's point of view as she walks through Cloud10. The sample shot for this chapter shows Zoey turning on the visibility of the characters' auras.

Interface Shapes Created in Adobe Illustrator

The dashboard element of the interface is first drawn in Adobe Illustrator. A rendered still shot at the final frame resolution is used as a reference background in Illustrator so the shapes of the dashboard can be drawn in the context of the footage they will be composited over. The Illustrator file of the dashboard consists of several shape elements. The layers that contain the shapes have their blending methods set to Overlay so that they are transparent. Finally, the temporary background image is removed and the file is saved as a Photoshop PSD image, which "bakes" the transparency information of the various elements down into one image.

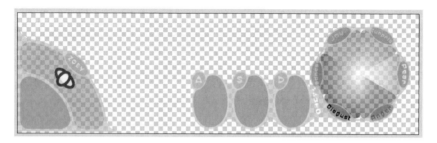

Rendering Source Footage

The foundation for this composite shot is the seventh shot of the sample animation from frames 2221 to 2316, for a total of 95 frames. This camera is from Zoey's point of view as she turns away from the balcony railing. This shot was rendered just like all the other shots in the film, as sequentially numbered 720×486, 24-bit TGA files.

The animation of Zoey walking on the right side of the dashboard is used to show her what her character is doing in the videogame. This 95-frame element was rendered from the same sequence in the original scene file. A fisheye camera is linked to Zoey's hip-control object, and all other objects in the scene are hidden. This footage was rendered as 32-bit Targa files at only 200×300 pixels. By rendering the footage as 32-bit TGA files with an alpha channel, transparency is saved with each frame.

The smaller animations of Zoey in the dashboard represent various gestures she can choose for her character to make. These animations were rendered in the exact same manner as the larger fisheye animation, but with a normal focal length and smaller still. Each gesture was rendered separately from different sequences of the main animation to separate out discrete snippets of body motion. This smaller animation of Zoey's walk cycle is only 30 frames long, but it can be made to loop in combustion. Also, 95 frames of Zoey's aura for the left side of the dashboard were rendered in the original aura max file from Chapter 15.

To create the animated "Auras On" alert, the new 3ds max 6 Blobmesh object was used. The Blobmesh was assigned an Ink and Paint material with colors to match the interface. Point helpers, the simplest max objects, were added to the Blobmesh object and animated moving upward. Max Text objects were linked to two of the point helpers so that they would move with the blobs. The blobs and text were then rendered as two separate sequences so that the blob sequence could be made transparent in combustion.

All these separate animation sequences were named carefully and rendered to a solidly constructed folder hierarchy so that they could be found later.

Working in Combustion

Now we'll build our composite from the separate footage elements that have been rendered. The first task is to make a workspace file in combustion. A workspace is essentially a container file for all the various pieces of footage combined in a composite. Here are the steps to follow:

1 In combustion's main menu, choose File | New Workspace. In the pop-up window, click the Custom button and choose NTSC / D1 Discreet edit NTSC from the drop-down list. Click the same drop-down button again and choose Custom this time. Now you can change the pixel aspect ratio from .9 to 1.0 (this will keep the footage from looking squashed in the combustion viewports).

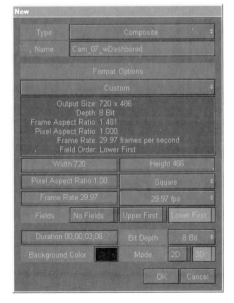

In the main menu, choose File | Import Footage. In the Import Footage dialog box that pops up, navigate to…\3dsmax6_CD\ Frames\Cam_07\. A single thumbnail of the rendered shot 7 will appear representing all 95 frame files. In combustion, clips are imported by choosing the first file of the sequence. Click once on the thumbnail, and the thumbnail will appear again at the bottom of the Import Footage dialog box. Click OK.

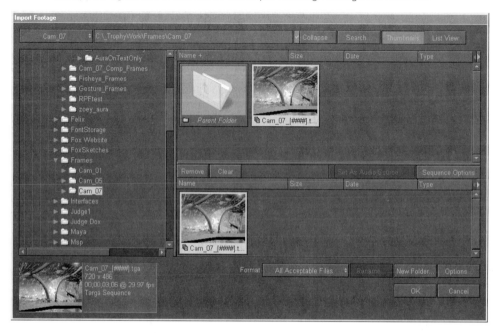

The first frame of the footage will now appear in the combustion viewport (see Figure 17-1). You can play the footage by clicking the Play button just below the viewport. On the first pass, the footage will play slowly as the video frames are being buffered into RAM. But after that, if you click the Play button again, the footage should play in real time.

Now we can continue importing the other pieces of footage for the shot.

2 Choose File | Import Footage again and import ...\3dsmax6\Composites\ interface_11_scaled.psd, which contains dashboard shapes created in Illustrator. This is a Photoshop file containing the shapes of the dashboard that were created in Illustrator.

3 Because the dashboard image appears in the center of the viewport, it needs to be moved into its proper position. At the bottom left of the combustion interface is the Toolbar tab. Click the Select button and then move the dashboard image so that its bottom-left corner is aligned with the bottom-left corner of the footage.

FIGURE 17-1   When the background footage for the sequence is imported into the workspace, it will show up in the viewport.

The Workspace tab is a hierarchical view that shows all the components of the combustion workspace file. The order of this workspace list directly affects the visibility of footage. Footage items at the top of the list will appear on top of the footage below them when viewed in the viewport. To experiment, you can drag the dashboard object in the Workspace tab beneath the Cam_07_2221 footage and see it disappear behind the background footage in the viewport. Press CTRL-Z to undo this. As each new piece of footage is imported into the workspace, it appears at the top of the list and therefore on top in the viewport.

Now we can add to any layer in our composite what combustion calls an *operator*. Operators can consist of a wide variety of manipulations, many of which will be very familiar to Photoshop users. However, 3-D effects are also available, as well as some video-specific operators. Operators are added to a specific piece of footage in the Workspace tab, located next to the Toolbar tab.

4 Add a color-correction operator to the dashboard image by right-clicking it in the workspace list and choosing Operators | Color Correction | Discreet Color Corrector from the right-click menu.

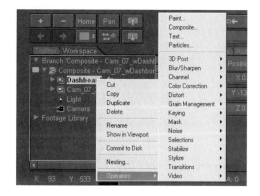

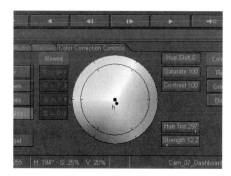

5 Controls for the Discreet Color Corrector operator will appear in the middle of the combustion interface. In the color wheel, drag the dot in the center slightly down and to the right. This will affect the saturation of the dashboard image.

6 In the Workspace tab, click the Dashboard entry again, and in the vertical row of buttons next to the Workspace tab, click the Surface button. Then click the button under the words *Transfer Mode* and choose Hard Light from the drop-down menu. This list of blending modes works almost identically to the layer blending modes found in Photoshop and Illustrator.

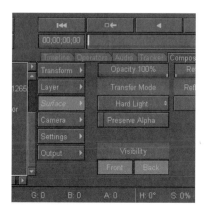

7 Now add a Glow operator to the dashboard. To do this, right-click the Dashboard entry in the Workspace tab again. This time choose Operators | Stylize | Glow in the right-click menu. Give the Glow operator the settings shown here:

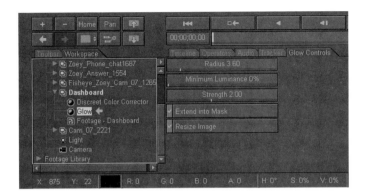

8 Import the fisheye clip from …\Composites\ Fisheye_Frames\Cam_07_Fisheye\. Make sure the Time slider is set to the first frame in the sequence. In the Toolbar tab, choose the Scale button. In the viewport, hold down the SHIFT key while scaling the fisheye footage object until it is the size of the "mood ring" circle on the right side of the dashboard. Use the Move tool to center it on the circle.

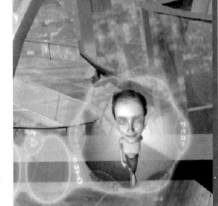

9 Now import all three clips in …\Composites\ Gesture_Frames\ at the same time. Do this by navigating to the Zoey_Answer gesture footage and clicking its thumbnail in the upper portion of the Import Footage window. Then navigate to the Zoey_Phone_chat footage and click its thumbnail. Do the same for the Zoey_Phone and Zoey_walk footage. Each of the thumbnails will appear in the bottom portion of the Import Footage window. Click OK.

10 Because all three pieces of animated gesture footage appear on top of each other, they can be scaled together to save time. CTRL-click each of the three gesture footage entries in the Workspace tab and then choose the Scale tool from the toolbar. Hold down the SHIFT key in the viewport to scale the three objects uniformly, until they are the size of the ellipses in the middle of the dashboard. Then select one gesture at a time in the Workspace tab and use the Move tool in the viewport to move it into place within the ellipses.

If you click the Play button to preview the shot, you'll see that the Zoey_walk footage disappears

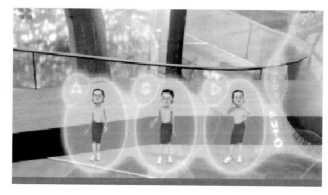

after a few frames. This is because this particular piece of footage is only 30 frames long, instead of 95 like the rest of the shot. To change that, you can make this footage loop.

11 In the Workspace tab, click the small arrow in the Zoey_walk_1370 entry. Below it will appear the Footage operator, which points to the external file sequence. Click this and then click the Output button to the right of the Workspace tab. Click the button under the words *Playback Behavior* and choose Loop from the drop-down menu. Enter a value of 3 in the field next to this button.

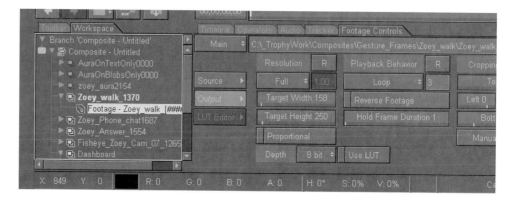

12 To change the actual duration of the footage, click the top-level entry in the Workspace tab. Then to the right of the Workspace tab click the Timeline tab. The bars in the timeline represent the duration of the various pieces of footage. Drag the right side of the bar for the Zoey_walk_1370 entry all the way to the right to make it last as long as the rest of the shot.

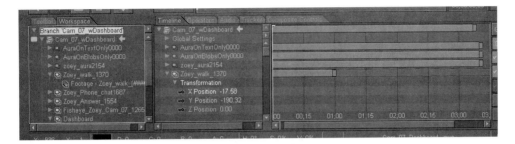

Now upon playback of the shot, the walking animation will loop.

13 Import the clip from …\Composites\ Zoey_Aura\. Scale and place it in the bottom-left corner of the dashboard.

The videogame interface has various alerts that pop up during the course of the film. These alerts pop up as animated blobs with text on top of them. The blobs come up from the bottom of the screen.

14 Import the AuraonBlobsOnly and then the AuraOnTextOnly clips from …\Composites\Blobs\AuraOn\. Because the first frame of the animation is what is initially visible, unless you have the Time slider set to a different frame, these pieces of footage are invisible. However, you can still scale them by placing their bounding boxes between the gestures in the ellipses and the aura border shapes.

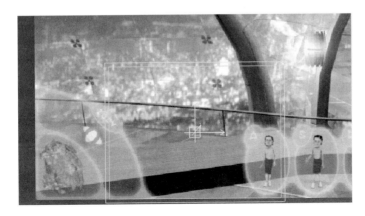

15 Add a glow to the blobs by selecting the Glow operator connected to the Dashboard entry in the Workspace tab. Right-click it and choose Copy from the right-click menu. Then right-click the AuraonBlobsOnly entry and choose Paste.

Now combustion must render all the video layers together to create the final composite shot. For previewing, the shot can be exported as a video file (AVI or QuickTime) using a typical compression codec, or it can be exported as sequential frames again to be imported into a video-editing package for final editing.

16 To export a sequence of TGA files, choose File | Render from the main menu. In the combustion RenderQueue dialog box, click the button next to the word *Format* and choose Target Sequence from the drop-down list. Then click the Process button.

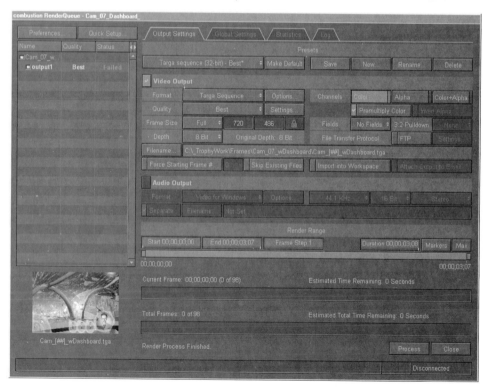

This exercise only touches on some of the capabilities provided by the integration of 3ds max and combustion. Combustion's support for 3ds max's G-buffer through the use of the RPF format allows for the next generation in special effects. Specific 3-D objects can be given effects within combustion, and two-dimensional elements can even be composited in between 3-D objects thanks to the G-buffer's depth information (Zoey's phone, shown in the color insert, was composited in that way). Also, as mentioned earlier, scenes can be rendered in max as individual elements for deep control over individual image components in combustion.

Combustion also contains a robust, vector-based painting program, not unlike Flash, that allows for sophisticated animated graphics. Combine this with the fact that combustion workspaces, with all their animated, layered complexity, can be used as "live" textures in 3ds max, and you have an enormous new set of possibilities.

Video Editing

The final postproduction task is to edit together your rendered shots, combine them with your finished soundtrack, and export them as digital video to create your final film. For CG animators, the editing process consists mainly of stringing the clips together, unless you both animate and render each shot with extra footage at the beginning and end. This extra footage takes extra time to create, but it allows you to take advantage of transition effects such as video wipes and fades that appear between shots.

Although Discreet's combustion 3 now allows for editing footage together, in addition to its compositing capabilities, we'll briefly examine the process of using Adobe Premiere for simple video editing.

Simple Editing with Adobe Premiere

Adobe Premiere is a workhorse video-editing package. This is a handy tool to use for assembling all the footage of the separate camera shots, combining them with the final soundtrack, and creating finished video files. The process is very straightforward in Premiere. We'll go through the steps of assembling some of the sample footage together to make a final video clip:

1 Create a new Premiere project by choosing File | New Project from the main menu. In the Load Project Settings window that pops up, click the Custom button and then click the Next button to get to the new project's video settings.

2 In the Pixel Aspect Ratio drop-down menu, choose the Square Pixels (1.0) setting. Then choose a video compression codec and click OK.

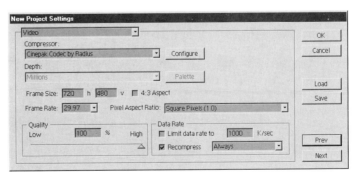

Video Compression Codecs

A codec is a video compression and decompression method or "coder" and "decoder". Codecs come in many flavors and need to be installed on your computer for you to be able to compress your video files into that particular flavor. When a codec is installed it will show up in 3ds max, Adobe Premiere, and in any other package that creates video files. Some codecs compress better than others, and some require specific video players to be viewed. Also, most video codecs will have their own specific settings that will allow you to customize how much the images and audio are compressed.

Among CG animators, the Divx codec is popular since it compresses video files to a relatively small size for Internet downloading while maintaining good image quality. Divx encoded video files have the AVI file extension and play on the standard Windows Media Player. Not only does the Divx Codec need to be downloaded and installed before you can author Divx encoded files, but viewers need to install the codec on their machines before Divx encoded files can be played. Typically, CG animators will include a link to the Divx web site (http://www.divx.com/) next to the link for downloading their films.

Other popular codecs, for example Sorensen, are only available when you create QuickTime MOV files, but QuickTime movies require that the QuickTime player be installed on a viewer's computer. The best way to choose a codec is to create several versions of your video file with different codecs and compression settings, and then compare image quality and file size.

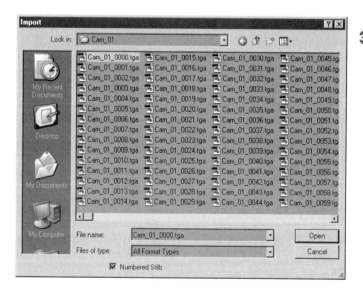

3 Right-click inside the Project window in the upper left of the Premiere interface. Choose Import | File from the right-click menu. Select the files for the first frame of the sequence for your first camera shot. Make sure that the Numbered Stills check box is checked and then click OK.

4 Repeat this for all of your camera shots.

5 Import the audio file for the film soundtrack in the same manner.

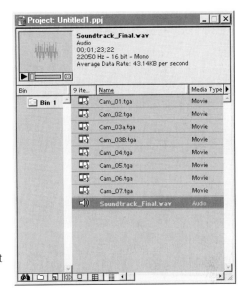

This now becomes the library of clips from which you can build the final film in the Timeline window.

6 Drag the first clip from the Project window into the Timeline window and drop it on the Video 1 track. If you drop it near the beginning, it should snap into place in the first frame. Then drag the clip for the second camera shot and drop it behind the first clip on the Video 1 track.

7 Drag the audio file from the Project window onto the Audio 1 track in the Timeline window.

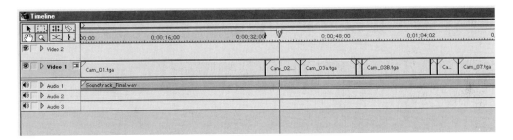

The film can be previewed by clicking the Play button at the right side of the Monitor window.

8 Now all the assembled frames can be rendered to final video. Choose File | Export Timeline | Movie from the main menu.

9 Because you gave the project file the desired output settings when it was created, all you need to do now is give the final video file a name and save it.

Obviously, Premiere can do much more than this, but because CG films are often created from camera shots that have exact frame lengths, the simplest approach to editing will often suffice. To be sure, fancy camera transitions are desirable in some cases, but Premiere's canned video transitions can look hokey if not used creatively.

Getting Your Films Out to the World

Now you will be presented with the most joyous task of all, presenting the fruits of your endless hours of isolated, hard work to the rest of the world. Distribution possibilities for independent filmmakers are better than ever before, thanks not only to the Internet, but to the myriad film festivals and the proliferation of cable television channels. Also making it easier is the flexibility you have for deploying your film. Streaming and nonstreaming Internet video, CD-ROMs, and DVDs are all extremely inexpensive and expedient ways to deliver your work.

Today, many of the best independent CG filmmakers are making extensive use of the Internet. Not only can a well-designed website be used to promote and deliver your film, but supporting materials can be provided to show your viewers more about your production process and other background information. The Internet is being used to create an active and vibrant community of filmmakers who collaborate and share their information.

Appendix

Resources

One of the threads throughout this book is that each chapter is a branching-off point to a deep and engrossing subject that could easily be its own topic of study. Fortunately, the art of creating 3-D animated films is mature enough so that ample information is available to aid the pursuit. An endless array of websites, books, and magazines exists for CG filmmakers. Following is a list of resources that I recommend as excellent starting points for further study.

The Internet: 1,001 Uses

Obviously, the Internet is a boundless source of information, but it also may be the prime conduit for showing your work to the world, sharing ideas and collaborating with other filmmakers as well as finding work.

Portals

Many portal websites cater to CG filmmakers. Each of the following websites offers a rich set of features, including industry news, feature stories, inspirational art galleries, and tutorials. Furthermore, each of these hubs has its own set of online forums, which are hosts to vibrant online communities. Although the sites are very similar, often covering the same news stories, I find each one has its own strengths and plenty of unique content:

▶ **CG Channel (http://www.cgchannel.com/)**

▶ **3D Total (http://www.3dtotal.com/)**

▶ **Inside CG (http://www.insidecg.com/)**

▶ **CGNetworks (http://www.cgnetworks.com/)**

▶ **Animation World Network (http://www.awn.com/)**   AWN is a portal website for the broader topic of animation in general. This site is packed with information relevant to CG filmmakers.

▶ **Gamasutra (http://www.gamasutra.com)**   Gamasutra is a portal website geared toward video game developers. Videogame development overlaps with CG filmmaking in many areas, making this an excellent resource.

3ds max-Specific Sites

Here are a few of the many sites dedicated to 3ds max:

▶ **Discreet 3ds max online forum (http://support.discreet.com/webboard)**
Discreet's official online forum for 3ds max is highly active with user-to-user communication.

▶ **Max Underground (http://maxunderground.com/)**   This is one of the best sources for 3ds max-specific news.

▶ **Script Spot (http://www.scriptspot.com/start.htm)**   The Script Spot is one of the most valuable resources for 3ds max filmmakers. This site is a comprehensive resource covering all aspects of 3ds max's built-in scripting language, MAXScript. It's also the most complete online repository of the hundreds of freely available maxscripts as well as an excellent source of information on creating MAXScripts.

▶ **Digimation (http://www.digimation.com/)**   Digimation is one of the key retailers of 3ds max plug-ins.

Venues and Online Animation Sites
The Internet is one of the best connections between filmmaker and audience. Here is a tiny sampling of online venues for short animated films. You can submit your finished films to these sites:

▶ **AnimWatch (http://www.animwatch.com)**   This excellent website highlights the best in independent CG filmmaking.

▶ **Atom Films (http://atomfilms.shockwave.com/)**   Atom Films is a large, high-profile website featuring hundreds of short films and reaching a large audience.

▶ **iFilm (http://www.ifilm.com/)**   iFilm is another large, high-profile short-film website.

▶ **Ten Second Club (http://10secondclub.net/)**   This website is created by animators for animators. All films created for this site are ten seconds long, making it a prime venue for quick, animated experiments and a showcase for animated talent.

Forums
Here are two of the more specific web forums:

▶ **Digital Sculpting Forum (http://cube.phlatt.net/forums/spiraloid/)**   This forum, dedicated exclusively to 3-D modeling, is a very focused community of dedicated artisans.

▶ **CGChar (http://cgchar.toonstruck.com/forum/)**   Dedicated to the art of making 3-D characters move, this forum is a rich resource and an active community.

≫ CAUTION ≪   *The forums listed here are valuable because of the people populating them, often top industry professionals. If the forums become oversaturated with rude and inane postings, the best artists and professionals will disappear from them and greatly diminish their value to you. It is best to post carefully and thoughtfully to help maintain these communities.*

Magazines

Here are a few magazines relevant to CG filmmaking:

▶ ***Cinefex*** (http://www.cinefex.com/)   *Cinefex* is a quarterly magazine dedicated to special effects films. It is an information-rich magazine, thoroughly chronicling the technical details of most of today's major effects films.

▶ ***Animation Magazine*** (http://www.animationmagazine.net/)   This monthly magazine covers the larger world of animation.

▶ ***3D World*** (http://www.3dworldmag.com/)   This monthly UK magazine is fairly expensive in the U.S. but is a nice, general 3-D magazine.

▶ ***Renter Node*** (http://www.rendernode.com/)   This online magazine is delivered in PDF format and is another good, general 3-D magazine.

Films Made with 3ds max

Here are a few websites of independent CG filmmakers who use 3ds max:

▶ **Fifty Percent Grey** (http://www.3dluvr.com/ruairi/)   Ruairi Robinson's Oscar-nominated short film, *Fifty Percent Grey*, is an excellent example of what one focused person can do with 3ds max.

▶ **The Cathedral** (http://www.platige.com/katedra/eng_\strona_glowna.html) This Oscar-nominated short film by Tomek Baginski clearly shows that rich, no-compromise production values can be achieved with 3ds max, even on small production films.

▶ **Respire** (http://www.respire-leclip.com/)   This emotive, French music video, by Stephane Hamache and Andre Bessy, shows a distinctive cartoon-rendered look used to tell a provocative story.

Books

Here are a few select books relevant to the various tasks with CG filmmaking:

▶ *The Five C's of Cinematography: Motion Picture Filming Techniques,* by Joseph V. Mascelli

This book on the basics of filmmaking in general is recommended by many different CG filmmakers as a good, concise grounding in fundamental cinematography techniques.

▶ *The Art of the Storyboard,* by John Hart

This is an in-depth book on the use of storyboards and visualizing films. It also serves as a good introduction to the basics of cinematography.

▶ *The Animator's Survival Kit,* by Richard Williams

This highly visual book by the Director of Animation for *Who Framed Roger Rabbit?* provides critical nuts-and-bolts knowledge on the basics of character animation.

▶ *The Artist's Complete Guide to Facial Expression,* by Gary Faigin

One of the prime resources for information on the different expressions a face can make and how it makes them.

▶ *Rendering with Mental Ray,* by Thomas Driemeyer

3ds max 6 comes with the industry-tested, industrial-strength renderer Mental Ray built in. Although this renderer can be used to create state-of-the-art CG imagery, this power comes at the price of a steep learning curve. This comprehensive book provides in-depth technical knowledge on using Mental Ray.

Author's Website

My website, http://www.barrettfox.com/, is the main spot for viewing this book's example film, *The Game to Save the World*. This site contains further material regarding the film, including concept imagery, stills, and other content related to the making of this film. The site also contains my portfolio, a demo reel, and links to other websites of interest.

Instructions for Using the CD-ROM

The CD-ROM accompanying this book contains the 3ds max, image and video files needed to work through the tutorials in the book and re-create a significant portion of the example film. This is an extensive array of materials, including characters that have been modeled, textured, and rigged for animation as well as the environment models in which to animate the characters. The scene files feature the characters within the environments, along with animations for those characters, providing a thorough illustration of the entire filmmaking process.

Installing and Using the Files

To be able to work through this book's tutorials, you should have the files located on your computer's hard drive. 3ds max files make references to other files for textures and sounds, so it is important to duplicate the CD-ROM's folder structure and to configure max to access their specific location. To do this, follow these steps:

1. Copy the folder \3dsmax6_CD\ to your hard drive. If space on your hard drive is limited, you can remove the subfolders called \Frames and \Composites. Both of these folders are used for Chapter 17, and the files in them can be accessed directly from the CD-ROM if needed.

2. Add the path of the \3dsmax6_CD\ folder to your 3ds max 6 path configuration. Do this by choosing Customize | Configure Path from 3ds max's main menu. Click the XRefs tab and click the Add button. Then navigate to the \3dsmax6_CD\ folder on your hard drive. Click the Use Sub Paths check box and then click the Use Path button.

3. For the path to the audio soundtrack files, choose Customize | Configure Path from the main menu again. In the General tab, click the Sounds entry in the list. Click the Modified button and navigate to \3dsmax_CD\Audio\folder. Then click the Use Path button.

4. In your 3ds max 6 installation folder, copy the MAXScript file \3dsmax6\scripts\PluginScripts\Modifier-AttributeHolder.ms to the folder \3dsmax6\stdplugs\stdscripts\.

NOTE ***When opening any 3ds max files from the CD-ROM, you may be presented with this dialog box. Be sure to always check the Adopt the File's Unit Scale radio button. Otherwise, the objects in the file may be scaled incorrectly and the files essentially broken (if this happens, simply don't save and reopen the file).***

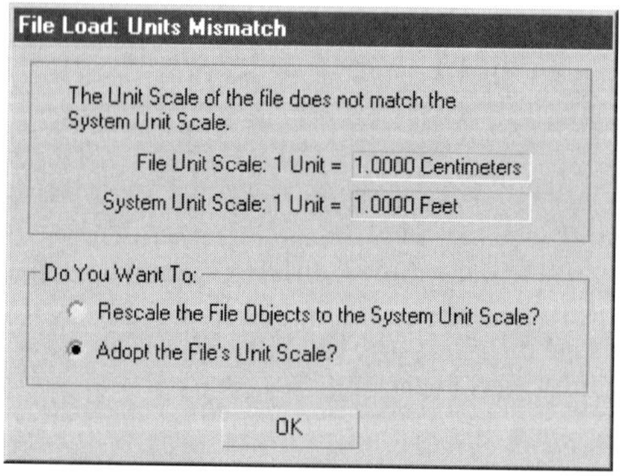

Index